# Economics and Engineering:
# Institutions, Practices, and Cultures

# Economics and Engineering: Institutions, Practices, and Cultures

**Annual Supplement to Volume 52**
*History of Political Economy*

**Edited by Pedro Garcia Duarte and Yann Giraud**

Duke University Press
Durham and London 2020

EXTENT AND NATURE OF CIRCULATION: Average number of copies of each issue published during the preceding twelve months; (A) total number of copies printed, 267.3; (B.1) paid/requested mail subscriptions, 94.5; (B.4) Paid distribution by other classes, 1 (C) total paid/requested circulation, 95.5; (D.1) samples, complimentary, and other nonrequested copies, 0; (D.4) nonrequested copies distributed through outside the mail, 83; (E) total nonrequested distribution (sum of D.1 & D.4), 83; (F) total distribution (sum of C & E), 178.5; (G) copies not distributed (office use, leftover, unaccounted, spoiled after printing, returns from news agents), 88.8; (H) total (sum of F & G), 267.3.

Actual number of copies of a single issue published nearest to filing date: (A) total number of copies printed, 224; (B.1) paid/requested mail subscriptions, 128; (B.4) Paid distribution by other classes, 1(C) total paid/requested circulation, 129 (D.1) samples, complimentary, and other nonrequested copies, 0; (D.4) nonrequested copies distributed through outside the mail, 80; (E) total nonrequested distribution (sum of D.1 & D.4) 80, ; (F) total distribution (sum of C & E), 209; (G) copies not distributed (office use, leftover, unaccounted, spoiled after printing, returns from news agents), 15 (H) total (sum of F & G), 224.

# Contents

# Economics and Engineering: A Foreword

David Blockley

Throughout history we humans have dreamed and *purposefully* and *ingeniously* turned new ideas, and new ways of doing things, into reality based on their *worth*. I use the word *ingeniously* to mean being inventive, resourceful, and skillful. I use the word *worth* to convey more than a monetary amount, that is, all aspects of quality as fitness for purpose such as functionality, safety, resilience, and sustainability as well as economic value for money, and working within budgets.

It is my contention that knowing and doing have become artificially separated in Western intellectual culture. The emphasis on scientific knowing has led to an overconfidence in our ability to predict the future and a neglect of the need to control complex and often unforeseen, unintended consequences of our practical actions.

It is my purpose here to explore the relationship between economics and engineering not in analogy but in actuality. The strategy is, first, to set the context for this discussion; second, to look at the nature of science and mathematics in relation to engineering; and third, to explore some of what I see as the main similarities and differences between engineering and economics.

## Preliminaries

Uncertainty is pervasive in the world, and it introduces a significant distinction between the scientific knowledge produced in and outside the laboratory. In classical physics we have controlled uncertainty through the precise conditions of laboratory testing. As we move outside the laboratory

*History of Political Economy* 52 (annual suppl.) DOI 10.1215/00182702-8717886

(world outside the laboratory, or WOL), we have to relax our grip on uncertainty. Here the uncertainty has a greater and variable impact on our ability to predict the more complex phenomena.

Engineering has largely been ignored by philosophers or subsumed under science (Mitcham 1999; Goldman 2004) because, Goldman argues, engineering employs contingency-based reasoning, in contrast to the necessity-based modeling of rationality that has dominated Western philosophy since Plato. Engineering is not just something-to-do-with-engines. To engineer is to solve problems as only we humans can.

Before the Renaissance, the same person might be an artist, artisan, architect, craftsman, mason, or engineer depending on the job he was doing—the distinctions we make nowadays were small. After the Renaissance, engineering disciplines fragmented (civil; construction; mechanical, railways and cars; electrical, power and electronics; aerospace; and computer science and software), as opportunities arose largely through the evolution of specialist scientific knowledge. Today, the engineers' professional duty of care for the safety and well-being of others requires them to examine the scope and dependability of all kinds of information, including science. However, there has been very little reflection on the way that knowledge is used and the "fit" between engineering and other disciplines. History, philosophy, economics, and politics have only a nominal role in the education of engineers. While almost all engineering societies have attempted to define the nature of engineering (e.g., Royal Academy of Engineering 2019), there is little in-depth critical discussion of the role of engineers in society. As a result, there is a plethora of different views about the nature of engineering.

Engineering is not a science: whereas the purpose of science is to understand, the purpose of engineering is to act and do something practical— usually but not always to create something physical—to meet a human need or want as expressed usually by a client (Blockley 2010). The physical results of engineering work are highly testable. Indeed, Mother Nature is the final arbiter. She is the most severe taskmaster—she will find any weak points. If a computer program has a bug, then at some point it will fail, although that failure has consequences in physical reality only when the software is used, for example, to control the flight of an airplane or to decide the proportions of a bridge structure.

## The Nature of Engineering

At the core there are four stages to engineering tasks: design, make, operate, and maintain. Through fragmentation between the different branches of engineering, these stages are handled differently in different disciplines. However, for the present purpose, we can divide them into two groups. The first are the "one-off" big engineering projects such as building a large dam or skyscraper. The second are the "mass-produced" projects such as computers and cell phones. In between are "small-quantity" production projects such as ships and airplanes, which show features of both. The essential difference between the two groups is the level of prototype testing that can be done before production. Mass-produced goods are extensively tested before being put into production, and heavy investment is made in factory production processes. By contrast, "one-off" products have to be "right the first time." So safety factors and conservative assumptions are necessarily greater in one-off industries, whereas margins are tighter in mass production.

The first stage of designing is turning a client brief into a clear purpose, and then coming up with possible solutions and criteria for choice between them. The criteria depend crucially on interactions between all stakeholders. Necessary criteria concern functional reliability, safety, and budgetary constraints. More recently, sustainability has become important together with resilience and robustness. Designing includes prototype testing for manufactured products but not for "one-off" products, although laboratory tests will be done for aspects of large projects (such as testing a physical model of a long span bridge in a wind tunnel).

Making, the second stage, is manufacture, construction, or building, usually performed in a factory or on-site with the participation of multiple contracting businesses in a supply chain. Operating and maintaining are given various levels of attention or inattention depending on the product. For example, software products get regular updates, whereas potholes in highways may go neglected for years due to political budget austerities. High-reliability systems like airplanes have sophisticated avionic control and maintenance systems. Feedback and feedforward from sensor data are used directly to help make decisions—sometimes automatically as in aircraft landing control systems.

Models

The relationship between engineering and science is reciprocal. As we do more (engineer), then we know more (science), and hence we can do more and know more in an ever upward spiral. At the heart of scientific knowing are models. The word *model* is important and controversial when used to describe scientific theory (Cartwright 1999). However, the idea of a model is particularly important in engineering. Nevertheless, there is no settled view as to the nature of what constitutes a model.

For the reasons given earlier, engineers only think intuitively about the models they use. Most engineers know that the science they use is incomplete and approximations are required. They typically require models to (a) work and (b) be tractable. The first is checked by experiment in laboratory conditions, but perhaps more important by practical use. Experience builds by trial and error. The tractability of theory has changed dramatically over the years chiefly through advances in mathematical techniques and computing. Almost universally, engineers see mathematics purely as a tool. Many practitioners are wary of what they see as "overly" complicated mathematical analysis and fight shy of adopting it. Researchers and academics are often frustrated by these attitudes. However, nowadays almost all calculations are done by computer, and therein lie some new risks. Many "pure" mathematicians find engineering methods to be ad hoc. The reason is that engineers have to approximate in order to get to solutions, and it is in these approximations that the new risks lie. The approximations are different in different applications but depend almost entirely on judgments about the uncertainties lying in approximations and other contextual assumptions.

## Managing Uncertainty

Uncertainty is analyzed and judged largely in two ways, pragmatically and theoretically. The first is through experience in practice and the trial and error of what has worked in the past with "built-in" simple safety factors. The second is through research techniques. These find little application in anything other than high-risk industries like nuclear and aerospace. One-off industries rely on various kinds of simple safety factors where parametric quantities are increased or reduced appropriately to make any assumptions conservative or safe. Systems are designed wherever possible to be "fail-safe," that is, to minimize consequences should failure occur. Defense in depth is used where safety is highly critical. Here many levels of protection are designed-in, so if one fails, the next takes over. Industries that require very high reliabilities and safety levels (e.g., aerospace and nuclear) are funding research into probabilistic methods taken rather uncritically from mathematicians. However, their use in practice is still controversial because of the intuitive feelings of experienced engineers that the methods are inadequate to deal with the vagaries of operations.

Engineers face three types of uncertainty in their models. First, *random* variations in parameters (e.g., variations in the weights of people in a building). These can legitimately be modeled by mathematical theories of probability and statistics (Blockley 1980). Second, *system* uncertainties stem from the physical context in which a tested theoretical model (to a degree in the laboratory or through the experience of practical usage) is used. These are very variable in quite different contexts and hence difficult to pin down. Some *systemic* differences are deliberately introduced to make a problem tractable (e.g., engineers model the load on the floor of a building as uniformly distributed when clearly it is not—but the model is fail-safe). Likewise, systems can be modeled at varying levels of definition and abstraction to account for emergent properties where the behavior of the whole is more than the sum of the parts. Applications of probability theory, using random error terms to account for systemic differences, have proved, in my view, inadequate (Blockley 1992). Third, uncertainties in *human* and social systems are even more difficult to control because of the tendencies for people to do the unexpected and to make mistakes (overweight vehicles crossing a bridge or a design calculation mistake). It is rare for engineers to scan for unintended consequences or to do a systematic scan for unknown unknowns. They are usually guided by previous practices that have worked and by legal guides such as regulations and codes of practice.

Engineers create models for a specific purpose, and what really matters is the quality of the model to deliver that purpose. Engineers succeed because when they have to approximate, they make assumptions that are "fail-safe," that is, always erring on the safe side when in doubt to make sure they stay in context. The dependability of models varies across engineering disciplines. For large "one-off" projects, theories are laboratory tested, but in the WOL great reliance is placed on previous practice, experience, and national regulations. For manufactured large-volume "mass-production" products, prototypes are extensively tested both in the laboratory and then in a simulated reality before being put on sale.

Attributes and Criteria—
How Do We Recognize Success?

If engineering is about delivering a purpose, then how do we know if and when that purpose is achieved? Strictly and rigorously, quality is "fitness for purpose," which does not mean only functionality. Quality should cover all attributes of purpose as safety and economy. In the past, engineers have understandably focused on functionality and safety because they are necessary (but not a sufficient condition) for practical success. For example, a building must stand firm against the elements and whatever the people interacting with it require of it. While buildings in a nonseismic zone are not normally designed to withstand earthquakes, it is a legal requirement that buildings in California are designed to do so, which does not ensure that all buildings are safe, as past events have shown.

Since the Renaissance, some other aspects of quality have been diverted into other professions, for example, aesthetics to architects, accounting to quantity surveyors, and management to project managers. The result has been even more fragmentation of the professions. Only in the recent past are we collectively beginning to realize (largely through some high-profile failures) that some important requirements such as robustness, lack of vulnerability and fragility (low-probability but high-consequence events), sustainability, and resilience have "fallen through the cracks" between the professions. Hence there are new calls to emphasize whole systems engineering approaches to improve performance—particularly cost and time overruns on big projects (Blockley and Godfrey 2017). These developments are patchy and controversial among engineers. Some dismiss systems thinking as "management speak," hence unworthy of consideration, against the views of the Royal Academy of Engineering (2007).

## How Are Economics and Engineering Similar and How Are They Different?

The similarities between economics and engineering seem profound. J. F. Hayford (1917: 59) noted this when he wrote, "Economics and engineering are closely related. Economics has been defined as the social science of earning a living. With the same appropriateness engineering may be defined to be physical science applied to helping groups of men to make a better living." The main sources of similarities and differences that I shall explore are (a) the understanding and importance of context, the dependability of the underlying models and the role of mathematics, and (b) the role of failure.

### Context, Testability, and Models

To explore the importance of context, it is worth pausing to consider how the philosopher Karl Popper (1978) explained the way we perceive, sense, and share our reality. He said that we effectively inhabit three worlds. World 1 is reality, the actual physical world of which we are a part. Next, he said that we can make sense of world 1 only through world 2, our own subjective world of mind. World 2 is where we think about the things that we cannot share with anyone else. Finally, he said that we also try to make sense of world 1 (and world 2) through world 3, the world of our shared experiences, the world of objective data. Tests on engineered physical systems are devised in world 3 and are repeatable in world 1—precisely in the laboratory and more or less imprecisely in the WOL.

The simple linear deterministic supply and demand model of econometrics, such as $S = a + bP$, where $S$ is supply and $P$ is price, is informative but not as dependable as the way engineers use an equivalent formula such as $S = a/b$, where $S$ is a safe breaking stress for a piece of steel, $a$ is a tensile force, and $b$ is a cross-sectional area of that piece of steel. The engineering relationship is accurate in the context of small forces up to an "elastic limit" for steel, though not for many other materials such as concrete. Nevertheless, engineers can use the linear elastic relationship to make fail-safe assumptions to work in the WOL, making calculations tractable even for concrete (a material with nonlinear properties). The econometric linear relationship between supply and demand is a statistical "fit" based on a regression with a great deal of inherent uncertainty and many potentially omitted variables because they are difficult to include. This model is therefore a very limited representation, but useful in understanding what is going on and what decisions need to be made to achieve purpose. Consequently, the relationship between the results and behaviors in practice is much more tenuous.

The Role of Failure

I have spent a lifetime of research looking at why engineering systems fail. The gaps between what we know, what we do, and why things go wrong are huge. The old adage "failure is an opportunity to learn" is often quoted but, in my experience, seldom appreciated sufficiently by practitioners. It has deep roots and far-reaching implications for the joining-up of theory and practice. In 1978 the sociologist Barry Turner showed that the preconditions to major disasters can incubate or develop in a way that it may be possible in some instances to identify before a final disastrous event. He pointed out that we need to develop methods for identifying those preconditions with sufficient dependability to enable decision-makers to make such politically difficult and potentially expensive decisions to avoid the even greater costs and consequences of a disaster. In subsequent research he and I and the psychologist Nick Pidgeon followed up this idea (Blockley 1992) but without much impact on practice, since the methods needed are not straightforward.

The same issues are alive in economics. For example, after the financial collapse of 2008 the queen of England, Elizabeth II, asked of the experts, "If these things were so large, how come everyone missed them?" In reply Tim Besley and Peter Hennessy (2009: 10) wrote, "The failure to foresee the timing, extent and severity of the crisis and to head it off, while it had many causes, was principally a failure of the collective imagination of many bright people." That such an event should "never happen again" is widespread across all systems, from criminal justice and social care to economics and engineering.

In my view, a systems-thinking approach is the only way to follow through Besley and Hennessy's conclusions—we have to find ways to integrate the professions. The historical fragmentation of specialisms has been spectacularly successful but has led to an inability to see the "big picture." To deal with the surprises, unexpected events, and unknown unknowns of a future of climate change, uncertain politics, religious strife, and pandemics we need systems that are resilient and sustainable. This can only happen if the professions work together to "join-up" their thinking, decision-making, and actions.

## References

Besley, T., and P. Hennessy. 2009. "The Global Financial Crisis—Why Didn't Anybody Notice?" *British Academy Review* 14 (November). www.thebritishacademy.ac.uk/sites/default/files/03--Besley.pdf.

Blockley, D. 1980. *The Nature of Structural Design and Safety*. Chichester, UK: Ellis Horwood.

Blockley, D. 2010. *Engineering: A Very Short Introduction*. Oxford: Oxford University Press.

Blockley, D., ed. 1992. *Engineering Safety*. London: McGraw-Hill.

Blockley, D., and P. S. Godfrey. 2017. *Doing It Differently: Systems for Rethinking Infrastructure*. 2nd ed. London: ICE Publishing.

Cartwright, N. 1999. *The Dappled World: A Study of the Boundaries of Science*. Cambridge: Cambridge University Press.

Goldman, S. L. 2004. "Why We Need a Philosophy of Engineering: A Work in Progress." *Interdisciplinary Science Reviews* 29, no. 2: 163–76.

Hayford, J. F. 1917. "The Relation of Engineering to Economics." *Journal of Political Economy* 25, no. 1: 59–63.

Mitcham, C. 1999. *Thinking through Technology: The Path between Engineering and Philosophy*. Chicago: University of Chicago Press.

Popper, K. 1978. *Three Worlds: The Tanner Lecture on Human Values*. University of Michigan. tannerlectures.utah.edu/_documents/a-to-z/p/popper80.pdf.

Royal Academy of Engineering. 2007. *Creating Systems That Work: Principles of Engineering Systems for the Twenty-First Century*. www.raeng.org.uk/publications /reports/rae-systems-report.

Royal Academy of Engineering. 2019. "What Is Engineering?" www.raeng.org.uk /education/what-is-engineering.

Turner, B. A. 1978. *Man-Made Disasters*. London: Wykeham.

# Introduction:
# From "Economics *as* Engineering"
# to "Economics *and* Engineering"

Pedro Garcia Duarte and Yann Giraud

## The Transformation of Economics
## into an Engineering Science:
## From Analogies to Interactions

In recent years, economists, who in the past had mostly insisted on their
discipline's strength as a rigorous social science, have turned to its larger
role in transforming society. As early as 2002, Alvin Roth, the Stan-
ford-educated economist who received the Nobel memorial prize in 2012,
has claimed that members of his community should think of themselves
as engineers rather than scientists. By this he meant that they should not
be interested solely in the making of theoretical models but also in con-
fronting these models with the complexities of real-life situations, which
is what engineering is allegedly about. He pointed to the rise of the new
subfield of market design, which he had helped develop, as characteristic
of an engineer's stance and provided several examples of engineering
practices applied to economics: the design of labor clearinghouses—such
as the entry-level labor market for American physicians—and that of the
Federal Communications Commission spectrum auctions (Roth 2002).

We want to thank the Center for the History of Political Economy and Duke University Press
for their support, as well as the many referees who helped us during the editorial process. Yann
Giraud wishes to point out that his research has been supported by the project Labex MME-DII
(ANR11–LBX-0023–01). Pedro Duarte acknowledges the financial support of the Institute for
Advanced Studies, at the Université de Cergy-Pontoise, for visiting professorships (2016, 2018)
that were critical for the shaping of this joint project.

*History of Political Economy* 52 (annual suppl.)  DOI 10.1215/00182702-8717898

More recently, the development economist and MIT scholar Esther Duflo, another recent Nobel awardee, built on Roth's (2002) and Abhijit Banerjee's (2007: chap. 3) contributions and reiterated the need for economists to venture outside academe. But she went further and introduced, in addition to the engineer, a new character: that of the plumber. For her, while scientists attempt to seek epistemic truths using theoretical models and engineers design the machine through which these models can be translated into policy devices, plumbers are the ones who are responsible for making that machine work. For instance, while economic scientists have shown that school vouchers help improve the education level of a population, it is the role of economic engineers to design a voucher system and an incentive structure that helps encourage the use of vouchers. In their turn, economic plumbers are the ones who will work with the population in order to make sure that those vouchers will be addressed to those, situated in a particular environment, who need them the most (Duflo 2017).

For both Roth and Duflo, engineering is the practice of designing policy interventions that requires a certain degree of tinkering in the application of preexisting theoretical models in order to adapt them to real-life practicalities. For them, the engineering and scientific aspects of economics complement each other. By contrast, the macroeconomist Gregory Mankiw (2006: 29) identifies a tension between science and engineering, contrasting two depictions of economics: that of a scientific endeavor, according to which "economists formulate theories with mathematical precision, collect huge data sets on individual and aggregate behavior, and exploit the most sophisticated statistical techniques to reach empirical judgments that are free of bias and ideology (or so we like to think)," with that of engineering. After all, "God put macroeconomists on earth not to propose and test elegant theories but to solve practical problems." Mankiw uses this dichotomy as a foil for him to appraise the development of macroeconomics and to indict new classical macroeconomics as a science while praising the engineering stance of New Keynesian macroeconomics. For him, while the rational expectation theory and calibration techniques conceived by Robert Lucas, Edward Prescott, and their allies exhibit the rigor of science, New Keynesian economics, while less accurate from a scientific standpoint, has the advantage of being easily amenable to policymaking. To gain relevance for policy purposes, therefore, economics as engineering needs to momentarily stray from scientific accuracy.

While Roth, Duflo, and Mankiw located the engineer's attitude at the policymaking level, other economists stationed it at the theoretical model building. Speaking of his "neoclassical growth model," the macroeconomist Robert Solow told our colleague Verena Halsmayer (2014: 241) that it could be considered engineering "in the design sense." What Solow meant was that this model could be conceived as a sort of prototype for more complex measuring devices, subject to simple manipulation, which enables "the modeler-economist to enter a new, unexplored, world" (241). In that case, the engineering aspect is enhanced by the fact that Solow's own institution, MIT, is an engineering school and that the model was partly intended as a pedagogical device for the students, most of whom were future engineers.[1] Solow's model is not the only macroeconomic device that was built using engineering techniques. In fact, as Esther-Mirjam Sent (1997) has shown, all branches of postwar macroeconomics have been using them. New classical macroeconomics emerged from the appropriation by Lucas et al. of Richard Bellman's dynamic programming and Kálmán filtering (Judy Klein and Marcel Boumans, in this volume, develop and qualify the history of this appropriation). These economists may well believe that they helped their field become a *science*, yet they did so using *engineering* mathematics.

Not only practitioners but also historians of the discipline have addressed this engineering characterization of economics. Writing for a history of social science audience and building on the *HOPE* volume she had coedited with Malcolm Rutherford in 1998, Mary Morgan provided an account of the development of twentieth-century economics as that of an engineering science, arguing that it implied two things: first, that economics "came to rely on a certain precision of representation of the economic world, along with techniques of quantitative investigation and exact analysis that were alien to the experience of nineteenth-century of economics"; second, that it is "best characterized as a science of applications and implies a technical art, one that relies on tacit knowledge and decidedly human input" (Morgan 2003: 276).[2]

Michel Armatte (2010) expanded on Morgan's argument and wrote a book-length depiction of the transformation of political economy into an

---

1. Economics was a compulsory subject for all MIT undergraduates, even those who were not enrolled in a social science program.

2. In fact, Morgan was not the first historian of economics to use the "economics as engineering" analogy. In his 1979 presidential address to the History of Economics Society, Craufurd Goodwin (1980: 619), then editor of this journal, wrote: "If economists do insist on taking models for the development of their subject from elsewhere rather than constructing new ones, a closer analogy than the physical sciences may be engineering. Much of what economists do is more comparable to the designing and fabricating of structures for social use than to the laboratory work of the physicist."

engineering science, covering several national experiences and various subfields—from econometrics to environmental economics. In his account, "economics as engineering" is characterized by the development of a unified body of doctrine (neoclassical economics), a new way of using evidence (quantitative and mathematical), the inclusion of economic theory into a socioeconomic environment (a new management of economic activities), and the rise of a new kind of economic expertise (in think tanks and other institutions).

While the economics as engineering analogy seems to work well as a backdrop to articulate a relatively cohesive narrative about the discipline's development, it also undermines some of the actual tensions that have existed between economics and engineering in that period. In the article mentioned above, Sent (1997: 277) summed it up by writing that "while economists attempted to develop scientific knowledge . . . engineers are practical people who are concerned with getting specific jobs done and who seek satisfactory solutions in the face of complexities and uncertainties. Engineers are known to use trial-and-error empiricisms and rule-of-thumb techniques that could not be generalized to a wide range of problems."

Most of these accounts of economics as engineering, whether written from an economist's or a historian's perspective, share a number of common traits: they point to the fact that the depiction of economics as a science leaves aside some important practical aspects involved in the application of economic knowledge to real-life situations; the necessity to have recourse to tinkering and trial-and-error procedures, both in modeling practices and in the use of these models for policy purposes; the characterization of economic issues as necessitating complex computational processes; and, more generally, the characterization of the economy as a machine. However, there is room for deeper scrutiny. For instance, while Roth characterizes the transformation of economics into an engineering science as a relatively recent—post-1980s—feature of the discipline, Morgan and Armatte locate that transformation at the turn of the twentieth century. Also, while Roth and Mankiw circumscribe the engineering attitude to certain aspects of the discipline, that of policymaking and market design, others consider the analogy as a more general take on economics. More important, what is more often left aside is the actual interaction between economists and engineers. How did the latter react to economists' appropriation of their tools, and were they themselves interested in taking into account economic knowledge as part of their professional activities?[3] This points to the fact that economics *as* engineering, taken as an analogy, while insightful, may not be the best way to grasp or assess, from a historical standpoint, the presumed transformation of economics into an engineering science. To do this, we might turn instead to the history of economics *and* engineering: accounts of how these two types of knowledge—and the communities who produce them—have interacted in various institutional and national contexts.

## Historicizing "Economics and Engineering": A *HOPE* Conference

The encounters between economics and engineering have been seldom documented in the existing historical literature, yet there are hints that these interactions may have been more significant than is currently acknowledged. Besides modern macroeconomics, one instantiation most familiar to historians of economics is the contribution by mid-nineteenth-century French engineers to the development of what would be later termed "microeconomics."[4] Robert Ekelund and Robert Hébert have argued on many occasions (most notably Ekelund and Hébert 1999) that Jules Dupuit, an engineer at the École des Ponts et Chaussées, should be considered the founder of neoclassical economics. However, because they look at past engineering from the perspective of modern economics, reading Dupuit's writings in search of evidence of antecedents to contemporary economic verities, the authors do not say much about the context in which the practices of French engineers occurred and their relation to the existing economists' community. On the other hand, when we move away from the economist's perspective and look at the literature in engineering, there is ample evidence that economic matters have constituted an object of interest for engineers since the end of the nineteenth century, mostly at the educational level—the "engineering economics" class that was compulsory in most US engineering programs (see Bix, this volume). After World War II, some engineers, like Arnold Tustin and A. W. Phillips, began to be interested in analyzing the economy as a mechanical system, inventing paper tools and physical devices to do so (see Klein, this volume). Some of

3. While pointing to these divergences between economists and engineers, Sent (1997) does not really attempt to put them in historical perspective.

4. Since that time, an important feature of the engineering curriculum in France is the strong background in mathematics. Not surprisingly, there has been a long tradition of studying the French engineers turned economists as originating a branch of mathematical economics. For a panorama of this literature, see Mosca 1998.

these attempts have been addressed in the existing literature (see, for instance, Morgan 2012 on the Phillips machine), but, on the whole, not much is known about the extent to which they actually participated in the transformation of economics or the reasons they failed to do so.

There also exist contributions standing outside disciplinary history that can be interpreted as implicit accounts of the interaction between engineering and economics (among other social sciences). Guy Alchon's (1985) history of planning in the 1920s depicts how social scientists collaborated with business managers in the creation of an American branch of planning, which the author labels "technocratic progressivism" (see also Layton 1986). The thought collective he describes associates institutionalist economists like Wesley Mitchell and Taylorites like the engineer Morris L. Cooke, who would later head the Rural Electrification Administration under President Franklin D. Roosevelt's legislature. Likewise, Erickson et al. (2013) told the story of how the Cold War transformed rationality, first seen as a human faculty associated with the enlightenment to its modern algorithmic, formal, and mechanistic version. Their narrative situates that change at the crossroads between engineering, operations research, economics, management, psychology, and the political sciences. In a quite similar vein, William Thomas's (2015) account of the sciences of policy in Britain and the United States during the twentieth century tells the story of how the nascent disciplines of operations research and management science—both neighboring to economics in some way—were grounded in military planning and engineering practices. All those contributions evoke economics knowledge to some extent, but because the economics discipline is not at the center of their narrative, not much is said about disciplinary exchanges between engineering and economics and how the latter has been transformed in the process.

Finally, several works in the history of engineering have sought to portray American engineers' conflicted relation to techno-capitalism over the past century. David Noble (1977) depicts their transformation into business managers during the first decades of the twentieth century, pointing to their role in the rise and defense of corporate capitalism. On the other hand, Matthew Wisnioski's (2012) study of engineering in the 1960s analyzes the debates among engineers during a period where technology ceased to be seen as an engine of liberation and progress. In response to this challenge, engineers became "socio-technologists" who would help society adjust to technological change. These stories do not specifically address economics as a discipline, yet they deal with the engineers' various visions of the economic system and their take on subjects such as growth and sustainability.

Although fragmentary, the preceding elements were enough for us to think that a more systematic investigation into the economics-engineering nexus would constitute a useful addition to the history of both disciplines. Under the patronage of the Center for the History of Political Economy and Duke University Press, we invited an eclectic group of historians of economics, historians of science, and engineering studies scholars to write papers on this topic. The resulting conference was held April 5–6, 2019, in the Breedlove Conference Room of the Perkins Library at Duke University. The present volume collects most of the papers that were presented there, with a foreword by the engineering scholar David Blockley and closing comments by the researcher responsible for drawing our interest in this topic in the first place, Mary Morgan.

## Identifying the Economics-Engineering Nexus: The Historiographical Challenge

We may not need to properly define "economics" and "engineering" in order to retrace the history of their relation in the twentieth century. Yet, because we need to start somewhere, we must at least identify the sites where economics and engineering knowledge are produced and the communities that produce them. Traditionally, historians of economics have studied the sort of economics that has been produced within academe and whose output is mostly found in treatises or scientific articles—but the practice turn has challenged this and opened up what we understand by economics (see Boumans and Duarte 2019). The question of whether economics taken in that sense is a unified field is subject to debate (see, for instance, Davis 2019), but at least when considered from an academic perspective, it is one discipline, and a relatively structured one—with journal rankings, *JEL* codes, and so on.

On the other hand, while there certainly exists engineering knowledge produced within academe, in engineering schools and departments, it is just a small part of what engineering is about. Blockley (2010) observes that engineering includes many subdisciplines, noting that in the UK alone there are more than thirty different professional institutions that qualify engineers. In his foreword to this volume, he seeks less to define engineering than to characterize it in opposition to science: whereas science is about "knowing," engineering is about "doing" things, that is designing and/or building a device—not necessarily a physical one—in order to satisfy human needs, those of a client, for instance. But while in the traditional conception of science, knowledge is created at an abstract level and then "applied" to solve practical problems, in engineering knowledge creation occurs as the by-product of practice itself (see also Vincenti 1990).[5] This horizontal character of engineering, as opposed to the more vertical nature of applied science, must be taken into account when we analyze knowledge transfer from engineering to economics. To do this, we must first ask ourselves what sort of engineering we are talking about—mechanical engineering, civil engineering, chemical engineering, electrical engineering, systems engineering—and, second, look outside academe. For instance, when we analyze the use of "engineering mathematics" in modern macroeconomics, we need to take into account that engineering mathematics itself has a history and that it may have evolved in accordance with the set of practical issues in which it was grounded. Borrowing one's mathematics from control engineering or from information engineering will therefore produce different sorts of macroeconomic knowledge (see Boumans, this volume).

Reciprocally, the more we study the relation between economics and engineering the more we realize that our traditional vision of economics as, first and foremost, an academic discipline might itself be unsatisfying. Admittedly, economists mostly identify themselves as academics. In the United States, even economists who act as experts for governments, businesses, and other sorts of nonacademic institutions draw their legitimacy for doing so from their success in a highly competitive academic environment (Fourcade 2009). The so-called applied turn in economics did not really compromise the discipline's academic anchorage. The typical applied economist may occasionally venture outside the university, but doing so is not a necessary condition to define one as an applied economist because most of her activities (the analysis of natural and controlled experiments and the building of databases, for instance) take place in the confines of the research center (Backhouse and Cherrier 2017).

However, when we move to the study of economics and engineering, we come up with a reversed situation. While there are occasional instances

5. The notion of applied science has been a controversial one among historians of technology and on characterizing engineering as such (see Alexander 2012). Besides, the reasoning style and the knowledge engineers produce possess elements that cannot be reduced to verbal descriptions and, thus, depend on a mental process that is visual and nonverbal, according to Eugene Ferguson (1992).

when economists have absorbed engineering knowledge without having
to do fieldwork, most of the engineering-economics nexus is located outside academe, and, at times, it does not even involve the sort of professionals we commonly identify as "economists." In other terms, the history of
that nexus cannot be fully grasped without having a fairly extensive view
of what economics is. Therefore, it is no wonder that many contributions
in this volume do not deal with academic economics, or when they do so,
they examine their practices in nonacademic settings. For instance, rather
than studying "price theory," Daniel Breslau's and Guillaume Yon's
respective chapters deal with "pricing," a practice that relates only partly
to theory, although it quite unintentionally ended up producing knowledge
that the economics profession has come to identify as part of its own
canon (the Ramsey-Boiteux pricing, for instance).

Seen from the perspective of engineering history rather than the history
of economics, there are two main reasons why historicizing the economics-engineering nexus is particularly challenging. The first is that engineering has evolved to display "extreme diversity of . . . jobs and realizations" that has clear national traits, as the engineering historian Antoine
Picon (2004: 422) argued:

> Engineering looks more like a continent marked by striking contrasts
> than like a unified field. On this continent, no self-evident link seems to
> exist between the organization of the profession and the various activi-
> ties engineers are involved in. In this context, it may be tempting either
> to define the engineer through his social identity and aspirations or to
> limit oneself to a relatively narrow domain of technological expertise.

The second reason is that engineers have attempted, since the Renaissance, to ground their practice on science and at the same time to distance
themselves from "down-to-earth practitioners" (Picon 2004: 429), which
implies that there is "some kind of intermediate know-how" between "the
formalized knowledge that can be traced through courses and treatises, and
the everyday decisions made by engineers" (424). As a consequence, Picon
argues, the temptation is "to define the engineers through a certain kind of
rational argumentation, either in design or in decision-making" (429).

While this could sound like music to the ears of economists, the historically contingent notion of rationality and of efficiency in engineering has
sharp contrasts to those in economics that came with the widespread
acceptance of Lionel Robbins's definition of economics.[6] Rationality in

---

6. Roger Backhouse and Steve Medema (2009) discuss the acceptance of Robbins's definition.

engineering "appears primarily as a guideline for action," revealing itself "primarily through the concrete practice of design, technological development and decision-making rather than in purely discursive structures" (Picon 2004: 429).[7] Picon then argues that "contrary to a long tradition in the social sciences, when confronted with science and above all technology, rational behavior cannot be separated from the objectives it aims at" (429–30), to conclude:

> This constant interaction means that rationality is not synonymous with a crystal-clear attitude consisting in the determination of the most appropriate means towards an end, whatever it is. In other words, rationality cannot be reduced to a sort of calculation. Ends and means do not follow similar paths. They are often somewhat contradictory. Their interaction is synonymous with perturbations that transforms rationality into something more muddy, so to say, than what one might expect a priori.
>
> Another reason for this muddy nature lies in the fact that the engineer's rationality is not a pure individual conduct. It emerges in a context of interaction with other partners. Beside the other engineers, it has to take into account the existence of entrepreneurs and workers, even if it tries to set its own agenda. Rather than the result of a solitary exercise of the mind, rationality is the product of interaction, communication, and conflict. (430)

Both Picon (2004) and Blockley (this volume) call attention to the fact that efficiency, or fitness for purpose, means to have a good representation of what matters in the physical world (given that engineers typically see themselves as mediators between nature and man). So both efficiency and rationality are central concerns to engineering and to economics, but they became understood very differently in those areas. Paying attention to the actual interactions of engineering and economics requires, therefore, handling historiographical challenges that are not minor.

### The Economics-Engineering Nexus Delivered

As its title suggests, the structure of this volume is tripartite. The contributions focus on the relation between economists and engineers within specific institutions, or on the way tools traveled from one area to the other, or

---

7. Picon (2004: 429) highlights that "rationality is not to be confused with logic at large. Contrary to logic, rationality is permeated by all sorts of historically determined factors like the representations of nature and man that prevail in a given society."

on how the engineering-economics relation operated in specific national cultures. Of course, these three aspects are necessarily interrelated, and several contributions ended up addressing them together.

Our volume, accordingly, starts, in part 1, with three chapters on interactions between economics and engineering knowledge in specific types of institutions. The set of institutions covered in Amy Bix's contribution is the American engineering school in the first half of the twentieth century. Showing that there is more to economics education intended for future engineers than Paul Samuelson's *Economics*, she analyzes how economic concerns were present in the engineering profession since the late nineteenth century, focusing especially on the attempt by the Society for the Promotion of Engineering Education to counter the widespread claim that engineers were deemed responsible for "technological unemployment" during the Great Depression. It is in that context that engineering educators developed their own version of economics knowledge and spread it through textbooks and courses, coming up with the subfield of "engineering economics."

While dealing with the same period of time, Thomas Stapleford's chapter explores economics and engineering knowledge developed not in academe but in private businesses. Depicting Malcolm Rorty's work for American Telephone & Telegraph Company, he argues that some of the distinct features of telephone engineering created opportunities for the interaction between economists and engineers, especially when it came to choosing the optimal amount of investment to respond to the demand. Trained as an electrical and mechanical engineer, Rorty helped develop market forecasting techniques and wrote about economics on the occasion of debates over the public ownership of utilities. Focusing on Rorty is interesting also because he, unbeknownst to most historians of economics, was one of the founders of the National Bureau of Economic Research with Wesley Mitchell. And yet, Rorty was only one engineer among a handful whose work for telephone companies contributed to the development of operations research and management science during World War II.

The last chapter in part 1, by Béatrice Cherrier and Aurélien Saïdi, is also the only one in this volume that deals with a particular place, Stanford University. Home of many self-professed "economic engineers" like Roth, David Kreps, Paul Milgrom, and Robert Wilson, Stanford has a long history of cross-fertilization between economics and engineering tools, merging economic modeling with statistics, optimal control, and game theory. None of those research programs, however, are specific to

Stanford. What is specific is how they were combined and infused with an entrepreneurial spirit later exhibited by Roth and the like. However, it was never a straightforward story, especially as economics was not considered an important force at Stanford until relatively recently and was scattered through many different and at times competing departments and schools there: the economics department and, most important for our purposes, the engineering department and the Graduate School of Business.

The second part of the volume deals with tool transfers. Building on many years of historical work on the military's influence on the mathematical social sciences, Judy Klein depicts the "shotgun weddings" between control engineering and applied mathematics that produced techniques eventually used in modern macroeconomics. In some ways, her narrative starts where Stapleford's left off, depicting the association between the engineering of long-distance telecommunication and that of regulators such as thermostats in the production of servomechanisms to control weapons during World War II. The new technologies, using negative feedback loops to enhance a system's stability, were soon extended to human areas such as economics. Both critics and defenders of state intervention to stabilize the economy shaped their discourse using concepts taken from feedback-loop engineering. By the time economists joined, though, a second shotgun wedding had occurred, one between optimization theory and the theory of stochastic processes, which would most notably nurture rational expectations theory in macroeconomics. This is where Marcel Boumans's chapter picks up. His contribution focuses on the macroeconomist Robert Lucas, who developed his models while at the Graduate School of Industrial Administration at the Carnegie Institute of Technology, in the wake of Charles Holt and Herbert Simon's research project on business forecasting and decision-making using engineering methods. Boumans argues that what permitted the rational expectations "revolution" was a shift from control to information engineering. This is not a neutral move: while control engineering depicted a world dominated by human-machine relationships, information engineering described one populated with information-processing robots.

The third chapter in part 2, by William Thomas, revisits a seemingly well-known episode in the history of economics, Kenneth Arrow's 1963 paper on the economics of medical care. While that article, which is considered a staple of information and uncertainty theory, is generally depicted as emanating from theoretical concerns over efficiency and rationality, Thomas connects Arrow's contribution to his research at RAND on military R&D.

There, Arrow developed the view that sequential information gathering could help reduce uncertainty. That work was qualitative and descriptive, emphasizing the tentative and approximate nature of decision-making. This descriptive character also pervaded Arrow's work on health economics. Therefore, Thomas argues that Arrow's place in the history of economic theory should not just be seen through the prism of his pushing for a more formalistic economic theory, as this would undermine the heterogeneous character of his methodology.

The fourth and last chapter on tool transfers, by Chung-Tang Cheng, explored another allegedly engineering-induced economic technique: microanalytic simulation (microsimulation), invented by Guy Orcutt. Cheng argues that Orcutt's approach was influenced by his engineering and physics backgrounds, and describes it as an alternative to the Cowles Commission econometric models. Microsimulation used the engineering of feedback loops, creating a model in which knowledge is derived not only from the study of aggregate data but from analyzing how components in an economic system work with one another and react to external changes. Used as a technique to simulate welfare policies, it became a tool to reengineer society.

The final part of our volume offers three chapters placing the engineering-economics nexus in specific professional practices and/or national contexts. Daniel Breslau's contribution deals with electricity pricing in the United States, depicting the efforts of a group of researchers—electrical engineers and economists—led by the control theorist Fred Schweppe to build an efficient marketplace for wholesale electricity. This followed the demise of the regulated load-following system, in which it was taken for granted that the dispatch of power—and therefore prices—should adjust to the changing demand. Schweppe came up with a new pricing method, called "locational marginal pricing," in which at each location prices are equal to the marginal cost of serving one additional unit of electricity. While this seems to match neoclassical price theory in a perfectly competitive market, Breslau argues that the Schweppe team reached that conclusion not by thinking in terms of deregulated, free markets but by introducing price signals and consumer participation into a self-correcting control scheme. Therefore, he presents a case study of market design where the designers were not the typical Roth-like economists but actual engineers.

The second contribution in this part, by Guillaume Yon, also deals with electricity pricing but in a different context: France in the immediate postwar period. The author presents electricity pricing at the crossroads between engineering, economics, and French politics. Focusing on Marcel Boiteux's work as a civil servant for Electricité de France, the state monopoly, from the late 1940s onward, it presents the development of long-term marginal cost pricing as a calculative technique that did not emanate from economic theory but from an equipment issue. Like in the United States at the same period, the pricing of electricity rested on assumptions about the growth in the load. But in postwar France growth was politically, not technologically induced, as it was a rule devised by the Commissariat général au Plan, the French planning agency, that the production of electricity should double every ten years. In addition to solving this equipment issue, long-term marginal cost pricing had two other roles in the economy: that of providing instructions to the users of electricity so that they would act according to the plan and that of constituting a social contract with the population, in which the burden of large-scale investment would be fairly distributed among citizens.

The final paper of part 3 explores the economics-engineering nexus in Soviet Russia during the post-Stalin era. Ivan Boldyrev studies the work of a group of engineers led by the control engineer Mark Aizerman at the Institute of Control Sciences in Moscow, who ended up developing knowledge in choice theory that, outside Russia, would be considered part of economics. Moving freely from one area to another is what permitted Aizerman and his team to be in contact with "bourgeois" economists in Western countries and develop knowledge that would have been otherwise considered subversive to the authorities.

Finally, Mary Morgan offers some concluding remarks. Reassessing her initial thesis that economics has transformed into an engineering science during the twentieth century, she now distinguishes between two engineering modes: the engineering design mode and the tool-based engineering mode of problem solving. Drawing on this distinction, she then comments on the articles in this volume.

## Building a New Metanarrative
## or Revisiting Old Ones?

It is not for us to judge whether these contributions, taken together, participate in the making of a new metanarrative in the history of economics.[8] On

8. One of the editors has argued (Giraud 2019) that metanarratives mostly belong to the past of the history of economics discipline and that the best we can do is to qualify and elaborate on already existing ones. Nonetheless, Roy Weintraub (2014: 4) revisited the "narrative approaches to telling the story of how economics changed in the postwar period" to then launch a new one that is important for understanding the rise of MIT economics.

the other hand, it is rather clear that they show that the economists' own metanarrative that their discipline has transformed into an engineering science in the second half the twentieth century cannot be accepted without a few qualifications. Indeed, most of the chapters can be read as evidence that while there were many interactions between economics and engineering knowledge, these exchanges have not always changed the scope and culture of each discipline. In substance, economists and engineers still retain their respective visions of technology and markets. At the risk of oversimplifying, we can say that whereas most engineers consider prices as either parameters or solutions to a problem essentially driven by technological characteristics, most economists see prices as conveying epistemic truths and the markets where they are determined as truth-generating engines.

Likewise, a word like *efficiency*, while used in both disciplines, will take a specific meaning in each of them. For engineers, efficiency is mostly a technical property, whereas for economists it is related to a certain allocation of resources. Of course, there are many ways in which economists and engineers can interact and make use of these concepts to solve practical issues, but it is unlikely they will leave each other with a better mutual understanding of such issues. The same could be said about those disciplines' respective professional attitudes and values. While economists are interested in solving practical economic and social issues, their career advancement is still based on scientific merits, as attested by publications in leading journals, and their sense of accountability regarding the economic and social consequences of the devices they help build is still limited. In other terms, economists' contacts with engineering did not prevent them from going on acting mostly as (applied) scientists.

Whether or not they may offer a new metanarrative, the chapters in this volume at least not only allow for a reconsideration of some of the main existing ones concerning the transformation of economics in the twentieth century but also invite engineering historians to better understand what Picon (2004: 421) presented as a still open-ended issue: what are the relations between engineering history and social history, or "what can we learn through engineering evolution that concerns society and culture at large?" For the side of economics, while the histories of the field's mathematization and more generally of its transformation into a more technical discipline have been mostly considered through the prism of theory (e.g., Weintraub 2002), the story of economics' relation with engineering reminds us that the technical turn also arose from the treatment of practical issues—Thomas's reconstruction of the engineering roots of Arrow's uncertainty and information theory provides compelling evidence of this, and so does Yon's depiction of Boiteux's long-term marginal cost.

Similarly, looking at the involvement of economics with World War II and Cold War military funding not from the viewpoint of its association with "big science" but through the prism of its interacting with engineering offers a fresher look. Whereas the military-industrial complex story is most often interpreted from the perspective of economists as an opportunity to assuage their science envy, Klein's chapter describes how some of these interactions came through the initiative of the engineers, who identified similarities between economics and problems in control engineering they had been used to deal with while participating in the war effort. Additionally, looking through the economics-engineering nexus helps us better understand how Samuelson's famous textbook, *Economics*, which developed a streamlined version of Keynesianism in order to make it fit for future engineers at MIT, should take into account Bix's study of the engineer's side of the story. Finally, looking at the engineering-economics nexus in certain national traditions helps qualify the simple history of the internationalization of economic knowledge. Being an engineer or an economist in France or in the USSR implies a social function that differs from that of US engineers and economists. While exhibiting a neutral and universal character, the knowledge that these people produce is most often embedded in their respective countries' politics.

Like most *HOPE* conference and annual volumes, this one does not seek completion. Instead, our role is to encourage further work. Therefore we hope that the reader will find herself sufficiently stimulated to want to expand the research to other topics and periods of time. One aspect that this volume did not cover and that may be of interest to both historians of economics and STS scholars is the competing views of engineers and economists about technology and, even most important, the environment. More generally, we also hope that this volume will encourage historians of both economics and engineering to move further away from disciplinary history and start considering the extent to which what they perceive as knowledge in their respective fields is in fact jointly produced.

## References

Alchon, Guy. 1985. *The Invisible Hand of Planning: Capitalism, Social Science, and the State in the 1920s*. Princeton, NJ: Princeton University Press.

Alexander, Jennifer. 2012. "Thinking Again about Science in Technology." *Isis* 103, no. 3: 518–26.

Armatte, Michel. 2010. *La science* économique *comme ingénierie*. Paris: Presses des Mines.

Backhouse, Roger, and Béatrice Cherrier, eds. 2017. *The Age of the Applied Economist: The Transformation of Economics since the 1970s*. Supplemental issue to vol. 49 of *History of Political Economy*. Durham, NC: Duke University Press.

Backhouse, Roger E., and Steve G. Medema. 2009. "Defining Economics: The Long Road to Acceptance of the Robbins Definition." *Economica*, n.s., 76 (supplement 1): 805–20.

Banerjee, Abhijit. 2007. *Making Aid Work*. Cambridge, MA: MIT Press.

Blockley, David. 2010. *Engineering: A Very Short Introduction*. Oxford: Oxford University Press.

Boumans, Marcel, and Pedro G. Duarte. 2019. "The History of Macroeconometric Modeling: An Introduction." *HOPE* 51, no. 3: 391–400.

Davis, John. 2019. "Specialization, Fragmentation, and Pluralism in Economics." *European Journal of the History of Economic Thought* 26, no. 2: 271–93.

Duflo, Esther. 2017. "Richard T. Ely Lecture: The Economist as Plumber." *American Economic Review* 107, no. 5: 1–26.

Ekelund, Robert, and Robert Hébert. 1999. *Secret Origins of Modern Microeconomics: Dupuit and the Engineers*. Chicago: University of Chicago Press.

Erickson, Paul, Judy Klein, Lorraine Daston, Rebecca Lemov, Thomas Sturm, and Michael D. Gordin. 2013. *How Reason Almost Lost Its Mind: The Strange Career of Cold War Rationality*. Chicago: University of Chicago Press.

Ferguson, Eugene. 1992. *Engineering and the Mind's Eye*. Cambridge, MA: MIT Press.

Fourcade, Marion. 2009. *Economists and Societies*. Princeton, NJ: Princeton University Press.

Giraud, Yann. 2019. "Five Decades of *HOPE*." *HOPE* 51, no. 4: 601–69.

Goodwin, Craufurd. 1980. "Toward a Theory of the History of Economics." *HOPE* 12, no. 4: 610–19.

Halsmayer, Verena. 2014. "From Exploratory Modeling to Technical Expertise: Solow's Growth Model as a Multipurpose Design." In *MIT and the Transformation of American Economics*, edited by E. Roy Weintraub. *History of Political Economy* 46 (supplement): 229–51.

Layton, Edwin. 1986. *The Revolt of the Engineers: Social Responsibility and the American Engineering Profession*. 2nd ed. Baltimore: Johns Hopkins University Press.

Mankiw, N. Gregory. 2006. "The Macroeconomist as Scientist and Engineer." *Journal of Economic Perspectives* 20, no. 4: 29–46.

Morgan, Mary S. 2003. "Economics." In *The Modern Social Sciences*, edited by Theodore M. Porter and Dorothy Ross, 275–305. Vol. 7 of *The Cambridge History of Science*. Cambridge: Cambridge University Press.

Morgan, Mary S. 2012. *The World in the Model: How Economists Think and Work*. Cambridge: Cambridge University Press.

Morgan, Mary, and Malcolm Rutherford, eds. 1998. *From Interwar Pluralism to Postwar Neoclassicism*. Supplemental issue to vol. 30 of *History of Political Economy*. Durham, NC: Duke University Press.

Mosca, Manuela. 1998. "Jules Dupuit, the French 'ingénieurs économistes,' and the Société d'Économie Politique." In *Studies in the History of French Political Economy: From Bodin to Walras*, edited by Gilbert Faccarello, 254–83. London: Routledge.

Noble, David F. 1977. *America by Design: Science, Technology, and the Rise of Corporate Capitalism*. New York: Knopf.

Picon, Antoine. 2004. "Engineers and Engineering History: Problems and Perspectives." *History and Technology* 20, no. 4: 421–36.

Roth, Alvin. 2002. "The Economist as Engineer: Game Theory, Experimentation, and Computation as Tools for Design Economics." *Econometrica* 70, no. 4: 1341–78.

Sent, Esther-Mirjam. 1997. "Engineering Dynamic Economics." In *New Economics and Its History*, edited by John B. Davies. *History of Political Economy* 39 (supplement): 41–62.

Thomas, William. 2015. *Rational Action: The Sciences of Policy in Britain and America, 1940–1960*. Cambridge, MA: MIT Press.

Vincenti, Walter. 1990. *What Engineers Know and How They Know It: Analytical Studies from Aeronautical History*. Baltimore: Johns Hopkins University Press.

Weintraub, E. Roy. 2002. *How Economics Became a Mathematical Science*. Durham, NC: Duke University Press.

Weintraub, E. Roy. 2014. "Introduction: Telling the Story of MIT Economics in the Postwar Period." In *MIT and the Transformation of American Economics*, edited by E. Roy Weintraub. *History of Political Economy* 46 (supplement): 1–12.

Wisnioski, Matthew. 2012. *Engineers for Change: Competing Visions of Technology in 1960s America*. Cambridge, MA: MIT Press.

# Economics and Engineering in Institutional Contexts

# The Wider Context of Samuelson's MIT Textbook— Depression-Era Discussions about the Value of Economics Education for American Engineers

Amy Sue Bix

"This book is written primarily as a textbook for those who will never take more than one or two semesters of economics," Paul Samuelson declared in the opening sentence of his 1948 work *Economics: An Introductory Analysis*. As a professor at the Massachusetts Institute of Technology, Samuelson had firsthand experience of the challenges involved in teaching economics to nonmajors. As other historians have noted, MIT explicitly pressed Samuelson to write his textbook to serve the school's particular audience, heavily made up of engineering students.

Historians of economics have tended to accept the impression that Samuelson and MIT undertook this project because nobody else was concerned with the need to help future engineers understand economic principles. In reality, engineering professionals and educators had been extensively discussing the issue of how to instill a good economics education in future engineers for years before Samuelson began writing his textbook. Samuelson was not the first economics professor to experiment with new methods aimed at teaching engineering majors. In the years before World War II, economics faculty had joined engineering faculty in sharing ideas and strategies for teaching economics to engineers through exchanges at

Thanks for research assistance to Kelsey Murphy of Iowa State University and to Matthew Brown and Joanne Dera of the New Jersey Institute of Technology. I thank Yann Giraud, Pedro Garcia Duarte, and other members of the spring 2019 *HOPE* conference at Duke for their helpful suggestions.

*History of Political Economy* 52 (annual suppl.)  DOI 10.1215/00182702-8717910

professional conferences and in journal publications. The engineering community's pre–World War II conversation regarding exactly when, how, and what engineering students should learn about economics thus situates this key episode of Samuelson's life, the authorship of one of the most influential textbooks in modern economics, in a broader intellectual context.

To trace this pre-Samuelson attention to the question of economics education for engineers, it is necessary to shift attention away from economics departments and toward the engineering world itself. Most notably, meetings, activities, and publications of the Society for the Promotion of Engineering Education (SPEE) in the years before World War II offered the most logical space for faculty and professionals to address the subject of filling what seemed to be a serious educational gap. As SPEE material from the 1930s shows, numerous professors and colleges worked to define an appropriate form of economics training for engineering majors and often created new courses or shaped curricula accordingly, though the resulting content and requirements varied widely.

The deepening economic catastrophe of the 1930s itself attached new urgency to discussions about the proper role of economics in engineering education, as the Depression undermined easy assumptions that technical innovation automatically ensured a steady rise in prosperity. Early twentieth-century development of cities, infrastructure, and the automobile, aviation, electrical, and entertainment industries had surrounded engineering with an exciting aura of modernization. The Depression suddenly destabilized such optimism, as a growing number of critics linked technological change to human misery, rather than rising living standards. President Franklin Delano Roosevelt, among others, warned about technological unemployment, the fear that mechanization had displaced workers faster than society and individuals could adapt.

In response, leading Depression-era engineers largely denied that mechanization-related job losses represented any real problem and constructed an alternative narrative of their world, one that directly credited engineering with civilization's advance from generations of poverty to modern abundance. Interpreting talk of technological unemployment as accusatory, seemingly making engineers and scientists into scapegoats for the Depression, professionals positioned themselves as national economic saviors, rather than saboteurs. By placing themselves at the center of historical "progress," engineering educators reinforced their self-image during a stressful period and embedded that moralizing in lessons on economic history for majors.

Such stories that engineering faculty, college administrators, and other professional leaders repeated with conviction, about "who we are," both reflected and shaped the Depression era's discussion of engineering and economics. In particular, engineers openly voiced a position of intellectual superiority, arguing that technical training instilled a precision of mind in students, more valuable than the less rigorous humanities and social sciences. Following that assumption, engineers argued that although they bore no blame for having instigated economic decline, their unique mental discipline made engineers America's best hope to ensure economic recovery. Leading educators again created a new self-aggrandizing narrative, of engineers as embodying trained rationality, problem-solvers who could reinstall the nation's progress toward well-being if given greater respect and influence. Some faculty believed that engineers were already well prepared to assume public leadership; others campaigned to increase and broaden students' economic education as preparation to shape the perfect policies for business, government, and society.

Thus the 1930s represented a watershed decade for discussion about increasing and reshaping economics education in engineering programs, because engineers' movement into business management had by then become naturalized, because public discussion of technological unemployment infuriated engineers and led them to promote more self-glorifying accounts, and because engineers regarded themselves as experts in logic who could and should straighten out less-well-trained policymakers. But though the Depression-era crystallized engineering educators' sense of the importance of teaching students more economics, there was no consensus over direction. Some faculty and programs focused on business-oriented learning, accounting work, and microeconomics; others advanced broader studies of macroeconomics and economic history. Some colleges created their own material to teach economics to engineers, even as they recognized students' open resentment of such requirements. Some adopted existing textbooks specifically geared to explain economics to engineering students, though others criticized their quality. Such developments thus fill in a wider backstory to the genesis of Samuelson's 1948 textbook.

## 1.  Engineering's Evolution as a Profession

The profession of engineering in the United States evolved quickly and significantly following the mid-1800s. Engineering education had become increasingly formalized, gaining a foundation in a growing number of

American colleges. The Morrill Act of 1862 specifically provided federal assistance to support teaching of "agriculture and the mechanic arts." Advocates promoted ideals of democratically accessible education offering practical value to set young people on rewarding paths in life while advancing knowledge of farming and manufacture for state and national economic benefit (Nienkamp 2008). By 1872, the United States had about seventy schools teaching engineering. Some degree programs maintained extensive shop-work requirements, to ensure that graduates would fit into employment, rather than seem like abstract bookworms unable to tell one tool from another (Calhoun 1960). Engineering education retained the influence of what the historian Monte Calvert has called "shop culture," an emphasis on practical hands-on problem-solving that indoctrinated young men into traditions of technical work and gave them an entrepreneurial-minded orientation. Increasingly, however, faculty promoted a "school culture" that aimed to improve engineering graduates' status and remuneration by stressing their exposure to higher mathematics and theoretical science (Calvert 1967).

During the late nineteenth and early twentieth centuries, the growth of new industrialization, electrification, and large-scale construction promoted expansion of academic engineering training and professional formalization. Growth of academic programs and employment opportunities fostered disciplinary specialization. Focused identities accordingly evolved, with the emergence of the American Society of Civil Engineers (1852), American Society of Mechanical Engineers (1880), American Institute of Electrical Engineers (1884), and American Institute of Chemical Engineers (1908). Inside American colleges, engineering programs developed parallel specialization, with related but distinct curricula in each discipline, increasingly offering the option of advanced degrees. Not coincidentally, the late nineteenth and early twentieth centuries also witnessed professionalization and formalized growth of multiple other fields, including economics, sociology, history, and political science. Processes of discipline formation advanced through establishment of new norms of intellectual and collegial exchange (national journals, annual conferences, expanded graduate education, etc.), which in turn served as gatekeeping mechanisms to reaffirm assertions of expertise.

With development of large-scale technological systems in the big-business world of mechanical, electrical, and chemical industries throughout the late 1800s and early 1900s, growing numbers of American engineering graduates secured jobs with General Electric, Westinghouse, DuPont,

AT&T, and similar giant corporations. The engineering "organization man," to use a later nickname, gained a new range of opportunities to enter relatively steady, prestigious managerial positions. Cognizant of those trends, American engineers and engineering educators voiced concerns about the best way to prepare new generations of students to master the bureaucratic hierarchy and function well within that establishment environment. Management skills, business awareness, and economic knowledge all seemed increasingly relevant (Grayson 1993; Lundgreen 1990; Downey 2007; Sinclair 1980; Reynolds 1983; Layton 1971; McMahon 1984; Noble 1977).

As the historians Edwin Layton (1971), Peter Meiksins (1996), and others have documented, engineers' expanding role in management raised tensions within the profession. Some specialties, such as chemical engineering, welcomed the lucrative connections to corporate production work. As Layton (1971: 57) documents, engineering organizations between 1895 and 1920 sought to define the boundaries of their profession by asserting "an ideology of engineering" that "portrayed the engineer in glowing terms . . . as a vital force for human . . . enlightenment, . . . a logical thinker free of bias . . . [with] a special social responsibility to protect progress." Society officers and prominent members declared that engineers' skill in creative, honest problem-solving made them the perfect stewards of civilization and positioned themselves to defend business interests as the foundation for progress.

That alliance between engineering and management connected engineers to economics, with embedded assumptions about business success and efficiency equating to human progress. The early twentieth century brought the emergence of industrial engineering as an increasingly influential discipline, naturally wedded to business operations. The origins of scientific management, in the work of Frederick Winslow Taylor and his disciples, focused on ideas about time and motion study, piece rate pay, planning systems, and reengineering factory layout. Henry L. Gantt, Frank Gilbreth, and other practitioners advanced these ideas through articles, speeches, and consulting arrangements, while engineering educators in turn picked up those concepts and embedded them in instruction. Advocates such as Lillian Gilbreth extended the field through connection to psychology, and in turn, engineering schools began assessing whether their curricula should allow more room for classes in psychology, social science, and economics. Penn State, Purdue, the Carnegie Institute, Cornell, MIT, and NYU led the creation of industrial engineering departments and substantive coursework prior to World War I (Lytle 1931).

The closeness of engineering and the business establishment disturbed some engineers who valued independence over expectations of conformity and unswerving loyalty to employers. But the "Roaring Twenties" prosperity and "return to normalcy" sidelined calls for progressive reform within the profession, solidifying engineers' conservative, corporate-friendly mind-set. "By 1929, the profession was dominated by business," Layton (1971: 225) writes, yet "despite the conservative reaction, the underlying ideas of the engineers' ideology showed a surprising vitality. . . . Engineers continued to identify their profession with scientific and technological progress, they portrayed themselves as impartial middle men, and they stressed the idea that engineers bore a social responsibility for solving modern problems." Layton interprets such positioning as mere feel-good rhetoric that "led to no action" even as the nation's economy worsened, "little more than a ritual" for engineers to comfort themselves during difficult times (236).

I would suggest a more complex reality behind the ideology asserted by engineers about themselves during the Depression. Some members, most notably those focused on engineering education, did indeed use the crisis as a catalyst for action. Specifically, they initiated intense discussion aimed at pinpointing what students should learn about economics and accordingly instigated some changes in their teaching and curricula.

## 2. Teaching Engineering Students More Economics

At the start of the 1930s, engineering educators were well aware that managerial positions represented a widening path for graduates, with up to 75 percent of engineers moving into administrative functions during their career (Norton 1935, 1936). That fact represented a source of pride among engineers who believed their profession cultivated superior skills. R. A. Seaton (1934: 13), Kansas State's engineering dean, asserted that the engineer predictably did well in management, "due in no small measure to the sound fundamental training he had received in the engineering schools in the scientific method of approach . . . in correct and logical thinking, and in the elimination of guesswork . . . [by] sound judgments."

Working engineers' opinions reinforced the sense that lack of economic skill posed a professional problem. In one survey, 90.6 percent of young engineering alumni, as well as 69 percent of those five or more years past graduation, admitted they "were not as well qualified to deal with eco-

nomic elements as with technical elements of their engineering problems."
There were 456 respondents who specifically lamented not having more
business-administration background in college, 226 who wished they had
received more economics training, and 179 who wanted better accounting
preparation (Lytle 1931: 836). Professional credentialing mechanisms,
such as New York State's engineering-licensing examinations, also had
evolved to expect economics mastery. To help candidates meet that requirement, the American Institute of Electrical Engineers and American Society of Mechanical Engineers offered a special lecture series covering "the
business cycle as it affects the engineer, business organization and finances,
financial math, economics election and replacement studies, valuation and
appraisal—depreciation theory," and more (Ayres 1939: 758).

Much of this concern among graduates, faculty, and professional engineers related more closely to topics that might be considered business
administration, in contrast to economics proper. But the era allowed for a
great deal of overlap between these subjects, and teaching of the 1930s
crossed this line without concern. Some faculty, programs, and textbooks
put more emphasis on practical accounting and business economics; others aimed to guide young engineers to comprehend fundamental economic principles and consider larger policy matters, especially those
relating to prosperity, employment, and technological development. The
intersections between the functional and the political orientation, and the
differing weight to give each, were the very matters that engineering faculty and professionals debated and negotiated during the 1930s.

During the Depression era, many colleges instituted specific courses
and modules designed to help budding engineers understand accounting,
contracts, managerial specifications, and costs. Armour Institute of Technology offered a two-course sequence of "business and engineering problems" and "social and engineering problems" to freshmen, drawing on
real-world study examples taken directly from Chicago and Illinois public
engineering offices (Hotchkiss 1935: 87, 89, 93). Cornell created a new
degree in "administrative engineering," which substituted forty class-hours
of teaching in banking, investments, corporation finance, accounting, statistics, business organization, and management for upper-level technical
work (Garrett 1933: 51). In late 1929, William Ennis, professor of economics of engineering at Stevens Institute of Technology, wrote, "Practically
all engineering schools—I know of no exception, except possibly Cooper
Union—have courses in engineering economics or industrial engineering,
or management, or some apparently related subject" (Ennis 1929: 706). He

praised his own school, Stevens, for making "economics of engineering [into] a department just as much as is Chemistry or Physics" (706). Ennis saw such knowledge as mandatory for professional excellence. "Where an engineering situation involves economic factors—that is, business or commercial factors—there we belong. If there is a problem of engineering practice which does not involve such factors, I have not encountered it. Our men must have at least as much respect for, and acquaintance with, the dollar sign as for, and with, the sign of integration" (708).

Fostering discussion about the proper level of economics studies for young engineers, the American Society for Engineering Education devoted sizable attention to that matter during the Depression. Established in 1893, the SPEE (later renamed the American Society for Engineering Education) started publishing the *Journal of Engineering Education* in 1896. In the *Journal*'s pages, at SPEE meetings, and in its presidential addresses of the 1930s, engineering educators exchanged ideas about how much and what type of economics and management studies to offer. That debate represented a specific new manifestation of earlier conversations about what engineering majors should learn. In 1918, the SPEE had produced the Mann Report, an extensive assessment of how engineering curricula were and should be shaped. That report noted that by 1918, humanities-based courses had fallen from 27 percent to 19 percent of the engineering curriculum on average. In reaction, many professors and administrators campaigned to swing the pendulum back, to give young engineers a more broadly based college background.

Stanford University's Eugene Grant (1931: 655) emphasized the significance of this change, in which previous generations of engineering-school administrators had approached economics with "anything from mild disapproval to active opposition." In the early 1920s, one dean had flatly told him, "I am absolutely opposed to putting such courses as engineering economics into the curriculum," Grant wrote (656). Yet by 1931 "that attitude has all changed, I think . . . . deans of engineering colleges and department heads . . . recognize quite clearly the importance of this field, though many of them feel . . . groping in the dark as to just what should be taught and how" (656).

By the early 1930s, at least fifty schools (state schools such as Alabama, Arizona, Arkansas, Delaware, Florida, and Wisconsin, as well as private schools such as RPI, Yale, and Harvard) required at least some engineering majors to take at least one management class, with additional elective options. At least thirteen others (including Stevens, Missouri, Tennessee,

NYU, Columbia, Brooklyn Polytechnic, Colorado School of Mines, and Worcester Polytechnic) required students to take more than one year's worth of management. Harvard and the University of Texas almost entirely omitted management studies from engineering, but students could add a fifth-year curriculum made up of full-time management work (Lytle 1931: 817–19). The junior year of Ohio State University's industrial-engineering curriculum required classes on "economics principles," "laws of engineering management," an "outline of accounting," and "accounting: factory costs" (829–31). Purdue's industrial-engineering option within the mechanical engineering program expected juniors to take one semester of economics and seniors one semester of cost accounting.

While engineering education embraced a trend toward more management-related economics requirements, details varied substantially across institutions. Surveying eighteen industrial-engineering departments in 1931, the NYU professor Charles Lytle calculated that time devoted to industrial history and economics ranged from two class-hours to seventeen, with a median of six. Those programs also required anywhere from zero to fifteen class-hours of finance courses, zero to twelve class-hours for marketing, zero to ten for statistics, and zero to sixteen for cost-control studies. Lytle recommended greater standardization of practice, to establish economics and management lessons as norms. His vision of an ideal industrial-engineering curricula proposed three class-hours of industrial history, seven class-hours of economics (three for theoretical, four applied), nine for accounting (covering bookkeeping, cost analysis, and budgetary control), five for statistics, with electives including marketing, finance, and business law. Lytle (1931: 822–23, 826) suggested that a proper applied-economics course should teach future engineers "the various trends leading to the best known measures for economic stability," along with "the history of business cycles" and "economic formulae" for equipment replacement, lot sizes, and living costs. Management classes should teach the purchasing of materials and equipment, plus wage theories and "the mathematical analysis and design of plans" for financial incentives for factory, office, and sales workers (828–32).

Within many institutions, precise expectations for economics learning also varied across the different engineering specialties. Charles Debleth (1933: 401), University of California engineering dean, emphasized that at his school, civil engineers studied "contracts and economics." Mining students learned "mine development and methods, economics of mining, mine cost accounting, mine valuation, cost accounting in petroleum production"

(401). For mechanical-engineering majors, an elective in "mathematical principles of investment as applied to engineering structures" covered "the relation of the engineer to investment, effects of the introduction of . . . automatic machines . . . difficulties of defining cost . . . depreciation . . . economic maximum for building heights," and more (400–3).

The Columbia civil engineering professor J. K. Finch (1935: 690) declared that any "satisfactory" engineering education must include "due attention" to economics. Columbia had experimented with assigning engineering majors to take an early general economics course, but realized that upper-level engineers "promptly forgot about it" once "swamped with a highly concentrated and exacting program of strictly technical subjects [in which] the economic and social consequences of engineering activity were seldom mentioned" (691). Instead, Finch aimed to incorporate practical economics directly into the civil-engineering course for freshmen, the "natural setting" to address matters such as "economy of design, construction, or operation" in bridge building (692). Columbia's sophomore "transportation economics" class focused on public works administration, as a rapidly growing element of New Deal civil-engineering work. The ultimate goal, Finch said, was in cultivating "the interest of the student in the economic and social problems of modern life, the hope being, of course, that in the future the engineer will take a more active part in formulating public policies in those fields with which he is professionally concerned" (696).

In 1934, the SPEE hosted a special conference on "the teaching of engineering economy." Reviewing the discussion, the SPEE concluded that "more attention should be devoted, in all engineering curricula, to the economic phases of engineering [but] there is no such unanimity with regard to the best method to use in reaching the desired objective" (Barnes et al. 1935: 678). The conference committee favored having all engineering majors take a general-economics course offered by economics faculty, followed by a class on "the fundamentals of engineering economy" (678–79) taught by an engineering-based specialist in that area. They cautioned that since "engineering students tend to concentrate on the technical parts of the curriculum" (679), professors would need to consciously push students to appreciate the significance of their economics studies, by underlining its relevance to their future careers.

As that report illustrated, disagreement remained over whether engineering programs should require students to take the standard introductory economics survey, or ask economics professors to customize classes for engineering students, or locate such courses in the business college, or have engineering faculty create their own specialized economics or industrial-management courses. Ennis, along with many engineering educators, wanted the subject under their control, expressing frustration that economics professors failed to adapt classes to an engineering-major audience. Future engineers needed economics primarily to provide "tools in their future work," NYU's Lytle (1931: 837) complained, but "the typical economist . . . seems to go at it as though he were trying to make every member of his class a professional economist." Some institutions arranged joint custody; at Columbia University, engineering and business schools shared oversight of industrial-engineering education. University of Iowa professor C. C. Williams (1935: 9) found that unacceptable, warning that "combination courses in engineering and commerce have usually resulted in a mixture of the water of science with the oil of business rather than a homogeneous preparation suitable for the purpose." Williams wanted all engineering education to include economics "more than previously," but found "classic" economics simply "too hypothetical to serve the more quantitative requirements of engineers" (11).

Not surprisingly, economics faculty disagreed. Wisconsin economics professor Don Lescohier (1933–34: 415) told an SPEE audience that "a year's work in general economics is of fundamental importance," so that engineers working on major projects could apply not just technical expertise but also a full understanding of public finance and taxation. As "an industrial leader of the next generation," Lescohier said, the engineer needed to assist economists, political scientists, bankers, and business and labor leaders in analyzing the complexities of business cycles (419).

Lescohier believed that engineering curricula could easily clear room for students to take a year of economics, by conducting a "cold-blooded analysis" to identify and eliminate "obsolete" courses that lingered due to "inertia" or professors' vested interests while deferring highly technical studies for graduate training (414, 420). Engineering professors felt ambivalent; while many wanted students to have more management and economics background, they also regarded engineering as continually deepening in complexity, forcing the addition of specialized new technical classes. Moreover, a patronizing element deterred too close an embrace of outside subjects regarded as less rigorous; NYU's Lytle (1931: 838) told fellow engineers that "economics and psychology, although partially scientific, are certainly not so wholly scientific as are the physical sciences underlying engineering."

Engineers' confidence in their subject's intellectual superiority infected undergraduates, who often openly resented humanities and social-science requirements. In 1939, the Northwestern economics professor Wilfred Lake said that surveys of his students showed that 18 percent approached general-economics classes in "antagonistic" fashion (754). Willard Hotchkiss (1935: 89), president of Armour Institute of Technology, said that engineering majors recognized mathematics, science, drawing, and English as useful for their careers, but took an "indifferent or critical attitude" toward the social sciences, since their worth seemed "indefinite." Hotchkiss attributed such "adverse traditions" of dislike to a clash of cultures, reflecting again a certain engineering arrogance. "To the extent that economics employs deductive reasoning with but meager opportunity for testing hypotheses objectively and without bias, it is likely to impress students as highly speculative," Hotchkiss said (89). "Forcing factual material into conformity with accepted theory, and the highly controversial character of much of the discussion do violence to mental processes which in other parts of their work engineering students are taught to regard as indispensable to sound thinking" (93). But the Depression context mattered; alarm over the national crisis pushed many engineering educators to seek new ways for helping students appreciate the value of understanding economics.

## 3. Defending Engineering against Technological Unemployment Alarms

Through the late nineteenth century and the early twentieth, Americans had celebrated technological developments from the Philadelphia Centennial's Corliss engine to the Brooklyn Bridge and electrification, all appearing as both visible advances and intangible symbols of progress. Innovation seemed the ultimate guarantee of modernized prosperity; manufacturing output practically doubled through the 1920s. The apparently endless stream of new refrigerators, automobiles with annual model changes, and other novel consumer goods made it tempting to believe that technological change provided the key to continual economic and social progress. But as the Depression sent unemployment soaring, the idea of technology as foundation for steady employment suddenly began to appear a bitter joke. Desperately seeking to explain national economic disaster, both professionals and the public expressed growing concern about workplace mechanization in industrial, agricultural, and service jobs displacing humans. Talk of "technological unemployment" filled labor union meetings, government offices, and professional conferences of economists and sociologists. Concerned Americans pointed to cigar makers apparently displaced by rolling machinery, switchboard operators replaced by telephone dial systems, steel workers made redundant in new continuous-strip mills. The popular economic writer Stuart Chase (1931) asked, "Is it not all tragically ridiculous? Men are to tramp the streets by the thousands because machines can provide *more* than enough to go around. From now on, the better able we are to produce, the worse we shall be off. This is the economy of a madhouse."

Technological unemployment, of course, was neither a uniquely modern nor peculiarly American consideration; economists from David Ricardo to John Stuart Mill and Thomas Malthus had long analyzed relationships between mechanization, productivity, and employment. But the Depression moved such questions from abstraction to urgency, out of economic theorization and into front-page headlines. Classic economic assumptions promised that mechanization would ultimately benefit labor and consumers alike, but Americans worried that perhaps the new Machine Age had changed the rules, destabilizing many areas of employment simultaneously and rendering workers obsolete faster than they could retrain (Bix 2000).

Government experts under Roosevelt's administration explicitly defined mechanization as a special concern, creating a major Works Progress Administration research project to collect information. After reviewing data showing significant declines in employment over recent years even as productivity rose, WPA officials concluded, "A substantial proportion of unemployment in any single year has probably consisted of workers displaced from their jobs by technological progress. Since our economic system has not evinced an ability to make the necessary adjustments fast enough, dislocations occasioned by technological progress will continue to present serious problems of readjustment" (Weintraub 1937). President Roosevelt himself declared in a 1935 press conference that technological unemployment might be a chronic machine age problem. Because mechanization had so greatly increased industrial efficiency over just the last five years, Roosevelt said, returning to 1929's peak production would only provide work for 80 percent of unemployed; 20 percent would remain displaced (*New York Times* 1935). Roosevelt's 1940 State of the Union address warned that America faced a crisis of "finding jobs faster than invention can take them away. We have not yet found a way to employ the surplus of our labor which the efficiency of our industrial processes has created" (Roosevelt [1940] 1967).

Defying challenges to the equation of technological change with progress, the National Association of Manufacturers and prominent business leaders such as Henry Ford maintained that only anecdotal evidence interpreted technological unemployment as a major problem. Chase National Bank defined machine-related labor displacement as merely temporary, reasserting that rapid technological change acted as a "dynamic and energizing factor" (Anderson 1937). Similarly, for Depression-era engineers, the technological-unemployment debate seemingly involved judging the "innocence and guilt of science" and technology themselves (Budington 1933). In 1936, President Roosevelt told America's Society of Arts and Sciences, "I suppose that all scientific progress is, in the long run, beneficial, yet the very speed and efficiency of scientific progress in industry has created present evils, chief among which is unemployment."

Roosevelt's qualified phrase "I suppose," along with his direct link between efficiency and misery, shocked scientists and engineers. At a 1934 American Institute of Physics symposium titled "Science Makes More Jobs," Caltech physicist Robert Millikan declared flatly, "There is no such thing as technological unemployment." MIT president Karl Compton (1934) added, "The idea that science takes away jobs is contrary to fact, based on ignorance, vicious in its possible social consequences, and yet has taken an insidious hold on the minds of many people."

Engineers joined scientists in defending the link between technological change and national progress. AT&T's chief engineer declared in 1933, "Not only have we had to stand our share of the grief of the depression, but adding insult to injury, we are blamed for the depression, while in reality we have raised standards of living, increased leisure and relieved drudgery" (Gherardi 1933). In 1938, the American Engineering Council organized a forum, "Employment and the Engineer," intended to explain "the constructive side" of technology in terms "understandable to the majority voter" (Fletcher 1938). Engineers felt acutely conscious of public perceptions; in 1933, William McClellan, former president of the American Institute of Electrical Engineers, casually remarked that "engineers are magnificent creators of unemployment." Roundly criticized by his fellows for giving critics ammunition, McClellan (1934) quickly revised his statement to "engineers are magnificent creators of leisure."

Within SPEE circles, educators expressed deep resentment of the criticism of engineering they saw implied in technological-unemployment accusations, which Seaton (1934: 14) dismissed as "a great deal of nonsense." Seaton maintained that innovation would perpetually generate more employment opportunities, since increasing wealth inevitably raised people's expectations and spurred demand for new luxuries, for which "human wants are insatiable" (14). Seaton asserted that engineers had brought the world within reach of unprecedented happiness, providing society could learn to handle that gift of utopian profusion. "It is only necessary that our economic system be modernized and brought into harmony with the condition of plenty provided by abundant production" (15).

In 1935, MIT's Dugald Jackson credited engineers with bringing humans from centuries of drudgery to modern "comfort," reading history as continual progress in forms that verged on ignoring the Depression's immediate suffering (69). Instead of fearing unemployment and poverty, Jackson maintained, "people of this nation ought to recognize themselves as enjoying a mutual prosperity, security, and happiness such as has not been associated with any other . . . history" (73). By contrast, he pointed to nineteenth-century peasants' near-starvation terrors (73). Modern Americans should not worry about technological displacement, Jackson insisted (69). "We [engineers] are proud of our offspring and stand warrantors of their serviceability to society" (67).

The SPEE community thus joined leading scientists in denying that technological unemployment represented a real Depression-era worry. When pressed, some acknowledged that mechanization could cause occasional temporary job loss. In 1934, for example, Case School of Applied Sciences president William Wickenden (1934: 153) told fellow engineering administrators that "the risk of supercession without warning has become one of the nightmares of industry. Economists agree that permanent technological unemployment is impossible but the hardships of transitional unemployment are known to be severe and are apparently increasing." The net effect of engineers' storytelling during the Depression, however, quickly glossed over such problems as insignificant, preferring to highlight claims for long-term gains in opportunity, work, and living standards generated by technological change.

## 4. Faith in Engineering as the Source of Civilization's Economic Progress

In 1930s writings, speeches, and professional activities, scientists and engineers overwhelmingly cast themselves as heroic figures, creating rather than destroying jobs and wealth. The decade's discussion of curriculum reform evolved to seek ways of instilling that defensive disciplinary

confidence in new professionals. Editors of *Mechanical Engineering* recommended that colleges teach all students celebratory history of technology courses, to show future engineers their profession's "dignity and significance" while "trac[ing] out for non-engineers" the moral of technology
as progress. As a counterweight to popular misconceptions of machines
as job destroyers, editors continued, professors should rhetorically ask students, "If we have progressed so far from the times . . . of tooth and claw,
shall we not proceed further through dependence on the intelligent use of
technology?" (*Mechanical Engineering* 1938: 527).

Engineering faculty themselves interpreted world economic history in
technology-centric terms, crediting the development of civilization itself to
engineers. In his 1929 SPEE presidential address, Cornell's engineering
dean, Dexter Kimball, told colleagues that since ancient times, humans had
prayed for security, but only received release from drudgery thanks to "a
comparatively small group of humble engineers" (11). Kimball declared,
"Suddenly out of a clear sky there came the Industrial Revolution, changing
all of our ideas of production, opening up a vista of hope and promise hitherto denied to humanity" (11). Yet after gifting modern people with sur-
pluses of food and other necessities, Kimball bemoaned, engineers were
repaid with "a chorus of complaints, criticisms" (12). Although "for the first
time we are within striking distance of the abolition of poverty . . . many
insist that we are making the world worse instead of better" (12). He dismissed those who blamed engineers for building a "Frankenstein" as
timid conservatives, alarmed by changes they felt unable to comprehend.
Kimball compared engineers to the Pied Piper, concluding, "Where we
lead all men will follow because only where we walk can there spring
up an industrial background, fair and fertile, without which there can be
no progress. . . . May God help us to realize our responsibilities and
possibilities!" (13–22).

As the Depression extended, engineers continued asserting historical
interpretations that defined engineering as the very "basis of our civilization," to quote Kansas State's Seaton (1934: 13). Twentieth-century technical innovation had upended centuries-old patterns of privation and misery
by "solving [all] of the problems of production," Seaton declared, and
"due credit for [this] . . . must be given to the schools in which engineers
have received their fundamental training and inspiration" (13). A Cornell
industrial economist, Seymour Garrett, wanted more schools' curricula to
replace the standard survey in general economics with classes in such
nakedly pro-engineering economic history. To reinforce new generations'

confidence in the social goodness of their work amid Depression questioning, Garrett (1933: 52–53) suggested that engineering students should learn "to visualize the sweep of our ancestors' progress in the fields of mechanical technique and in business practice."

Joseph Roe, an industrial engineering professor at NYU, presented the most detailed reading of engineers' progress-minded reading of history while acknowledging occasional tensions in technology's effects on society. Roe (1929: 78) saw the Industrial Revolution as humanity's turning point, insisting that "knowledge of it is essential to a wise handling of the problems of today." Production had soared thanks to "great inventions," Roe declared (80), but British people suffered under terrible factory conditions, child-labor abuses, and neglect of the poor, until legislative measures corrected such horrors. "Machinery has ultimately enriched and benefited society as a whole, both earner and worker, but the selfishness and brutality of its introduction made the Industrial Revolution in England . . . tragic," he wrote (86). "All this has direct and profound bearing today. The same old forces are at work although under vastly better conditions" (86). In the twentieth century, "new products like the automobile and radio start major industries, dislodging and re-aligning vast numbers of workmen. The cry has even been raised that invention, while enormously increasing production, has actually decreased employment. No mechanical engineer can be indifferent to this situation because the machines he designs have caused it" (78). Just as Britain had eventually recognized the need for intervention to redress the harmful side of industrial advance, Roe declared, modern America must also remain conscious of its most vulnerable citizens. Roe praised what he considered socially aware business executives, such as leaders of one rubber company that adopted a machine replacing 140 expert workmen, who then reassigned those men to other positions without penalty. Technical innovations could "*make possible* a higher state of physical and social well-being, but . . . by no means insure it. Whether or not these work out as a blessing depends largely on the spirit and manner in which they are introduced," Roe concluded (87–88). "It is our task to get this across to every mechanical engineer" (88).

Doubling down on his ideas as the Depression deepened, Roe told fellow engineering educators in 1932 that the clear "advance" of Western history gave humans unprecedented leisure and ever-rising living standards, but with associated casualties. "It has been proved repeatedly that ultimately labor is benefitted by labor-saving machinery . . . but the first impact . . . may be devastating, and it is cold comfort to a jobless worker to tell him it will be all right in the next generation" (Roe 1933: 702). Roe assessed current distress associated with technological change as "a very real factor and one to which an engineer, if he has any red blood, must give thought . . . [so it may] be minimized as far as possible, in individual enterprises as well as in industry as a whole" (702). Roe believed that conscientious engineers and businessmen could and should avoid Industrial Revolution–age mistakes through voluntary measures to improve workers' lives, which would "increase a man's confidence in our basic industrial structure" (707) and thus stabilize society and discourage radicalism. All engineers needed to know this history, Roe declared, and "should be keenly alive to the economic factors in their work even if they never take over managerial duties . . . [to] be more socially minded . . . for their own interest as well as for that of society" (699). Beyond comprehending principles of overhead, the nature of partnerships and corporations, "valuation and rate making, obsolescence, the economics of capacity, sinking funds," Roe said (699), engineers needed to master political economy. "Ignorance of, and indifference to, the economic elements in engineering has been a characteristic weakness of the engineer. His influence today would be greater and his position in society stronger if he had been . . . better informed about them" (707). Roe's classes at NYU, as at other schools, embedded that narrative of economic history, revolving around engineering as the spark of civilization, in teaching engineering majors about the value of their work.

## 5. Positioning Engineers as Economic Leaders

Roe's wish to see engineers assume larger influence in national affairs followed on the community's assumptions that engineering education trained graduates for rational problem-solving better than the more fuzzy-minded social sciences and that technological change represented the dominant force shaping human history. Multiple colleagues echoed such sentiments during the Depression. Seaton (1934: 15–16) declared that while "larger economic problems of industry and of society . . . do not fall exclusively within the field of the engineer . . . his fundamental training in the scientific approach to his problems and in clear and logical thought processes, as well as his experience in the organization and administration of vast industrial enterprises, may well justify the hope that he can make a very considerable contribution to their solution." Seaton believed that engineering education should prepare future professionals not just for "the operation and administration of industries" but also for "the control and direction of industrial operations in the interests of society," with post-undergraduate education in industrial economics to prepare "a considerable percentage" of the best for "careers of leadership in industrial and economic affairs" (16–17).

Some engineers saw themselves as already perfectly positioned to provide economic expertise. MIT's Jackson (1935: 66) presumed fundamental differences between engineering and social sciences, to the latter's detriment; he complained that in economics, "exact data . . . are so hidden behind a barricade of allegations and assumptions that it is very difficult . . . to carry on an investigation which detects . . . unmixed facts and thereby clears the ground for discovery of . . . exact conclusions." He complained that economic and sociological analysis tended to "neglect exact reasoning" in favor of "prejudices" (79). By contrast, Jackson declared, "our engineering training helps us to distinguish between specific differences and generic differences, even in very complex situations, and therefore we should be able to aid in untangling some of the difficulties in economics" (67). Accordingly, Jackson called for giving students more exposure to "sound and comprehensive thinking in the economics and sociology relating to our field, such as we have not yet introduced into our teaching" (67). With such improvements to foster "encouragement of independent-mindedness associated with exact thinking, [and] elimination of flabby-mindedness," Jackson said, engineering education could institute "the improvements of economic thought which should be aroused on account of the influence of engineering activities on society" (82). Just as engineers had come to work closely with mathematicians and physicists, Jackson hoped to see more cooperation between economists and engineers, with the former focusing on theory and the latter on application, to yield "improved results" for society. Cornell's Kimball echoed the sentiment that engineers offered important perspective to improve social-science analysis, praising President Herbert Hoover's National Bureau of Economic Research for consulting with engineers in writing the report *Recent Economic Changes*. "Never before, as far as I am aware, have economists or any persons interested in economic studies, called on engineers to help them write such a report. It is the first recognition of the fact that our industrial basis is complex and changing rapidly in a manner best known to engineers" (Kimball 1929: 21).

Engineers interpreted economic decisions as turning purely on application of correct facts and thus proclaimed that evaluative expertise made them "better equipped" than others to prevent or correct economic problems, as Walter Colpitts declared. "Engineers are analysts by training, and both in the design and erection of engineering works of all kinds are required to practice the art of the diagnostician . . . continually observing the relationship between cause and effect and acting upon his conclusions with a sure step" (Colpitts 1930: 152). If engineers applied that superior "training and mental makeup" (152) to economic issues, industry and the public would all benefit, Colpitts declared. "Nowadays business is largely run by charts. . . . Charts are the engineer's middle name and he is schooled in his technical work to be unbiased" (152). Colpitts suggested that "a permanent fact-finding body composed of engineers, economists, and financiers" specializing in "the dissemination of authoritative economic information concerning our principal industrial activities" (154) could have prevented the stock market crash and resulting depression.

Others in the profession took a different angle, arguing that while technical education uniquely sharpened men's minds, engineers needed better socioeconomic training to prepare them for policymaking leadership. In his 1935 SPEE presidential address, C. C. Williams warned that "severe testing of the past five years" had revealed "defects and inadequacies" of engineering programs as having "fallen short of their responsibilities," with serious "omissions" in economics training (8). Condemning what he called "the present paralysis of economic agencies," Williams wanted to institute a new "Epoch of Economic Adjustment" in engineering curricula, expanding students' administrative capacity as "preparation for assuming those functions wherein other agencies have been proved incompetent" (8–9). He too visualized having new generations of engineers correct large-scale economic errors of industrial overcentralization, lack of diversification, and "ill-conceived labor relations" (8). Williams wanted universities to teach what he labeled "technonomics," representing his ideal of "the orderly management of technical affairs, just as economics means the orderly management of a farm or business" (11). In his vision, new university-based research institutes, " 'technonomic' experiment stations," would correct what Williams viewed as the woolly-mindedness of social sciences by deploying "engineering methodology, viz., thoroughness of analysis, rigorous scrutiny and test of new proposals, strict evaluation of the so called 'economic laws' before applying them, conservatism in design and planning, and insistence on economic justification as a condition precedent for most public works" (11). Once the immediate "disorder" of depression had "passed," Williams said, "progress" would automatically resume as engineers turned their "inventive genius" to generating new consumer temptations whose purchasing could prevent "economic lopsidedness" (12–14).

The most direct application of these theories to educational change during the Depression came at Newark College of Engineering, where Roy Wright devoted special attention to elaborating concepts of "the engineer's duty as a citizen." Instituting a required upper-level course under that title, Newark College explicitly steered the young engineer to cultivate "his special training and abilities" for vital "civic responsibilities." Wright's (1935: 686–87) class taught students the progress-centric historical moral that engineers had done wonders "for humanity" in breaking centuries-old patterns of miserable toil, but also detailed "the economic, social and political complications and evils growing out of his work; the engineer's responsibility for those results."

This narrative positioned engineers as the nation's rescuers, ensuring permanent prosperity through both inventive brilliance and rational decision-making. In striking ways, it recapitulated the rhetoric that Layton (1971) argues defined the profession's ideology from 1895 to 1920 in which engineers similarly credited themselves with superhuman rationality that made them the proper guardians of public welfare. In his 1932 presidential address to the SPEE, University of Colorado's engineering dean, H. S. Evans, declared that an engineer of past eras was "expected to do his job . . . well and leave the result to be used" by others, but that new generations must become "more sensitive to the needs of society." Once alerted to that obligation, Evans (1932: 8–9) promised, engineers would "be able to lead industrial processes out of the wilderness of depressions, and society into a more stable existence." A rare cautionary voice came from 1934 SPEE president William Wickenden, who regarded engineers as possessing "gifts" but also "limitations" (157). Wickenden warned that "the engineer's habit of factual, analytical, and constructive thinking [was] . . . inadequate for the broader phases of public leadership," since engineers failed to appreciate the importance of "insight" and "values" in human society (157). Such knowledge came only through "study of history, economics, sociology, and political science, intangible though they may seem," Wickenden continued (156). He also challenged his profession's self-credited role as the driver of historical progress: "The contributions of science and technology to the making of our present social structure are great, beyond all calculation, yet I wonder if we engineers do not at times overestimate our part in the planning of the edifice, as if those who quarried the stone . . . were to claim credit for the design of the state capitol" (157–58). Ultimately, Wickenden suggested, the social sciences "must have a more generous place" in engineering curricula, "taught by men whose major interest is in human beings and society and not by engineers," but that the full complexity of economic issues meant that engineers should leave policymaking to others (160).

## 6. The Road to Samuelson

While engineering educators devoted substantial time to debating what and how their programs should teach future professionals about their role in past, present, and future society, they still resented hints of blame for Depression-era crisis. In 1936, President Roosevelt released a letter to over one hundred college presidents, advocating engineering curriculum reforms. Specifically, the president called for transforming technical education to become more "balanced" and so prepare students to "cooperate in designing accommodating mechanisms to absorb the shocks of the impact of science" in relation to "unemployment." Though engineering professors and administrators themselves argued for preparing students to assume wider leadership, the repeated reference to technological unemployment galled them. Hypersensitive to outside criticism, leaders protested that Roosevelt failed to appreciate the strengths of engineering education, while reiterating that technological unemployment was mythical.

Newark College created its special engineering-citizenship centerpiece-requirement, and some professors elsewhere moved to incorporate more economic, historical, and social-science commentary into engineering programs, but radical education change proved slow. The president of the Carnegie Institute of Technology, Robert Doherty, told the SPEE in 1939 that "a few [curricula] show revision toward the end of greater social and humane understanding, but by and large the portion of the curriculum assigned to this end is distressingly meagre" (28). Doherty denied that an engineer was "endowed with special intellectual gifts," but like others, asserted that his training instilled special "care and objectivity," superiority in "the impartiality of his decisions, the firmness of his execution" that offered something missing in different fields (31). Economics and policymaking needed "a pervasive infiltration" by "socially literate" engineering professionals "who will feel the responsibility that goes along with advantage and privilege," he concluded (31). Once educators awakened the young engineer through "an appropriate leavening of his mind with human appreciation and social understanding," Doherty said, future "socially literate" graduates could contribute more to policymaking commissions and government administration, both individually and through professional engineering organizations (32).

Through the 1930s, the SPEE held regular conferences devoted to "engineering economy," where professors shared and compared approaches to handling economics for majors. Those meetings only underlined differences of opinion and difficulties in figuring out what students should learn and why, taught by whom, and at what point in their already overstuffed curricula. Back in 1929, Ennis declared that the defining trait of engineering economics was its lack of consensus. "There is nothing in our subject analogous to Ohm's law in electrical engineering, to the laws of thermodynamics in power engineering, or to Newton's laws of equilibrium and motion in structural and machine engineering. Economics of engineering is really not a subject at all; it is a point of view." Professors simply chose to teach whatever aspects of economics they judged most interesting or relevant, Ennis concluded. He viewed such lack of standardization as advantageous, rather than flawed, allowing institutions to customize a focus around particular topics. His school, Stevens, for instance, had moved to specialize in economic studies of airplane travel and the nature of invention (Ennis 1929: 707).

But by decade's end, continued incoherence about substance weakened discussion of engineering economics, and only a few textbooks existed. One of the more prominent ones, *Principles of Engineering Economy*, by Eugene Grant (1931: 657), prioritized teaching students to master the practical question, "Will it pay?," along with "background subjects of corporation finance, public utilities, and economics of government work." Grant's (1933: 602–5, 608) approach emphasized applied accounting-centric lessons, delving into details of depreciation, compound interest, operating costs, and estimated-life use for "anything from a million-dollar project such as a power-plant costing millions to a minor choice in a detail of design." Grant (1937: 580) emphasized that seemingly-simple calculations of sunk costs and instrumental costs proved amazingly complicated, complaining that he had seen "horrible examples" of error even in textbooks.

Grant's emphasis on technical problem-solving, of course, did not satisfy engineering educators who wanted to cover broader issues of technology's social implications and engineering's relationship to economic well-being. The idea of sending all majors into general economics courses still displeased many faculty, administrators, and undergraduates themselves.

Compounding the difficulty of handling that hostile audience, no economics professors actually liked the textbooks available to teach engineering majors. "Even those ostensibly designed primarily for engineering students make but a few concessions in the title, preface, and in omissions which in one instance results in an incomplete theoretical framework." Warning that an overly "academic" or "excessively abstract" slant "repels" engineering majors, Lake (1939: 754) recommended making engineering students more comfortable by offering number-dense, "concrete problem situations with definite solutions." But others warned against catering to engineering students' comfort in plugging figures into formulas and emphasized the need to cultivate their "power of interpretation and expression." Without well-constructed guidance to inspire their interest in economics, William Ennis (1929: 709) complained, the typical engineering major "rarely reads a newspaper" and cared little about subjects such as tariffs or the Federal Reserve.

The SPEE's debates over whether, how, when, and why to teach economics to engineering majors paused during World War II, superseded by urgent discussions about temporary wartime reforms aimed at solving manpower shortages in the military and defense industries. But in peacetime, tensions resurfaced, especially following the influx of GI Bill veterans with little patience for requirements they judged irrelevant to employment, as E. Roy Weintraub (2014) has noted for the Massachusetts Institute of Technology. Like prewar professors at Newark College and other places, MIT economics professors compiled their own instructional material targeted to engineering students, since they found that textbooks purporting to serve that need did not either interest future engineers or serve them well. Still, expectations for providing service courses to resentful engineering majors frustrated MIT economists. Paul Samuelson recalled the department's chair, Ralph Freeman, agonizing, "Eight hundred MIT juniors must take a full year of compulsory economics. They hate it. We've tried everything. They still hate it." Making what Samuelson called "an offer I couldn't refuse," Freeman offered Samuelson time off to "write a text the students will like," adding, "Whatever you come up with, that will be a vast improvement" (quoted in Samuelson 1997: 154).

As Samuelson later explained, he deliberately opted not to make his text "heavily mathematical," since "MIT engineers were very good at the routine math, but they wouldn't see the forest for the trees. Everything would just become a little homework problem of how to mix two gasolines so as to get the best diesel fuel, and I wanted them to see the big principles involved" (quoted in Solman 2009). Samuelson's initial material "included a quite detailed introduction to the theory of supply and demand and, more surprisingly, an incursion into business management, including some elements of accounting and a 1941 business report," as Yann Giraud (2014: 138) has observed. The 1948 edition of *Economics* contained a section that explained sample balance sheets and income statements, described the handling of depreciation, and discussed earnings, dividends, and asset classes (Samuelson 1948). In historical context, that "incursion into business management" should not seem surprising. Educators throughout the 1930s had sought to make engineering majors more comfortable with business economics. Many of their courses and class materials had similarly offered sample business reports, seeking to prepare engineering majors for future shifts into management.

In his biography of Samuelson, Roger Backhouse (2017: 319) quotes MIT's 1940 catalog as crediting itself with becoming "the first technological institution to recognize and provide for the important place of economics in the training of the engineer." Full historical context makes this claim dubious; as shown above, prewar Stevens, Newark, and many public institutions also judged economics valuable for engineers and moved (in different ways) to incorporate such training. By the Depression era, engineering educators widely expressed interest in expanding their majors' economics education for practical professional reasons, validating, and supporting the career pattern for engineers moving into management, and for ideological self-promotion, countering talk of technological unemployment by crediting engineering with all human progress. In asserting that historical centrality and defining engineers as possessing mental discipline superior to other educated people, engineers thus demanded more respect from American society and claimed rightful jurisdiction to more direct influence on public economic policy.

## References

Anderson, Benjamin, Jr. 1937. "Technological Progress, the Stability of Business, and the Interests of Labor." *Chase Economic Bulletin* 17 (April 13): 1–35.

Ayres, Edmund. 1939. "Engineering Economy Page." *Journal of Engineering Education*, no. 29: 758.

Backhouse, Roger. 2017. *Becoming Samuelson, 1915–1948*. Vol. 1 of *Founder of Modern Economics: Paul A. Samuelson*. Oxford: Oxford University Press.

Barnes, R. M. 1935. "Report of the Committee on Industrial Engineering." *Journal of Engineering Education*, no. 25: 678–81.

Bix, Amy Sue. 2000. *Inventing Ourselves Out of Jobs? America's Debate over Technological Unemployment, 1929–1981.* Baltimore: Johns Hopkins University Press.

Budington, Robert. 1933. "The Innocence and Guilt of Science." *Ohio Journal of Science* 33, no. 4: 259–20.

Calhoun, Daniel. 1960. *The American Civil Engineer: Origins and Conflict.* Cambridge, MA: MIT Press.

Calvert, Monte. 1967. *The Mechanical Engineer in America.* Baltimore: Johns Hopkins University Press.

Chase, Stuart. 1931. *Men and Machines.* New York: Macmillan.

Colpitts, Walter William. 1930. "The Engineer and Finance." *Journal of Engineering Education*, no. 21: 149–55.

Compton, Karl. 1934. "Science Makes Jobs." "The Contributions of Science to Increased Employment." Special issue, *Scientific Monthly* 38 (April): 297, 299.

Debleth, Charles. 1933. "Instruction in Industrial Relations on the Pacific Coast." *Journal of Engineering Education*, no. 23: 395–414.

Doherty, Robert. 1939. "Social Responsibility of the Engineer." *Journal of Engineering Education*, no. 30: 27–36.

Downey, Gary Lee. 2007. "Low Cost, Mass Use: American Engineers and the Metrics of Progress." *History and Technology* 23, no. 3: 289–308.

Ennis, William. 1929. "Economics of Engineering." *Journal of Engineering Education*, no. 20: 706–11.

Evans, H. S. 1932. "Coordinated Engineering Education." *Journal of Engineering Education*, no. 23: 5–14.

Finch, J. K. 1935. "The Economic Sequence in the Civil Engineering Curriculum." *Journal of Engineering Education*, no. 24: 690–96.

Fletcher, Leonard. 1938. "Contributions of Technology." *Employment and the Engineer's Relation to It.* Supplement to AEC Bulletin for July: 13–16. Washington, DC: American Engineering Council.

Garrett, Seymour. 1933. "A Course in General Economics for Engineering Students." *Journal of Engineering Education*, no. 23: 50–57.

Gherardi, Bancroft. 1933. "Engineers and Progress." *Bell Telephone Quarterly* 12, no. 1: 7–9.

Giraud, Yann. 2014. "Negotiating the 'Middle-of-the-Road' Position: Paul Samuelson, MIT, and the Politics of Textbook Writing, 1945–55." In *MIT and the Transformation of American Economics*, edited by E. Roy Weintraub. *History of Political Economy* 46 (supplement): 134–52.

Grant, Eugene. 1931. "The Business Side of Engineering." *Journal of Engineering Education*, no. 22: 655–59.

Grant, Eugene. 1933. "Methods of Teaching Economics of Engineering." *Journal of Engineering Education*, no. 23: 602–9.

Grant, Eugene. 1937. "Practicable Objectives in Teaching Engineering Economy." *Journal of Engineering Education*, no. 27: 580–84.

Grayson, Lawrence. 1993. *The Making of an Engineer.* New York: Wiley.

Hotchkiss, Willard. 1935. "Social Sciences in Engineering Schools." *Journal of Engineering Education*, no. 26: 86–95.

Jackson, Dugald. 1935. "Objectives of Engineering Education." *Journal of Engineering Education*, no. 26: 60–85.

Kimball, Dexter. 1929. "The Economic and Social Significance of Engineering." *Journal of Engineering Education*, no. 20: 10–22.

Lake, Wilfred. 1939. "Vitalizing Instruction in Economics for Engineering Students." *Journal of Engineering Education*, no. 29: 751–54.

Layton, Edwin, Jr. 1971. *The Revolt of the Engineers: Social Responsibility and the American Engineering Profession.* Cleveland: Case Western Reserve Press.

Lescohier, Don. 1933–34. "The Place of the Social Sciences in the Training of Engineers." *Journal of Engineering Education*, no. 24: 414–21.

Lundgreen, Peter. 1990. "Engineering Education in Europe and the U.S.A., 1750–1930." *Annals of Science* 47, no. 1: 33–75.

Lytle, Charles. 1931. "Collegiate Courses for Management: A Comparative Study of the Business and Engineering Colleges." *Journal of Engineering Education*, no. 22: 806–39.

McClellan, William. 1934. "The Engineer a Creator of Leisure." *Electrical Engineering* 53 (May): 777–78.

McMahon, A. Michel. 1984. *The Making of a Profession: A Century of Electrical Engineering in America.* New York: IEEE.

*Mechanical Engineering.* 1938. "History of a Culture." 60, no. 7: 527.

Meiksins, Peter. 1996. "Engineers in the United States: A House Divided." In *Engineering Labour: Technical Workers in Comparative Perspective*, edited by Peter Meiksins and Chris Smith, 61–97. London: Verso.

Millikan, Robert. 1934. "The Service of Science." "The Contributions of Science to Increased Employment." Special issue, *Scientific Monthly* 38 (April): 306.

*New York Times.* 1935. "Works Relief Disputes Laid Before Roosevelt: . . . President Says Recovery to 1929 Basis Would Still Leave 20 Per Cent Unemployed." September 12.

Nienkamp, Paul. 2008. "A Culture of Technical Knowledge: Professionalizing Science and Engineering Education in Late Nineteenth-Century America." PhD diss., Iowa State University.

Noble, David. 1977. *America by Design: Science, Technology, and the Rise of Corporate Capitalism.* New York: Knopf.

Norton, Paul. 1935. "Engineering Economy." *Journal of Engineering Education*, no. 26: 266–68.

Norton, Paul. 1936. "Engineering Economy." *Journal of Engineering Education*, no. 27: 118–20.

Reynolds, Terry. 1983. *Seventy-Five Years of Progress: A History of the American Institute of Chemical Engineers.* New York: AIChE.

Roe, Joseph. 1929. "The Industrial Revolution." *Journal of Engineering Education*, no. 20: 78–88.

Roe, J. W. 1933. "Industrial Economics." *Journal of Engineering Education*, no. 23: 699–707.

Roosevelt, Franklin Delano. 1936. Letter to Carl Byoir, May 20, file PPF 700 "Science." Franklin D. Roosevelt Presidential Library and Museum, Hyde Park, New York.

Roosevelt, Franklin Delano. (1940) 1967. State of the Union message, January 3. In vol. 3, 1905–1966, of *The State of the Union Messages of the Presidents*, edited by Fred Israel, 2853–54. New York: Chelsea House.

Samuelson, Paul. 1948. *Economics: An Introductory Analysis*. New York: McGraw-Hill.

Samuelson, Paul. 1997. "Credo of a Lucky Textbook Author." *Journal of Economic Perspectives* 11, no. 2: 153–60.

Seaton, R. A. 1934. "Function of Engineering Schools in the Economic Life of the Country." *Journal of Engineering Education*, no. 24: 10–18.

Sinclair, Bruce. 1980. *A Centennial History of the American Society of Mechanical Engineers, 1880–1980*. Toronto: ASME.

Solman, Paul. 2009. "Samuelson on Whether Economics Is a Science." PBS interview transcript, December 24. www.pbs.org/newshour/economy/samuelson-on-whether -economics.

Weintraub, David, 1937. *Unemployment and Increasing Productivity: National Research Project on Reemployment Opportunities and Recent Changes in Industrial Techniques*. Report G-1. Philadelphia: US Government Printing Office.

Weintraub, E. Roy. 2014. "Introduction: Telling the Story of MIT Economics in the Postwar Period." In *MIT and the Transformation of American Economics*, edited by E. Roy Weintraub. *History of Political Economy* 46 (supplement): 1–12.

Wickenden, William. 1934. "Engineering Education in the Light of Changed Social and Industrial Conditions." *Journal of Engineering Education*, no. 24: 148–61.

Williams, C. C. 1935. "The New Epoch in Engineering Education." *Journal of Engineering Education*, no. 26: 6–17.

Wright, Roy. 1935. "Training for Citizenship." *Journal of Engineering Education*, no. 26: 686–89.

# Engineering the "Statistical Control of Business": Malcolm Rorty, Telephone Engineering, and American Economics, 1900–1930

Thomas A. Stapleford

In 1922, Malcolm C. Rorty, an assistant vice president with American Telephone & Telegraph (AT&T), published a slender volume titled *Some Problems in Current Economics*. As Rorty explained in the preface, "The substance of the present volume of essays on industrial economics is taken almost without change from a series of economic, financial, and statistical studies undertaken by the writer as an incident to his connection with a large public utility organization [i.e., AT&T]" (5). A few years earlier, Rorty had played a central role in establishing what would become one of the major institutions in economics: the National Bureau of Economic Research. According to one early tribute, Rorty was *the* founder of the NBER: it was Rorty who developed the initial idea of a multipartisan organization that would generate consensus, nonpartisan research; Rorty who enlisted Wesley Mitchell, Edwin Gay, and other economists; Rorty who reached out to various executives and foundation officials to gain their support; and Rorty who eventually raised the necessary funds "single-handed" (Stone 1945: 5–10, esp. 10).

I am very grateful for the comments of participants at the 2019 *HOPE* conference and especially for those of my two anonymous reviewers whose insights and suggestions made this a much stronger essay. I also owe particular debts to the archivists Sheldon Hochheiser (AT&T Archives) and Renee Pappous (Rockefeller Archive Center) for their help in locating materials and general advice, and to Karen Russell for sharing the final draft of her excellent forthcoming book, *Promoting Monopoly*.

*History of Political Economy* 52 (annual suppl.)  DOI 10.1215/00182702-8717924

Rorty's interest in economics would have been difficult to predict from his early career. Graduating from Cornell University in 1896 with degrees in mechanical and electrical engineering, Rorty first worked as a lineman on the construction of an ambitious electrical transmission line from Niagara Falls to Buffalo, New York. One year later, he joined the New York Telephone Company as an installer's assistant, and he spent the next twenty-five years moving between various Bell system affiliates and AT&T. (AT&T was originally established to handle long-distance connections for the local and regional Bell affiliates; in 1899 it became the parent company for the entire Bell system.) Well into the early 1910s, Rorty would have described his professional role as "engineering." So how did this erstwhile engineer become closely involved with economics?

To understand this transition, I find it helpful to draw on the theoretical concept of a *practice*.[1] As I use the term, a practice refers to a collection of actions that have been rendered intelligible by understanding them as aiming at some goal (*telos*). Critically, for our purposes, any set of actions can simultaneously be renarrated (reunderstood) as aiming at different goals. For example, my actions right now can situated within the practice of writing English prose (goal: construct prose that is comprehensible and elegant to other readers of English) but also within the practices of history (goal: making a contribution to the field of history as I and my colleagues understand it) and of being a faculty member at a research university (goals: strengthen the scholarly reputation of the university and fulfill my contractual obligations to the university). It is precisely this ability to renarrate actions—to situate them within different practices—that enables overlap between those practices and allows us to understand the same set of actions as being part of multiple fields. Of course, it also creates the possibility for tensions. Precisely because a set of lower-level actions can be renarrated as serving different ends, those ends might pull practitioners in conflicting directions. Or again, as these larger social practices change, overlaps that once existed may disappear.

To return to Rorty, the development of telephone engineering at AT&T created a context whereby the actions of an engineer could be renarrated as economics, and vice versa. Moreover, both could be equally situated as contributions to a new field, the "science of business." At the center of the science of business were a series of lower-level practices such as standardized accounting, surveys, tabulation, graphical presentation, curve fitting,

1. I have elaborated on my concept of a practice in Stapleford 2017; for a more general treatment, see Nicolini 2013.

correlation, and so forth—all of which could loosely be grouped as part of a fourth emerging field, statistics. It was precisely the overlap between these larger social practices that enabled Rorty to move fluidly between multiple professional roles: from being a lineman on the Niagara Falls transmission project, to modeling demand for telephone service as a "commercial engineer," to spearheading the creation of the NBER, to being chief statistician for AT&T, and finally to being a prominent executive in the telephone industry. That movement culminated in the development what Rorty (1923) called the "statistical control of business activity"—the use of data collection and statistical analysis to illuminate both the internal workings of a firm and external market conditions in order to guide executive decisions.

It was no accident that this vision and professional mobility emerged from within the practice of telephone engineering at AT&T. The engineering departments in the Bell system had cultivated employees who were primed to use mathematics to analyze complex systems. Initially focused on the human use of telephone networks, telephone engineers such as Rorty soon turned these same techniques—the collection of quantitative data, their graphical presentation, the construction of simplified models—in directions that would overlap with economics. First, AT&T engineers began forecasting consumer demand. The telephone industry (like railroads before them) featured capital-intensive, geographically fixed assets that created a premium on projecting future demand. In AT&T's early days, that task was handed by default to the engineers responsible for designing local Bell Telephone systems, who not surprisingly found it natural to construct mathematical models to predict market behavior. Second, AT&T's quasi-monopoly status from the 1910s to 1970s created pressure for rationalization both within the company (as a tool for creating profits by improving operating efficiency) and as a persuasive strategy (as AT&T had to justify its rates and policies to regulatory bodies and the public). The "statistical control of business" looked in both directions. On the one hand, it presented markets as dynamic but rule-governed systems whose fluctuations could be partially predicted and thereby incorporated into business planning. On the other, it depicted the actions of statistically guided firms as rational and efficient.

It was an engineer's view of management and markets, much as Thorstein Veblen (1921) had suggested. Nonetheless, by the 1920s, Rorty chose to narrate this view as a triad of business, economics, and statistics, leaving out engineering. In this respect, Rorty perhaps proved prescient: though the roots of "statistical control" may have lain in engineering, the key technical discipline for a science of business would be statistics.

## Projecting Demand for Telephone Service

The strongest early overlaps between the practice of engineering and that of economics in the United States came in the late nineteenth century through large civil engineering projects that required engineers to think carefully about fixed costs, operating costs, and future revenues as part of their design decisions—indeed, in some cases as the crucial factors. Railways were the first example of what eventually would be called "engineering economics" (Lesser 1969), but similar design problems existed in electrical power and new communications systems such as telegraphs and telephones: companies had to invest substantial capital into extensive technological systems that would be fixed in specific geographic locations. One critical component of those calculations involved market analysis: because these systems represented long-term investments that could not easily be relocated, companies faced intense pressure to identify both current and future demand for service in various areas.

Today, we would think of this as a project in market research, but there was no such field in the late nineteenth century (Wells 1999: 41–49). Instead, engineers stepped into the gap. In many ways, this was a logical move: whether in railways, telegraphs, electrical systems, or telephones, engineers were responsible for designing, selecting, and installing the equipment that would form the network. Since the technical capabilities of the equipment also placed important constraints on the system, engineers would have to play a central role in the network design. Moreover, they were one of the few groups of employees with experience using quantitative data for design decisions through basic techniques such as graphing and extrapolation.

The telephone industry in particular faced a thorny set of problems: there were no comparable existing technologies, and the engineers had to make both macro-level decisions about inter-city connections and micro-level choices about how to organize citywide networks. In this respect, AT&T and its Bell affiliates confronted challenges that were faced independently by railroads (city-to-city connections) and electrical power companies (intracity networks). Fortunately, the scale and integration of the Bell system also made it possible to develop and share techniques for grappling with these problems.

In 1892, AT&T's Engineering Department established a toll data bureau under Thomas Doolittle, who collected call data from local Bell companies and created a model that predicted service demand based on expected population growth (Miranti 2002: 739). Data collection and extrapolation were familiar practices for Bell system engineers, who used the practices to make inferences in other network design decisions as well. In this same period, for example, Bell engineers began collecting data on call volume at hourly intervals, as well as duration for long-distance calls, hoping to use that data to estimate the ideal number of trunk lines (i.e., lines between switchboard exchanges) to minimize delays without creating excess capacity (Wilkinson 1956: 796–98).

Unfortunately, Doolittle's efforts to estimate demand for telephone service struggled, both because his census population data was soon outdated and because he had ignored the effects of household income (Miranti 2002: 739). But Rorty would soon take the project further. After working on the Niagara transmission line, Rorty had joined the New York Telephone Company (a Bell affiliate) in 1897, moving from installer's assistant to switchboard repairman to "wire chief" (essentially the supervisor for operating and maintaining a telephone network and its equipment).[2] In 1899, he moved to American Bell in Boston (then the controlling company for Bell system), where the archival records show that he initially worked on inspecting equipment at Bell affiliate switchboard exchanges and assessing the manufacturing processes at Western Electric (the Bell subsidiary responsible for constructing its telephone equipment).[3] But Rorty soon put the mathematical skills he had honed at Cornell to work on new problems.

In 1902, Rorty collaborated with a fellow engineer, W. F. Patten, to overhaul Doolittle's approach to estimating future demand for telephone service. Like Doolittle, Rorty and Patten took population to be the primary driver of overall telephone service in a city, suggesting that engineers should expect the total number of telephone stations in a city to be roughly 10 percent of the population. To estimate future population, Rorty and Patten divided cities into three categories—those with a slowing rate of growth, those with a steady linear increase, and those growing or shrinking geometrically—and assigned a separate extrapolation technique to each. For intracity planning, they recommended subdividing urban areas into residential and business districts, each of which could be expected to expand in specific ways. Service demand in business districts was predicted to increase in parallel with the square root of the city's population.

2. These details on Rorty's early career come from Rorty 1920.
3. See correspondence between Rorty and Hammond Hayes in 21-06-03, folder 04, and Hayes to Joseph P. Davis, April 12, 1901, 137b-06-07, folder 04, both in AT&T Archives, Warren, NJ.

But the residential districts were further split into three categories based on income: high income (projected to demand full service); mid-income (50 percent service); and low income (5 percent).[4] By explicitly linking demand for telephone service to income, Rorty and Patten made a crucial departure from Doolittle's population-based model and set AT&T on a path to examining the growth and distribution of household income, eventually creating overlaps with economics.

For Rorty, the shift from installing or assessing equipment to creating predictive mathematical models seems to have sparked his imagination and opened new career paths. One year later, he analyzed AT&T call data and partnered with two other engineers to write a lengthy memo, "Application of the Theory of Probability to Traffic Problems," in which the team created sixteen carefully drawn graphs that allowed users to estimate the probability of various call volumes within intervals as small as thirty seconds. From these, Rorty showed how one could address various practical system design problems.[5] The project drew an enthusiastic response from traffic engineers across the Bell system (Anonymous 1905) and led to Rorty's appointment as traffic superintendent for Pittsburgh in Pennsylvania's Central District Telephone Company that same year (Rorty 1920).

Rorty and Patten's proposal for projecting telephone demand initially faced a cooler reception from upper management. While recognizing the crude nature of Rorty and Patten's model, AT&T's lead engineer, Joseph Davis, could see the promise of supplementing qualitative judgments with formal rules. He forwarded Rorty and Patten's notes to AT&T's president, Frederick P. Fish, whose response indicated the ambiguous place of mathematical models in managerial decisions at the turn of the century. Fish praised the "distinctly scientific" character of Rorty and Patten's method, but also conceded that he was "hardly able to say how complete or accurate" the results might be. Indeed, Fish's short response suggests that he was genuinely impressed with the engineers' work but also entirely unsure what to do with it or how much faith to place in the projections, contenting himself with sharing the "pleasure" he derived from "see[ing] work of this sort."[6]

If Fish saw the engineers' efforts as an interesting experiment, his successor, Theodore N. Vail, took a much stronger line. Inefficient overexpansion

4. W. F. Patten and Malcolm Rorty, "Note on Development Plan," pp. 1–5, encl. in Joseph P. Davis to Frederick P. Fish, August 28, 1902, 137-09-01-14, AT&T Archives.

5. M. C. Rorty to Joseph P. Davis and attachment, October 22, 1903, box 1360, AT&T Archives.

6. Fish to Davis, September 4, 1902, 137-09-01-14, AT&T Archives.

led to the near collapse of AT&T in the financial panic of 1907, with the company saved only by the intervention of a group of bankers led by J. P. Morgan. Morgan brought back Vail, AT&T's first president, to resurrect its fortunes, and Vail soon began bolstering the company's quantitative resources. In 1909, he formed the Statistical Division within AT&T's central offices to gather information about independent telephone companies (i.e., Bell competitors) and internal data on the Bell affiliates.[7] Sometime in 1910, Vail recalled Rorty from the Central District company to help organize a Commercial Engineering Department within AT&T (Rorty 1920).

In broader usage, "commercial engineering" could refer to everything from estimating costs and potential revenues for a project (much like the engineering economics) to developing new markets for products to the full suite of "commercial" activities entailed by running an engineering firm. Within AT&T, commercial engineering initially had a tight focus, charged with expanding the analysis of telephone demand that Rorty and Patten had pursued eight years earlier. As explained in an internal memo (likely from sometime in 1910–12, and possibly written by Rorty himself), the Commercial Engineering Department was responsible for producing a "Development Study" for each community that would "show the number and distribution of subscriber's lines, private branch exchange trunks and power circuits required for the most desirable telephone development in any community fifteen or twenty years hence," as well as "the probable rates of calling and percentages of trunking [use of trunk lines] in different parts of the community." With the Development Study in place, the traffic and plant engineers could then create a "Fundamental Plan" that would describe the equipment and network needed to meet the demand projected by the Development Study. In addition to this long-term planning, each year the Commercial Engineering Department would project an annual "Forecast of Year's Growth" focusing on service expansions and resulting gross revenue. These estimates, the memo recognized, required technical engineering knowledge, but also went beyond that, encompassing "large questions of business administration, judgment and foresight."[8]

In these early steps, therefore, AT&T's commercial engineers were already beginning to overlap with the practices of business management; indeed, the very title "commercial engineering" implied such multivalence.

7. Seymour L. Andrew, "The Work of the Chief Statistician's Division," pp. 3, 7, *General Accounting Conference* (1921), 185-03-01, folder 01, AT&T Archives.

8. "The Telephone Plant—Department Responsibilities in Connection with Its Design and Construction," pp. 1, 2–3, 140-04-01, folder 02, AT&T Archives.

Simultaneously, though, in attempting to estimate future demand, the Commercial Engineering Department was undertaking a task that could readily be categorized as part of the practice of economics. Nonetheless, it was a different approach than the work that dominated economics in the 1910s: whereas economists focused on estimating demand curves, showing how demand would change with price (Morgan 1991: 133–89), AT&T's commercial engineers were trying to predict how structural changes in population and household income would affect demand for telephones at a given price. What initially drew Commercial Engineering, and Rorty, into much closer overlap with the practice of contemporary economics was AT&T's fraught and delicate status as a privately owned, near monopoly.

### Fair Rates, Economic Facts, and the Formation of the National Bureau of Economic Research

In its earliest days, the Bell companies used their patents to maintain a de facto monopoly on American telephony. After those patents expired in 1894, however, the company faced an explosion of competition. More than three thousand new telephone companies formed in the next decade, and Bell's market share fell to almost 50 percent by 1910 (Vietor 1994: 168–70).

When Vail was installed as AT&T's new president after the company's near bankruptcy in 1907, he took swift action to restore the company's dominance. Beginning in his 1907 *Annual Report*, Vail proclaimed the company's new doctrine of "One System, One Policy, Universal Service," arguing that telephone service should be an integrated system controlled by a single company, thereby allowing all customers to connect with each other efficiently (Mueller 1997: 96–103). Rather than rates set directly by market competition, Vail conceded that subscription costs would require some degree of "public control" from an expert commission, "provided that it is independent, intelligent, and considerate," and that such a commission would recognize the need for "fair rates" through a careful analysis of costs and a "fair return" on investment (AT&T 1908: 18, 16). Over the next several decades, the federal government ceded AT&T a regulated monopoly on telephone service throughout much of the United States, a monopoly that began to crumble only in the 1950s before collapsing entirely with the forced divestiture of the Bell companies in 1984 (Vietor 1994: 167–233).

AT&T's unusual status as a national, quasi-monopoly created distinct pressures that would push the firm to engage with economists and economic practice. First, AT&T had justify its private ownership. If telephone service formed a natural monopoly, as Vail insisted, why not make it a government-controlled enterprise? Second, aside from these general arguments, AT&T had to justify the rates it charged customers, to show that they were "fair" (in Vail's terms), equivalent in some sense to what would prevail in a competitive market. Moreover, as a national company with regional affiliates, AT&T faced regulatory oversight at both the federal level (like railways) and within individual states (like electrical power companies). But if AT&T's position as a national monopoly created challenges, its extraordinary scale also created distinct advantages, namely, the resources and manpower to develop its own economic expertise to meet those regulatory challenges. At the center of AT&T's efforts was the Commercial Engineering Department, and though the National Bureau of Economic Research did not grow directly from those projects, it nonetheless fit squarely into the approach to political economy that the company espoused.

The roots of these ties lay in AT&T's response to the end of its patents. The Bell companies initially reacted to the explosion of competition by closing off their system: independent companies who wished to connect to Bell exchanges had to become de facto Bell franchisees, using Western Electric equipment (i.e., Bell equipment) and eschewing connections to other independents. After the 1907 financial crisis, Vail adopted a more liberal approach, sublicensing noncompeting independents (i.e., companies operating in areas that Bell did not serve) without requiring Bell equipment or tightly restricting connections to non-Bell exchanges. The result was a fourfold increase in interconnecting telephones in two years and just shy of tenfold by 1914, encompassing two-thirds of all independent telephones (Mueller 1997: 107–10). Simultaneously, AT&T began acquiring independents that were competing with established Bell companies in urban areas. From 1907 to 1913, the number of cities with a population over five thousand that had competing telephone companies fell from 59 percent to 37 percent (Mueller 1997: 111–12).

Not surprisingly, the Bell System's rapid expansion provoked a fierce backlash. According to Milton Mueller (1997: 129), by 1913, "AT&T was mired in lawsuits regarding rates or antitrust issues in almost every state," the federal government was preparing litigation, and Congress was considering nationalizing long-distance lines. From Vail's perspective, these lawsuits undoubtedly appeared as just one piece of a broader series of threats to corporate capitalism that accelerated after the 1907 financial crisis, from the clamor for government intervention (whether Roosevelt's antitrust campaigns or Woodrow Wilson's demand for regulated "New Freedom") to growing union power, violent strikes, and socialist protests (Dubofsky 1994: 38–51; Adams 1966). Small wonder, then, that in 1912 Vail gathered "some of the largest financial interests of this country" (including John D. Rockefeller Jr. and J. P. Morgan) to strategize. In the account of one participant, Vail proposed "a sort of publicity bureau" that would correct the "misinformation" about economic matters that (in Vail's view) plagued the "middle and lower classes on which the demagogues chiefly prey."[9]

Vail probably envisioned something like AT&T's earlier work with one of the first public relations firms (actually called the Publicity Bureau), which had written pro-Bell articles and placed them in newspapers across the country in the early years of the twentieth century. Vail had terminated AT&T's contract with the Publicity Bureau in 1908, but only because he was internalizing some of the same functions within AT&T, even hiring away the Publicity Bureau's main agent for the account, James Ellsworth (Russell forthcoming, chaps. 3, 4). Whereas the Publicity Bureau had focused on AT&T's battle with independent telephone companies, Vail's new venture, what one historian has called "the first, most persistent, and most celebrated" corporate public relations campaign in US history, would aim to insulate the company from antitrust attacks by promoting a positive image of AT&T's allegedly "natural" monopoly (Marchand 1998: 48–87, esp. 48; Russell, forthcoming). By uniting with Rockefeller, Morgan, and other corporate magnates to subsidize a general economic publicity bureau, Vail undoubtedly hoped to complement the specific AT&T campaign with broader economic arguments.

Vail's compatriots, however, could reach no consensus on whether the proposed bureau would merely publicize what Vail implied was well-established economic knowledge or whether it would conduct new research, and the project ultimately went nowhere (Grossman 1982: 61–76). But although Vail failed to get his independent publicity bureau for economic analysis, he had his own internal resource: the Commercial Engineering Department. Around this same time (per a later account), Vail directed Commercial Engineering "to keep informed as to all movements toward public ownership in the United States and other countries in general, and toward public ownership of public utilities in the Unites States in particu-

9. Jerome Greene, "Principles and Policies of Giving: Memorandum," Rockefeller Foundation Draft Report 12 (1913), pp. 16, 15, folder 163, box 21, SG 3.1, Rockefeller Archive Center.

lar, to advise the executives of the Company as to the significant developments in these fields, and to be prepared to furnish pertinent information on this subject."[10] Along with tracking efforts to promote government control of utilities, Commercial Engineering also began compiling a "Brief of Arguments against Public Ownership" in a binder containing one-hundred-plus pages of "related statistics and quotations from economic and other authorities" that AT&T would distribute across the country for use in articles, speeches, and community debates about public ownership (Kielbowicz 2009: 682).[11]

Vail's program paid big dividends in 1913 when AT&T faced a federal antitrust investigation and perhaps the strongest threat to a public takeover in its history. In the midst of the antitrust investigation, Rep. David Lewis (D-MD) began working with the US Postal Service to prepare a proposal for federal ownership of American telegraph and telephone services as part of the postal system (a common arrangement in several European countries). Per an early account from the *New York Times*, Lewis had been working "secretly" at the Post Office Department for some time gathering extensive data on US and European systems, eventually bringing "voluminous tables to the White House" and leaving President Wilson "greatly impressed by Mr. Lewis's ability to marshal his facts" (*New York Times* 1913a). After the release of the proposal, and just days before a major congressional speech by Lewis, AT&T reached a settlement with the Department of Justice in which the company would divest its controlling interest in Western Union (the major US telegraph company) and open its long-distance lines to independent companies. Lewis, however, was not deterred and gave a lengthy speech drawing on his detailed studies to persuade his colleagues that privately owned American telephone and telegraph services were inefficient and exploited consumers (*New York Times* 1913b, 1913c, 1913d).

AT&T's Commercial Engineering Department provided the empirical backbone to the company's response. By this time, Rorty had left the department: beginning in 1912, he had been part of a committee exploring how to integrate the Bell system with Western Union's network of telegraph offices. In the summer of 1913, he had shifted to an executive position at Western Union, becoming "Manager, Joint Telephone Services"

10. Andrew, "Work of the Chief Statistician's Division," p. 4. Per Andrew, AT&T started these efforts in 1912, though they seem to be an extension of a project begun by the AT&T statistician Walter S. Allen in 1902 (Russell, forthcoming: chap. 3).

11. Quotations are from the copy of the "Brief" held at the University of Michigan library.

and eventually an assistant to Vice President Belvidere Brooks.[12] In his absence, the new top staff member in Commercial Engineering took the lead: Chester I. Barnard.

Born in 1886, Barnard had studied economics at Harvard for three years. However, financial constraints drove him to leave Harvard for AT&T without a degree in 1909. Courtesy of a family connection to AT&T executive Walter Gifford, Barnard found a position in AT&T's new Statistical Division under Gifford's leadership, where his broad classical education (including reading multiple languages) and training in economics proved a major asset for the division's core task of gathering and analyzing information about foreign telephone and telegraph services and domestic Bell competitors (Wolf 1961; Scott 1992: 61–67). At some point in the early 1910s, Barnard transferred to the Commercial Engineering Department, becoming a counterpoint to the engineer Rorty: an economist who had moved into the overlapping world of commercial engineering.

Barnard's response to Lewis's arguments, issued as Commercial Bulletin no. 7, drew on all the resources collected by the Statistical Division and Commercial Engineering over the preceding years. The report was a rhetorical tour de force, containing fifty-six pages of close critique of Lewis's claims, jam-packed with statistics and supported by seven additional appendices and nearly two hundred endnotes to various journal articles, government reports, company bulletins, and letters from across Europe and the United States. The basic argument of Barnard's analysis was that Lewis had misunderstood both the data that he cited and the intricacies of telephone and telegraph operations. When corrected, a purely "statistical treatment of the subject" led to "general conclusions which are directly contrary to those reached by Mr. Lewis," namely, that the privately owned American telephone and telegraph services were more efficient than public counterparts and provided lower rates for customers (Barnard 1914: esp. 1). Per a retrospective account, the work of the Commercial Engineering Department "was exceedingly useful" in combating the "agitation" led by Lewis.[13]

---

12. For Rorty's work on integrating AT&T and Western Union, see minutes and memos from January 1912—fall 1913 in 126-09-02, folder 07, AT&T Archives. On Rorty's appointment to Western Union, see *Telegraph and Telephone Age* 1913. In May 1914, he was appointed assistant to Belvidere Brooks, vice president, Commercial Engineering Department (*Telegraph and Telephone Age*, May 1, 1914, p. 249; June 16, 1914, p. 348). By October, he had left the company and was presumably back at the Bell system.

13. Andrew, "Work of the Chief Statistician's Division," 5.

Rorty, who at the time was still working at Western Union, does not appear to have been directly involved in responding to Lewis. But the broad questions posed by AT&T's position were inescapable for anyone like Rorty who was now part of the company's management. For example, when Rorty returned to AT&T's New York offices later in 1914, he became involved in a long-running debate about reduced rates for nighttime calls. Everyone agreed that reduced night rates would cost Bell affiliates money; the question was how much and whether the loss would be outweighed by the public relations benefit of voluntarily making reductions that might otherwise be ordered by regulatory bodies. Rorty worked with Barnard's commercial engineers on several empirical studies to devise a rate schedule that Rorty felt would strike an appropriate balance.[14]

Sometime during this same period, Rorty struck up a friendship with Nahum I. Stone, a Russian-born economist with socialist leanings who had worked as a statistician in the US government and was at the time a consultant for labor arbitration and various industrial investigations (Fabricant 1984: 3–4; *New York Times* 1966). Per Stone's (1945: 5) retrospective account, the two met as dueling experts in several New York hearings, though the details are hard to verify.[15] Regardless, the catalyst for their friendship was Stone's lengthy and critical 1916 review in the *Intercollegiate Socialist* of the economist Scott Nearing's (1915) book on the distribution of income in the United States.

Rorty was impressed that a "radical" like Stone would evince so much integrity and care in statistical analysis, even at the expense of a potential political ally, and so he invited Stone to lunch, marking the beginning of a long friendship. Per Stone's account, Rorty lamented the lack of agreement "on the purely arithmetical question of what part of the national income goes to each element of society" (the very subject of Nearing's recent book and a core question in debates over socialism) and suggested

14. See correspondence in 125-06-01, folder 04, AT&T Archives, especially letters of July 10, 1915, August 28, 1915, December 23, 1915, August 30, 1916, October 21, 1916, March 3, 1917, and March 9, 1918.

15. Stone reports first meeting Rorty at the hearings of the New York State Factory Investigating Commission, created in the wake of the infamous 1911 "Triangle fire." Stone did testify at those hearings; Rorty does not appear in the official transcripts. (He could, of course, have attended the hearings.) Stone dates their second encounter to a consultation before the Mayor's Unemployment Committee; the committee did not publish transcripts or summaries, so this cannot be verified. Stone and Rorty did serve on the US Chamber of Commerce Committee on Statistics and Standards in late 1915, which issued a sharp critique of US trade statistics (*New York Times* 1916).

creating "an organization that devoted itself to fact finding on controversial economic subjects of great public interest" (Stone 1945: 6). Stone concurred, and after brainstorming about potential collaborators, Rorty enlisted the economists Edwin Gay (Harvard) and Wesley Mitchell (Columbia), offering to provide AT&T data on "a complete classification of families according to rents paid and rental value of properties occupied for the majority of cities of over 50,000 population in the United States" (Stone 1945: 6–7).

Whether by luck or previous knowledge, Gay and Mitchell were an inspired choice: when Vail had proposed forming a "publicity bureau" back in 1912, Jerome Greene at the Rockefeller Foundation had suggested a rival plan for a research bureau and had enlisted Gay as an ally. Gay, working with a small committee arranged by the foundation, had suggested Mitchell as the director. The program went nowhere at the time, derailed by internal divisions within the foundation (Grossman 1982: 61–76). But when approached by Rorty, both economists quickly agreed, and with Rorty courting business leaders and funding, they formed the Committee on the Distribution of Income. Though plans were temporarily suspended by the war, Rorty returned with gusto after the armistice, raising the necessary money and spearheading the foundation of the NBER at the December 1919 meeting of the American Economics Association in Chicago.

The extant documentation does not give much direct insight into Rorty's motivations, but placed in the context of his experience in the telephone industry, his actions make a great deal of sense. First, as seen earlier, AT&T's need for market research meant that its commercial engineers had experience and expertise in gathering and analyzing economic data. It is striking (though not surprising) that the data Rorty offered to Gay— details on household rent data and property values in large cities—were precisely the data that AT&T was using as a proxy for household income in order to project demand for residential telephone service.

Second, Vail's vision of AT&T as a lightly regulated monopoly that would offer "fair rates" in exchange for "fair returns" resonated perfectly with Rorty's belief in the purportedly neutral, quantitative economic facts that could be produced by the future NBER. In Vail's depiction, "fair rates" were not a matter for negotiation; they could be calculated from the extensive statistical data gathered by AT&T's Commercial Engineering Department and its Statistical Division. Moreover, such calculations would not be merely a hypothetical dream; the entire premise of Vail's approach rested on the company's ability to present quantitative arguments that could withstand close scrutiny in regulatory hearings. It is telling that the mix of professionals who formed the early boards of the NBER—business leaders, labor officials, lawyers, academic economists—reflected precisely the group of experts who frequently appeared in legislative or commission hearings on industrial matters.

How deeply Rorty had imbibed that vision became apparent in his 1922 volume *Some Problems in Current Economics*. The book began as a series of pamphlets (printed between 1920 and 1922) "to be distributed primarily to executives and other employees of the telephone industry."[16] In turning the pamphlets into a book for a general audience, Rorty kept the main text largely intact but replaced discussions of the telephone industry with nearly identical commentaries on public utilities. On that topic, Rorty repeated Vail's line: wages in utilities should mimic "comparable occupations" in the same localities, returns to capital should be "reasonably comparable" to those in other industries, and rates should be set accordingly (keeping in mind actual costs and depreciations). In short, regulating utilities simply required gathering economic statistics (14–17).

But Rorty's core argument went well beyond the economics of utilities. The book opened with a folksy anecdote about a West Virginian feud headed for "shootin's, an' murders, an' burnin's for three generations" that was defused when a diplomatic judge gathered the antagonists for a conversation about their disagreements and helped them recognize that their disagreements did not warrant wanton violence. The "point of this incident" for "the present economic situation," Rorty explained, was a parallel need for "a clear dividing line between what should be the basis for a feud and what the basis for a temperate and constructive difference of opinion." This "clear dividing line" would come from a "full and dispassionate understanding of the real facts," especially about wages, production, and the distribution of national income. The book culminated in a fourth chapter, "Some Pertinent Statistics," about these topics, which then led naturally to the conclusion, "Facing the Facts" (Rorty 1922: 11–13, esp. 12–13).

Against the backdrop of the recent Russian revolution and the American Red Scare, Rorty's reference to a violent "feud" between "employer and employee" was clear. The contrast between a "feud" and a "constructive difference of opinion" marked the distinction in Rorty's mind between Bolshevik revolutionaries and a socialist like Stone, between intransigent ideology and the self-critical empiricism that he envisioned for NBER.

16. The original printed pamphlets can be found in 127-09-03, folder 07, AT&T Archives. Quotation from the "Prefatory Note."

Indeed, in a 1917 address to the American Statistical Association, Rorty argued that a "true and widespread knowledge of income distribution" would undercut "the extremist and the I.W.W. [Industrial Workers of the World] agitator" (796). Likewise, in an early fund-raising letter for the still-nascent NBER, Rorty touted the potential value of the proposed bureau for "a campaign of education in opposition to Bolshevism in this country."[17]

If Rorty believed that "facing the facts" could defuse revolutionary tendencies, he also upheld the NBER's new tradition of gathering a politically diverse group of experts to scrutinize those facts. Although the book was not an official NBER publication, Rorty thanked Gay, Mitchell, and the prominent socialist Harry W. Laidler (who had commissioned Stone's 1916 book review and served on the NBER board) for "helpful comments and pertinent criticisms." Perhaps most remarkably, Rorty shared the pamphlets with "certain of his more radical friends, . . . inserting the substance of their comments as footnotes" in the published book. Most of these, he explained, had come from "a specially well-informed and temperate socialist" (likely Stone), and some turned into lengthy commentaries running across multiple pages (Rorty 1922: 8–9).

That Rorty could find common ground with socialists like Laidler or Stone is no surprise, for neither Rorty nor anyone else associated with the monopolistic AT&T could be a radical promoter of free markets. Rorty's book had two dominant analogies for what he called "our present industrial organization." The first, an "industrial" or "economic machine," was perhaps natural for an engineer. Rorty conceded that the current machine had "periodical partial breakdowns," but that it would be foolish "to condemn the whole machine because of a dirty spark plug or a choked gasoline feed, or to hammer blindly at the mechanism in the hope that a chance blow or turn of the wrench will remedy the difficulty." The better option was to learn "how the present machine works and how to adjust it and keep it in good running order" (59–61).

But Rorty's second analogy highlighted a different set of associations. He began with a contrast between the "highly individualistic state" of classical liberalism (which protected "individual liberties" but was "inca-

17. Rorty to Max Farrand, August 9, 1919, Series 18, box 223, folder 2099, Commonwealth Fund Papers, Rockefeller Archives Center, New York. Stone and the labor members of the planning committee objected to any direct ties to the anti-Bolshevik campaign; see Stone to Frey, August 19, 1919, and Frey to Rorty, August 22, 1919, both in the same folder.

pable of successfully directing the administration of large public or semi-public enterprises") and the "highly socialistic state" (which "sacrifice[s] . . . individual liberty and individual energy"). As a possible "compromise between these two extremes," Rorty proposed "the organization of the human body," where "the brain thinks, reasons, and plans—but although it is served by the vital organs, it has no control over their routine operations," that is, basic autonomic functions like breathing or digestion (44–47). In this analogy, the brain was the federal and state governments, while the "vital organs" were "our great corporations" (48). If individualism left the body uncoordinated and undirected, socialism would be "like a man who was compelled to order each heart beat and each breath by an effort of the will" (47–48).

For public utilities, Rorty conceded that some "small saving" might result from government ownership, but this "would not be much more than offset by the wastes that seem to be inseparable from governmental operation of complicated enterprises." As he insisted, *The question of capital ownership is, in itself, of minor importance, and the controlling point of view must be that of efficiency of operation and adequacy of service*" (51). Provided that the governmental "brain" deployed its regulatory power according to the kinds of neutral facts Rorty was offering, leaving "our great corporations" in private hands would bring efficiency and innovation (57–58). It was a vision that paralleled the voluntary corporatism championed by America's most famous engineer in the early 1920s, Herbert Hoover, who was simultaneously leading the Department of Commerce to collaborate with the NBER to mitigate the economic inefficiencies of business cycles through voluntary corporate planning based on economic statistics (Alchon 1985).

In all these respects, *Some Current Economic Problems* synthesized Rorty's experience at both AT&T and the NBER. Of course, in working with Stone to establish the NBER, and in helping to lead it over its first decade, he was acting on his own behalf rather than as an official agent of AT&T; indeed, in 1923, Rorty left AT&T for the International Telephone and Telegraph Company while retaining his role in the NBER. Yet it is highly unlikely Rorty would have offered AT&T's data on household rents without Vail's approval, and it is equally clear that the vision for the NBER resonated perfectly with how Vail and like-minded executives understood the regulation of monopolies: grounded in neutral facts about the larger economy (wages, returns to capital, shares of national income) that had passed through the purifying fire of experts representing various economic and political interests. In this respect, it is no surprise that AT&T and its affiliates were the largest corporate donors to the NBER in its early years.[18]

### From Commercial Engineering to Statistics: Business Cycles at AT&T

If one intersection between AT&T telephone engineering and the NBER lay in the form of the NBER—its dedication to producing impartial economic facts that could both constrain debates in political economy and guide the "fair" regulation of a privately owned monopoly—a second lay in the core intellectual content of the NBER's work for its first several decades, namely, the study of business cycles. Business-cycle research had close ties to forecasting and hence to one function of the Commercial Engineering Department examined earlier: producing an annual "Forecast of Year's Growth" to guide immediate decisions about investment and expansion. But in the aftermath of the First World War, this work was placed in a new institutional context: statistics rather than commercial engineering.

When Rorty returned to AT&T after the war (having reached the rank of colonel by serving in the Ordinance Department and then as head of the Supplies Accounting Section of the General Staff), he was appointed chief statistician (Rorty 1920). While taking the role, however, Rorty also absorbed some of the previous functions of the Commercial Engineering Department. By 1921, the Statistical Division was a broad operation with eight different sections. Telephone Statistics and Foreign Telephone and Telegraph Statistics continued the work of monitoring AT&T domestic competitors and international peers while also maintaining internal data on Bell system operations and its employees. The latter was aided by a

---

18. AT&T and Western Electric gave $2,500 combined to the NBER from 1922 through 1923, the only years with detailed donation records in the archives. The next closest contributor was J. P. Morgan at $1,500. Records of the Carnegie Corporation, III.A, box 243, folder 7, Rare Book and Manuscript Library, Columbia University. For an account that posits greater continuity between Vail's 1912 proposal for a "publicity bureau" and the NBER, see Cook 2017: 255–63. However, David Grossman (1982) argues that the early plans for an economic research bureau were rejected by proponents of the "publicity" model in Rockefeller circles. Certainly, the $2,500 AT&T gave to the NBER in 1922–23 pales in comparison to the $250,000 per year Vail had originally offered for a publicity bureau. See Rockefeller Jr. to Gates, July 27, 1912, pp. 1–2, Office of the Messrs. Rockefeller, Series F, box 18, folder 143, Rockefeller Archives Center.

Special Statistical Analyses section intended to study aspects of Bell operations. In a sign of the division's general role as an information clearinghouse, it also maintained the corporate library and the photostat services. Finally, the Statistical Division pulled two functions from Commercial Engineering: Public Ownership (dedicated to monitoring and intervening in debates about public ownership of utilities) and Economic and Financial Statistics (analyzing and using these data for internal decisions and public arguments). To this, Rorty added a new section on statistical methods, which, as the name implied, focused on the "origination and application of statistical methods," including "Probability, Sampling, Correlation," and so forth.[19] The entire division was a massive operation: by 1923, it employed twenty-eight main staff members and close to sixty clerks, secretaries, and messengers.[20]

The study of business cycles intersected the work of Economic and Financial Statistics, as well as Statistical Methods. Rorty's general views on business cycles—presented in *Some Problems in Current Economics* and recycled in internal presentations by the Statistical Division—followed fairly conventional lines: overexpansion leading to higher interest rates and high prices, followed by a reactive contraction. Rorty (1922: 73–84) hoped that timely restrictions on credit would prevent overexpansion, though he recognized the challenges of implementing that practically.[21] For the individual firm, the solution lay not in preventing fluctuations but in anticipating them, and that became the task of Economic and Financial Statistics.

In 1918, Statistical Methods began publishing a monthly "Summary of Business Conditions in the United States." Much of the thirty-plus-page report contained summary tables and charts of various financial and trade statistics compiled from other sources. But the summary also included several time-series graphs charting various indices as a percentage of their "normal" levels. The most basic of these was titled "General Business," being "a composite of important indices of business activity" running from 1903 to the present. As the accompanying text explained, each time series had been adjusted in three ways: (1) deflated by a price index; (2) removal of "long-term growth" trends; and (3) adjustment for seasonal

19. Andrew, "Work of the Chief Statistician's Division," 3–13, esp. 11.

20. See Comptroller's Department organizational chart, appended to General Accounting Conference (1923), 185-03-01, folder 02, AT&T Archives.

21. Andrew, "Work of the Chief Statistician's Division," follows Rorty's account, including the use of a diagram from his book. See esp. 16–22.

variation (AT&T, Office of the Chief Statistician 1921: 12).[22] In the eyes of the AT&T statisticians, the latter two steps effectively defined the "normal" levels; any remaining fluctuations in the time series were thus deviations from normal.

Developing and improving the "General Business" index and its components became the responsibility of the Statistical Methods section, led by Donald Belcher (a mathematician). Although we do not have the full details of how the section made its adjustments to the raw data, the more general discussions were sophisticated[23] and clearly aware of relevant contemporary literature; when explaining to business executives about the need to adjust data for seasonal variation, for example, Rorty (1920) referred them to Warren Person's work in the *Review of Economic Statistics*. Perhaps for that reason, the Statistical Division was also not naive about the limits of quantitative analysis; as Rorty's successor as chief statistician, Seymour Andrew, put it in 1921, "Much of the output of [Economic and Financial Statistics] is necessarily in the form of reasoned judgment of a qualitative character based on incomplete data,"[24] and the monthly summary gave equal space to narrative assessment of business conditions from division staff and local Bell affiliates. In Rorty's (1923: 158) assessment, "There is . . . no complete substitute for that instinctive knowledge, or 'feel,' of a business that comes in time to the experienced executive, and this knowledge, in combination with a relatively simple statistical analysis, will produce results that cannot be secured from the most elaborate sets of figures when the practical touch is lacking."

All told, the "Summary of Business Conditions" was a remarkable monthly publication—unique for the time period, so far as I am aware. Though other "business barometers" and forecasting services proliferated after the war (including the Harvard Economic Service), AT&T's monthly summary was the most elaborate internal analysis from a private corporation.[25] The summary was made possible both by the scale of AT&T (which allowed it to house such a large statistical division) and by its long tradition of data gathering and market analysis through the Commercial Engi-

22. The "Explanatory Note" first appears in the March 1921 summary; however, the description appears to match previous usage.

23. See also Belcher, "Discussion of Statistical Analysis and Its Application to Certain Phases of the Telephone Business," General Accounting Conference (1921), 185-03-01, folder 01, AT&T Archives.

24. Andrew, "Work of the Chief Statistician's Division," 13.

25. On the history of forecasting, see Friedman 2014.

neering Department. In that context, it should be no surprise that Rorty was one of the founding members of the Econometric Society in 1930—dedicated to the intersection of economics, mathematics, and statistics—or that Belcher and Andrew would join in the first year. Still, the affiliation of Belcher and Andrew—statisticians rather than engineers—pointed to an important realignment in which the older overlap between the practices of commercial engineering and economics would be replaced by a new configuration of economics, statistics, and management.

## Engineering, Economics, and the Statistical Control of Business

By the late 1910s, two key domains in which AT&T commercial engineering had once overlapped with economics (market forecasting and debates about public ownership of utilities) had been recategorized as part of a general Statistical Division. Outside the central office, this break was not so sharp: the Commercial Engineering Department of Southwestern Bell, for example, produced several "Economic Surveys" that analyzed the telephone market and its potential growth in its region in the late 1920s (e.g., Holsen 1927). For Rorty himself, though, the old category of commercial engineering had been completely subsumed by a new and more general practice, the "statistical control of business" that he promoted in talks and essays (e.g., Rorty 1920, 1923).

Rorty's own career had jumped fully onto the executive pathway: in 1921, he became vice president of Bell Telephone Securities; in 1922, he returned to AT&T as an assistant vice president; and in 1924, he became vice president of the International Telephone & Telegraph Company. His vision for the "statistical control of business" thus formed a synthesis of his past experience and current responsibilities. At its heart, he explained, the "essence of statistical control" involved the "picturing of a whole business, so that the essentials stand out sharply from the mass of detail" (Rorty 1923: 166). The task of the statistician, as he explained in another essay, was fundamentally inference: "Accounts are a systematic record and summary of what has happened. Operating statistics should show exactly *where* it has happened, *why* it has happened, and *who* or *what* is responsible" (Rorty 1920). The scope was broad—involving "personnel and wage studies" (what we might regard as human resources), budget projections (accounting), and topics that intersected closely with economics, such as "market and price analyses" and, above all, "general business forecasts" (much of which drew on the work of AT&T, with a reference to the Harvard Economic Service and the research of the NBER) (Rorty 1923). This new role demanded someone familiar with the practices of statistics, of economics, and of a given business (156).

The remainder of Rorty's career exemplified the power of that overlap. In 1930, he was elected president of the American Statistical Association (ASA); in 1934, he became president of the American Management Association, a post he held until his early death in 1936. Throughout this period, he continued to write about economics while also being the ASA's appointed director for the NBER from 1924 onward and serving terms as the NBER treasurer, president, and chairman of the board. This triple intersection of statistics, management, and economics in the telephone industry was not unique to Rorty. Donald Belcher, the mathematician who had run the Statistical Methods section in the Statistical Division, later became comptroller and then treasurer for AT&T, and also served on the NBER Board of Directors in the 1940s and 1950s. Even in the mid-1920s, Belcher's list of research areas for Bell system statisticians sounded nearly identical to tasks taken up by economists: "the problems of supply and price trend of raw materials; manufacturing costs; distributing costs; markets and market structures; labor supply; wages; living costs; interest rates; the future trend of wages, prices, and interest rates; [and] the cyclical ebb and flow of present and future general business conditions" (Glover 1926: 425).

But Belcher, of course, had never been an engineer. Nor did Rorty's essays from the 1920s and 1930s make reference to his engineering past; he spoke of statistics, executive decision-making, and economics, but not engineering. That absence is striking because the early 1920s were the very moment in which American engineers, led most visibly by Hoover, were promoting themselves as experts in efficient management for both business and government (Layton 1986: chaps. 7, 8). Veblen (1921) had similarly predicted that engineers' professional obsession with eliminating inefficiency through careful design would lead them to challenge bankers and more traditional capitalists for control of the modern industrial economy (Knoedler and Mayhew 1999). And indeed, Rorty's vision for the "statistical control of business" shared close similarities with the contemporaneous push for "scientific management" led by the Taylor Society, a movement that also had its origins in engineering (Chandler 1977: 272–81) and its own ties to institutional economics and to the NBER (Bruce and Nyland 2001).

Yet Rorty's decision to emphasize statistics over engineering was prescient. In truth, the lower-level practices linking engineering to both economics and management involved data collection and mathematics:

graphing, curve-fitting, regression, simple mathematical models, and so forth. Thus there was no reason that someone like Belcher, a mathematician with no substantive engineering experience, could not pursue those practices equally effectively. Indeed, Rorty's predecessor as chief statistician at AT&T was a perfect model of the intersection Rorty envisioned. Walter S. Gifford, a 1905 graduate of Harvard, had started as a clerk at Western Electric before Vail tapped him to be chief of AT&T's new Statistical Department. Gifford parleyed that experience into a leading role in US wartime planning before returning to AT&T as comptroller, then vice president, and eventually president from 1925 to 1948 (Marshall 2000).

Nonetheless, Veblen may have been correct that patterns of action and thought enculturated in engineering settings predisposed engineers to employ mathematical practices toward particular ends, namely, the characterization, analysis, and control of complex systems. It was surely no accident, for example, that scientific management and cost-benefit analysis both developed among engineers, or that key pioneers in statistical testing worked in applied agriculture (Ronald Fisher) or quality control for industrial processes (William Sealy Gosset). Although the mathematical practices could be separated from these origins, the decision to apply them as tools for control arose in specific institutional contexts that habituated such goals.

Indeed, the potential of AT&T's Commercial Engineering Department in this regard is well illustrated by Rorty's one-time subordinate, Barnard, who had led AT&T's response to Lewis's campaign for government ownership of the telephone system. Trained in economics, Barnard spent over ten years in commercial engineering before making his own jump to the executive ranks, becoming assistant vice president of the Pennsylvania Bell company in 1922 and then president of New Jersey Bell in 1927. In 1938, he published *The Functions of the Executive*, a text widely heralded as one of the pioneering works in the study of managerial organization. Herbert Simon called the book "a major influence upon my thinking about administration," and thanked Barnard for his "extremely careful critical review" of Simon's (1947: xv–xvi) preliminary draft of *Administrative Behavior*, the book that helped Simon earn his Nobel Prize.

By the late 1910s, the fecundity of AT&T's Commercial Engineering Department had come to an end as Rorty absorbed several of its broader functions into the Statistical Division. Yet the decline of Commercial Engineering was not the end of the intersection between economics and the practice of telephone engineering. Perhaps serendipitously, the early 1920s also saw the formation of Bell Labs, a joint venture between AT&T

and Western Electric that would forge a new set of ties to economics around a different set of lower-level practices: the operations of probability theory to systems analysis and decision-making (Klein 2000; Miranti 2005). Four members of Bell Labs involved with these projects would become early members of the Econometric Society (Harold Dodge, Thornton Fry, R. L. Jones, and Walter Shewhart). Later in the postwar era, Bell Labs would launch the *Journal of Economics and Management Science*, intended "to encourage and support research in the issues and problems of regulated industries" (Garlinghouse 1970: 3). It was a new era for the interlocking of engineering, economics, and business, founded on a different set of overlapping practices, yet both the pressures and resources that produced it would have been very familiar to Malcolm Rorty.

### References

Adams, Graham. 1966. *Age of Industrial Violence, 1910–1915*. New York: Columbia University Press.

Alchon, Guy. 1985. *The Invisible Hand of Planning: Capitalism, Social Science, and the State in the 1920s*. Princeton, NJ: Princeton University Press.

Anonymous. 1905. "How the Theory of Probability May Be Applied to Telephone Traffic." *Western Electrician*, May.

AT&T. 1908. *1907 Annual Report of the Directors of the American Telephone & Telegraph Company*. Boston: Alfred Mudge & Son.

AT&T, Office of the Chief Statistician. 1921. "Summary of Business Conditions in the United States, March 1921." New York.

Barnard, Chester I. 1914. "An Analysis of a Speech of the Hon. D. J. Lewis Comparing Governmental and Private Telegraph and Telephone Utilities." Commercial Bulletin no. 7. New York: AT&T, Commercial Engineering Office.

Barnard, Chester I. 1938. *The Functions of the Executive*. Cambridge, MA: Harvard University Press.

Bruce, Kyle, and Chris Nyland. 2001. "Scientific Management, Institutionalism, and Business Stabilization: 1903–1923." *Journal of Economic Issues* 35, no. 4: 955–78. doi.org/10.1080/00213624.2001.11506422.

Chandler, Alfred D. 1977. *The Visible Hand: The Managerial Revolution in American Business*. Cambridge, MA: Belknap Press of Harvard University Press.

Cook, Eli. 2017. *The Pricing of Progress: Economic Indicators and the Capitalization of American Life*. Cambridge, MA: Harvard University Press.

Dubofsky, Melvyn. 1994. *The State and Labor in Modern America*. Chapel Hill: University of North Carolina Press.

Fabricant, Solomon. 1984. "Toward a Firmer Basis of Economic Policy: The Founding of the National Bureau of Economic Research." www.nber.org/nberhistory/sfabricant.pdf.

Friedman, Walter A. 2014. *Fortune Tellers: The Story of America's First Economic Forecasters*. Princeton, NJ: Princeton University Press.

Garlinghouse, F. Mark. 1970. "About This Journal." *Bell Journal of Economics and Management Science* 1, no. 1: 3.

Glover, James W. 1926. "Requirements for Statisticians and Their Training: Statistical Teaching in American Colleges and Universities." *Journal of the American Statistical Association* 21, no. 156: 419–46. doi.org/10.2307/2276978.

Grossman, David M. 1982. "American Foundations and the Support of Economic Research, 1913–29." *Minerva* 20, nos. 1–2: 59–82. doi.org/10.1007/BF01098190.

Holsen, James N. 1927. *Economic Survey of Missouri*. St. Louis, MO: General Commercial Engineering Department, Southwestern Bell Telephone.

Kielbowicz, Richard B. 2009. "AT&T's Antigovernment Lesson-Drawing in the Political Economy of Networks, 1905–20." *History of Political Economy* 41, no. 4: 673–708. doi.org/10.1215/00182702–2009–037.

Klein, Judy L. 2000. "Economics for a Client: The Case of Statistical Quality Control and Sequential Analysis." In *Toward a History of Applied Economics*, edited by Roger E. Backhouse and Jeff Biddle. *History of Political Economy* 32 (supplement): 27–69.

Knoedler, Janet, and Anne Mayhew. 1999. "Thorstein Veblen and the Engineers: A Reinterpretation." *History of Political Economy* 31, no. 2: 255–72.

Layton, Edwin T. 1986. *The Revolt of the Engineers: Social Responsibility and the American Engineering Profession*. Baltimore: Johns Hopkins University Press.

Lesser, Arthur, Jr. 1969. "Engineering Economy in the United States in Retrospect—an Analysis." *Engineering Economist* 14, no. 2: 109–16. doi.org/10.1080/001379 16908928799.

Marchand, Roland. 1998. *Creating the Corporate Soul: The Rise of Public Relations and Corporate Imagery in American Big Business*. Berkeley: University of California Press.

Marshall, Stephen G. 2000. "Gifford, Walter Sherman." In *American National Biography*. New York: Oxford University Press. www.anb.org/view/10.1093/anb /9780198606697.001.0001/anb-9780198606697-e-1000628.

Miranti, Paul J. 2002. "Corporate Learning and Traffic Management at the Bell System, 1900–1929: Probability Theory and the Evolution of Organizational Capabilities." *Business History Review* 76, no. 4: 733–65. doi.org/10.2307/4127708.

Miranti, Paul J. 2005. "Corporate Learning and Quality Control at the Bell System, 1877–1929." *Business History Review* 79, no. 1: 39–72. doi.org/10.2307/25096991.

Morgan, Mary S. 1991. *The History of Econometric Ideas*. New York: Cambridge University Press.

Mueller, Milton. 1997. *Universal Service: Competition, Interconnection, and Monopoly in the Making of the American Telephone System*. Cambridge, MA: MIT Press.

Nearing, Scott. 1915. *Income: An Examination of the Returns for Services Rendered and from Property Owned in the United States*. New York: Macmillan. catalog .hathitrust.org/Record/001309983.

*New York Times*. 1913a. "Wilson Gets Facts on Wire Control." October 3.

*New York Times*. 1913b. "Government Accepts an Offer of Complete Separation." December 20.

*New York Times*. 1913c. "Federal Ownership Halts." December 21.

*New York Times*. 1913d. "Lewis Opens Fight for U.S. Telephones." December 23.

*New York Times*. 1916. "Attacks Reports on Foreign Trade." January 13.

*New York Times*. 1966. "Dr. Nahum Stone, Economists." October, 26.

Nicolini, Davide. 2013. *Practice Theory, Work, and Organization: An Introduction.* Oxford: Oxford University Press.

Rorty, Malcolm C. 1917. "Income Statistics." *Publications of the American Statistical Association* 15, no. 119: 794–800. doi.org/10.2307/2964965.

Rorty, Malcolm C. 1920. "Making Statistics Talk." *Industrial Management* 60 (December): 394–98.

Rorty, Malcolm C. 1922. *Some Problems in Current Economics.* Chicago: A. W. Shaw. hdl.handle.net/2027/hvd.hnarfl.

Rorty, Malcolm C. 1923. "The Statistical Control of Business Activities." *Harvard Business Review* 1, no. 2: 154–66.

Russell, Karen. Forthcoming. *Promoting Monopoly: AT&T and the Politics of Public Relations, 1876–1941.* New York: Peter Lang.

Scott, William G. 1992. *Chester I. Barnard and the Guardians of the Managerial State.* Lawrence: University Press of Kansas.

Simon, Herbert A. 1947. *Administrative Behavior: A Study of Decision-Making Processes in Administrative Organization.* New York: Macmillan.

Stapleford, Thomas A. 2017. "Historical Epistemology and the History of Economics: A View through the Lens of Practice." *Research in the History of Economic Thought and Methodology* 35A: 113–45.

Stone, Nahum I. 1916. "Review: Income, by Scott Nearing." *Intercollegiate Socialist* 4, no. 3: 30–35.

Stone, Nahum I. 1945. "The Beginnings of the National Bureau of Economic Research." In *The National Bureau's First Quarter Century*, edited by Wesley C. Mitchell, 5–10. New York: National Bureau of Economic Research.

*Telegraph and Telephone Age.* 1913. "M. C. Rorty, Manager Joint Telephone Arrangements, Western Union Telegraph Company, New York." July 16.

Veblen, Thorstein. 1921. *The Engineers and the Price System.* New York: B. W. Huebsch.

Vietor, Richard H. K. 1994. *Contrived Competition: Regulation and Deregulation in America.* Cambridge, MA: Belknap Press of Harvard University Press.

Wells, Coleman Harwell. 1999. "Remapping America: Market Research and American Society, 1900–1940." PhD diss., University of Virginia.

Wilkinson, R. I. 1956. "Beginnings of Switching Theory in the United States." *Electrical Engineering* 75, no. 9: 796–802. doi.org/10.1109/EE.1956.6442128.

Wolf, William B. 1961. "Chester I. Barnard (1886–1961)." *Journal of the Academy of Management* 4, no. 3: 167–73.

# A Century of Economics and Engineering at Stanford

Beatrice Cherrier and Aurélien Saïdi

In 2018, the prestigious John J. Carty Award for the Advancement of Science was, for the first time, awarded to economists.[1] The laureates, Robert Wilson, David Kreps, and Paul Milgrom, came from Stanford University. Together with a fourth colleague, John Roberts, they pioneered "economic engineering," which Kreps describes as "adapt[ing] what is learned from the stylized models and apply them to real-world contexts." Examples range "from auctions of the radio spectrum to models for school choice to kidney exchanges . . . licenses for mobile communications and other uses." In a seminal 2002 paper titled "The Economist as Engineer," Al Roth, a former student of Wilson, further argued that this research program created a shift in the identity of economics. He explained that "design economics" exhibited relationships between theory and applications akin to those of physics and engineering:

> Bridge design also concerns metallurgy and soil mechanics, and the
> sideways forces of water and wind. . . . These complications, and how

We are grateful to Pedro Duarte and Yann Giraud, Al Roth, two referees, and the participants in the 2019 *HOPE* conference, as well as Oliver Beige, Philippe Fontaine, David Kreps, Eddie Nik-Khah, and Bob Wilson for their very helpful comments. Errors remain our own. We are also indebted to Rebecca Pernell, Paul Reist, and all the librarians, archivists, and warehouse workers of the Stanford Libraries and Special Collections for their helpful assistance.

1. It had been awarded to Elinor Ostrom in 2004. Though she later received the Bank of Sweden economics prize in honor of Alfred Nobel, the Carty award was conferred to her as representing "social/political science."

*History of Political Economy* 52 (annual suppl.)  DOI 10.1215/00182702-8717936

they interact with the parts of the physics captured by the simple model, are the domain of the engineering literature. Engineering is often less elegant than the simple underlying physics, but it allows bridges designed on the same basic model to be built longer and stronger over time, as the complexities and how to deal with them become better understood. (Roth 2002: 1342)

The comparison was not merely metaphorical. Wilson, Kreps, and Roth shared a background in operations research (OR). And it was his contributions to this same field that earned the famed Stanford theorist Kenneth Arrow the 2014 "Stanford Engineering Hero" prize, alongside Google's Serguei Brin and Larry Page, and Sally Ride, the first American woman in space. Historians of economics (Armatte 2010; Morgan 2003; Klein 2015) have long pointed to some cross-fertilization between economics and engineering, and the purpose of the present volume is to document and characterize it more systematically. Our article raises the question of the role specific institutions played in nurturing such cross-fertilization and takes Stanford as a case study.

Previous research has documented diverging intra-university dynamics. At MIT, Paul Samuelson and Robert Solow tapped the administrative requirements that all students receive substantial training in mathematics and physics to support the development of a more formalized "new economics," but the lack of substantial collaboration between economists and engineers in OR or energy pricing is striking (Weintraub 2014; Thomas 2014; Breslau, this volume). At Carnegie, Judy Klein (2015; this volume) documents remarkable tool transfers, with optimal control and dynamic programming techniques developed for missile guidance finding their way into macroeconomic modeling. Most of the cross-disciplinary ventures examined by historians, however, took place in extra-university environments (Fontaine 2015).[2] The Statistical Research Group or the RAND Corporation, among others, cradled decision theory, statistics, linear programming, operations research, system analysis, and game theory.[3] In this

2. Fontaine 2015 proposes to use the word *multidisciplinary* to convey a process where disciplines coexist, *interdisciplinary* to denote exchanges between disciplines, *transdisciplinary* to characterize a desire to build a common overarching framework, and *cross-disciplinary* as a general term without special emphasis on a type and degree of relation between discipline. What we document is the existence of interdisciplinary transfers between economics and engineering. The two communities of scholars did more than just coexist in departments and workshops, but retained some disciplinary identity throughout their work.

3. See Jardini 1996 and Bessner 2015 on the RAND Corporation, Erickson et al. 2013 and Mirowski 2002 on decision science, Erickson 2015 on the history of game theory, and Thomas 2015 on the history of OR.

respect, the existing literature on Stanford exhibits an interesting gap. Though the university was home to Arrow's contribution to OR and to economic engineering, Stanford is largely overlooked in accounts of Cold War economics or the rise of market design (Mirowski and Nik-Khah 2017). At the same time, economists are altogether absent from the histories of how RAND, the Cold War military, the federal government, and the rising electronic and computer industry borrowed from and shaped Stanford engineering and fostered the rise of a "Cold War University" (Leslie 1993; Lowen 1997; Gilmore 2004; O'Mara 2019). Our article attempts to bridge this gap through documenting and explaining a paradox. We argue that though economics was, for a long time, given little attention, esteem, and resources by Stanford administrators, Wilson, Milgrom, Kreps, and Roth were nevertheless heirs to a century-long intellectual tradition and operated within an institutional structure designed to foster the kind of cross-disciplinary exchanges they built on. Engineers borrowed economists' normative decision tools. Economists retained engineers' mathematical tools and modeling strategies, but also a fine-grained knowledge of production and innovation processes, and ultimately, a "design" epistemology whereby scientific knowledge is shaped by clients' needs, and theoretical and applied work arc articulated with the purpose of *designing* and *building* (economic) systems that work rather than just modeling them.

We document the key role played by engineers like Herbert Hoover and Frederick Terman in defining the university's strategy, its long-standing intellectual, financial, and cultural association with the developing Californian industrial milieu, and the ability to attract a flow of scientists for short-term visits and permanent positions. Terman's view of research, in particular, was entrepreneurial and relied on the ability to attract public and private contracts. A consequence was that those economists modeling allocation, decision, production, growth and innovation, later pricing, competition and business strategies with statistics, optimal control, or game theory found a home at the School of Engineering and the Graduate School of Business (GSB) more than in the long-neglected Department of Economics.

This article should not be read as a history of economics, engineering, or management science at Stanford and their idiosyncrasies.[4] None of the research programs or institutional arrangements we describe were unique

4. Accordingly, we leave out large chunks of the history of Stanford economics: the rise of macroeconomics and of political economy in the 1980s, the labor economics tradition, the contested influence of the Hoover Institution, the type of agricultural, environmental, and development economics engineered at the Food Research Institute, and the role of the Center for Advanced Studies in the Behavioral Sciences in fostering the cross-fertilization of economics and psychology.

to Stanford. Rather, we document how some of the engineering and economics theories, tools, and epistemologies developed elsewhere were *recombined* in a specific institutional setting and entrepreneurial culture, and thus came to infuse the vision that some Stanford economists developed and spread in the last decades.

## Prologue: Economics and Engineering in the Wild Wild West

From Stanford's early days, economics held an ambiguous and paradoxical position. On the one hand, the discipline was not a priority, though a School of Humanities and Social Science was immediately established. It was even regarded with suspicion by trustees and administrators. The university was opened in 1891 by Jane and Leland Stanford, railroad barons, with the purpose of competing with eastern universities.[5] It was built ex nihilo on sunny rural land. A remote area in an already isolated state, Stanford was immediately given a devoted train station. Drawing inspiration from the development of Cornell, the Stanfords had an ambition to retain the scientists and especially engineers meant to foster the economic development of the West in California. Its motto, taken from German, praised the "Wind of Freedom" and embodied a pioneering spirit whereby frontiers, geographic, social, and economic, were meant to be pushed.[6]

Not only did the university prioritize engineering training and equipment during its first fifty years of existence, but its strategy, orientations, and culture were largely shaped by engineers. After the death of the Stanfords, Herbert Hoover, trained as an in-house geologist at Stanford and a successful mining engineer before being elected president, quickly ascended as the key trustee and donor. He managed to get his friend Ray Wilbur elected as Stanford president and campaigned for the establishment of a graduate school of business, which opened in 1925. It coincided with the recruitment of the electrical radio engineer Frederick Terman, trained at MIT by Vannevar Bush. Hoover, Wilbur, Terman, who was soon nominated chairman of the Department of Civil Engineering, General Secretary Paul Davis, and trustee and future Stanford president Donald Tresidder all shared a common vision: research was to be developed for and

5. Leland Stanford presided over the Southern Pacific Railroad and cofounded the Central Pacific. This history of Stanford is largely taken from Leslie 1933, Elliott 1937, and Nash 1988.

6. The university charter likewise stated that its goal was to "qualify students for personal success and direct usefulness in life."

funded by industrial partners. Terman thus encouraged students, among them William Hewlett, David Packard, and the Varian brothers, to set up new firms to develop and commercialize advances in radio engineering, vacuum tubes, and circuits, like the klystron tube and the audio oscillator.

None of these key prewar administrators held economics in high esteem, despite the Department of Economics and Sociology housing Allyn Young, Thorstein Veblen, Frank Fetter, and Harold Hotelling. None, however, stayed more than a few years, and some resigned amid controversies. That the first appointed sociologist, Edward A. Ross, attacked railroad patrons (including Stanford himself) for undermining efforts from Chinese workers to unionize did not help. Hoover also resented economists' support for Senator Robert La Follette and their campaign for public management of utilities like railroads and water power. As they would continue to do after World War II, economists also resisted pressures to fund research through industrial and business partnerships, which they believed threatened their independence. Administrators, who rather conceived *public* funding as threatening, retorted with (aborted) plans to place the Department of Economics within the business school, "where its professors might properly focus on issues of concerns to industry" (Lowen 1997: 71). The institutional and intellectual independence of economics within Stanford was thus constantly challenged, a trend that did not abate with the establishment of a stand-alone Department of Economics in 1948.

At the same time, Stanford engineers insisted that economic and management knowledge were key to sound engineering "design." The first two economics courses offered by the Department of Civil Engineering in 1891 were Economic Theory of Railroad Location, based on Arthur M. Wellington's 1887 *The Economic Theory of the Location of Railroad*, and Railroad Operations and Management (Stanford University Annual Register 1891–92: 60, 84). Wellington (1887: 1) opened his book with the warning that "engineering . . . is rather the art of not constructing . . . the art of doing that well with one dollar." The course bulletin described bridge design as "bridge location, economic relation between the cost of superstructure and substructure" (Stanford University Annual Register 1891–92: 86), and electrical engineering students were likewise instructed to focus on "the economics, design and management of central station systems" (136).

The set of economic courses for engineers soon became articulated and important enough to be established as an independent curriculum called Engineering Economy, then a whole Industrial Engineering program during the 1930s, and a Civil Engineering Administration two-year graduate curriculum co-taught by the School of Engineering and the GSB.[7] The course offering was developed by John C. L. Fish, author of a 1915 principles book titled *Engineering Economics*. It was then taken over by Eugene Grant, a professor of civil engineering also trained in economics. Grant was influenced by Fish's (1915: v) idea that "every engineering structure, with few exceptions, is first suggested by economic requirements . . . the so-called principles of design are subordinate to the principles which underlie economic judgment." He applied the techniques Fish had developed to study railroads to telecommunications. In 1930, Grant published an influential textbook, *Principles of Engineering Economy*, in which he used cost-benefit analysis to compare business alternatives. It borrowed from cost accounting and finance more than microeconomics.

The war entailed a shift in the university patronage, from industrial clients to the military, but this in fact strengthened the reliance on external funding and the insistence that teaching and research should be oriented toward clients' needs. Efforts to embed the new interdisciplinary war science into a university structure did not raise the status of economics *as a discipline* within the university, but it created new institutional spaces that nurtured theoretical, epistemological, and practical transfers between *some* economists and engineers.

### Nesting the New Sciences of Decision, Allocation, and Production into Engineering (1945–67)

Embedding the New Cold War Science into
a University Disciplinary Structure

The war and the ensuing Cold War prompted a massive metamorphosis of all sciences, hard, social, and humanities. Historians have extensively documented how the demands for more efficient allocation algorithms, new accounting systems, and new decision rules to produce planes and submarines, to schedule bombing strategies, and to guide missiles were channeled into extra-university entities like the Statistical Research Group (SRG), the RAND Corporation (aka the air force research group), the Office of Naval Research (hereafter ONR), and the Cowles Commission.[8] This fostered interdisciplinary interactions between mathematicians, physicists, psychologists, economists, and so on.

7. See Bix, this volume, on the integration of economics in engineering curricula in this period.
8. See note 5, as well as the references in Cravens and Solovey 2012.

The science they came up with was of quantitative, mathematical, and applied nature. Linear programming, statistical decision theory, operations research, optimal control theory, inventory theory, game theory, and sequential analysis were all born out of the need to deal with pressing practical problems. In the summer of 1948 at Santa Monica, for instance, Arrow, the statistician Abraham Girshick, and the mathematician David Blackwell joined forces to solve a mathematical problem they had encountered as they worked on inventory decision rules, that is, how to balance the costs and benefits of gathering information through sequential testing (Erickson et al. 2013: chap. 2). Like other universities, in particular nearby Berkeley, Stanford was eager to tap this pool of new methods. Arrow and Girshick would soon move to Stanford, Blackwell to Berkeley.

The challenge was to convince those scientists used to working in interdisciplinary settings to comply with the more disciplinary structure of the university. Stanford's move was to create new interdisciplinary programs, or even departments. One example was the Department of Statistics, founded in 1945 within the School of Humanities. Upon returning from Harvard, where he had led the prestigious Radio Research Lab, Terman, now dean of the School of Engineering, applied the contract-capturing and "steeples of excellence" development strategy he had successfully implemented during the war (O'Mara 2019: chap. 2). He helped recruit the statistician Al Bowker in 1947 at the instigation of ONR's mathematical division head, Mina Rees. The purpose was to draw funding from the military and lure top scientists into a new research environment. Bowker modeled the new department he headed on SRG, where he had worked with scientists from all disciplines during the war. We are "hopefully having a series of problems come in from either government or industry, having enough space so that all of the young scholars, graduate students and the faculty could be housed in the same building, easily accessible to each other," he explained (quoted in Olkin 1987: 473). He recruited Girshick in 1948, Wald's student Herman Chernoff in 1950, Herbert Scarf in 1957, and Herbert Solomon in 1959. Stanford increasingly resembled an annex of the RAND offices in Santa Monica.

As dean of the School of Engineering and chairman of the Department of Statistics, Terman and Bowker, respectively, relied on joint appointments and shared course sequences to create an environment in which the science military patrons needed could be produced, and to create bridges between schools and departments. A mechanical engineer and former SRG staffer, Gerald Lieberman, was jointly recruited in 1953 by the Departments of Statistics and Industrial Engineering, and quickly found himself in charge of the engineering economy and quality control courses. Samuel Karlin was recruited three years later in mathematics and statistics, and set out to develop courses not just for statisticians but also for engineers, businessmen, psychologists, and economists. Most important, Bowker managed to recruit Arrow from the Cowles Commission on a joint appointment at the Departments of Statistics and Economics.[9]

Arrow's influence in bridging disciplines was enormous. He spent his summers at RAND and later organized workshops with political scientists and philosophers. He developed sequential decision with Blackwell and Girshick, optimal inventory policy with Thomas Harris and Jacob Marschak, and mathematical modeling of allocation, broadly considered, with Patrick Suppes and Karlin. Arrow applied most of these tools to economic topics—general equilibrium theory, endogenous growth, production. But unlike other contemporary economists covering a wide range of topics and tools (such as Paul Samuelson), he was, by every account, also interested in the institutional architecture of science. He sat on dissertation, departmental, and university committees, and chaired research centers. He acted as a transmission channel between the tools produced by mathematicians and statisticians, the applications promoted by engineers and the knowledge about actual production processes they generated, and the topics favored by economists.

Terman's client-focused strategy was immediately successful (see Gilmore 2004: 344–47). By 1947 already, the School of Engineering was receiving more money from military contracts than from the university itself. An institution builder, he founded the Stanford Research Institute (SRI) in 1946, a nonprofit organization designed to allow commercial contracts too risky for industry and promote science education. He then opened the Electronic Research laboratory and the Stanford Research Park in 1951 to house growing companies funded by former students to commercialize research innovation. His and Bowker's recruits drew millions in small and large grants to the university. For instance, the Varian brothers, Terman's former mentees, offered eleven thousand dollars to establish a fellowship in economics for students "with engineering or scientific training" (Trustees 1958: 24). Arrow brought a huge ONR contract on the efficiency of decision-making from the ONR totaling more than two hundred thousand dollars by 1958. He also received NSF and Rockefeller foundation grants, housed in various programs, departments, and

9. Arrow was meant to replace Allen Wallis, who left Stanford in 1947. Part of Arrow's appointment was also at the School of Engineering after it established an OR program in 1962.

labs at the university. The contract-focused and entrepreneurial strategy Terman was allowed to spread throughout the university as provost between 1955 and 1965 created space for disciplinary transfers, yet would also further marginalize scholars from the Department of Economics.

## From Economists Contributing
## to Engineering . . .

In 1945, Industrial Engineering was formally established as a separate undergraduate program "for students who wish to emphasize the business aspects of engineering" within the Department of Civil Engineering (Stanford University Annual Register 1945–46, 257–58). The set of courses offered included Statistics and Accounting for Engineers, Production Engineering, and Machine Design.[10] By the early 1960s, the Engineering Economy course, now compulsory for industrial engineering undergraduates, was advertised as "economic decision making for engineering alternatives" (Stanford University Annual Register 1962–63, 60). The shift highlights that the rise of the sciences of decision created a new role for economics within engineering. At that time, economics was itself in the process of being reframed as the science of rational decision-making under uncertainty (Erickson et al. 2013; Backhouse and Medema 2009). Beyond Arrow, who initially nurtured those research lines, economists at Stanford as elsewhere collectively understood that rational decision theories was what they had to propose in cross-disciplinary ventures. This was clearly articulated by the Stanford econometrician Marc Nerlove in a letter to the chief of the Johns Hopkins Operations Research Office:

> Economics has two general aspects: (1) the first relates to the economy, that is, to a complex of producing, marketing, distributing and consuming institutions and activities. (2) the second relates to economizing, that is, to a certain kind of rational choice and behavior, to making the most of one's resources in achieving one's objectives, in whatever kind of institutional framework. It is the second aspect of economics which I believe especially qualifies economists for work in operations research, *for almost all problems of operations research are problems of rational choice in the sense described above.* (emphasis added)[11]

10. The program was given its own budget, and the power to award a master's degree, in 1952, under the leadership of William Ireson.

11. Nerlove to Simcox, 04/11/1960, box 146, Marc Nerlove Papers, Duke University, Durham, NC.

Nerlove's perspective was shared—albeit with a managerial bent—by Alan Manne, who was recruited from Yale at the GSB in 1961 and spent most of his career at Stanford. A former RAND analyst, Manne had just published a textbook titled *Economic Analysis for Business Decisions*, which he explicitly located in the tradition developed by Grant. The mix of linear and integer programming, inventory models, and sequential decision theory covered in the book could be indifferently called engineering economics, operations research, or management science, and reflected the convergence of economic analysts and business executives when it came to analyze "the internal operation of the business enterprise" (Manne 1961: v–vii). In the introduction, he presented a Dantzig transportation problem where the most efficient route between several factories needed to be determined to make the case that the economist should be considered an efficiency expert "concerned with finding ways to increase the organization's profitability" (Manne 1961: 1–5). Some of the dissertations defended at the School of Engineering in these years were thus clearly economic in their topic, such as Eric Thain's 1968 thesis on "the spatial distribution of public investment in a dual economy," supervised by Arrow, Manne, and Richard Cottle.

The above quotes attest that the combination of mathematics, statistics, engineering, and economics into a new science of decision (military, business, and public) had produced a set of new disciplines sometimes called operations research, sometimes called systems analysis. Though close in their content, mathematical tools, and RAND origins, the two research programs and associated communities responded to different client demands and were stabilized in distinct communities (Thomas 2015). OR programs were established throughout the country during the 1950s, in particular in those business schools undergoing scienticization under the patronage of the Ford Foundation (Khurana 2007; Augier and March 2011). The archetypal example of this transformation was Carnegie Tech's Graduate School of Industrial Administration, headed by the economist Georges Leland Bach, where Herbert Simon, Richard Bellman, Franco Modigliani, John Muth, and the likes of Robert Lucas crafted new models of decision, from bounded rationality to dynamic programming and rational expectations. Systems analysis grew out of the need to rationalize air warfare analysis, but the willingness to model how much human pilots deviated from rationality during aerial combats led RAND social scientists to focus more on "moral" factors. They strove to apply their "science of warfare" to large-scale policy problems of all stripes and established a separate society for management science in 1953, the Institute of Management Sciences (TIMS). At the same time, efforts to sell OR to industry clients who had long housed operations engineers resulted in a growing emphasis on its "scientific" aspect, understood as its theoretical foundations.

At Stanford, these two branches of the new science of rational decision-making tapping economists' knowledge for engineering and business needs were institutionalized in two separate departments. In 1960, the School of Engineering received $3.4 million from the Ford Foundation to develop programs focused on "decision-making in the field of public works engineering, operations research, systems optimization, reliability of engineering systems and components and man-machine systems" (Cottle 2010: slide 29). Arrow pushed for the establishment of an interdepartmental committee on the future of OR, which led to the creation of an interschool program in 1962, turned into a degree-granting department in 1967. Chaired by Lieberman, its faculty was drawn from the Departments of Electrical Engineering (Arthur Kalman, William Linvill), Industrial Engineering (Frederick Hillier, Arthur Vienott), Mathematics (Samuel Karlin), Statistics (Herbert Scarf, Herman Chernoff, Herbert Solomon), Economics (Arrow, Hirofumi Uzawa, Nerlove), and the GSB, where Bach had just been recruited. He shared Terman's client-oriented strategy of selecting a few elite quantitative applied research programs to which researchers from various disciplines contributed. This is what business students needed to be taught, he reflected (Augier and March 2011).[12]

At the same time, a distinct institute in Engineering-Economic System (EES) was established, covering close topics: "engineering economy, operations research, system theory and the planning of engineering works" (Stanford University Annual Register 1962–63). It was chaired by Linvill and staffed with another set of researchers drawn from the GSB, civil, electrical, and engineering economics but also the Food Research Institute, whose trademark was an interdisciplinary structural and institutional approach to development and political sciences. Arrow (2011: 80) later complained that it was like "having two economic departments, one Keynesian and one anti-Keynesian, which is wrong; they both should be working together." Yet, for EES professor Ronald Howard, there was a clear difference between the two programs: "Our discipline was engineering. Theirs [at OR] was applied mathematics," he explained (quoted in

12. George Dantzig himself was poached from UC Berkeley on a joint appointment in operations research and computer science in 1966.

Garber 2009: 267). According to the 1962 registrar, the goal was to "develop improved . . . methodology for decision making in public works." Most EES dissertations emphasized a desire to produce "real-world applications" and were completed in specific firms, in line with the distinctive internship requirement pushed by Linvill.[13] "A unique feature of the program is the internship, a period of experience in the real world that allows a student to test theory in the face of reality . . . [and] formulate meaningful research problems. . . . Problems of broad scope requiring a system viewpoint and thus suitable for the internship experience are found in large industrial firms, in companies and research groups concerned with the design and operation of civilian and military systems, and in government agencies planning and executing public works and economic development projects," the EES registrar read (124).

### . . . to Engineers Turned Economists

The interactions between economists and engineers described above were largely located in the School of Engineering, yet they also affected the kind of topic and methods pursued at the Department of Economics. Shifts in orientation are visible in the database of economics theses defended at Stanford between 1940 and 1990 that we have assembled.[14] The dominant characteristic of the 1950s was diversity. The welfare economist Tibor Scitovsky supervised or sat on the committee of seven dissertations during the 1950s. Other active faculty included Keynesian Lorie Tarshis (five); the finance macroeconomist Edward Shaw (four), who trained John Gurley; Arrow (four); and Moses Abramovitz (four), who supervised an engineering dissertation on the political economy of petroleum conservation in Oklahoma. Topics ranged from international to labor economics and institutional economic history. The 1960s figures show a clear dominance of Arrow, who supervised or sat on the committee of thirty-two dissertations, versus fifteen for Ronald McKinnon and Tarshis and fourteen for Melvin Reder and Gurley. Some of these were

13. Yaw Ansu (1984), for instance, acknowledged his principal adviser (the economist Ronald McKinnon), whose "insistence that [his] work stay in touch with real world economic problems has done much to shape both substance and form of the final product."

14. We have reconstructed a database of the Stanford dissertations defended between 1891 and 1990 (including titles, dates, and committee members) based on the Stanford archives manuscripts. These volumes have been identified through the SearchWorks catalog, from which we have extracted 457 entries in economics, 523 in operations research or engineering-economic systems, and 401 from the GSB.

formally defended in the OR department. Arrow supervised technical work on "simultaneous equations and correlation theory," or "mathematical programming in allocation over time," but also dissertations on trade, migration, health, and insurance.

Though topics researched and taught at the department spanned international economics, public finance and taxation, labor economics, and economic history and development, the main research program was focused on production and growth. It was carried at the department's Research Center for Growth, opened in 1960 to "consolidate a number of research and training activities in the fields of economic development and comparative economics" (Ballandonne 2012: 455). The center was the offspring of two previous projects: the Stanford Project for Quantitative Research in Economic Development launched around 1954 by faculty members Hollis Chenery, Hendrick Houthakker, and Abramovitz, then taken over by Emile Despres, and the Quantitative Project on Production Functions, coordinated ten years later by Arrow, Chenery, Bagisha Minhas, and MIT's Robert Solow. The first of these projects had allowed Chenery, recruited by Stanford in 1953, to study scale economies in specific industries, and he, Arrow, and others were looking to draw general laws on the shape of production functions from industry-specific processes that could be modeled by power-law distributions. At about that time, Nerlove proposed an early implicit empirical application of duality of production and costs to estimate returns to scale in electricity supply.[15] All this research was informed by the engineering-friendly environment in which it was conducted.

Chenery's work on production functions drew on his background as a former petroleum engineer. Author of a 1949 Harvard dissertation, "Engineering Bases for Economic Analysis," supervised by Leontief, he meant to bridge the gap between an engineering and an economic conception of the production function: "The essential difference between the engineer and the economist lies in the variables that each uses to describe the process of production," he later reflected. "The inputs into the engineering production function include pumps, pipe, energy sources, and skilled labor . . . main outputs are the movement of natural gas over varying distances and at different pressures . . . design laws [*for pipelines*] can be used to construct a production function linking inputs and outputs. The economist's cost function can then be derived by replacing some of the engineering variables

---

15. Nerlove (1993: 125) remembered that when he presented a version of the electricity supply at a seminar, Uzawa said, "You can always recover production function from cost function. I thought it was a question, but Uzawa said . . . 'not a question. Always true.'"

with economic variables which conceptualize output as a function of the types of capital goods, labor and raw material," he went on (Chenery 1992: 373).

The interdisciplinary institutional setting also favored the transfer of mathematical tools to economics in the Stanford context (and possibly beyond). The many models of optimal growth written by faculty, including Arrow and Uzawa and graduate students like Menahem Yaari, Karl Shell, David Cass, and David Starrett, were struggling to be solved. Uzawa's two-sector model and Cass's optimum growth model included infinite-horizon maximizing agents and constraints, the kinds of problems that are hardly solved with the classical calculus of variations in use in economics since Frank Ramsey. The interdisciplinary environment in Stanford provided the adequate generalization of these techniques: it was Karlin who suggested that Uzawa check Lev S. Pontryagin's *Mathematical Theory of Optimal Processes*, just translated into English in 1962. Growth economists tapped engineering knowledge in other ways. In his learning-by-doing paper, Arrow (1962) modeled the learning process by a log-linear equation. He borrowed this idea from research on the learning processes in the airframe industry carried at RAND and the SRI (Ballandonne 2012: 470–72; Ballandonne 2015; however, see Thomas, this volume, for a different perspective).

The kind of interdisciplinary research drawing hundreds of thousands of dollars from clients Arrow spearheaded, one that Terman supported as chairman then provost, fit the culture of the School of Engineering (especially the Department of Operations Research). Yet it remained an exception in the Department of Economics. Only the research in economic development (with a growing industrial focus) and international economics led by Chenery, Houthakker, and Tarshis drew an equivalent amount of funding from the Ford Foundation (Stanford University Board of Trustees 1958: 402). The much smaller grants that Shaw, Tarshis, Haley, Baran, and Abramovitz received from the SSRC, Brookings, and the NBER did not convince Stanford administrators to endow the department with more human and space resources, to the growing dismay of economists. After a bitter 1955 battle between Terman and Shaw, then chairman, Arrow had already warned Stanford president Wallace Sterling that it was "a mistake to channel all research into the particular lines for which outside support is available and into relatively large projects. . . . the Individual Scholar, working in a field which may or may not be currently fashionable plays a very vital role in economics" (quoted in Lowen 1997: 161). By the mid-

1960s, Scarf, Uzawa, and Nerlove, having fought with Terman over recruit-ment, were gone, and emerging stars Zvi Griliches, Franklin Fischer, and Dale Jorgenson had turned down offers. Arrow blamed it on the lack of cooperation from the university in opening full professorships and aligning salaries with other universities, warning that such brain drain in economic theory reduced Stanford's status in the field considerably.[16] He finally left for Harvard in 1967, amid speculation that he resented the university's lack of support to economics or simply wanted to be closer to policy deci-sion-making circles (see the many interviews in Feiwel 1987).

## Crisis and Renewal (1967–90)

A Twofold Crisis

Arrow's departure threw a "demoralized and deteriorating" Department of Economics in disarray, so much so that the associate dean of the School of Humanities and Sciences, Richard Lyman, appointed a committee in 1971 and invited Nerlove, now at Chicago, to propose a plan for renewal.[17] His report stressed that Stanford economics suffered from fragmentation. Economists were institutionally and geographically scattered across the university, at the School of Engineering, the School of Medicine, the Food Research Institute, the Center for Advanced Study in the Behavioral Sci-ences (CASBS), the Hoover institution, the rising GSB, and the Institute for Public Policy.[18] He suggested that some unification was in order, that full professorship be established in the department, that economists be given control over fund-raising and appointments of peers across the university (deans were those with the real power), and physically housed in one place.

In response, economists were allowed to increase their faculty from about fifteen to thirty, attracting Joseph Stiglitz, Michael Spence, Theo-dore Anderson, Roger Noll, Robert Hall, and so on and succeeding in getting Arrow back. Yet by the mid-1980s, little had changed. Many of the new recruits only stayed a few years.[19] In 1985, the faculty sent Nathan

16. Nerlove to Abramovitz, February 26, 1964; Abramovitz to Griliches, undated, folder "Correspondence: Jan 1964–March 64," Arrow to full professors, memorandum, undated; Arrow to full professors, June 6, 1963, all from box 146, Marc Nerlove Papers, Duke University.

17. See news.stanford.edu/news/2005/july13/memlrosse-071305.html.

18. Nerlove to Arrow, September 20, 1973; "Innovation and Change in the Social Sciences at Stanford University," Nerlove, undated, box 5, folder "Marc Nerlove," Kenneth Arrow Papers, Duke University (hereafter cited as KAP).

19. Spence, for instance, stayed at the economics department only from 1973 to 1975. He came back in the 1990s, but at the GSB.

Rosenberg, then chairman of the department, a long collective letter titled "The Priority of Economics at Stanford: An Urgent Need for Change."[20] They complained about their lack of attractiveness. Not only did they have to deal with the "Cambridge Mystique" (competing job offers from East Coast departments were always selected), but as the NSF was widely slashing support to social sciences, business schools were on the rise throughout the country, cannibalizing funding, recruits, and students: "The paradoxical outcome is that the same Economics which has been subjected to current political hostility and severe resource cut backs in the School of Humanities and Sciences has been declared desirable by the business community and lavishly endowed with financial support when conducted in a school of business." To compete, they had no building and too little university funding for research, visiting scholars, or yearly seminars, and no computer facility.

The lingering departmental crisis was simmering in the context of a larger social and financial crisis. The late 1960s and 1970s were troubled times at Stanford, as elsewhere. Students' ire targeted the preferred institution whereby military money was channeled into academic research, the Stanford Research Institute (Mody 2017). The Applied Electronics laboratory was occupied and classified research was banned, resulting in a two-million-dollar budget shortfall. This prompted a reorientation of Stanford's research toward interdisciplinary problem-solving research related to transportation, urban, population, and environmental issues. While economists were not directly targeted by the protests, the ensuing gradual withdrawal of military patrons (including the reorientation of RAND's research agenda toward social and urban studies) affected their research programs. The financial, institutional, and intellectual relationships with industrial business clients, while overshadowed by the weight of the military demands of the postwar decades of the 1960s, needed to be reinforced.

## The Rise of the Economist as a Market Designer

At the time Stanford economists were searching for a consistent vision, a wealth of new theories, tools, and research questions was emerging in the profession. None of these were devised at Stanford, but they were brought together through the university's summer workshop tradition, combined by a handful of scholars, including Robert Wilson, who blended them with a

20. Arrow et al., May 29, 1985, "Economics Department 1983–1985" folder, box 65, KAP.

focus on applied theory borrowed from OR and an awareness to business applications characteristic of the GSB, which housed his research group.

In the 1960s, game theory experienced a renewal under the guise of an evolution from its cooperative to its noncooperative species (Erickson 2015: chap. 7). Thomas Schelling's research on armed conflict resolution led John Harsanyi to transform the analysis of games with incomplete information into games with complete but imperfect information. Richard Selten studied what kinds of strategies and resulting equilibria emerged from playing such games in dynamic settings. Interest in the consequences of information imperfections and asymmetries on market outcomes was pervasive, with Arrow contributing the foundational paper in the analysis of the health market before leaving for Harvard (see Thomas, this volume). Another set of questions came from Minnesota's theorist Leonid Hurwicz, who pointed out the destabilizing effects of information asymmetries. A long-term coauthor of Arrow, he began to rethink informational efficiency in resource allocation processes while visiting Stanford in 1958–59.[21] In 1973, he suggested that economists should not merely take existing market settings as objects of study but also study which "mechanism" (i.e., which procedure that uses messages received from agents to select an outcome, the decision to produce a public good or a market allocation) was optimal. The challenge was to identify "incentive compatible" mechanisms inducing participants to reveal information about their true beliefs.

These new research orientations launched a race to analyze new types of dynamic games and develop all sorts of equilibrium refinements, with the soon-thwarted hope to identify unique equilibria. While the hothouse of game theory in the 1970s was Northwestern, most of this flourishing literature was brought to Stanford through the large number of visitors who came through the CASBS, and in particular through the summer workshop, organized annually by Mordecai Kurz, at the Institute for Mathematics in the Social Sciences (IMSS) from 1969. Initially funded by the Ford Foundation and later supported by the Hoover Institution, this workshop brought together mathematical economists for a six-to-eight-week program combining presentations and daylong courses. In 1982, for instance, July workshops were taught by Eric Maskin ("Incentive Theory") or Hurwicz and Marschak ("Resource Allocation Mechanism in Discrete Spaces"). Rogerson presented on the role of reputation in repeated agency problems,

21. His resulting paper was published in 1960 in the book on mathematical models for social sciences edited by Arrow, Karlin, and Suppes.

Drew Fudenberg on sequential equilibria, and Roger Myerson on the value of games with incomplete information.[22]

Economists then looked for applications beyond international warfare, among them Robert Wilson. Trained under Howard Raiffa at the Harvard Business School, Wilson had participated in the famous "Decision under Uncertainty" seminar held between 1961 and 1964, in which Bayesian games were forged. In 1963, he defended a dissertation presenting an algorithm to solve nonlinear programming problems before taking a position at the Stanford GSB. Though he "was still considered partly an operations researcher" by the late 1960s and kept training students in that area (Jennergren 2002: 1), he gradually turned to problems of bargaining and auctions. As then explained by Michael Rothkopf (1969: 362), "Operations researchers are starting to construct bidding models that are realistic and that consider simultaneously the optimality of the decisions of all bidders." "Only Wilson has begun to take account of the uncertainty of a bidder about the value of the subject of the auction to himself," he continued. Building on Bayesian assumptions on how economic agents use new information to revise their beliefs across time, Wilson modeled a no-regret strategy whereby each agent would use the information revealed by other players leaving the auction to recalibrate her own reservation value, and studied the resulting bidding equilibrium.

In line with his OR background and the business school environment in which he was operating, Wilson paired his theoretical interests with a distinctive concern for real-world applications. His work on auctions was aimed at providing better strategies to bid for offshore oil tracts to the oil companies he was advising, so as to escape the "winner's curse"—winning as a result of having *ex ante* overestimated the value of the commodity.[23] Likewise, his work on the pricing of public utilities, culminating in the publication of the book *Nonlinear Pricing* in 1983, was fueled by his consulting work for the Analysis Research Group at the Xerox Palo Alto Research Center and for the Electric Power Research Institute.[24] Applying

22. The workshop is still active under a new heading, SITE. Another workshop series important in the development of game theory and market design was the Conference on Econometrics and Mathematical Economics, inaugurated at Berkeley in the early 1970s. It was instigated by Arrow and divided in two branches, general economics and decentralization, first coordinated by Debreu and Radner (then Kreps took over, and by the early 1980s, Wilson and Milgrom were also regular presenters).

23. The problem had been clearly outlined (and christened) in a seminal 1971 paper by three oil engineers from Atlantic Richfield Co., E. C. Capen, R. V. Clapp, and W. M. Campbell.

24. Former Stanford PhD student Samuel Oren, a Xerox staffer, remembers that in 1979, "we became interested in broadband communication . . . there were no customers, so how do you do market research? . . . Wilson introduced us to the whole area of non-linear pricing, market design." See also Rothkopf 2000.

game-theoretic concepts of strategy and equilibrium to real-world situations often meant relaxing informational requirements, dealing with the fact that equilibrium are indeterminate, multiple, and very sensitive to players' beliefs, that outcomes can be non-budget-balanced and manipulated by coalitions, that the computational burden for solutions is often intractable, and that preparing bids is often extremely costly. Wilson took these constraints into account in his theoretical work. In the end, his economics, though building on game-theoretic rather than financial accounting, programming, or optimal control tools, was in the spirit of the work of the likes of Grant and Manne: it was knowledge built with the purpose of making practical industrial management decisions more efficient.[25]

This blend of theoretical rigor and practical bent Wilson imparted on the stream of students he directed, as well as those many more who attended, often several years in a row, his graduate lectures. The graduate students he trained in the 1970s and early 1980s included Roth, Milgrom, Holmström, Armando Ortega-Reichert, Claude d'Aspremont, and Peter Cramton. Many of them shared an OR background with Wilson, and several built on prior professional experience as they entered the graduate program. Milgrom had worked as an actuary, and Holmström had worked as an OR analyst at a Finnish conglomerate. "My interest in incentives had been raised by the problems I had encountered when trying to implement a large-scale corporate planning model at Ahlstrom," he later explained (Holmström 2002: 1). Many of them were trained within a newly founded "Decision Sciences Group" headed by Wilson and a cluster of researchers interested in OR, applied mathematics, and economics at the GSB.[26]

It was within the GSB, the summer workshops organized by the IMSS and other newly established interdisciplinary spaces, that the moribund

25. In the introductory essay to a tribute volume, Bengt Milgrom, Paul Holmström, and Alvin Roth (2002: 1) pointed to Wilson's emphasis that "the value of theory is its usefulness in addressing practical problems," which Roth (2018) called "the Wilson Doctrine." Mirowski and Nik-Khah (2017) claim that it was only the "experimental school" of market design led by Roth which "designed" markets, and that the two previous schools, Hurwicz's "walrasian school" and Wilson's "bayesian school," remained highly theoretical. What we argue here is that, though theoretical, Wilson's approach was applied in that it was aimed at solving business clients' issues, and therefore already was a "design" practice akin to what engineers were doing.

26. They included the OR specialist Evan Porteus, who was working on Markov decision processes, and later his student Kreps, who had completed a dissertation in the theory of dynamic programming. In the 1970s, the GSB was organized into "groups" including the Economic Policy Analysis Group run by GSB's Bach, Accounting, Finance, Marketing, and Organizational Behavior. It was a structure more fluid and less hierarchical than a departmental one, and facilitated interdisciplinary transfers (Wilson, correspondence with authors).

tradition of introducing students to game theory's applications was gradually renewed. While Karlin had published a two-volume book, *Mathematical Methods and Theory in Games, Programming, and Economics*, in 1959, by the late 1960s, the topic was not taught anymore. It was (re)taught by IMSS visitors like Aumann (courses offered in 1971 and 1975), as well as Michael Maschler (1973). In his business course Competitive Strategies, based on business cases, Wilson suggested that students read references by Melvin Dresher, Duncan Luce and Raiffa, John von Neumann and Oskar Morgenstern, Martin Shubik, Robert Aumann, Cottle, and Dantzig and Karlin.[27] He then set up a course on "multi-person decision theory," in which he was teaching the modeling strategy and key results of the sixteen papers from the previous year that he had found most noteworthy.

As hinted above, the operationalization of Hurwicz's hope to "design" markets required permanent trade-offs between theoretical purity, information requirements, concepts of equilibria, the legal and institutional characteristics of the real world, and the computational abilities of real players and the scientists who advised them. The development of experimental economics (see Svorenčík 2016) afforded new ways for testing auction and matching designs. Developed at Arizona State, Caltech, and other experimental economic labs, these techniques were brought to Stanford through, again, the creation of new workshops. Upon moving back to California in 1979, Arrow, whose interest in decision theory and applied and interdisciplinary bent had not abated, organized an interdisciplinary seminar in applied decision analysis with Wilson, Amos Tversky from the Department of Psychology, and the organization theorist James March. It was advertised as the "study of normative and descriptive decision making particularly in the face of uncertainty . . . problems arising in making decisions analyses in applied policy contexts" (Stanford University Register 1980–81: 341), and featured Vernon Smith on risk aversion auction, as well as Charles Plott, Richard Thaler, and political scientists and law scholars. In subsequent years, presentations focused on conflict and negotiations.[28] As highlighted in our introduction, Roth largely contributed to

27. "Lectures on Cooperative Game Theory," Aumann, July 1971; "Analysis of Competitive Strategies" Wilson, Spring 1973, all box 21, Al Roth Papers, Duke University. In his syllabus, Wilson noted the lack of treatment of uncertainty and applications to "the practical context of managerial decisions."

28. Arrow came back to Stanford with an ONR grant to establish a Center on Decision and Conflict in Complex Organizations, for which he got a grant from the Hewlett Foundation in 1988. He also participated in the development of a program in political economy.

blend game-theoretic tools, experiments, and a concern for design he had inherited from his engineering background and continued discussions with his wife, Emily Roth, a psychologist specializing in cognitive engineering (Roth and Wilson 2018).

What emerged from this outline is not just a two-way street between economics and engineering but a three-legged nexus of engineering, economics, and management, each discipline growing closer to the other two. When Milgrom was brought back to Stanford in the early 1980s, Arrow pointed out that "in the field of managerial economics (the common part of decision analysis and microeconomic theory), it is hard to find anyone to compare him with."[29] At the same time, industrial administration PhD and marketing professor Seenu Srinivasan was setting up a GSB joint course on the design of new product with the business administration professor William Lovejoy and the mechanical engineer David Beach. Called Integrated Design for Marketability and Manufacturing, it illustrated the complementarities of engineering and business. One knew "how to understand consumers and how to market a product," the second "how to manufacture," and the third "how to design." The course combined two MBAs and two engineers in each team (Srinivasan 2017).

### Rethinking Innovation and Operations Managements

The overhaul of industrial relations by game theorists and the nascent field of market design were not the only spaces where yet other types of interactions between economics and engineering flourished. Though still centered on decision theory, OR's and EES's course offerings evolved with the pressing issues of the time. EES advertised its expertise in the "economics of depletable resources; impact of government policies on economic growth . . . econometrics with particular emphasis on passenger car use of gasoline." Course programs in health policy and energy modeling and analysis were set up (Stanford University Annual Register 1981–82). In OR, too, environment had become a major topic, as a new optimization system lab promised to help students "learn about modeling complex systems dealing with energy, the economy, water." Arrow taught a "theory of information and organization course" throughout the 1980s and 1990s, and OR students were also allowed to attend the conflict

29. Arrow to William Breen, June 3, 1981, folder "Milgrom, Paul," box 5, KAP.

resolution seminar, a course on welfare economics by Starrett, or another interdisciplinary seminar in risk management organized by Arrow and Lieberman (Stanford University Annual Register 1990–91: 216).

Beginning in the 1970s, interactions between economics and engineering were not merely largely mediated and unified by management (both the client-oriented approach and the GSB flexible group structure) but also increasingly by computer science. In the 1950s, Terman, Bowker, mathematicians, and engineers had established a Computation Center and a graduate program in data processing and scientific computation, and recruited George Forsythe to head a small group in the mathematics department (Cottle 2010). By the late 1960s, it has evolved into an independent department in the School of Humanities with a strong interdisciplinary bent. Several economists, including Manne and Wilson, were associated with some of its projects in mathematical programming languages. By the mid-1980s, computer science had become so central that it was seen as a basis on which to merge the still-independent departments of OR, EES, and industrial engineering. In 1985, a failed proposal to establish a joint research center in decision analysis suggested merging "elements from the social (people, organizations), analytic (logic, mathematics), and technological (enabling technologies) domains to develop and explore new concepts that will be relevant in solving the complex problems of modern businesses and industries. Jim March saw these domains as analogous to empires competing for power and the center enabling them to make trade agreements."[30] The report pointed out that "a theme emerged based on the idea that it is tough to manage companies and this management can be made easier with computers." The term *intelligent management systems* was thus chosen by the proposal authors as the rallying idea to "express ties to both engineering and business."[31]

At the Department of Economics, a distinct "economics of industry" program was taking shape, one that was also influenced by proximity with engineering. It also dealt with health, environment, and market structures, but it was of a more institutional nature. Roger Noll, Tim Bresnahan, and others wanted to study oligopoly and the antitrust status of joint ventures, contracts negotiations, and property rights in collaboration with the GSB and political scientists, through a detailed study of actual institutional arrangements. Under the leadership of the economic historian Paul David

30. James March was a Stanford sociologist and organization theorist who developed the behavioral theory of the firm with Richard Cyert.
31. "Engineering research center proposal 1985" folder, box 66, KAP.

and Nathan Rosenberg, economists' traditional concern with the explanation of growth had morphed into a "new economics of science" that drew on case studies to understand the production and dissemination of knowledge and the determinants of innovation (David and Dasgupta 1994).

David had been teaching a course on the determinants and consequences of the diffusion of technological innovations in the economic history of the West from the ninth to the nineteenth centuries.[32] Rosenberg was teaching a course on "technology and modern industrial society," studying the "socio-economic processes" influencing the rate and direction of technological changes. Some of his knowledge was taken from a seminar, "Science, Technology and Society," organized by an aeronautics engineer, Walter Vincenti (see Rosenberg and Vincenti 1978).[33] The latter published an influential 1990 book titled *What Engineers Know and How They Know It*. It used examples from the history of aeronautical engineering to construct an epistemology of engineering and to sketch a model of how new technologies are produced. The gist of the argument was to explain what engineers do when they "design"—design variation is affected by "blindness" and selection by "unsureness," so engineers are left combining theoretical knowledge and trials and errors in various ways. Market designers would not have rejected that characterization of their work.

## Epilogue

In the past two decades, the much-covered 1994 FCC auctions for radio spectrum acted as a test for the market designer's epistemology of applied economics.[34] The OR, EES, and industrial engineering departments were eventually merged into a new management science and engineering department, covering decision analysis and risk analysis, economics and

32. The key takeaway was the notion of "innovation clusters." His research combined economic theory, history, and microeconometrics to analyze technological change, studying the failure of innovation like the reaper to disseminate, on the establishment of standards like the QWERTY keyboard.

33. Rosenberg and Vincenti 1978 coauthored a book, *The Generation and Diffusion of Technological Knowledge*. David and Vincenti appear to have read each other's course material, though the extent of their exchanges and mutual influences will be studied from archives in the future. In the 1980s, Rosenberg and David Landau chaired a workshop on technological innovation sponsored by the Department of Economics and the Center for Economic Policy Research.

34. The Stanford economists involved in the process subsequently founded Market Design Inc. For historical and methodological analyses of the auctions, see the references listed in Mirowski and Nik-Khah 2017.

finance, information science and technology, production and operations management, and system modeling and optimization.

The continuing intellectual cross-fertilization and joint institutional redevelopment in economics, engineering, business, and more recently computer science illustrate the paradoxical history of economics at Stanford in the past hundred years. On the one hand, this history was one of a long, protracted battle between economists and an administrative hierarchy they felt neglected them, to strengthen their disciplinary boundaries, emphasize their specificities, and get control over funding and recruitment. At the same time, what was crucial to the import of mathematical tools, an engineering perspective on innovation and a "philosophy of design" into economics, and to the export of economists' contributions to the postwar science of decision and allocation to OR and EES was the constant institutional innovations whereby these disciplines were combined and recombined. This involved a long tradition of supporting joint appointments and of constantly updating a rich and complex network of interschool and interdisciplinary training "programs" and workshops.

In the end, none of the ingredients that shaped the relationships between economics and engineering were specific to Stanford (except the weather), from the rise of statistics and OR to the Cold War context and associated stream of military and federal financial support. If what later came to be called the Silicon Valley formed a unique intellectual and industrial environment, a university forging ties with its industrial milieu was nothing original, nor was retaining the best students as educators, researchers, or business partners. Yet these ingredients were stirred by a few scientists with an interdisciplinary bent like Bowker, Forsythe, Arrow, and Wilson as well as engineers-turned-administrators like Hoover and Terman, who upheld a strong vision of which grants and contracts-capturing research programs should be prioritized. They created an institutional structure in which theoretical, tool, and epistemological cross-fertilization between disciplines and between researchers, and public and business clients, was nurtured on a long-term scale. This included interdisciplinary programs like OR, teams at the GSB and other extradepartmental structures like the Stanford Research Park for electrical engineering and computer science, or the IMSS workshop for mathematical science. Though economics was not a priority in itself, the skills developed by some economists in the context of the Cold War allowed them to become central resources in engineering education and research fostered by the army, then the large-utilities energy industry, then the Silicon Valley companies. The

Stanford Department of Economics has eventually managed to rank in the US top-ten departments, many years after the engineering and computer science departments did so.

## References

Ansu, Yaw. 1984. *Monetary and Exchange Rate Policies for an Economy with Parallel Markets: The Case of Ghana.* Stanford, CA: Department of EES, Stanford University.

Armatte, Michel. 2010. *La science* économique *comme ingénierie.* Paris: Presses des Mines.

Arrow, K. 2011. "Oral History Interview Conducted by Jane Hibbard." Stanford Oral History program.

Augier, M., and J. March. 2011. *The Roots, Rituals, and Rhetorics of Change: North American Business Schools after the Second World War.* Stanford, CA: Stanford Business Books.

Backhouse, Roger, and Steven Medema. 2009. "On the Definition of Economics." *Journal of Economic Perspectives* 23, no. 1: 221–33.

Ballandonne, M. 2012. "New Economics of Science, Economics of Scientific Knowledge and Sociology of Science: The Case of Paul David." *Journal of Economic Methodology* 19, no. 4: 391–406.

Ballandonne, M. 2015. "Creating Increasing Returns: The Genesis of Arrow's 'Learning by Doing.'" *History of Political Economy* 47, no. 3: 448–79.

Bessner, Daniel. 2015. "Organizing Complexity: The Hopeful Dreams and Harsh Realities of Interdisciplinary Collaboration at the RAND Corporation in the Early Cold War." *Journal of the History of the Behavioral Sciences* 51, no. 1: 31–53.

Chenery, H. 1992. "From Engineering to Economics." *BNL Quarterly Review*, no. 183.

Cottle, R. 2010. "The Building of Management Science and Engineering at Stanford." PowerPoint. Msande.stanford.edu/sites/default/files/history_masande.ppt.

Cravens, H., and M. Solovey. 2012. *Cold War Social Science: Knowledge Production, Liberal Democracy, and Human Nature.* London: Palgrave Macmillan.

David, P., and P. Dasgupta. 1994. "Toward a New Economics of Science." *Research Policy* 23: 487–532.

Elliott, Orrin Leslie. 1937. *Stanford University: The First Twenty-Five Years.* Stanford, CA: Stanford University Press.

Erickson, P. 2015. *The World the Game Theorists Made.* Chicago: University of Chicago Press.

Erickson, P., J. Klein, L. Daston, R. Lemov, T. Sturm, and M. Gordin. 2013. *How Reason Almost Lost Its Mind: The Strange Career of Cold War Rationality.* Chicago: University of Chicago Press.

Feiwel, G., ed. 1987. *Arrow and the Foundations of the Theory of Economic Policy.* London: Palgrave Macmillan.

Fish, John C. 1915. *Engineering Economics: First Principles.* New York: McGraw Hill.

Fontaine, P. 2015. "Introduction: The Social Sciences in a Cross-Disciplinary Age." *Journal of the History of the Behavioral Sciences* 51, no. 1: 1–9.

Garber, Russ. 2009. "An Interview with Ronald A. Howard." *Decision Analysis* 6, no. 4: 263–72.

Gilmore, G. Steward. 2004. *Fred Terman at Stanford: Building a Discipline, a University, and Silicon Valley*. Stanford, CA: Stanford University Press.

Grant, Eugene. (1930) 1938. *Principles of Engineering Economy with Problems*. New York: Ronald Press.

Holmström, B. 2002. "Introductory Essay to Groves Scheme on Restricted Domains." In Holmström, Milgrom, and Roth 2002.

Holmström, B., P. Milgrom, and A. Roth. 2002. *Game Theory in the Tradition of Bob Wilson*. services.bepress.com/wilson/.

Jardini, D. R. 1996. "Out of the Blue Yonder: The RAND Corporation's Diversification into Social Welfare Research: 1946–1968." PhD diss., Carnegie Mellon University.

Jennergren, L. Peter. 2002. "Introduction to a Paper Inspired by Bob Wilson, Well-Known Optimization Theorist." In *Game Theory in the Tradition of Bob Wilson* 7. services.bepress.com/wilson/art7.

Khurana, R. 2007. *From Higher Aims to Hired Hands: The Social Transformation of American Business Schools and the Unfulfilled Promise of Management as a Profession*. Princeton, NJ: Princeton University Press.

Klein, J. 2015. "The Cold War Hot House for Modeling Strategies at the Carnegie Institute of Technology." Institute for New Economic Thinking Working Paper Series No. 19. papers.ssrn.com/sol3/papers.cfm?abstract_id=2667883.

Leslie, S. W. 1993. *The Cold War and American Science: The Military-Industrial-Academic Complex at MIT and Stanford*. New York: Columbia University Press.

Lowen, R. S. 1997. *Creating the Cold War University: The Transformation of Stanford*. Berkeley: University of California Press.

Manne, A. 1961. *Economic Analysis for Business Decisions*. New York: McGraw-Hill.

Mirowski, P. 2002. *Machine Dreams: Economics Becomes a Cyborg Science*. Cambridge: Cambridge University Press.

Mirowski, P., and E. Nik-Khah. 2017. *The Knowledge We Have Lost in Information*. Oxford: Oxford University Press.

Mody, C. 2017. "Interdisciplinarity at Vietnam-Era Stanford." In *Investigating Interdisciplinary Collaboration*, edited by S. Frickel, and B. Prainsack, 171–93. New Brunswick, NJ: Rutgers University Press.

Morgan, Mary S. 2003. "Economics." In *The Modern Social Sciences*, edited by Theodore M. Porter and Dorothy Ross, 275–305. Vol. 7 of *The Cambridge History of Science*. Cambridge: Cambridge University Press.

Nash, Georges H. 1988. *Herbert Hoover and Stanford University*. Stanford, CA: Hoover Institution.

Nerlove, M. 1993. "The ET Interview by Eric Ghysels." *Econometric Theory* 9: 117–43.

Olkin, I. 1987. "A Conversation with Albert H. Bowker." *Statistical Science* 2, no. 4: 472–83.

O'Mara, M. 2019. *The Code: Silicon Valley and the Remaking of America.* New York: Penguin.

Rosenberg, N., and W. Vincenti. 1978. *The Britannia Bridge: The Generation and Diffusion of Technological Knowledge.*

Roth, Alvin E. 2002. "The Economist as Engineer: Game Theory, Experimentation, and Computation as Tools for Design Economics." *Econometrica* 70, no. 4: 1341–78.

Roth, A., and R. Wilson. 2019. "How Market Design Emerged from Game Theory." *Journal of Economic Perspectives* 33, no. 3: 118–43.

Rothkopf, M. 1969. "A Model of Rational Competitive Bidding." *Management Science* 15, no. 7: 362–73.

Srinivasan, V. Seenu. 2017. "Interview by Leigh McAlister, October 24, 2017." Working paper.

*Stanford University Annual Register.* 1891–92, 1945–46, 1962–63, 1981–82, 1990–91. Stanford University Bulletins. Palo Alto, CA: Leland Stanford Junior University.

Stanford University Board of Trustees. 1958. *Minutes of the Board of Trustees of the Leland Stanford Junior University,* vol. 39. Palo Alto, CA: Leland Stanford Junior University.

Svorenčík, A. 2016. "The Experimental Turn in Economics." PhD diss., Utrecht University.

Thomas, W. 2014. "Decisions and Dynamics: Postwar Theoretical Problems and the MIT Style of Economics." In *MIT and the Transformation of American Economics,* edited by E. Roy Weintraub. *History of Political Economy* 46 (supplement): 295–314.

Thomas, W. 2015. *Rational Action: The Sciences of Policy in Britain and America, 1940–1960.* Cambridge, MA: MIT Press.

Vincenti, W. G. 1990. *What Engineers Know and How They Know It: Analytical Studies from Aeronautical History.* Baltimore: Johns Hopkins University Press.

Weintraub, R., ed. 2014. *MIT and the Transformation of American Economics.* Supplemental issue to volume 46 of *History of Political Economy.* Durham, NC: Duke University Press.

Wellington, Arthur M. 1887. *The Economic Theory of the Location of Railroad.* New York: John Wiley and Sons.

**Trading Tools and Practices
at the Boundary between
Economics and Engineering**

# Shotgun Weddings in Control Engineering and Postwar Economics, 1940–72

Judy L. Klein

> Many machines already run themselves by feedback.
> A new species of engineer is now required to orchestrate a whole
> technological process and its controls in a unified system.
> —Gordon S. Brown and Donald P. Campbell, "Control Systems" (1952)

> It is not by coincidence that in some advanced phases of his work
> the modern economist resorts to systems of differential equations
> similar to those used by the designers of self-regulating machinery.
> —Wassily Leontief, "Machines and Man" (1952)

Control engineering is engineering for design. In particular, it is an analytic framework for the design of self-regulated dynamic systems that respond automatically to new inputs, such as disturbances or changes in environmental factors, to move the system to a new stable state. The stability criterion usually entails the incorporation of feedback of information from previous system outputs. Time lags inherent with dynamic feedback can themselves be sources of instability because they could lead to "hunting," or in the case of communications engineering "singing," such that the

I am grateful for research support from the Institute for New Economic Thinking (grant number IN011-00054). An earlier version of this article was discussed at the April 2019 *History of Political Economy* conference, "Engineering and Economics." I appreciated comments from participants at that conference and an anonymous referee for *HOPE*. I thank in particular Pedro Duarte, Yann Giraud, Mary Morgan, Paul Dudenhefer, and Claude Misukiewicz for their effective editorial support.

*History of Political Economy* 52 (annual suppl.) DOI 10.1215/00182702-8717948

amplitude of the output oscillations become explosive, never reaching a steady state. The articulation, measurement, and testing of stability were therefore essential components of control engineering.

The post–World War II fluidity of exchange of ideas between control engineering and economics was enhanced by their shared interest in cyclical behavior, dynamic system stability, and self-regulation.[1] The desire to steer the economy away from another economic depression, as well as conceptual compatibilities in Keynesian theory, led several engineers, including the British engineer Arnold Tustin, the Australian engineer Bill Phillips, and the American engineer Charles Holt, to apply their newly forged tools to economics after World War II.[2]

In a 1992 interview for the Institution for Electrical Engineers' series "Pioneers of Control," Tustin used his decades of experience to reflect on the writing of the history of control engineering:

> And if I might make a comment about the study of the history of engineering—in general, not just control engineering—it seems to me that the major task is to try to understand how and why technological advance occurs. Is it a result of education, for example, or is it by chance, or due to the personal characteristics of particular inventors? What are the effects of particular circumstances, such as the pressure of war? and so on. These important questions shouldn't be smothered by the "who-did-what-first" attitude, because as far as I'm concerned that's neither here nor there! But the study of how scientific advance relates to the prevailing circumstances influencing developments seems to me a fascinating and important undertaking. (quoted in Bissell 1992: 226)

1. Also, economists' use of empirical graphs and schematic diagrams for intradiscipline communication yielded a "natural affinity" for the visual tools of control engineering (see Goodwin 1955: 210).

2. High unemployment in the industrial economies, high indebtedness, falling prices and incomes fueling deflationary spirals, and runs on failing banks characterized the world-wide Great Depression of the 1930s. The prolonged severity of the crisis led to paradigm shifts in economic theory. Residue from debates over causes and solutions to the Great Depression has lingered into the twenty-first century. One explanation for what precipitated an end to the economic crisis is the major increases in government's expenditures in the late 1930s as several countries, starting with Germany, began rearming for another major war.

Many historians see Nazi Germany's invasion of Poland on September 1, 1939, as the start of World War II. Germany surrendered to the Allied powers on May 8, 1945. Japan surrendered on December 15, 1945, after the United States dropped atomic bombs on the cities of Hiroshima and Nagasaki. During the course of World War II, over twenty-five countries sent military forces into battle and seventy to eighty-five million people lost their lives due to the war.

"Pressures of war" were indeed major stimuli to developments in control engineering. US scientific research during World War II and the subsequent Cold War space race spurred two key conceptual leaps in the theory and practice of control engineering.[3] The driving force of military exigencies led to control engineers and applied mathematicians labeling both qualitative turning points as "shotgun weddings." The first marriage led to standardized analytic tools to improve and speed up the design of servomechanisms for gunfire control, particularly with World War II anti-aircraft guns. During the 1960s there was another shotgun wedding, again named as such by participants. This Cold War marriage, of optimization theory with stochastic control theory to maintain optimal trajectories of missiles and space vehicles, led to what engineers claimed was the "modern theory of optimal control." These two jumps to new disciplinary frameworks in turn influenced macroeconomic theory and policy debates in the 1950s, 1960s, and 1970s.

Several historians of economics and science, including Nancy Wulwick (1995), Esther-Mirjam Sent (1997), Judy Klein (2002, 2007, 2015), and Marcel Boumans (this volume) have investigated the influence of optimal or state-variable control engineering on the economics discipline in the 1960s and 1970s. This investigation concentrates on the earlier stage of control engineering with its emphasis on a systems' perspective, the important role of feedback of information to control systems, and the visual, empirical examinations of systems and stability criteria.

## Gunfire Control and the First Shotgun Wedding

Reflecting on his World War II work as a communications engineer at Bell Laboratories, Hendrik Bode (1960: 17) asserted that "the war emergency produced a sort of shotgun wedding" of two originally separate technical approaches.[4]

3. Most historians date the Cold War from 1947 to December 1991, when the Union of Soviet Socialist Republics disbanded into fifteen independent nation-states.

4. In New York in the late nineteenth century, Alexander Graham Bell used funds from a research prize for his invention of the telephone to set up the research laboratory and patent office targeting sound communication. Bell used the profits of those operations and near-monopoly market position to rapidly expand the company. In 1925, Bell Laboratories was formally established to work on research projects for the American Telephone and Telegraph Company and the Western Electric manufacturing division. Thomas Stapleford, in this volume, examines how the distinct structural features of telephone engineering in general, and the Bell system in particular, created intersections between the practices of engineering and economics in the early twentieth century.

One area is the classic field of regulators, as exemplified by the house-hold thermostat or the Watt centrifugal governor. The other is the comparatively recent theory of negative feedback amplifiers, originally developed to meet the problems of long-distance telephony. The two fields were brought together by military servomechanism and computer problems which arose during the war. (1)

Before the war, Bode and his colleagues at Bell Laboratories, including Harold Black and Harry Nyquist, were electrical engineers confronted with the problems associated with maintaining the integrity of the verbal communication transmitted over telephone lines spanning great distances. In 1915, heavy conducting cable and vacuum tube amplifiers and repeaters facilitated the first effective transcontinental line from New York to San Francisco. The trade-off was the more lines/channels covered, the more repeaters required, but the more noise and distortion created. The solution developed by Black and his colleagues was the negative feedback amplifier. In December 1937, the US Patent Office awarded Patent 2,102,671 for Black's "Wave Translation System" employing negative feedback loops to repeat and amplify electric waves without major distortion. As long as the feedback was not destabilizing, such systems would enable high load capacity in long-distance telephone networks. As Bode (1960: 8) explained in his history, "We needed a practical criterion which would tell the design engineer what properties he should seek to ensure a stable system." The Nyquist diagram, developed by Black's and Bode's colleague at Bell Laboratories enabled control engineers to empirically test the stability of their feedback loops (see figure 1).[5]

A postwar conceptual framework narrating a sketch of a steam engine with James Watt's 1784 design for a flyball, centrifugal governor for steam engines (see figure 2) illustrates the advantages of the wartime union Bode discussed. Steam from the engine in the frame drives the flywheel and the large belt that transmits the output of energy to other large machines. The movement of the flywheel also transmits a small representation of the output back along the narrow belt to a more delicate instrument, Watt's fly-ball

5. The kernels of control engineering—focus on stability in feedback loops and its determination by studying the effects of transient inputs on output—are evident in Nyquist's (1932: 126) opening sentences: "When the output of an amplifier is connected to the input through a transducer the resulting combination may be either stable or unstable. The circuit will be said to be stable when an impressed small disturbance, which itself dies out, results in a response which dies out. It will be said to be unstable when such a disturbance results in a response which goes on indefinitely, either staying at a relatively small value or increasing until it is limited by the non-linearity of the amplifier."

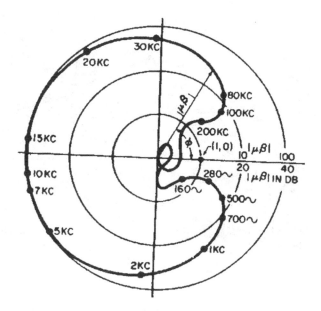

**Figure 1** A Nyquist diagram is used to determine whether a configuration of a closed-loop sequence is an unstable system. Information from the transfer function (the Laplace transform of the output divided by the Laplace transform of the input) is plotted for all significant frequencies. If the locus of points passes through the critical point (1,0) the amplitude and phase of the sinusoidal output remains identical to that of the input. If the locus encircles the point (1,0), the oscillations become cumulative and the system is unstable. If the locus fails to circle the critical point (as in this case), the oscillations will dampen and the system will be stable (Bode 1960: 8).

governor. The governor responds to that representation of output as a new input. The greater the pressure in the steam engine, the more energy transmitted to the flywheel and belts. As pressure builds, the increased speed of the narrow belt increases the angular velocity of the shaft of the governor, and thus the centrifugal force on the fly-ball mechanism, which causes the fly balls to move farther from the shaft. This movement out causes a throttle valve to close more, and the steam pressure is reduced until the desired pressure, which was previously set by the operator, is achieved. The steam engine plus governor is what control engineers call an "error-actuated" device. The more the engine pressure exceeds the desired set point, the more the throttle valve closes, thus reducing the pressure. The wider belt on the flywheel transmits energy. The narrow belt to the governor transmits

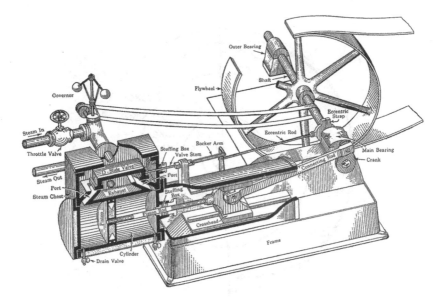

**Figure 2** Sketch of main components of a steam engine with a centrifugal governor designed by James Watt (Leonard and Maleev 1949: 98).

messages or information about the speed of the flywheel and thus the pressure of the steam engine. The entire system, including the feedback loop of the narrow belt and governor, was a "servomechanism."

The concepts of feedback, the transmission of messages, or information in a closed loop, and error-actuated automatic control mechanism are war-related appropriations from communication and information engineering. Before World War II, this conceptual structure would not have been applied to large energy-generating mechanisms such as a steam engine or the movement mechanisms on large antiaircraft guns.[6]

### Scientific Research on Mechanisms of Warfare

Concerned about the possibility of US engagement in the war in Europe, President Franklin D. Roosevelt signed an order on June 27, 1940, creat-

6. The *Oxford English Dictionary* definition of a servomechanism is a good expression of its essential properties: "A powered mechanism in which a controlled motion is produced at a high energy or power level in response to an input motion at a lower energy level; esp. one in which feedback is employed to make the control automatic, and generally comprising a measuring device, a servo-amplifier, and a servo-motor."

ing the National Defense Research Committee (NDRC) to "correlate and support scientific research on the mechanisms and devices of warfare" (*Order Establishing the National Defense Research Committee*, reproduced in Baxter 1946: 451). Initially, Division D-2, under the directorship of Warren Weaver, was responsible for all research on the control of anti-aircraft guns. "A basic program of development of servomechanisms" was at the top of the agenda for the first formal meeting of "Division D-2 on August 1, 1940" (*Gunfire Control* 1946: 38).

Gordon Brown and Donald P. Campbell, two NDRC researchers at the Massachusetts Institute of Technology Servomechanism laboratory, described the scientific hothouse climate at the NDRC in which control engineering developed:

> During World War II great numbers of men were brought together from different fields to pool their abilities for the design of weapons and instruments. As a result, the specialists on engineering and science found themselves talking to one another for the first time in generations. Mechanical engineers exploited techniques of circuit theory borrowed from the communications engineers; aeronautical engineers extended the use of electrical concepts of measurement and of mathematical presentation; mathematicians working with engineers and experimental scientists discovered entirely unsuspected practical uses for forgotten theorems. The enforced collaboration soon focused attention on the essential principles that apply to all control systems. The general theory of control systems which now emerged was enriched in turn with the lore of experience from many different technologies. With the theoretical means at hand to write the equations for motors, amplifiers and hydraulic transmissions, it became possible to design control-system components with entirely new properties to meet predetermined needs. Moreover, these new parts could be used in many different types of control systems, and they could be manufactured in quantity. (Brown and Campbell 1952: 59)

Under the reorganization and expansion of the NDRC in the fall of 1942, Division 7, based mainly at MIT under Harold Hazen, took of responsibility of "Fire Control," particularly in destroying enemy aircraft. Communications engineers from Bell Labs, including Ralph Blackman, Bode, and Claude Shannon, and the mathematician Norbert Wiener, were among those working with Division 7. As the Division 7 researchers stated in their summary report at the end of the war:

Superficially there is no apparent relation between fire control and electrical communications. More fundamentally, however, both are concerned with the separation of useful information or data from the unwanted but unavoidable data in the form of "noise" or rough tracking. In fact, ultimate performance of equipment in both fields is limited fundamentally by the extent to which these two, the wanted information and the unwanted or spurious information can be separated. The adaptation of methods already highly developed for this purpose in the communications field into a form useful in the fire-control field constitutes one of the important contributions of World War II to fire Control. (*Gunfire Control* 1946: 5)

Most of the research of Division 7 was on control systems in large land-based or ship-based antiaircraft guns. The 1942 reorganization of the NDRC had also led to the establishment of the Applied Mathematics Panel (AMP), directed by Weaver. The AMP contract with the military included the improvement of the instrumentation and operation of the smaller antiaircraft guns in airplanes. The small analog computers of their control systems precluded optimization and in many cases led to marksmen having to be an integral part of the feedback loop in the servomechanisms (see Klein 2016). AMP researchers formulated exponential smoothing equations to model the information flows between gunner, analog computer, and gun that aided in the prediction of where the enemy plane would be by the time the marksman's bullet intersected with it. In June 1944, Weaver appointed LeRoy MacColl, from Bell Telephone Laboratories, to write a mathematical text on servomechanisms. The preexisting literature, which had been directed to engineers, was mechanism specific, and often proprietary. By the end of the war, mathematicians could refer to one equation that described all servomechanisms whether they were electrical, gyroscopic, or mechanical (see Klein n.d.).

The mathematicians and engineers in D-7 appropriated stability tests from communication engineers. They investigated a system's response to either an instantaneous switching on and off of voltage or the application of an alternating current. The determination of the frequency response and stability conditions of a closed-loop system subject to either this transient or sinusoidal input initiated an essential mathematical approach to control engineering and to the study of dynamic processes in general. In evaluating the output of a system in response to a transient or sinusoidal input, an engineer could treat one closed loop or even the entire system as a "black box." One did not have to construct equations for every structural feature of the circuits or loops. In the case of linear models, the use of Laplace transform operators enabled the comparison of output to input formalized as a transfer function.[7] In addition to the constructed ratio of output to input, engineers, following Nyquist's lead, plotted the relationship between the phases and magnitudes of sinusoidal input and output waves on a diagram that could indicate whether the output oscillations would dampen, stay identical to the input oscillation, or explode, rendering the system unstable. The Nyquist diagram (see figure 1) thus visually determined whether a system met the stability criterion.

The rapid speeds of enemy aircraft introduced new types of errors of observation due to the difficulty of steady tracking of the moving target. The communication engineers from Bell Labs introduced their data smoothing framework to servo control of antiaircraft fire in order to minimize "the consequences of observational error by, in effect, averaging the results of observations taken over a period of time" (Blackman et al. 1946: 71). The communication engineers saw data smoothing as a special case of the "transmission, manipulation, and utilization of intelligence" (72). They argued that their data-smoothing approach was operationally better than Wiener's statistical approach because the military was "interested only in increasing the number of very well aimed shots" (73).[8]

Wiener was not interested in good-enough solutions, or as Herbert Simon would come to call it, "satisficing." The visual "practical" criteria for stability embodied in a Nyquist or Bode diagram were after-the-fact legacies of the empirical arts of cut-and-try engineering. Wiener's statistical approach was in pursuit of formulating the optimal properties of servomechanisms and the optimal method of prediction that combined the complex plane analysis of the communication theory with probability theory and autocorrelation. This combined with the minimization techniques derived from the calculus of variations yielded a science of information.[9]

7. A transfer function is the ratio of the Laplace transform of the output to the Laplace transform of the input, assuming that all initial conditions are zero. The transfer function is used only with linear relationships. Engineers calculate a transfer function for each closed loop in a system, as well as a transfer function for the system as a whole.

8. Blackman, Bode, and Shannon (1946: 73) did allow for the superiority of a statistical approach in the form of minimizing the probability of making large misses.

9. In Wiener's (1948: 9) words, "In general engineering design has been held to be an art rather than a science. By reducing a problem of this sort to a minimization principle, we had established the subject on a far more scientific basis.... We have made of communication engineering a statistical science, a branch of statistical mechanics." Some NDRC resources went into improving predictors as well as the directors (the servomechanisms). Peter Galison (1994) details Wiener's design for an antiaircraft predictor, based on the autocorrelation function of the enemy pilot's positions in the past, and he discusses the tests, comparing Wiener's stochastic predictor with Bode's simpler geometrical, deterministic predictors.

Because of the relatively large analog computing capacity in the land- or sea-based guns, Wiener could entertain hope of synthesizing optimal control systems using both predictors and directors. His answer—*Extrapolation, Interpolation, and Smoothing of Stationary Time Series with Engineering Applications*—was published as a classified NDRC document in 1942 and as a declassified book in 1949. For decades, Wiener's book on his time-series approach as well as his 1948 book *Cybernetics or Control and Communication in the Animal and the Machine* were required reading in most top-level courses in control engineering (see Kalman 1978).[10] Wiener's goal of optimal prediction, his emphasis on the intimate relationship between filtering and prediction, the ostensible elegance of his mathematical approach, and the fact that his often impenetrable mathematics was difficult to comprehend fostered an appealing mystique. For military and industrial needs, however, Wiener's optimal approach was too restrictive and therefore rarely operational. For example, it could only be applied to stationary time series data amenable to linear modeling. Operational optimal control finally flourished with the second shotgun wedding in the late 1950s and early 1960s aided by the larger computing capacity of digital computation.[11] In both Cold War superpowers, Richard Bellman's, Rudolf Kalman's, and L. S. Pontryagin's research on optimal trajectories of missiles and space ships enabled this qualitative leap.

In most cases engineers in World War II had to proceed with trial and error in designing their systems—they changed a component, calculated

10. Wiener named the study of humans and machines communicating within closed-loop systems of control "cybernetics." In some cases, such as with the small turrets in bombers, it was still necessary for humans to be a part of the feedback loop. Indeed, despite all the mechanization, the enemy pilot had to be considered one of the servomechanisms in the system. The addition of the human element necessitated a stochastic rather than a deterministic approach to such problems, and this in turn led to new developments in time-series analysis. More specifically, as Galison (1994) has documented, Wiener's research into the enemy's reactions indicated that while it was difficult to predict one enemy pilot's reflexive behavior to gunfire based on another pilot's behavior, the individual's immediate past behavior was a good predictor of his future response. In other words, the appropriate way to model this feedback loop was through autocorrelation.

11. One of the biggest stimuli to the wartime development of the digital computer was the need to solve the equations necessary to design optimal servomechanisms, which were usually analog computers. At Bell Telephone Laboratories, George Stibitz designed and Samuel Williams supervised construction of what the Bell engineers called a "complex computer" to multiply and divide complex numbers. These computations were essential in designing feedback amplifiers, wave filters, transmission networks, and analog computers. The first prototype electronic digital computer went into operation on January 8, 1940. In his first encounter with the Bell digital computer, Wiener tried, on September 11, 1940, to stump the computer with difficult complex variable computations. The computer triumphed (Bell Telephone Laboratories 1978: 166).

the transfer function, and determined with the aid of a Nyquist diagram whether the system was still stable. The transfer function was analogous to a black-box reduced-form model in forecasting or econometrics. In the 1960s this input-output approach gave way to a modeling of the structural equations in the time domain. Control engineers describe this post-1960 state-variable or state-space approach as optimal or modern control theory (see Bellman and Kalaba 1964). Digital computation combined with mathematical solutions in the form of algorithms, and sampled sequential data, made recursive optimization possible without assumptions of stationarity, linearity, or time-invariant constant coefficients as equation parameters.

### The Conceptual Framework of Control Engineering in the Late 1940s

By the end of the World War II, the formalized principles and protocols for the practice of control engineering were in place:

- The analytic focus was on a system.
- Automatic control—self-regulation of a *system* required feedback of *information* (i.e., signals, or messages, not energy) that engendered stability.
- The information that was fed back often took the form of the error between the actual value and the desired, or predicted value of the output.
- In the context of error-actuated servo mechanisms, negative feedback occurs when some function of the output of a system is fed back in a way that tends to reduce the oscillation in the output. This damping enhances stability by countering the output.
- Positive feedback increases fluctuations and augments the noise leading to explosive oscillations, instability, and the inability to comprehend the signal.
- The mathematics for designing negative feedback amplifiers in the electronic relay of telephone messages could be applied to feedback loops that included humans, direct current electricity, gyroscopes, mechanical gears, or electrical motors.
- The stability of the system was to be ascertained by drafting block diagrams of every closed loop, and studying what would happen to each loop if it was subjected to a sinusoidal or transient input. If the input-output relationship was a linear one, engineers would compute the transfer

function for each loop and one for the entire system then map out the transfer function on the complex plane of the Nyquist diagram.

- Feedback could make matters worse by causing explosive oscillations. The greater the time lags in information flows and/or the higher the gain from input to output, the greater the potential for self-excitation.
- Critical, rapid damping to the desired value could be achieved by reducing time lags and/or adding more feedback loops. The additional loops would take into account that the output often needed to respond not just proportionally to the error but also to the rate of change of the error or even the rate of change of the rate of change of the error.
- The proportion of the output fed back as a new input was usually a very small quantity, and in the absence of new large external disturbances, the feedback necessary to maintain a finely tuned system was slight.

### "Using These Borrowed Weapons in Economics"

In the United States and the UK, the refined concepts of feedback and control took on facilitating qualities between society and scientific cultures in ways reminiscent to those of force and work in Victorian Britain (see Wise and Smith 1989). Control engineering was an interdisciplinary systems-approach to problems of self-regulation, and its postwar dissemination was thus closely linked to that of operations research and cybernetic research. All three of these areas received US military support after the war and captivated the interest of academics and industrial managers.[12]

The insights gleaned from the interdisciplinary work on the problem of control can be found in comments by Warren McCulloch, a psychologist turned physiologist, at MIT's Research Laboratory of Electronics. In his summary of points of agreement in nine interdisciplinary meetings of the Macy Foundation study of cybernetics, McCulloch ([1953] 1955: 60, 70) stated,

> Our meetings began chiefly because Norbert Wiener and his friends in mathematics, communication engineering, and physiology, had shown the applicability of the notions of inverse feedback to all problems of regulation, homeostasis, and goal-directed activity from steam engines to

12. Several writers have explored the wartime creation of cybernetics and its postwar diffusion including Donna Haraway (1981–82, 1985), Steve Heims (1991), Andy Pickering (1995), Paul Edwards (1996), Katherine Hales (1999), and Philip Mirowski (2002). Donald MacKenzie (1990) examines the postwar appropriation of a "gyro culture" and "black box" mind-set for the design of guidance systems for nuclear missiles. Also, several papers in Hughes and Hughes 2000 discuss operations research and the systems aspect of control engineering.

human societies. . . . we had already discovered that what was crucial in all problems of negative feedback in any servo system was not the energy returned but the information about the outcome of the action to date.

As early as 1949, economists took an interest in cybernetics. Harry Johnson (1949) of Cambridge University and M. M. Flood (1951) of the RAND Corporation were among those who reviewed Wiener's *Cybernetics or Control and Communications in the Animal and the Machine*. Although Wiener had expressed skepticism about the applicability of cybernetics to the social sciences, Johnson (1949: 575) believed that "the notion of society as a communicating rather than an energy-conserving system, and the associated concepts of amount of information and feedback, are capable of throwing a great deal of light on a wide range of economic problems."[13] Johnson speculated that trade (business) cycles could be due to excessive feedback, and he argued that central bank control should be seen as a communications problem with signal effects. That notion was taken up so readily by economists that Johnson (1968: 984) eventually questioned whether the application of control-system engineering to monetary policy suffered "somewhat from taking stabilization per se as the objective of policy and the measure of success."

By the early 1950s these notions of system homeostasis, stability, and negative feedback of information based on deviation from desired outcome were no longer confined to government research for the military. The lead article in the September 1952 special issue of *Scientific American* on automatic control was an essay by the philosopher Ernest Nagel, who explained that only recently had scientists formalized the principles of automatic control, which as a general notion had been around since ancient times. In an article on the economic and social impact of automatic control systems, Wassily Leontief reported on the "progressive 'instrumentation' of the U.S. economy." He also argued that the modern industrial economy was like a feedback mechanism, and it was "not by

---

13. The rotation of perspective to economic systems as communications systems is also evident in microeconomics. Kenneth Boulding (1952: 36), for example, argued that economists should only model behavior of the firm that was compatible with feasible information flows: "The Maximization of profits is unrealistic because firms cannot possibly know when profits are at a maximum. Hence firms must adopt rule-of-thumb methods of behavior (like full-cost pricing) which do not necessarily maximize profits but which fit into their information systems. Profit maximization is ruled out because there is nothing in the information system of the firm which reveals the marginal inequalities which would be indicative of failure to maximize profits. The information system reveals average costs; it reveals sales, production, inventory, debt, and other figures in the balance sheet and income statements. It does not, however, generally reveal marginal costs and still less does it reveal marginal revenues."

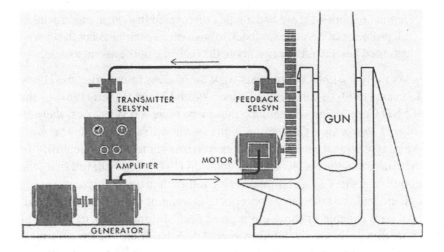

**Figure 3** Arnold Tustin's (1952: 52) diagram of the electrical feedback system used to change the elevation of a gun on a ship. The term *selsyn* is a portmanteau of *self* and *synchronizing*. Selsyns or syncros, whether mechanical or electrical, transmit messages about angular rotation. In the diagram above, the feedback selsyn sends information on the current angle of elevation of the gun to a differential above the transmitter selysn. The predictor (not pictured) transmits the newly computed desired angle to the differential. Any discrepancy between the actual and desired angles is transmitted via the transmitter selsyn as an AC signal to the amplifier, which transmits the message to the motor controlling the gun to change the angle of elevation.

coincidence that in some advanced phases of his work the modern economist resorts to systems of differential equations similar to those used by the designers of self-regulating machinery" (Leontief 1952: 150).

The articles in the control issue dealt mainly with the principles of automatic control and its potential for industrial applications, but several authors mentioned possible applications in social science. Tustin asserted that understanding feedback was essential for comprehending all self-regulating systems in "not only machines but also the processes of life and the tides of human affairs." Using the example of the automatic antiaircraft gun director on a ship (see figure 3), Tustin explained the beauty of a closed-loop system revealed in gunfire control.[14]

14. During the war, Tustin had worked on control of antiaircraft guns on British naval ships for the Metropolitan Vickers Company. He also served as the company's representative to the British Ministry of Supply "Informal Panel on Servomechanisms."

Tustin (1952: 51) also elaborated on the ugly side of automatic control: feedback could in itself cause unstable, explosive oscillations—"self-excitation" was "the chief enemy of the control-system designer." In a linear system, the options open to the engineer to minimize these destabilizing oscillations in negative feedback loops were to minimize response time lags, introduce "time-lead" devices that anticipated time lags, or add additional feedback loops. Tustin gave several examples of natural feedback systems, including time-lead, anticipatory responses of human synapses, and the rabbit and lynx predator-prey cycle. Tustin gave prominence, however, to the boom-bust business cycles that he considered a "major example of oscillatory behavior due to feedback" (53).

Tustin asserted that although John Maynard Keynes did not use or indeed have access to the terminology of control-system theory, he gave "the first adequate and satisfying account of the essential mechanisms" that could explain undamped oscillations in the economy including the fact that economic activity depended on the rate of investment, which in turn also depended on economic activity (53, 54). Tustin presented a full-page block diagram of Keynes's notions of dependency constructing an analogy between Keynes's notions of economic interdependency and electrical feedback circuits (figure 4).

Tustin's 1953 book *The Mechanism of Economic Systems: An Approach to the Problem of Economic Stabilisation from the Point of View of Control-System Engineering* was the most extensive illustration of the control engineers' direct entry into macroeconomics. In the preface to his book, Tustin (1953: v) asserted that the time was ripe to bring "the analysis of engineering systems and the understanding of economic structure . . . into a potentially fruitful marriage." In an additional reverberation of shotgun weddings, Richard Goodwin's (1955: 109) review of Tustin's book made mention of economists "using these borrowed weapons in economics."

From the mid-1950s to the mid-1960s, the influences of control engineering on economics were evident in a variety of forms:

1.  Economists began to see the economy as a communicating system, with information being a major flow within the system.
2.  Economists began to use the term *feedback* as a noun—an entity to be diagrammed, measured, manipulated, and institutionalized.
3.  Economists used the schematic diagrams of closed loops, Nyquist diagrams, and equations of control engineering to construct abstract models of money and information flows. Transfer functions described linear relationships; electrical and hydraulic analogues of closed

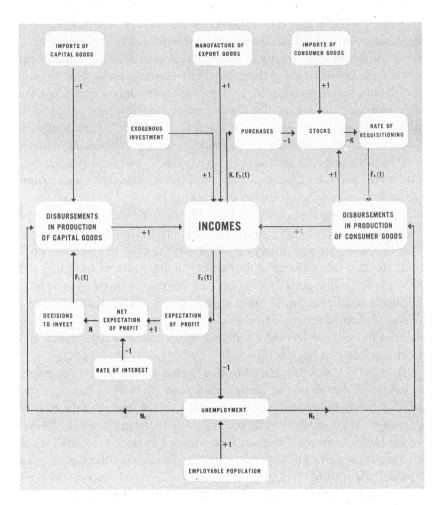

**Figure 4** Tustin (1952: 55) used this block diagram of John Maynard Keynes's ideas to illustrate how an economic system functions through feedback loops for consumer goods and capital goods and the relationship between them. Tustin's hope was to design an electrical analog of the economic system. K represents Keynes's propensity to consume; $F_1(t)$ is the time-lag between the decision to invest and the purchase of capital goods; $N_1(t)$ and $N$. stand for nonlinear functions that diminish increases in production as unemployment approaches zero.

loop systems served as material models for examining nonlinear relationships.

4. Macroeconomists made stabilization of income, employment, and/ or interest rates a major goal of government policy. Measuring and minimizing variance in macroeconomic aggregates became as important as establishing a level.

5. Even before the war economists had perceived time lags as a major source of instability, for example in a market for an agricultural good like hogs. Closed-loop models, however, gave them ideas for structuring and critiquing mathematical and physical models of the macroeconomic system.

6. Economists began to use the communication engineering term of *fine-tuning* as a noun. Advocates of government intervention used the equations of control engineering to demonstrate that fine-tuning could be relatively effective and painless. Critics of discrete fiscal and monetary policy used the equations of control engineering to demonstrate that government intervention could exaggerate economic oscillations thus destabilizing the economy.

7. Engineers and economists applied the diagrams and models of control engineering retroactively. Block diagrams of views of economic systems from those of David Hume to John Maynard Keynes were seen as embodying the principles of feedback and self-regulation.

8. Under the umbrella of "cybernetics," economists in centrally planned economies adopted the focus and tools of automatic control in their research on planning.

9. For economists on both sides of the Cold War, control lost its status as villain and acquired a near-heroic one in its association with harmony, coordination, and the natural feedback mechanisms embodied in all animals.

Tustin and other engineers became quite zealous in their promotion of schemas of automatic control for economic modeling. The year before the special *Scientific American* issue on control, the British Department of Scientific and Industrial Research, in cooperation with the Institution of Electrical Engineers and the Institution of Mechanical Engineers, held a conference on automatic control in Cranfield, England (see *Automatic and Manual Control* 1952). More than three hundred engineers, military personnel, mathematicians, and economists attended the July 1951 meeting. In a session called "Analysis of the Behaviour of Economic Systems," Richard Stone demonstrated the usefulness of electrical analogs in understanding transactions within Leontief's framework of input-output analysis. Tustin presented a paper titled "An Engineer's View of the Problem of Economic Stability" (reproduced in Tustin 1951–52) in which he demonstrated that the engineer's "scheme of dependence" was the equivalent of the economist's "model." He used an engineer's block diagram (similar to that of figure 4) to represent the scheme of dependence in Keynes's *General Theory*. The independent variable was the rate of investment, the feedback was Keynes's marginal propensity to consume, and the multiplier captured the effect of the feedback and investment on income. That scheme pinpointed nonlinear relationships, for which Tustin asserted the necessity of using physical analogs. Tustin envisioned that an accurate analog might take up to five years to construct, at a cost of tens of thousands of pounds. He sketched out how a circuit that included rectifiers and capacitors could "compute" the present value of Keynes's expectation of profitability. Tustin declared that he and other engineers skilled in analog devices would be willing to offer their services in the construction of a more complete physical analog of the economy.

Control engineers took delight in finding examples of a feedback mindset in a myriad of economic theories.[15] Keynes's theory was an obvious example, as was the business cycle model of the Polish economist Michal Kalecki. In 1951 and 1952, the American Institute of Electrical Engineers published papers on electrical analogs of economic models of inventory oscillations, Goodwin's nonlinear national income model, and Kalecki's macrodynamic system (see Strotz, Calvert, and Morehouse 1951; and Smith and Erdley 1952). The engineers argued that the electrical analogs could reveal the topological features of the economic models, including stability conditions, the quantitative behavior of certain parameters, and estimates of parameters. Analogs were particularly useful in modeling nonlinear relationships that could not be captured with transfer functions.

In 1955, the Control Systems Division of the Association of German Engineers (VDI-VDE) held a meeting in Essen on the topic of "economic control processes in comparison with technological control processes." Engineers presented most of the papers on the applications of servomechanism theory to understanding and controlling the economy, including reinterpretations of David Ricardo and François Quesnay (see Geyer and

15. This delight with using a new framework to delve into a variety of contexts was similar to that of the nineteenth-century natural philosophers who relished their new perception of the Gaussian law of error in frequency distributions in observations arising from diverse phenomena (see Klein 1997: 161–94).

Oppelt 1957; Föhl 1957; and Fels 1957). In this conference, as in other forums, engineers presented schematic closed loops that diagramed the economic relationships posited by famous economists. The list would eventually include David Hume and Adam Smith as well as the representations of Ricardo, Keynes, Kalecki, and Goodwin.

Why would engineers be so willing to apply their tools to economic issues? There was obviously an element of zeal that snowballed as more disparate disciplines were captured in the "essential unity" of automatic control theory (see Lockspeiser 1952; and Brown and Campbell 1950, 1952). As George J. Thaler and Robert G. Brown (1953: 25) explained in their postwar text *Servomechanism Analysis*, almost all analysis and design of servomechanisms "must be carried out on a mathematical basis in order that time must be saved in reaching an optimum design." There was one basic general equation for all servomechanisms. In addition to the wartime acknowledgment of this common formalization, there was the realization that the feedback circuits, whether they be hydraulic, translational mechanical, or rotational mechanical, had an analog in some electrical circuit (see, e.g., the Table of Analogous Elements in Thaler and Brown 1953: 38). So even when the operational calculus of Laplace transforms could not handle the nonlinear elements, the electrical analog could serve as a useful model by which one could test the stability of a system. By the end of the war, these engineers were experienced and comfortable in moving from a model of a system to its analogy in another type of system.

There was also concern among engineers that periodic depression was becoming more pronounced and that capitalism could be preserved only if stability could be achieved. In his book *The Mechanism of Economic Systems*, Tustin (1953: 1), for example, asserted that "the nature of the instability of an unregulated free-enterprise system is only now beginning to be clearly understood." Engineers like Tustin were struck by remarkable analogies between the economic reasoning of Keynes, Hicks, and Kalecki, and key elements of control engineering theory. Tustin, Head of the Department of Electrical Engineering in the University of Birmingham, offered his engineering expertise in what he perceived as the most urgent economic problem—"the guidance of government departments in the implementation of a full-employment policy." That sentiment resonated with many economists who were, at the same time, engaged in offering guidance on the goals of full employment stability of output and prices. Goodwin, for example, called for economists to use the analogy of servomechanisms to understand both the process of *tâtonnement* in markets (1951a) and the role of the nonlinear accelerator in the persistence of business cycles (1951b). Goodwin (1955: 209, 210) asserted that there was a "natural affinity" between control engineering and postwar macroeconomics:

> Since the advent of the New Economics these has been a distinct shift of emphasis from reform to quantitative action of the counter-cyclical fiscal policy variety. It is interesting that the communications engineers have made a similar change in their technique for stabilizing their networks. They do it by adding a "supplementary feed-back loop," and this is precisely what a successful Council of Economic Advisers would be. Modern high-fidelity amplifiers were the first great success of these techniques, and the extraordinary quality of their performance (based on heavy negative feedback loops) shows how well it can work in the proper conditions.

The initial stimulus to the economics profession taking up the goals, vocabulary, diagrams, and equations of control engineering came primarily from engineers or physicists who turned their sights on economics, including Tustin (1953), Phillips (1954, 1957), and Holt (1962).

Phillips's early works illustrate the double-edged reaction that accompanied applications of the analogies of control engineering to macroeconomics. In his first article on stabilization policy (1954), Phillips argued the case for monetary policy to stabilize the economy:

> Some may doubt whether it is a sufficiently powerful instrument; but if the right type of stabilisation policy is being applied continuously, comparatively small correcting forces are sufficient to hold the system near the desired position once that position has been attained. It is quite likely, therefore, that a monetary policy based on the principles of automatic regulating systems would be adequate to deal with all but the most severe disturbances to the economic system. (315)

Subsequent work on the electronic simulators at the UK National Physical Laboratory with the use of more elaborate time lags and Nyquist diagrams led Phillips (1957: 276) to conclude that "it is unlikely that the policy applied will be the most appropriate one, it may well cause cyclical fluctuations rather than eliminate them."[16] The lessons from control engineering included the acknowledgments that first, long time lags followed by high gain from input to output (great, abrupt effects after the delay) engendered

16. In addition to using electronic simulators, Phillips constructed a hydraulic model of the UK economy that is discussed in detail in Morgan and Boumans 2004 and Morgan 2012.

instability, and second, derivative controls (feedback based not just on the error but also the rate of change of the error) enhanced stability.

For many economists, the most thorough introduction to the tools of control engineering came from R. G. D. Allen (1955, 1956). Allen used mathematics to examine cyclical fluctuations and the potential of government policy in damping fluctuations. He constructed schematic closed-loop diagrams of the economics models of Phillips, Goodwin, Hicks, and Kalecki, and explained the use of Laplace transforms and transfer functions. He argued that "until the engineer's experience is appreciated and assimilated, there is little hope that the economist can develop macro-dynamic models to the point where there is a chance of practical application" (Allen 1955: 168).

The engineer Charles Holt was instrumental in cultivating the blending of control engineering and economics at the Graduate School of Industrial Administration at the Carnegie Institute of Technology (GSIA at CIT; see Klein 2015, 2016; and Simon 1952). Holt and Herb Simon (1954: 75) took an early interest in the application of servomechanisms to decision-making under uncertainty without the need resorting to forecasting.

> It happens that there is a class of mechanical and electrical automatic control mechanisms usually referred to as servo mechanisms that can be said to "make decisions" by reacting rather than by forecasting and planning, and there is a body of theory available for predicting their behavior. In studying the inventory and production problem it may prove useful to examine the servomechanism analogy for the points of view that may be suggested and the analytical tools that may be borrowed.

Holt introduced the Carnegie group to the exponential smoothing model from the analog computers in the gunsights of World War II B-17 bombers and generalized the exponentially weighted moving averages forecasting model to incorporate seasonal fluctuations (see Holt 1957; and Holt et al. 1960). In a similar vein, Phillips introduced Milton Friedman to the exponential smoothing model. Friedman handed it to Philip Cagan, who developed the model of adaptive expectations that would dominate macroeconomic theory from 1956 until the late 1960s (Cagan 1956; Friedman 1957; and see Klein 2016).

At CIT, John Muth, whose undergraduate degree was in industrial engineering, used Wiener's wartime statistical approach research to reveal what structural model of random processes ended in the solution taking the form of the exponentially weighted moving averages being the conditional expected value. Muth (1960) demonstrated that the model that yielded the EWMA as an optimal solution was composed of two random processes: a random walk whose influence persisted through all subsequent time periods plus white noise whose influence did not persist past a single time period.[17]

Both advocates and critics of government intervention rested their case on the engineer's experience. On the one hand, some economists, like Goodwin, saw new institutions such as the US Council of Economic Advisers as the additional feedback loop necessary to foster stability through frequent but relatively slight countercyclical adjustments. On the other hand, F. A. Hayek used the principles of cybernetics and negative feedback to highlight complex self-regulating behavior (see Caldwell 2004 and Oliva 2016).

Within the vigorous debates on the time lags and feedback loops of stabilization policies, economists acknowledged that their attitude to control had changed. In reviewing Stanley Beer's book *Cybernetics and Management*, Maurice Kendall (1959: 392, 391) stated that although economists "have been talking cybernetics for centuries without realising it," they were only now seeing control in a new light—"not control in the repressive sense which we have all come to hate, but control in the sense of the co-ordination and harmonious working of interacting components." Similarly, in his *American Economic Review* essay on mechanisms and models in economic thought, Gregor Sebba (1953: 268) asserted that men in general and economists in particular were redefining control:

> They have to. They use control every day and are proud of it. When they look at their economic environment, they find the scene dominated by vast economic and political combines smoothly operating by a thoroughly rational system of internal controls. This is why programming theory is more realistic than the traditional theory of the firm and why the theory of games, if it can explain the behavior of "coalitions," will be more realistic than the traditional theory of market behavior. Control can no longer be identified with interference and with disturbing the natural harmony of the economy. The new models reflect the economy of our day as surely as Adam Smith's model reflected that of his time.

Economists in centrally planned economies took up the analytic tools of control engineering as readily as their counterparts in capitalist econo-

---

17. Subsequent researchers such as Andrew Harvey applied the Kalman filter from the second "shotgun wedding" in control engineering to Muth's model. This was the starting point for developing structural time-series analysis. Muth (1961) also articulated the modeling strategy of "rational expectations" (see Klein 2015).

mies (see, e.g., the entry "Cybernetics, Economic" in volume 12 of the 1973 English translation of *The Great Soviet Encyclopedia*). As the ideas of Smith and Keynes were put into closed-loop schemas, so too were those of Marx and Lenin. As Western historians of technology looked to Watt's 1784 steam engine governor as a stunning early example of a self-regulating mechanism, so did Soviet historians look to Ivan Polzunov's 1765 invention of a "shaker" to regulate his steam boiler. Beer's (1959) treatise on feedback and self-regulation within the firm, which urged capitalist industrial managers to espouse cybernetics to avoid a socialist revolution, was translated into Russian and highly regarded in the centrally planned economies.[18] Economists at the Institute of Cybernetics of the Academy of Sciences of the Ukrainian SSR considered the economy an information system and investigated automatic control of industrial processes, economic sectors, and the national economy. The Polish economist Oskar Lange ([1965] 1970) argued that the theory of automatic control was an "indispensable tool" for management of the socialist economy. Indeed, Lange asserted that cybernetics had little potential for managing economic processes in capitalism because "in capitalism the organization of economics processes is elemental and cannot be based on rational principles" (173). In their cold war ideological battles, economists aligned with capitalism and economist aligned with socialism turned to the lessons of control engineering.[19] This competition in divergence culminated in an intellectual convergence.

18. In the preface to *Cybernetics and Management*, Beer (1959: xv) explained the context for the urgency of the capitalist economies adopting the theories of automatic control: "The highly industrialised societies of the West are due to meet intense pressure, economic and ethnic, from the East. It is difficult to speak of these matters in a sophisticated society without sounding absurdly sententious, but somehow we have to survive in a world where the opposition is prepared to throw human comfort, security and dignity into the balance—which we are not. . . . The tremendous rate of advance in Russia, for instance, has not been the product of iron resolve and self-abnegation alone. Sputniks are not sent into orbit by fasting and prayer. In Britain there is little to claim in such fields as space research, because there is never enough money for the programmes required. In the field of industrial production, new methods and inspired management are sometimes said to have transformed British industry. The fact remains that the index of industrial production has not moved up for four years. We desperately need some radical new advance, something qualitatively different from all our other efforts, something which exploits the maturity and experience of our culture. A candidate is the science of control. Cybernetic research could be driven ahead for little enough expenditure compared with rocketry, for example. And if we do not do it, someone else will."

19. Ivan Boldyrev, in this volume, asserts that after World War II, the Soviet Union was a "country of engineers." Boldyrev examines how a group of control engineers led by Mark Aizerman at the Institute of Control Sciences in Moscow turned from the cybernetics of mechanical systems to an abstract theory of choice and rationality.

The meeting of enemies in the discipline of control is perhaps best exemplified in the simultaneous emergence, during the height of the Cold War, of a common new front. Bellman (1956) and Kalman (1960) in the United States, and Pontryagin (see Boltyanskii, Gamkrelidze, and Pontryagin [1956] 1964) in Russia, applied the calculus of variations to what was celebrated as a "modern theory of optimal control" (see, e.g., Samuelson 1970). As Bellman and Robert Kalaba (1964: 2) described it from their RAND offices in Santa Monica, the "Russian School" and the "American School" both officiated at the "shotgun wedding of the classical optimization theory and the classical theory of stochastic processes." This renewed focus on a minimization principle through an accessible, computable algorithmic approach addressed Wiener's search for a scientific foundation. Optimization also greatly increased the compatibility of control engineering with economic theory. By the time of that second shotgun marriage, the economist had joined the wedding party in the celebration of the military art of control engineering and readily took up the fruits of Bellman's and Kalman's work on optimal trajectories for their modeling of recursive macroeconomic dynamics.

## References

Allen, R. G. D. 1955. "The Engineer's Approach to Economic Models." *Economica* 22, no. 86: 158–68.

Allen, R. G. D. 1956. *Mathematical Economics*. London: Macmillan.

*Automatic and Manual Control: Papers Contributed to the Conference at Cranfield, 1951*. 1952. New York: Academic Press.

Baxter, James Phinney. 1946. *Scientists against Time*. Boston: Little, Brown.

Beer, Stafford. 1959. *Cybernetics and Management*. London: English University Press.

Bell Telephone Laboratories, Technical Staff. 1978. *A History of Engineering and Science in the Bell System: National Service in War and Peace 1925–1975*, edited by M. D. Fagen. Muray Hill, NJ: Bell Telephone Laboratories.

Bellman, Richard. 1956. *Dynamic Programming and Its Application to Variational Problems in Mathematical Economics*. Santa Monica, CA: RAND Corporation.

Bellman, Richard, and Robert Kalaba, eds. 1964. *Selected Papers on Mathematical Trends in Control Theory*. New York: Dover.

Bissell, Christopher. 1992. "Pioneers of Control: An Interview with Arnold Tustin." *IEE Review* 38, no. 6: 223–26.

Blackman, Ralph Beebe, Hendrik Wade Bode, and Claude E. Shannon. 1946. "Data Smoothing and Prediction in Fire-Control Systems." In *Gunfire Control*, vol. 1 of *Summary Technical Report of Division 7, NDRC*, 71–159. Washington, DC: Office of Scientific Research and Development, National Defense Research Committee.

Bode, Hendrik W. 1960. "Feedback—the History of an Idea." In *Proceedings of the Symposium on Active Networks and Feedback Systems*, edited by Jerome Fox, 1–17. New York: Interscience Publishers.

Boltyanskii, V., R. Gamkrelidz, and L. Pontryagin. (1956) 1964. "On the Theory of Optimal Processes." In *Selected Papers on Mathematical Trends in Control Theory*, edited by Richard Bellman and Robert Kalaba, 170–76. New York: Dover.

Boulding, Kenneth. 1952. "Implications for General Economics of More Realistic Theories of the Firm." *American Economic Review* 42, no. 2: 35–44.

Brown, Gordon S., and Donald P. Campbell. 1950. "Instrument Engineering: Its Growth and Promise in Process Control." *Mechanical Engineering* 72: 124–27.

Brown, Gordon S., and Donald P. Campbell. 1952. "Control Systems." *Scientific American* 187, no. 3: 57–67.

Cagan, Philip. 1956. "The Monetary Dynamics of Hyperinflation." In *Studies in the Quantity Theory of Money*, edited by Milton Friedman, 31–54. Chicago: University of Chicago Press.

Caldwell, Bruce. 2004. *Hayek's Challenge: An Intellectual Biography of F. A. Hayek*. Chicago: University of Chicago Press.

Clark, John, Arthur Smithies, Nicholas Kaldor, Pierre Urie, and E. Ronald Walker. 1949. *National and International Measures for Full Employment: A Report by a Group of Experts Appointed by the Secretary General*. New York: United Nations.

Edwards, Paul N. 1996. *The Closed World*. Cambridge, MA: MIT Press.

Fels, Eberhard M. 1957. Review of *Volkswirtschaftliche Regelungsvorgange im Vergleich zu Regelungsvorgangen der Technik*. *American Economic Review* 47, no. 6: 1014–15.

Flood, M. M. 1951. Review of *Cybernetics* by Norbert Wiener. *Econometrica* 19, no. 4: 477–78.

Föhl, C. 1957. "Volkswirtschaftliche Regelkreise höherer Ordnung in Modelldarstellung." In *Volkswirtschaftliche Regelungsvorgänge im Vergleich zu Regelungsvorgängen der Technik*, edited by H. Geyer and O. Winfried, 25–120. Munich: R. Oldenbourg.

Friedman, Milton. 1957. *A Theory of the Consumption Function*. Princeton, NJ: Princeton University Press.

Galison, Peter. 1994. "The Ontology of the Enemy: Norbert Wiener and the Cybernetic Vision." *Critical Inquiry* 21, no. 1: 228–66.

Geyer, Herbert, and Winfried Oppelt, eds. 1957. *Volkswirtschaftliche Regelungsvorgänge im Vergleich zu Regelungsvorgängen der Technik*. Munich: R. Oldenbourg.

Goodwin, Richard M. 1951a. "Iteration, Automatic Computers, and Economic Dynamics." *Econometrica* 19, no. 2: 196–98.

Goodwin, Richard M. 1951b. "Nonlinear Accelerator and the Persistence of Business Cycles." *Econometrica* 19, no. 1: 1–17.

Goodwin, Richard M. 1955. Review of *The Mechanism of Economic Systems—an Approach to the Problem of Economic Stabilization from the Point of View of Control-System Engineering*. *Review of Economics and Statistics* 37, no. 2: 209–10.

*Gunfire Control*. 1946. Vol. 1 of *Summary Technical Report of Division 7, NDRC*. Washington, DC: Office of Scientific Research and Development, National Defense Research Committee.

Hales, Katherine N. 1999. *How We Became Posthuman: Virtual Bodies in Cybernetics and Informatics*. Chicago: University of Chicago Press.

Haraway, Donna. 1981–82. "The High Cost of Information in Post-World War II Evolutionary Biology: Ergonomics, Semiotics, and the Sociobiology of Communication Systems." *Philosophical Forum* 13, nos. 2–3: 244–78.

Haraway, Donna. 1985. "A Manifesto for Cyborgs: Science, Technology, and Socialist Feminism in the 1980s." *Socialist Review* 15, no. 2: 65–107.

Heims, Steven J. 1991. *The Cybernetics Group*. Cambridge, MA: MIT Press.

Holt, Charles C. 1957. "Forecasting Seasonals and Trends by Exponentially Weighted Moving Averages." Office of Naval Research memorandum, ONR 52. Pittsburgh: Carnegie Institute of Technology.

Holt, Charles C. 1962. "Linear Decision Rules for Economic Stabilization and Growth." *Quarterly Journal of Economics* 76, no. 1: 20–45.

Holt, Charles C., Franco Modigliani, John F. Muth, and Herbert A. Simon. 1960. *Planning Production, Inventories, and Work Force*. Englewood Cliffs, NJ: Prentice-Hall.

Holt, Charles C., and Herbert A. Simon. 1954. "Optimal Decision Rules for Production and Inventory Control." Paper presented at Operations Research in Production and Inventory Control, Case Institute of Technology, Cleveland, OH, January.

Hughes, Agatha C., and Thomas P. Hughes, eds. 2000. *Systems, Experts, and Computers: The Systems Approach in Management and Engineering, World War II and After*. Cambridge MA: MIT Press.

Johnson, Harry G. 1949. Book review of *Cybernetics: Control and Communication in the Animal and the Machine* by Norbert Wiener. *Economic Journal* 59, no. 236: 573–75.

Johnson, Harry G. 1968. "Problems of Efficiency in Monetary Management." *Journal of Political Economy* 76, no. 5: 971–90.

Kalman, Rudolf E. 1960. "On the General Theory of Control Systems." In *Automatic and Remote Control: Proceedings of the First International Congress of the International Federation of Automatic Control*. Moscow: International Federation of Automatic Control.

Kalman, Rudolf E. 1978. "A Retrospective after Twenty Years from the Pure to the Applied." In *The Application of Kalman Filter to Hydraulics and Water Resources: Proceedings of AGU Chapman Conference at University of Pittsburgh*, 31–54. Pittsburgh, PA: American Geophysical Union.

Kendall, M. G. 1960. Review of *Cybernetics and Management*, by S. Beer. *Economic Journal* 70, no. 278: 391–92.

Klein, Judy. 1997. *Statistical Visions in Time: A History of Time Series Analysis*. Cambridge: Cambridge University Press.

Klein, Judy. 2002. "Optimization and Recursive Residuals in the Space Age: Sputnik and the Kalman Filter." Paper presented at the Allied Social Science Association annual meeting, Atlanta, GA, January 5, 2002.

Klein, Judy. 2007. "Cold War Dynamic Programming and the Science of Economizing: Bellman Strikes Gold in Policy Space." Paper presented at the History of Science Society annual meeting, Crystal City, VA, November 3, 2007.

Klein, Judy. 2015. "The Cold War Hot House for Modeling Strategies at the Carnegie Institute of Technology." Institute for New Economic Thinking Working Paper Series No. 19. papers.ssrn.com/sol3/papers.cfm?abstract_id=2667883.

Klein, Judy. 2016. "Material Origins of Adaptive Expectations and Exponentially Weighted Moving Averages." Paper presented at History of Economics Society annual meeting, Duke University, Durham, NC, June 18, 2016.

Klein, Judy. n.d. "Protocols of War and the Algorithmic Invasion of Policy Space, 1940–1960."

Lange, Oskar. (1965) 1970. *Introduction to Economic Cybernetics*. Translated by J. Stadler. Oxford: Pergamon.

Leonard, Carroll Mendenhall, and Vladimir Leonidas Maleev. 1949. *Heat Power Fundamentals*. New York: Pitman.

Leontief, Wassily. 1952. "Machines and Man." *Scientific American* 187, no. 3: 150–60.

Lockspeiser, Sir Ben. 1952. "Presidential Address." In *Automatic and Manual Control: Papers Contributed to the Conference at Cranfield, 1951*, edited by Arnold Tustin, 1–3. New York: Academic Press.

MacKenzie, Donald. 1990. *Inventing Accuracy: A Historical Sociology of Nuclear Missile Guidance*. Cambridge, MA: MIT Press.

McCulloch, Warren S. (1953) 1955. "Summary of the Points of Agreement Reached in the Previous Nine Conferences on Cybernetics." In *Cybernetics: Circular and Feedback Mechanisms in Biological and Social Systems; Transactions of the Tenth Conference, April 22, 23, and 24, 1953*, edited by Heinz Von Foerster, Margaret Mead, and Hans Lukas Teuber, 69–80. New York: Josiah Macy Jr. Foundation.

Mirowski, Philip. 2002. *Machine Dreams: Economics Becomes a Cyborg Science*. Cambridge: Cambridge University Press.

Morgan, Mary. 2012. *The World in the Model: How Economists Work and Think*. Cambridge: Cambridge University Press.

Morgan, Mary, and Marcel Boumans. 2004. "The Secrets Hidden by Two-Dimensionality: Modelling the Economy as a Hydraulic System." In *Models: The Third Dimension of Science*, edited by Soraya de Chadarevian and Nick Hopwood, 369–401. Stanford, CA: Stanford University Press.

Muth, John F. 1960. "Optimal Properties of Exponentially Weighted Forecasts." *Journal of the American Statistical Association* 55, no. 290: 299–306.

Muth, John F. 1961. "Rational Expectations and the Theory of Price Movements." *Econometrica* 29, no. 3: 315–35.

Nyquist, H. 1932. Regeneration Theory. *Bell System Technical Journal* 11, no. 1: 126–47.

Oliva, Gabriel. 2016. "The Road to Servomechanisms: The Influence of Cybernetics on Hayek from the Sensory Order to the Social Order." *Research in the History of Economic Thought and Methodology*, no. 34A: 161–98.

Phillips, A. W. 1954. "Stabilisation Policy in a Closed Economy." *Economic Journal* 64, no. 254: 290–323.

Phillips, A. W. 1957. "Stabilisation Policy and the Time-Forms of the Lagged Responses." *Economic Journal* 67, no. 266: 265–77.

Pickering, Andrew. 1995. "Cyborg History and the World War II Regime." *Perspectives in Science* 3, no. 1: 1–48.

Samuelson, Paul. 1970. "What Makes for a Beautiful Problem in Science?" *Journal of Political Economy* 78, no. 6: 1372–77.

Sebba, Gregor. 1953. "The Development of the Concepts of Mechanism and Model in Physical Science and Economic Thought." *American Economic Review* 43, no. 2: 259–68.

Sent, Esther-Mirjam. 1997. "Engineering Dynamic Economics." In *New Economics and Its History*, edited by John B. Davis. *History of Political Economy* 29 (supplement): 41–62.

Simon, Herbert A. 1952. "On the Application of Servomechanism Theory in the Study of Production Control." *Econometrica* 20, no. 2: 247–68.

Smith, Otto J. M., and H. F. Erdley. 1952. "An Electronic Analogue for an Economic System." *Electrical Engineering* 71, no. 4: 362–66.

Strotz, R. H., J. F. Calvert, and N. F. Morehouse. 1951. "Analogue Computing Techniques Applied to Economics." *Transactions of the American Institute of Electrical Engineers* 70, no. 1: 557–63.

Strotz, R. H., J. C. McAnulty, and J. B. Naines Jr. 1953. "Goodwin's Nonlinear Theory of the Business Cycle: An Electro-Analog Solution." *Econometrica* 21, no. 3: 390–411.

Thaler, George J., and Robert G. Brown. 1953. *Servomechanism Analysis*. New York: Macmillan.

Tustin, Arnold. 1951–52. "An Engineer's View of the Problem of Economic Stability and Economic Regulation." *Review of Economic Studies* 2, no. 49: 85–89.

Tustin, Arnold. 1952. "Feedback." *Scientific American* 187, no. 3: 48–56.

Tustin, Arnold. 1953. *The Mechanism of Economic Systems: An Approach to the Problem of Economic Stabilisation from the Point of View of Control-System Engineering*. Cambridge, MA: Harvard University Press.

Wiener, Norbert. 1948. *Cybernetics or Control and Communication in the Animal and the Machine*. Cambridge, MA: MIT Press.

Wise, M. Norton, and Crosbie Smith. 1989. "Work and Waste: Political Economy and Natural Philosophy in Nineteenth Century Britain." *History of Science* 27, no. 3: 263–301.

Wulwick, Nancy J. 1995. "The Hamiltonian Formalism and Optimal Control." In *Measurement, Quantification, and Economic Analysis*, edited by Ingrid H. Rima, 406–35. New York: Routledge.

# The Engineering Tools That Shaped the Rational Expectations Revolution

Marcel Boumans

In 2011, a panel discussion was held marking the fiftieth anniversary of John Muth's "Rational Expectations and the Theory of Price Movements" (1961), with Michael Lovell, Robert Lucas, Dale Mortensen, Robert Shiller, and Neil Wallace in the panel and Kevin D. Hoover and Warren Young (2013) as moderators. To open the discussion, Hoover remarked: "Fifteen years later, it was commonplace to speak of a rational expectations revolution. And within another fifteen years, rational expectations had been fully integrated into macroeconomics" (Hoover and Young 2013: 1169–70). In his response, Lucas made clear that he did not like the term *revolution*, because of its political connotation (see also Klamer 1984: 55–56), but when used in a Kuhnian sense, to mark a scientific change, however, he considered this term appropriate to denote what has happened since the 1970s: a change in scientific worldview, research strategies, vocabulary, and questions.

At least on two occasions, Lucas explained what he saw as the nature of this revolution; it should be seen not as a change of theory but as a technical development.

I would like to thank the editors, Pedro Garcia Duarte and Yann Giraud, for encouraging me to revisit my earlier work on engineering and for nudging me to make it fit into this volume. I would also like to thank the other participants of the conference and the two anonymous referees for their thoughtful comments. Special thanks go to Mary S. Morgan, who helped me enormously with the struggle I had to convey this article's main claim.

*History of Political Economy* 52 (annual suppl.) DOI 10.1215/00182702-8717960
Copyright 2020 by Duke University Press

One would expect developments to arise from two quite different kinds of forces outside the subdisciplines of monetary economics or business cycle theory. Of these forces the most important, I believe, in this area and in economic generally, consists of purely technical developments that enlarge our abilities to construct analogue economies. Here I would include both improvements in mathematical methods and improvements in computational capacity. (Lucas 1980: 697)

We got that view from Smith and Ricardo, and there have never been any new paradigms or paradigm changes or shifts. Maybe there will be, but in two hundred years it hasn't happened yet. So you've got this kind of basic line of economic theory. And then I see the progressive—I don't want to say that everything is in Smith and Ricardo—the progressive element in economics as entirely technical: better mathematics, better mathematical formulation, better data, better data-processing methods, better statistical methods, better computational methods. (Lucas 2004: 22)

Considering the development of economics mainly driven by technical innovations, the rational expectations revolution should, however, be distinguished from an earlier technical development, called the "Keynesian," which was "the evolution of macroeconomics into a quantitative, scientific discipline, the development of explicit statistical descriptions of economic behavior, the increasing reliance of government officials on technical economic expertise, and the introduction of the use of mathematical control theory to manage an economy" (Lucas and Sargent 1979: 50).

In two mainly reflective papers (1977, 1980), Lucas discussed the outlines of the new methodology that he supposed to be needed for the kind of macroeconomics he was promoting. The first thing that stands out when reading both articles is the terminology Lucas used. Agents are "processing noisy signals" by "smoothing" them for which they use "information systems." Elsewhere (Boumans 1997, 2005), I have shown that Lucas introduced in these two articles Turing's approach by looking upon models as imitation games, and hence they should be validated by a Turing test.

When a description of the information system is seen as an essential element of a macroeconomic model, the modeler should provide an explicit account of the nature of expectations-formation. It is only in this context that Lucas (1977: 15) suggested that expectation is "rational" in the sense of Muth:

To practice economics, we need *some* way (short of psychoanalysis, one hopes) of understanding *which* decision problem agents are solving. John Muth (1961) proposed to resolve this problem by identifying agents subjective probabilities with observed frequencies of the events to be forecast, or with "true" probabilities, calling the assumed coincidence of subjective and "true" probabilities *rational expectations.*

While one can question one part of Lucas's historical claim that scientific development in macroeconomics is only technical—which will not be discussed here—the article instead shows and thereby confirms Lucas's claim that what he called the Keynesian revolution was based on a different technical development than the rational expectations revolution. This article shows that the rational expectations revolution is based on the introduction of a different type of engineering mathematics. Control engineering was replaced by information engineering, that is to say, the framework of feedback loops was replaced by a framework of information processing. The rational expectations revolution was not only based on the introduction of Muth's idea of rational expectations to macroeconomics; the introduction of Muth's hypothesis cannot explain the more drastic change in macroeconomics, namely, the change of the mathematical toolbox and concepts in macroeconomics since the 1980s.

The claim that the major shift from "Keynesian economics" to "new classical economics" is based on a shift from a control engineering approach to a different kind of engineering methodology is not new. Esther-Mirjam Sent (1997: 57) makes a similar claim: "New classical economists criticized the use of control engineering in economics and adopted other engineering techniques instead . . . tools of optimal prediction and filtering." I, however, disagree with her view that "new classical economists realized that the use of control techniques was not only possible but essential under rational expectations" (58). Although some of the control techniques may still be used by the new classical economists, they were not "essential" anymore to their new approach. In my view, the "revolution" was even more radical. The change of tools has changed macroeconomics more deeply, not only its methodology but also its epistemology and ontology.

To show this 1970s shift in epistemology and ontology, the history of economics needs first to be interwoven with the history of engineering mathematics, which cannot be untangled from the emergence of the digital computer and the influence of this emergence on the changed nature of mathematics: "The single most impressive thing that has happened is the arrival on the industrial, and the mathematical, scene of the large high speed digital computer" (McMillan 1962: 86). In his presidential address to the Society for Industrial and Applied Mathematics in 1961, Brockway McMillan presented an overview of what he considered the major trends since 1940.[1] It is in particular the rise of new domains such as statistical theory of communication, the theory of feedback and control, the theory of games, and linear programming that were relevant for the change of the nature of mathematics. Connected to this change, McMillan observed a new "attitude" to mathematical problems:

> Mathematicians, both the applied and some of the pure ones, have caught up with the logicians and have adopted a new concept of solution, a concept of what it means to solve a problem. A solution is no longer a number, a formula, or a function describing dependence upon a parameter. A solution may simply be an algorithm which is known to terminate in a reasonable number of steps and is available on cards or tape for one's own brand of computer. (McMillan 1962: 89)

The result of this new concept of solution is a new approach, which McMillan called the "operational method in human affairs": "the approach to a process in terms of its observables, its inputs, outputs, criteria, choices, without anthropocentric references to intentions, purposes, authority, or even 'meaning.' This is the way we have been forced to approach the mechanization of routine human data handling activities" (90). This method had a stronger influence on a new field called information engineering than control engineering. Control engineering maintained the anthropocentric references, by focusing on the human-machine relationship, and references to intentions and purposes.

The term *information engineering* will be used in this article to distinguish a specific domain within mathematical engineering from control engineering. Because both engineering branches are not uniquely specified, my distinction is based on the differences between control theory and information theory. Control theory is the theory of feedback systems. According to Andrei (2005: 3), there are three fundamental concepts in control theory: feedback, need for fluctuations, and optimization. A textbook on information theory (Yeung 2008: 3) describes information theory as "the science of information" that "studies the fundamental limits in

---

1. This paper was brought to my attention when reading Klein 2001.

communication regardless of the technologies involved in the actual implementation of the communication systems" and finds its origins in Claude E. Shannon's "Mathematical Theory of Communication" (1948). To clarify the core concepts, tools, and strategies of information engineering, they are discussed as they were first introduced into mathematical engineering and computer science. The next section shows how these tools have shaped Lucas's papers of the early 1970s. This article focuses on five papers by Lucas (1971, with Prescott; 1972a, 1972b, 1973, 1975). This suffices for the main claim of this article that the rational expectations revolution was based on a change of engineering tools. It does not mean to suggest that others did not co-create the rational expectations revolution and thus contributed to the development of the new tools, but it was Lucas alone who received the Nobel Prize in 1995, "for having developed and applied the hypothesis of rational expectations, and thereby having transformed macroeconomic analysis and deepened our understanding of economic policy" (Nobel Media AB 2019).

## 1. The Rise of the Operational Method in Human Affairs

> Our task as I see it . . . is to write a FORTRAN program that will accept specific economic policy rules as "input" and will generate as "output" statistics describing the operating characteristics of time series we care about.
> —Robert E. Lucas, "Methods and Problems in Business Cycle Theory" (1980)

To understand which tools Lucas used to shape a new ontology for macroeconomics, particularly in relation to the emergence of the computer, one can choose between two starting points: John von Neumann and Alan Turing. It has already been shown that for game theory and linear programming, von Neumann is the most appropriate starting point, but for statistical theories of communication and information, it is better to start with Turing.

In his 1936 paper, "On Computable Numbers, with an Application to the Entscheidungsproblem," Turing introduced the idea of an idealized human computer. According to Robert Soare (1996: 291), this paper is "monumental" because

(1) Turing analyzed an idealized *human* computing agent (a "*computer*") . . . ; (2) Turing specified a remarkably simple formal device

(*Turing machine*) and proved the equivalence of (1) and (2); (3) Turing proved the unsolvability of Hilbert's *Entscheidungsproblem* . . . ; (4) Turing proposed a *universal* Turing machine, one which carried within it the capacity to duplicate any other.

This idealized human computing agent, a "computing machine," which is only capable of a finite number of conditions, called "*m*-configurations," is supplied with a "tape," "the analogue of paper" (Turing 1936: 231), moving back and forth past the machine. The tape is divided into "squares," each capable of bearing a "symbol." At any moment there is just one square, which is "in the machine," which is called the "scanned square." "The 'scanned symbol' is the only one of which the machine is, so to speak, 'directly aware'" (231). The possible behavior of the machine at any moment is determined by the *m*-configuration and the scanned symbol. The machine is able to erase the symbol on the scanned square, to print a symbol on the scanned square, and to move the tape to the left or right, one square at a time. In addition to these operations, the *m*-configuration may be changed. This device of *m*-configurations functions as a simple memory. As Turing writes, "By altering its *m*-configuration the machine can effectively remember some of the symbols which it has 'seen' (scanned) previously" (231).

Turing (1936: 249) emphasized that the behavior of the machine is similar to the computations of a human being. "Computing is normally done by writing certain symbols on paper. We may suppose this paper is divided into squares like a child's arithmetic book." The behavior of a *human* computer, then, "at any moment is determined by the symbols which he is observing, and his 'state of mind' at that moment" (250).[2] Each "state of mind" corresponds to an *m*-configuration. Turing aimed not to define "computing" as a psychological process but to externalize it as operations on paper. He therefore wished to define the "state of mind" by a "more physical and definite counterpart": "It is always possible for the computer to break off from his work, to go away and forget all about it, and later to come back and go on with it. If he does this he must leave a note of instructions (written in some standard form) explaining how the work is to be continued" (Turing 1936: 253). This "note of instructions" is therefore the counterpart of the "state of mind."

2. In the 1930s the term *computer* always referred to a human making computations. In the late 1940s it became common to use this term as a reference to a machine, though Turing still used the term *computer* to refer to a human with paper (Soare 1996: 291).

In Turing's 1936 paper, machine operations were taken as being similar to a specific domain of human thinking, namely, computations. With the building of real machine computers, the comparisons became more ambitious and were extended to "thinking" more generally. In the same year as Turing published "Computing Machinery and Intelligence," in which he introduced what later came to be known as the Turing test, Shannon published two papers on a chess-playing machine. In the one written for a more general audience, Shannon ([1950] 1988: 2099) explicitly discusses the question "Could a machine be designed that would be capable of 'thinking'?" Chess-playing machines were considered "an ideal one to start with," because "chess is generally considered to require 'thinking' for skillful play; a solution of this problem will force us either to admit the possibility of a mechanized thinking or to further restrict our concept of 'thinking'" (Shannon 1950: 257).

A comparison of their discussions of the question whether machines can think shows how similar the views of Shannon and Turing were:

> From a behavioristic point of view, the machine acts as though it were thinking. It has always been considered that skillful chess play requires the reasoning faculty. If we regard thinking as a property of external actions rather than internal method the machine is surely thinking. The thinking process is considered by some psychologists to be essentially characterized by the following steps: various possible solutions of a problem are tried out mentally or symbolically without actually being carried out physically; the best solution is selected by a mental evaluation of the results of these trails; and the solution found in this way is then acted upon. It will be seen that this is almost an exact description of how a chess-playing computer operates, provide we substitute "within a machine" for "mentally." (Shannon [1950] 1988: 2107)

Shannon is, however, better known for "A Mathematical Theory of Communication" (1948), which aims to extend the theory of communication by including "the effect of noise in the channel" (1). The "fundamental" problem of communication, according to Shannon, is that of "reproducing at one point either exactly or approximately a message selected at another point," but the "semantic aspects of communication are irrelevant to the engineering problem" (1).

Shannon (1948) discusses three categories of communication systems: discrete, continuous, and mixed. A discrete system is one in which both the message and the signal are a sequence of discrete symbols. As an example of such a system, Shannon mentions telegraphy, where the message is a sequence of letters and the signal a sequence of dots, dashes, and spaces. A continuous system is one in which the message and signal are both treated as continuous functions, for example, radio or television. A mixed system is one in which both discrete and continuous variables appear. The largest part of this 1948 paper discusses the discrete case, which has "applications not only in communication theory, but also in the theory of computing machines" (3).

The discrete information source is considered a stochastic process, a sequence of symbols governed by a set of probabilities. In particular it is a Markov process, which can be described as follows: there exist a finite number of possible "states" of a system $S_1, S_2, \ldots S_n$, and there is a set of transition probabilities; $p_i(j)$ the probability that if the system is in state $S_i$ it will next go to state $S_j$. Among the possible discrete Markov processes there is a group with special properties of significance in communication theory, namely, the "ergodic" processes. Ergodic processes have transition probabilities with the same constant values.

In his discussion of continuous systems, Shannon refers to Norbert Wiener as an important source for his own work:

> Communication theory is heavily indebted to Wiener for much of its basic philosophy and theory. His classic NDRC report, "The Interpolation, Extrapolation and Smoothing of Stationary Time Series," to appear soon in book form [Wiley 1949], contains the first clear-cut formulation of communication theory as a statistical problem, the study of operations on time series. This work, although chiefly concerned with the linear prediction and filtering problem, is an important collateral reference in connection with the present paper. (Shannon 1948: 326–27)[3]

Published in book form as *Extrapolation, Interpolation, and Smoothing of Stationary Time Series*, Wiener's report is restricted to continuous systems, and therefore Shannon discusses filters only in terms of these systems.

The purpose of Wiener's NDRC report is to "unite" time series in statistics and communication theory. Communication theory, according to Wiener, is the "study of messages and their transmission," and because a "message to be transmitted is developed into time series" (2), fusing statis-

---

3. In addition to this, Shannon (1948: 52) mentions in the acknowledgments that "credit should also be given to Professor N. Wiener, whose elegant solution of the problems of filtering and prediction of stationary ensembles has considerably influenced the writer's thinking in this field."

tical techniques with communication engineering, such as Fourier analysis, into a "common technique" is "more effective than either existing technique alone" (9).

Wiener mentions three "things which we can do with time series or messages" (9): prediction, filtering, and answering questions of policy. Prediction is the estimation of the continuation of a series that is most probable, and filtering or "purification" (9) is the estimation of what the data would have been without being corrupted or altered by mixture with other time series. While prediction and filtering operate on data without direct information as to how these data might have been altered, questions of policy require an "intrinsic" study of time series: "to ascertain how certain series dealing with the economics of a country might have changed if a different system of taxation had been adopted" (11).

To commemorate the twenty-fifth anniversary of the publication of Wiener's 1949 monograph, the *IEE Transactions on Information Theory* published a survey of "three decades of linear filtering" (Kailath 1974). According to Thomas Kailath, Wiener's work was "the direct cause for the great activity of the last three decades in signal estimation, but it was perhaps the greatest factor in bringing the statistical point of view clearly into communication theory and also control theory" (146).

The key problem of linear filtering is the determination of the linear least squares (i.e., optimal) estimate of a signal process corrupted by additive white noise. For information theorists and communication engineers at that time, the conventional specification of the filtering problem was in terms of signal and noise covariance functions, and the Wiener filter, designed to tackle this kind of problem, was an obvious method to use. Rudolf Emil Kálmán replaced this approach by one in which state-space models—borrowed from Richard Bellman—instead of covariance functions were specified for the signal and noise, and "it seemed to many that this difference in specification was the chief reason for the success of the Kalman filter" (153): "The fact that the Kalman filter dealt with state-estimation made it comparatively easy to include it in books and courses in state-variable theory, without having to go very deeply into estimation theory or even into Wiener filtering" (152).

The Kalman filter is not given by an explicit formula for the impulse response of the optimal filter—as in the case of Wiener filters—but as an algorithm suitable for direct evaluation by computers. As Kálmán (1960: 35) noted, the Wiener filtering methods were subject to "a number of limitations which seriously curtail their practical usefulness":

(1) The optimal filter is specified by its impulse response. It is not a simple task to synthesize the filter from such data.
(2) Numerical determination of the optimal impulse response is often quite involved and poorly suited to machine computation. The situation gets rapidly worse with increasing complexity of the problem.
(3) Important generalizations (e.g., growing-memory filters, nonstationary prediction) require new derivations, frequently of considerable difficulty to the nonspecialists.
(4) The mathematics of the derivations are not transparent. Fundamental assumptions and their consequences tend to be obscured.

Kálmán's "new approach" introduced "a new look at this whole assemblage of problems, sidestepping the difficulties just mentioned" (35): the filtering problem is approached from the viewpoint of conditional distributions and expectations, so all statistical calculations and results are based on first and second moments, and no other statistical data are needed.

To clarify later in this article how much Lucas's approach was based on Kálmán's "new approach," I now discuss it in more detail: in this approach, the random signals are represented as the output of a linear dynamic system excited by independent or uncorrelated random signals (white noise). The behavior of this system is described through a quantity known as the system "state," which is specified by what is called the "system equation":

$$x_{t+1} = F_t x_t + \eta_t \tag{1}$$

where $x_t$ is an $(n \times 1)$ vector of state variables, $F_t$ an $(n \times n)$ state transition matrix, and $\eta_t$ an $(n \times 1)$ vector of system noise. Associated with the system equation is what is called the "measurement equation":

$$y_t = H_t x_t + \varepsilon_t \tag{2}$$

where $y_t$ is an $(m \times 1)$ vector of measurements, $H_t$ an $(m \times n)$ measurement matrix, and $\varepsilon_t$ an $(m \times 1)$ vector of measurement noise. To complete the model specification, a description of the noise terms $\eta_t$ and $\varepsilon_t$ is required; their means and variance-covariance matrices are given as $\mathrm{E}[\eta_t] = \mathrm{E}[\varepsilon_t] = 0$, $Q = \mathrm{Var}(\eta_t)$, and $R = \mathrm{Var}(\varepsilon_t)$.

Given the state-space representation of a discrete linear dynamic system and the measurement equation, the problem is to estimate the state $x_t$ from the noisy measurements $y_1, y_2, \ldots, y_t$. The estimation of the state will also be based on the estimate of $x_{t-1}$. Let $\hat{x}_{t|t-1}$ denote such an estimate, where the subscript $t \mid t - 1$ denotes that the estimate at time $t$ used the information available up to time $t-1$. The estimate of $x_t$ using all available information at time $t$ is, then,

$$\hat{x}_{t|t} = L_t\hat{x}_{t|t-1} + K_t y_t \tag{3}$$

where $L_t$ and $K_t$ are time-varying weighting matrices to be specified by imposing on the filter the conditions that the estimate should be unbiased and of minimal variance.

The unbiasedness is ensured by having

$$L_t = I - K_t H_t \tag{4}$$

which, when substituted in (3) gives

$$\hat{x}_{t|t} = \hat{x}_{t|t-1} + K_t[y_t - H_t\hat{x}_{t|t-1}] \tag{5}$$

To meet the requirement of minimal variance $K_t$, called the Kalman gain, should be of the following shape:

$$K_t = P_{t|t-1}H_t^T[H_t P_{t|t-1} H_t^T + R]^{-1} \tag{6}$$

where $P_{t|t-1} = Var(\hat{\varepsilon}_{t|t-1})$, that is to say, the variance-covariance matrix of the estimation error $\hat{\varepsilon}_{t|t-1} = \hat{x}_{t|t-1} - x_t$.

As mentioned above, Kálmán's state-space models are based on Bellman's (1954: 1) theory of dynamic programming. Bellman had developed his theory "to treat the mathematical problems arising from the study of various multi-stage decision processes," which he described in the following way:

> We have a physical system whose state at any time $t$ is determined by a set of quantities which we call state parameters, or state variables. At certain times, which may be prescribed in advance, or which may be determined by the process itself, we are called upon to make decisions which will affect the state of the system. These decisions are equivalent to transformations of the state variables, the choice of a decision being identical with the choice of a transformation. The outcome of the preceding decisions is to be used to guide the choice of future ones, with the purpose of the whole process that of maximizing some function of the parameters describing the final state. (1)

According to Bellman, the difficulty and complexity of a multistage decision process require new methods instead of the conventional "enumerative" methods that only work well in a "computational nirvana." In the conventional formulation, the multistage decision process, that is, an

*N*-stage process where *M* decisions are to be made at each stage, is considered an *MN*-dimensional single-stage process. The fundamental problem is, then, "How can we avoid this multiplication of dimension which stifles analysis and greatly impedes computation?" (Bellman 1957: xi). The answer is that it is the structure of the policy, which is essential. By structure Bellman meant the characteristics of the system, which determine the decision to be made at any particular stage of the process: "In place of determining the optimal sequence of decisions from some *fixed* state of the system, we wish to determine the optimal decision to be made at *any* state of the system" (xi). This approach makes the decision problem analytically more tractable and computationally vastly simpler.

Bellman (1957) outlines the "structure of dynamic programming processes" by first enumerating the features of these processes:

    a.   In each case we have a physical system characterized at any stage by a small set of parameters, the *state variables*.

    b.   At each stage of either process we have a choice of a number of decisions.

    c.   The effect of a decision is a transformation of the state variable.

    d.   The past history of the system is of no importance in determining future actions.

    e.   The purpose of the process is to maximize some function of the state variables. (Bellman 1957: 81–82)

In this context, a "policy" is defined as "any rule for making decisions which yields an allowable sequence of decisions; and an optimal policy is a policy which maximizes a preassigned function of the final state variables" (82). An optimal policy is obtained by applying the "principle of optimality":

> An optimal policy has the property that whatever the initial state and initial decision are, the remaining decisions must constitute an optimal policy with regard to the state resulting from the first decision. (83)

The resulting functional equation for optimal policy, then, is

$$f(p) = \max_q f(T_q(p)) \tag{7}$$

where $T_q$ is the transformation as a result of the first decision, obtaining in this way a new state vector $T_q(p)$.

Existence and uniqueness theorems were proved for this kind of functional equations, not by applying fixed-point theorems, but by Bellman's own method of successive approximation. He showed that a particular sequence of successive approximations

$$f_N(p) = \max_q f_{N-1}(T_q(p)) \tag{8}$$

converges to the unique solution.

The tools designed by Turing, Shannon, Wiener, Kálmán, and Bellman created a new world populated by machines that communicate with each other by exchanging information. This information does not, however, contain only signals about the system states but also noise that needs to be filtered out. It is not a deterministic world, but one governed by stochastic processes. The decisions these machines take is conditioned on the (noisy) information they have about the current state of the world but at the same time will affect future states. Policy in this world therefore means tracing an optimal trajectory taking all these issues into account.

## 2. What Lucas Took from the Carnegie Institute of Technology

> This is what I mean by the "mechanics" of economic development—the construction of a mechanical, artificial world, populated by the interacting robots that economics typically studies, that is capable of exhibiting behavior the gross features of which resemble those of the actual world that I have just described.
> —Robert E. Lucas, "On the Mechanics of Economic Development" (1988)

As is well acknowledged by Lucas, he borrowed not only the tools from the field of information engineering but also those that were developed at the Graduate School of Industrial Administration of the Carnegie Institute of Technology, in particular Muth's "rational expectations hypothesis." When Lucas introduced the concept of rational expectations in his early papers, he, however, also indicated that his interpretation of the rational expectations hypothesis differed from Muth's:

- "[Muth] applied it to the case where the expected and actual price (both random variables) have a common *mean value*. Since Muth's discussion of this concept applies equally well to our assumption of a common *distribution* for these random variables, it seems natural to adopt the term here." (Lucas and Prescott 1971: 660n4)
- "The main difference is in what superficially appears to be a fine mathematical point. Muth defines solutions to be elements of the space of sequences of realizations, as opposed to being elements of the space of functions of current state variables. The definition used here is much more restrictive." (Lucas 1972b: 55)

To clarify how much of Lucas's work of the early 1970s was based on the tools of information engineering and how much on Muth's rational expectations hypothesis, the background of the rational hypothesis is briefly discussed. This background was shaped by the research project Planning and Control of Industrial Operations conducted by Charles C. Holt, Franco Modigliani, Muth, and Herbert A. Simon. The project resulted in the volume *Planning Production, Inventories, and Work Force* (1960). Because the historical context of this research is excellently covered by Klein 2015, I focus briefly on only one aspect of this research, namely, adaptive expectations and Muth's own specific response to it.

According to Holt et al. (1960: 258), forecasts (of sales) must meet the following "tests":

> They must be made quickly, cheaply, and easily. The forecasting technique must be clearly spelled out, so that it can be followed routinely, either manually or using an electronic computer. The number of pieces of information required to make a single forecast must be small so that the total amount of informant required for all products will not be expensive to store and to maintain. It should also be possible to introduce current sales information easily.

The authors were quite explicit about the nontheoretical aspect of the forecasting techniques they were interested in: "do not 'explain' sales changes, but simply extrapolate a sales time-series" (258). The only relevant input is the past history of sales; "no direct information concerning the market, the industry, the economy, sales of competing and complementary products, price changes, advertising campaigns, and so on is used" (258).

The technique that is primarily discussed is the "exponentially-weighted moving-average forecast," because it meets the above tests: it "extrapolates sales in the forthcoming period by correcting for observed error in the preceding forecast" (259). This technique can be described as follows:[4] let $y_t$ represent that part of a time series which cannot be explained by trend, seasonal, or any other systematic factors; and let represent the expectation of $y_t$ on the basis of information available through the $(t-1)$st period. Then, the expectations are adapted from one period to the next proportional to the latest observed error:

$$y_t^e = y_{t-1}^e + \beta(y_{t-1} - y_{t-1}^e), \ 0 \leq \beta \leq 1 \qquad (9)$$

---

4. This description is based on Muth 1960.

The solution of this equation gives the formula for the exponentially weighted forecast:

$$y_t^e = \beta \Sigma_{i=1}^{\infty} (1 - \beta)^{i-1} y_{t-i} \qquad (10)$$

Muth 1960 studies the statistical properties of time series for which this forecasting method would work well and concludes that this is for the case where $y_t$ consists of a permanent component, $\bar{y}_t$, and a transitory component, $\eta_t$, so that $y_t = y_t + \eta_t$. The transitory components are assumed to be independently distributed with mean zero and variance $\sigma_\eta^2$, and the permanent components are defined by $\bar{y}_t = \bar{y}_{t-1} + \varepsilon_t = \Sigma_{i=1}^{t} \varepsilon_i$, where the $\varepsilon$'s are serially independent with mean zero and variance $\sigma_\varepsilon^2$. The optimality condition is to minimize the error variance $E(\bar{y}_t - y_t^e)^2$. By applying this condition, Muth (1960) shows that the weight $\beta$ has to be a specific combination of the variances $\sigma_\varepsilon^2$ and $\sigma_\eta^2$.

One year later, *Econometrica* published Muth's (1961) paper on rational expectations. Contrary to the aims of the *Planning* book (Holt et al. 1960)—namely, forecasting and not explaining—the intention of this paper was "to explain fairly simply how expectations are formed" (Muth 1961: 315). To do so, Muth suggested the "hypothesis" that "expectations, since they are informed predictions of future events, are essentially the same as the predictions of the relevant economic theory" (316). This hypothesis was "a little more precisely" rephrased as the following: "That expectations of firms (or, more generally, the subjective probability distribution of outcomes) tend to be distributed, for the same information set, about the prediction of the theory (or the 'objective' probability distributions of outcomes)" (316).[5]

Muth's discussion of an isolated market shows nicely the difference and similarity of optimal adaptive expectations and rational expectations. Suppose the market equations take the form

$$C_t = -\beta p_t \qquad \text{(Demand)}$$
$$P_t = \gamma p_t^e + u_t \qquad \text{(Supply)}$$
$$P_t = C_t \qquad \text{(Market equilibrium)}$$

where $P_t$ represents production, $C_t$ consumption, $p_t$ market price, $p_t^e$ expected market price, and $u_t$ an "error term." If these latter error terms $u$ can be represented by a linear combination of the past history of normally

5. Hence the interpretation of rational expectation in Lucas and Prescott 1971 is in this respect not different from Muth's—contrary to what Lucas and Prescott 1971 claims (see quotation above).

and independently distributed random variables $\varepsilon_t : u_t = \Sigma_{i=1}^{\infty} \varepsilon_{t-i}$, then the price and expected price will be linear functions of the same independent disturbances: $p_t = \Sigma_{j=1}^{\infty} W_i \varepsilon_{t-i}$ and $p_t^e = \Sigma_{i=1}^{\infty} W_i \varepsilon_{t-i}$. Because the aim is to write the expectations in terms of the history of observable variables, the result is that the expected price is a geometrically weighted moving average of past prices:

$$p_t^e = \frac{\beta}{\gamma} \Sigma_{j=i}^{\infty} \left(\frac{\gamma}{\beta+\gamma}\right)^j p_{t-j} \tag{11}$$

Comparing this equation (11) with equation (10), the prediction formula is the exponentially weighted forecast, but with different weights: "The only difference is that our analysis states that the 'coefficient of adjustment' in the expectations formula should depend on the demand and the supply coefficients" (320). In the case of optimal adaptive expectations, the coefficient of adjustment depends on the variances $\sigma_\varepsilon^2$ and $\sigma_\eta^2$ of the disturbances, whereas for rational expectations the coefficients are determined by using knowledge of the structure of the system describing the economy, namely, the model parameters, $\beta$ and $\gamma$.

## 3. What Kinds of Mathematical Engineering Tools Did Lucas Use?

> If Wesley Mitchell could view agents as "signal processors"
> in 1913, then I saw no reason to regard my own adoption
> of this viewpoint in 1972 as unduly speculative.
> —Robert E. Lucas, Studies in Business-Cycle Theory (1981)

Although Lucas made all kinds of references to the information engineering literature, as shown below, these references could be dismissed as rhetoric. This section shows that this is not the case. To apply the rational expectations hypothesis to macroeconomics, Lucas needed and therefore was in search for new mathematical tools that could enable this implementation.

In his first paper on rational expectations, "Investment under Uncertainty" (1971), Lucas and Prescott were very clear about their mathematical approach: "It is shown, first, that the equilibrium development for the industry solves a particular dynamic programming problem (maximization of 'consumer surplus')" (659). This was reconfirmed ten years later: "The idea of defining an equilibrium as a point in a space of functions of a few 'state variables' was one that Prescott and I had utilized in 'Investment under Uncertainty'" (Lucas 1981: 7).

To obtain a theory of the development of the industry through time, Lucas and Prescott considered it "natural" to define an anticipated price process as a sequence $\{p_t\}$ of functions of $(u_1, \ldots, u_t)$, where $\{u_t\}$ is a Markov process (664). Similarly the investment-output plan $\{x_t, q_t\}$ is also considered a sequence of functions of $(u_1, \ldots, u_t)$. To link the anticipated price sequence to the actual price sequence—also a sequence of functions of $(u_1, \ldots, u_t)$—it was assumed that the expectations are "rational" in the sense that "the anticipated price at time $t$ is the same function of $(u_1, \ldots, u_t)$ as is the actual price. That is, we assume that firms know the true distribution of prices for all future periods" (664).

Equilibrium, then, was defined as an element $\{q_t^0, x_t^0, p_t^0\}$ such that the market condition is satisfied for all $(t, u_1, \ldots, u_t)$ and such that

$$E\{\textstyle\sum_{t=0}^{\infty} \beta^t [p_t^0 q_t^0 - x_t^0]\} \geq E\{\textstyle\sum_{t=0}^{\infty} \beta^t [p_t^0 q_t - x_t]\} \tag{12}$$

for all $\{q_t, x_t\}$ satisfying certain conditions. The largest and central section of their paper proved that this equilibrium is unique and exists by "using the techniques of dynamic programming" (665), that is to say, by utilizing the "method of successive approximation as applied in [Bellman 1957]" (668). Therefore an "operator" $T$ was defined such that solutions to equation 12 coincides with solutions to $Tf = f$. Then, it was proved that $Tf = f$ has a unique solution, $f^*$, and for any $g$, $lim_{n \to 0} T^n g = f^*$.

This framework of dynamic programming was a year later again applied—"exactly the [same] way" (Lucas 1981: 7)—in the "Expectations and the Neutrality of Money" paper:

> The substantive results developed below are based on a concept of equilibrium which is, I believe, new (although closely related to the principles underlying dynamic programming) and which may be of independent interest. In this paper, equilibrium prices and quantities will be characterized mathematically as *functions* defined on the space of possible states of the economy, which are in turn characterized as finite dimensional vectors. (Lucas 1972a: 104)

In this article, the state of the economy in any period is entirely described by three variables $m$, $x$, and $\theta$, representing money supply, global money shocks, and local allocation shocks, respectively. The "motion of the economy from state to state is independent of decisions made by individuals in the economy" (106), and is given by $m' = mx$, and the densities $f$ and $g$ of $x$ and $\theta$. As a result, the equilibrium price was considered a function $p(m, x, \theta)$ on the space of possible states and was defined to satisfy a specific functional equation. And again, the largest and central section (plus appendix) was spent on proving the existence and uniqueness of the equilibrium price as a solution to the equation $Tf = f$.

In several of his papers, Lucas (1972b, 1973, 1975) introduced other mathematical tools in his analysis than those of dynamic programming used in the two articles (1971, 1972a) discussed above. Actually, his paper "Econometric Testing of the Natural Rate Hypothesis" is the only one in which rational expectations are formed as "originally proposed by Muth" (Lucas 1972b: 51) and hence were shaped by the same mathematical tools.

The aim of the "Econometric Testing" paper is to compare two different models of expectations-formation, adaptive and rational, to investigate which one can give an adequate formulation of the natural rate hypothesis. To show that the model of rational expectations-formation in this paper is indeed the same as Muth's (1960), I discuss this model in more detail.

Letting $y_t$ be the log of real output in $t$, $P_t$ be the log of the price level, and $P_t^*$ be the log of an index of expected future prices, the aggregate supply function is $y_t = a(P_t - P_t^*)$, and aggregate demand is assumed to be $y_t + P_t = x_t$, where $x_t$, the log of nominal GNP, is viewed as a "shift parameter." Policy is defined as a "rule" giving the current value of $x_t$ as a function of the state of the system. Lucas considered the following particular rule: $x_t = \rho_1 x_{t-1} + \rho_2 x_{t-2} + \varepsilon_t$, where $\{\varepsilon_t\}$ is a sequence of independent random variables that are distributed identically and normally, each with zero mean. Expectations were defined as rational:

$$P_t^* = E\{P_{t+1} \mid x_t, x_{t-1}, \eta_t\} + \eta_t \tag{13}$$

where $\eta_t$ is the forecast error, with the same properties as $\varepsilon_t$. To solve this system of four equations, Lucas used Muth's solution method by considering $P_t$ and $P_t^*$ linear combinations of the disturbances $x_t$ and $x_{t-1}$ and forecast error $\eta_t$.

Lucas's "Some International Evidence on Output-Inflation Trade-offs" (1973) was based on the main result of his "Expectations and the Neutrality of Money." This latter paper showed that an economic system in which "all prices are market clearing, all agents behave optimally in light of their objectives and expectations, and expectations are formed optimally" (Lucas1972a: 103) still could give rise to business cycles. This result was achieved by "the removal of the postulate that all transactions are made under complete information" (104). Information was incomplete because the economy was divided into two physically separated markets ("islands"), and information on the current state of these real and monetary disturbances is transmitted to agents only through prices in the market where each agent happens to be. In the particular framework presented below, prices convey this information only imperfectly, forcing agents to hedge on whether a particular price movement results from a relative demand shift or a nominal (monetary) one. (103)

This idea of incomplete information was taken over in his 1973 empirical study of real output-inflation trade-offs. To model "suppliers' lack of information on some of the prices relevant to their decision" (326), "where agents are placed in this situation of imperfect information" (327), Lucas "imagined" suppliers as located in a large number of scattered competitive markets, indexed by $z$. The information available to suppliers in $z$ at $t$ comes from two sources. First, traders enter period $t$ with knowledge of the past course of demand and supply shifts. While this information does not permit exact inference of the (log of) current general price level, $P_t$, it does determine the distribution on $P_t$ common to all markets. It is assumed to be normal with mean— $\bar{P}_t$ "depending in a known way on the above history" (328)—and a constant variance $\sigma^2$. It is supposed that the observed price in market $z$ deviates from the general price level $P_t$ with mean zero and variance $\tau^2$. Then the observed price in $z$, $P_t(z)$ is the sum of independent, normal variates

$$P_t(z) = P_t + z \tag{14}$$

The information $I_t(z)$ relevant for estimation of the unobserved $P_t$ consists, then, of the observed price $P_t(z)$ and the history summarized in $\bar{P}_t$. This information is used to infer the value of $P_t$:

$$E(P_t \mid I_t(z)) = E(P_t \mid P_t(z), \bar{P}_t) = (1-\theta)P_t(z) + \theta\bar{P}_t \tag{15}$$

where $\theta = \tau^2/(\sigma^2 + \tau^2)$, and variance $\theta\sigma^2$.

Although this result was apparently obtained by "straightforward calculation" (328), the same result would have been attained by framing this information processing as a Kalman filter. To see this, consider first equation (14) as the measurement equation (2), so that $H_t = I$, $y_t = P_t(z)$, $x_t = P_t$, $\varepsilon_t = z$, $R = \tau^2$. If one, subsequently, equates $\hat{x}_{t|t}$ with $E(P_t \mid I_t(z))$ and $x_{t|t-1}$ with $\bar{P}_t$, then $P_{t|t-1} = \sigma^2$, and thus the Kalman gain $K = \sigma^2/(\sigma^2 + \tau^2) = 1-\theta$ and $P_{t|t} = (1-K)\sigma^2 = \theta\sigma^2$. It can now be seen that the expectation of the general price level using information $I_t(z)$ as represented in equation (15) is equal to the Kalman-filtered signal as represented in equation (5).

Lucas's 1975 paper "An Equilibrium Model of the Business Cycle" dealt with the same problem: "The expectations of agents are rational, given the information available to them; information is imperfect, not only in the sense that the future is unknown, but also in the sense that no agent is perfectly informed as to the current state of the economy" (1113). And similar to his 1972a and 1973 papers, he adopted "the device proposed by Phelps (1969) and, since utilized in similar contexts by Lucas (1972[a], 1973) . . . , of thinking of trading as occurring in distinct markets, or 'islands'" (Lucas 1975: 1120).

The aggregate state of the economy is fully described by the variables $k_t$, $m_t$, and $x_t$, representing capital stock, money, and nominal government spending. The situation of an individual market $z$ is described by its capital relative to average, $u_t(z)$, and the government spending it receives relative to average, $\theta_t(z)$. Agents observe none of the variables directly. The only source of information is the history of market clearing prices $p_t(z)$, $p_{t-1}(z), p_{t-2}(z), \ldots$ of the markets in which traders happened to be currently and in the past. This information is used to form unbiased estimates of the current values of the aggregate state variables. On the basis of this information, the agents have a "well-informed opinion" of the relevant variables they cannot observe: $s_t = (k_t, m_t, x_t, \theta_t(z), u_t(z))$.

When new information is available, $p_t(z) - \hat{p}_t$, agents form an a posteriori conditional mean on the state vector to be used in forecasting: $\tilde{s}_t$. And again, according to Lucas, "a straightforward calculation yields the conditional means" (1125)

$$\tilde{s}_t = \hat{s}_t + \sigma_p^{-2} V(p_t(z) - \hat{p}_t) \tag{16}$$

which again can be interpreted as a Kalman filter.

## 4. Evaluation

Lucas has never made clear and explicit what the larger background is from which his new methodology was developed. The early 1970s papers were written when he was at Carnegie Mellon University, from 1963 to 1974. At several occasions, Lucas explained that the people who were around at Carnegie at that time had influenced him, but not in what way. When he, for example, clarified that he saw models as a "parallel or analogue system," he noted that "I do not know the background of this view of theory as physical analogue, nor do I have a clear idea as to how widely shared it is among economists. An immediate ancestor of my condensed statement is [Simon 1969]" (Lucas 1980: 697).

Also, with respect to the kind of mathematics, he never made clear where it came from. In relation to Arjo Klamer's question about his collaboration with Prescott on the first paper in which rational expectations was introduced, Lucas answered: "We thought [the investment problem] was a pretty straightforward applied problem, but then we got in way over our heads technically. We didn't want to quit, so we read tons of difficult mathematical economics and mathematics, even though none of us had any prior familiarity with it" (Klamer 1984: 32–33).

The only exception with respect to more precise referencing to the mathematical literature is to be found in his 1975 paper. To clarify how he arrived at the above presented equation 16, Lucas refers in a footnote to a theorem in a textbook on statistics: Franklin Graybill's *Introduction to Linear Statistical Models* (1961), namely, theorem 3.10 on page 63. To receive more clarification about the mathematical resources Lucas had used in his early 1970s papers, I wrote in March 9, 2005, an email to Lucas with the following question:

> When carefully reading your work from the early 1970s, I found it striking that the way rational expectations is defined in these early papers differs from one paper to the other. While your papers written together with Prescott and your Neutrality paper is closely linked to dynamic programming, the 1973 paper "Some International Evidence on Output-Inflation Tradeoffs" and your 1975 paper "An Equilibrium Model of the Business Cycle" show a different approach—in the sense of mathematical concepts and techniques. In section 6, page 1125, of the 1975 paper, you refer to a theorem in a statistics textbook, which is an ordinary conditional expectations theorem. However, your specific application of it, namely taking expectations conditioned on information which give a noisy signal of unobserved prices, is in fact a Kalman filter.

On April 20, 2005, Lucas responded:

> I don't understand the distinction you are drawing here. I think of Kalman filtering as a recursive method for updating Bayesian posteriors as time passes that works in certain dynamic models. It, too, is an application of ordinary conditional expectations to a particular context. The linear set-up I used in these papers and some others is similar to Muth's, in his two papers on rational expectations. I suppose I just took it from him. But of course I knew about Kalman filtering at this time too.

The above references and answers show an instrumental relationship to mathematics. Consistent with his instrumental view on theory, namely, to be considered "an explicit set of instructions" (Lucas 1980: 697) for build-ing a model, Lucas searched the mathematical literature for useful con-cepts and tools, and picked out the ones that solved his technical problems.

The present article shows that the mathematical "instructions" came from information engineering, which should be distinguished from those of control engineering. This could, however, not be shown by exhibits from the Lucas archive[6] or from his published work, or from remarks made at interviews or in panel discussions. Evidence to show that the "rational expectations revolution" would have been better called the "information revolution" has to be constructed in another way. The recon-struction method applied here is actually closer to forensic research, in the sense that I have looked for mathematical traces, that is to say, mathemat-ical concepts and tools that I could trace back to original sources.[7] These original sources are the works where these concepts and tools for the first time were presented and discussed. But the present article does not claim that Lucas used these original sources directly. By the time Lucas started to use these tools, they already had found their way into textbooks and other handbooks where they could be picked up for use.

But this forensic tracing is not sufficient to make any claim about the relevance of an information engineering background for Lucas's new methodology. My email exchange with Lucas shows that Lucas himself saw no sense in making any distinction between the various backgrounds of the tools he had used. In his view they are neutral with respect to the original context from which they were developed and neutral with respect to the context of application. Mathematical tools are like hammers and screwdrivers; the usage of them does not change one's worldview. Con-trary to this viewpoint, this article shows that this distinction is relevant because the tools of control engineering shape a different world, namely, one consisting of human-machine relationships, rather than those of infor-mation engineering, which is populated by information-processing robots.

As Mary Morgan (2020) discusses in a paper on diagrams, but also in her earlier work on models (2012), a mathematical tool, such as a diagram or model, becomes a description or representation of the economic mate-

6. I searched the Lucas collection in the Economists' Papers Archive held in the David M. Rubenstein Rare Book and Manuscript Library at Duke University to no avail.

7. The possibility of this kind of tracing is not limited to mathematics. In Boumans 2004 I was able to show that the Hodrick-Prescott is actually a Kalman filter, by deconstructing the Fortran subroutine that was published in a research memorandum, "A Fortran Subroutine for Efficiently Computing HP-Filtered Time Series," by Finn E. Kydland and Edward C. Prescott in 1989.

rials in the sense that economists cannot think of the materials without that description: the tool becomes wedded to the materials. What economists think is in the world, or in the way the world works—their ontology of what is in the world—can be understood only through this mathematically expressed projection. The mathematical form is essential to the way economists think of the world and how it works. Although originally the choice of a tool depends on the economist seeing the problem in a particular way to which that tool fits that epistemological purpose, over time that choice has ontological implications as the tool and subject matter become more closely intertwined: tools "have implications for the way they think about their materials and subject matters and so the objects that they think exist in the world" (Morgan 2020: 250). Due to the innovations of the 1970s, the (economic) world came to be seen as an "informational structure," providing "signal processors" with noisy information that needs therefore to be "filtered" (see, e.g., Lucas 1977). With the rational expectations revolution, Lucas and the other new classical economists have changed the world such that in that new world, control techniques have lost their essence.

## References

Andrei, Neculai. 2005. "Modern Control Theory: A Historical Perspective." Center for Advanced Modeling and Optimization. camo.ici.ro/neculai/history.pdf.

Bellman, Richard. 1954. "The Theory of Dynamic Programming." Working paper P-550. Santa Monica, CA: RAND.

Bellman, Richard. 1957. *Dynamic Programming*. Princeton, NJ: Princeton University Press.

Boumans, Marcel. 1997. "Lucas and Artificial Worlds." In *New Economics and Its History*, edited by John B. Davis. *History of Political Economy* 29 (supplement): 63–90.

Boumans, Marcel. 2004. "The Reliability of an Instrument." *Social Epistemology* 18, no. 2–3: 215–46.

Boumans, Marcel. 2005. *How Economists Model the World into Numbers*. London: Routledge.

Graybill, Franklin A. 1961. *An Introduction to Linear Statistical Models*. New York: McGraw-Hill.

Holt, Charles C., Franco Modigliani, John F. Muth, and Herbert A. Simon. 1960. *Planning Production, Inventories, and Work Force*. Englewood Cliffs, NJ: Prentice-Hall.

Hoover, Kevin D., and Warren Young. 2013. "Rational Expectations: Retrospect and Prospect." *Macroeconomic Dynamics* 17: 1169–92.

Kailath, Thomas. 1974. "A View of Three Decades of Linear Filtering Theory." *IEEE Transactions on Information Theory* IT-20, no. 2: 146–81.

Kálmán, Rudolf Emil. 1960. "A New Approach to Linear Filtering and Predictions Problems." *Journal of Basic Engineering* 82: 35–45.

Klamer, Arjo. 1984. *The New Classical Macroeconomics: Conversations with the New Classical Economists and Their Opponents*. Brighton, UK: Wheatsheaf.

Klein, Judy L. 2001. "Optimization and Recursive Residuals in the Space Age: Sputnik and the Kalman Filter." Working paper, Mary Baldwin College, Staunton, VA.

Klein, Judy L. 2015. "The Cold War Hot House for Modeling Strategies at the Carnegie Institute of Technology." Institute for New Economic Thinking Working Paper Series No. 19. papers.ssrn.com/sol3/papers.cfm?abstract_id=2667883.

Lucas, Robert E. 1972a. "Expectations and the Neutrality of Money." *Journal of Economic Theory* 4: 103–24.

Lucas, Robert E. 1972b. "Econometric Testing of the Natural Rate Hypothesis." In *The Econometrics of Price Determination Conference*, edited by O. Eckstein, 50–59. Washington, DC: Board of Governors of the Federal Reserve System.

Lucas, Robert E. 1973. "Some International Evidence on Output-Inflation Tradeoffs." *American Economic Review* 63, no. 3: 326–34.

Lucas, Robert E. 1975. "An Equilibrium Model of the Business Cycle." *Journal of Political Economy* 83, no. 6: 1113–44.

Lucas, Robert E. 1977. "Understanding the Business Cycle." In *Stabilization of the Domestic and International Economy*, edited by Karl Brunner and Allan H. Meltzer, 7–29. Amsterdam: North-Holland.

Lucas, Robert E. 1980. "Methods and Problems in Business Cycle Theory." *Journal of Money, Credit, and Banking* 12, no. 4: 696–715.

Lucas, Robert E. 1981. *Studies in Business-Cycle Theory*. Oxford: Basil Blackwell.

Lucas, Robert E. 2004. "Keynote Address to the 2003 HOPE Conference: My Keynesian Education." In *The IS-LM Model*, edited by Michel De Vroey and Kevin D. Hoover. *History of Political Economy* 36 (supplement): 12–24.

Lucas, Robert E., and Edward C. Prescott. 1971. "Investment under Uncertainty." *Econometrica* 39, no. 5: 659–81.

Lucas, Robert, and Thomas Sargent. 1979. "After Keynesian Macroeconomics." *Federal Reserve Bank of Minneapolis Quarterly Review* 3, no. 2: 1–16.

McMillan, Brockway. 1962. "Mathematicians and Their Uses." *SIAM Review* 4, no. 2: 79–90.

Morgan, Mary S. 2012. *The World in the Model*. Cambridge: Cambridge University Press.

Morgan, Mary S. 2020. "Inducing Visibility and Visual Deduction." *East Asian Science, Technology and Society* 14, no. 2: 225–52.

Muth, John F. 1960. "Optimal Properties of Exponentially Weighted Forecasts." *Journal of the American Statistical Association* 55, no. 290: 299–306.

Muth, John F. 1961. "Rational Expectations and the Theory of Price Movements." *Econometrica* 29, no. 3: 315–35.

Nobel Media AB. 2019. "Robert E. Lucas Jr.: Facts." NobelPrize.org, August 23. www.nobelprize.org/prizes/economic-sciences/1995/lucas/facts/.

Sent, Esther-Mirjam. 1997. "Engineering Dynamic Economics." In *New Economics and Its History*, edited by John B. Davis. *History of Political Economy* 29 (supplement): 41–62.

Shannon, Claude E. 1948. "A Mathematical Theory of Communication." *Bell System Technical Journal* 27: 379–423, 623–56.

Shannon, Claude E. 1950. "Programming a Computer for Playing Chess." *Philosophical Magazine* 41, no. 314: 256–75.

Shannon, Claude E. (1950) 1988. "A Chess-Playing Machine." In vol. 4 of *The World of Mathematics*, edited by James R. Newman, 2099–108. Redmond, Wa.: Microsoft Press.

Simon, Herbert A. 1969. *The Sciences of the Artificial*. Cambridge, MA: MIT Press.

Soare, Robert I. 1996. "Computability and Recursion." *Bulletin of Symbolic Logic* 2, no. 3: 284–321.

Turing, Alan M. 1936. "On Computable Numbers, with an Application to the Entscheidungsproblem." *Proceedings of the London Mathematical Society* 42: 230–65.

Wiener, Nobert. 1949. *Extrapolation, Interpolation, and Smoothing of Stationary Time Series: With Engineering Applications*. New York: Wiley.

Yeung, Raymond W. 2008. *Information Theory and Network Coding*. New York: Springer US.

# Research and Development, Testing, and the Economics of Information, 1937–63

William Thomas

In the United States during World War II, engineers worked rapidly to develop and produce weapons and equipment for the military, but they were also under intense pressure to ensure these products functioned well and met the immediate needs of combatant personnel. This pressure spurred the use of enhanced equipment tests, which could help to guide the design process, evaluate prototypes, and vouchsafe the quality of mass-produced items. Yet, with tight constraints in time and resources, it was also important to make the most of available testing opportunities. To cope with the situation, the military consulted with mathematicians and statisticians, who responded with an array of ideas and methods to improve R&D and testing processes. Much of this work seemed to also harbor considerable intellectual and practical potential, and after the war it flourished and diversified within mathematical statistics, economics, and such emerging fields as operations research, systems engineering, and systems analysis. Judy Klein's contribution to this volume explores another branch of this same history.

One strand of this work, centered at the new RAND Corporation, employed formal analysis to anticipate how well a particular design could be expected to fare in combat. Such analyses promised to make the engineering process less haphazard by informing selections among competing design proposals and by pinpointing the most critical uncertainties bearing on specific design choices, which helped engineers decide what sorts

*History of Political Economy* 52 (annual suppl.) DOI 10.1215/00182702-8717977

of tests to conduct and what kinds of performance data to acquire. A second strand of work, also closely connected to RAND, conceptualized testing less as something to be economized and optimized than as an option that engineers and military authorities could invoke when they needed empirical information to decide which designs to pursue and procure and which to abandon. This conceptualization corresponded with a view of development engineering as a trial-and-error process that carries an inherent risk of failure. In the hands of some economists, the question became how to design policies that would encourage military contractors to take such risks, thereby allowing the military to benefit not only from a wider variety of R&D projects but also the information that even failed development projects yielded.

A key figure in this second strand of work was Kenneth Arrow, who worked intensively on it during the same period in which he produced some of his better-known achievements, including his theory of social choice and his general equilibrium proof with Gérard Debreu (Düppe and Weintraub 2014). Building on the theory of sequential analysis, which had been developed during the war to inform the conduct of quality control tests (Klein 2000), Arrow focused on the idea that conducting a test entails costs that must be balanced against the benefits of the information expected to be gained from it. During the 1950s, he wrote a series of memoranda for RAND that leveraged a conception of R&D as a kind of testing or information-gathering process that market incentives tend to discourage due to the ways in which information fails to function as a typical commodity. This view of information also led him to reflect more broadly on how its peculiarities undermine the functioning of market mechanisms that might otherwise allocate risk among market actors in an economically efficient way. Notably, in the early 1960s, he reapplied this view of information in his foundational work on the economics of medical care, arguing the inevitable information disparity between patients and physicians inhibits market behavior and establishes a need for strong institutional and policy interventions.

How all this work may have influenced engineering and R&D management remains to be fully evaluated. In the 1950s, military contracting represented a large, rapidly changing, and intensely powerful component of the US economy, which President Dwight Eisenhower famously described in his 1961 farewell address as the American "military-industrial complex." Because the work of the complex has not been thoroughly mapped, it is difficult to distinguish whether a particular expression of an idea constitutes an origin point or merely an exposition of the ideas inhabiting an emerging practice elsewhere. However, we do know that both the first and second strand of work identified here, along with a number of other lines of inquiry, found a canonical expression in the 1960 book *The Economics of Defense in the Nuclear Age*, written by the RAND economists Charles Hitch and Roland McKean. In 1961, Hitch became comptroller at the Defense Department, where he implemented a new defense budgeting framework called the Planning, Programming, and Budgeting System (PPBS) and created an accompanying Office of Systems Analysis that Defense Secretary Robert McNamara used to exert stronger control over weapons systems acquisition. President Lyndon Johnson soon ordered PPBS extended to cover all federal agencies. While a modified version of PPBS remains central to US defense budgeting to this day (McGarry and Peters 2018), economic controls have never fully tamed defense R&D and weapons systems acquisition, and they notoriously failed when applied to nondefense agencies (Young 2010). To whatever degree this work may have influenced practice and to whatever degree it crashed up against the shoals of practical and political realities, it certainly was at the heart of an enduring discourse surrounding pressing, high-profile problems at the intersection of engineering and economics.

## Formal Modeling and Engineering Design

Prior to World War II, engineers who developed military technologies assembled designs exhibiting favorable qualities that could be measured under laboratory conditions or at proving grounds: high lethality, high speed, precise and accurate firing, low weight, ease of use, low failure rates, and so forth. However, sometimes design decisions made to enhance one quality required accepting limitations in, or even detracting from, other qualities. To decide which trade-offs were worth making entailed considering the consequences the trade-offs would have for how the design would perform in its intended purpose, not in a controlled test. For airplane-mounted weapons, to take the most commonly considered example, the question was: how would different weapons configurations bear on the probability of achieving victory in typical instances of aerial combat?

L. B. C. Cunningham, a ballistics instructor with the British Air Ministry, first considered these issues in 1937. Having earned a doctorate in mathematics under Edmund Whittaker at the University of Edinburgh, he formulated a simple model of air duels that integrated mathematical expressions of each aircraft's "stated tactical methods either of approach or withdrawal" with expressions representing armament specifications such as rapidity of fire, accuracy, and so forth, as well as vulnerabilities of the target. After sending this model to the Royal Aircraft Establishment, the Air Ministry's main manufacturing facility and laboratory, Cunningham was encouraged to further develop his ideas, because, while they could not determine final design decisions, they did prove capable of rooting out design fallacies and resolving certain quandaries. By the summer of 1939, Cunningham had worked out the fundamentals of what he called a "Mathematical Theory of Combat." In February 1940, he was named the head of a new organization called the Air Warfare Analysis Section, which continued working throughout the war.[1]

Two of Cunningham's early papers on the mathematical theory of combat came into the hands of the American mathematician Warren Weaver in early 1942. In peacetime, Weaver directed the New York City–based Rockefeller Foundation's philanthropic activities in the natural sciences. During the war, he was recruited by the newly established National Defense Research Committee to lead a New York–based group set up to advise military suppliers on the design of fire control mechanisms, which are used to aim large weapons such as antiaircraft guns at moving targets. In this position, Weaver routinely received technical reports from across American and British military agencies. Immediately impressed by Cunningham's papers, Weaver later recalled he "showed and praised" them to various military officers until they asked him to "try to digest and simplify" them, and to explain their contents "in terms not so formidably mathematical." In summer 1942, Weaver approached the Columbia University statistician and economist Harold Hotelling to help him recruit a team to undertake the task. Hotelling referred Weaver to his former students Allen Wallis, who had gone on to the Stanford University economics department, and Jacob Wolfowitz, who was teaching in the New York public school system. They formed the core of a new Columbia-based Statistical Research Group.[2] It became one of several specialist mathe-

---

1. Original materials in National Archives of the UK, Public Record Office AIR 13/879. For synthesis of these and other materials, see Thomas 2015: chap. 4.

2. National Archives and Records Administration, Record Group 227, Applied Mathematics Panel: General Records, 1942–1946, box 13, "Project No. 7—Columbia University SRG-C," folders 1 and 2. Quotes in this and the following three paragraphs are from Warren Weaver, "Comments on a General Theory of Air Warfare," AMP Note No. 27, January 1946, Library of Congress, Papers of Edward L. Bowles, box 43, folder 5 (hereafter cited as Weaver, "Comments").

matical groups operating under the umbrella of an organization called the Applied Mathematics Panel, which Weaver led for the duration of the war.

The Columbia group's first application of the theory sought to determine whether eight 0.50-inch guns or four 20mm guns constituted a preferable armament configuration for a fighter making a tail attack on a bomber. Weaver later explained the work entailed integrating theory and data pertinent to the problem, including "estimates" and "guesses," and then discussing the relevant figures and the nature of the problem "at very considerable length with experienced officers." He recalled that the mathematical exercise allowed the team to pinpoint whether various uncertainties would affect the final choice between the two configurations. Ultimately, the group found that, for most assumptions about the vulnerability of the bomber, the 20mm guns had the advantage. In cases of remaining uncertainty, the exercise identified what sorts of data could be obtained and tests performed to resolve the matter. While Weaver was clearly impressed by the potential of the method, the pressures of the war were such that there were few opportunities to develop and make full use of it.

It was not until late 1944 that Weaver spotted such an opportunity when the US Army Air Forces sought advice on how to make best use of its new, cutting-edge B-29 bomber, which had been rushed through design and production. Under a contract referred to as AC-92, Weaver set up a large, multipronged study. The air force proved interested in field testing undertaken under the auspices of AC-92 at the air base near Alamogordo, New Mexico, as well as in certain other aspects of the project. However, Weaver found to his dismay that the military was "totally (and in most cases emphatically) uninterested" in a Princeton University–based integrative mathematical analysis that he regarded as the "crowning jewel" of the whole endeavor. Compiling his final report on AMP's activities, Weaver consolidated his thinking on the potential of mathematical theories of combat into a long and rambling document called "Comments on a General Theory of Air Warfare." In it, Weaver imagined such a theory embedded in the analog mechanisms of a "Tactical-Strategic Computer." The computer would assist engineers and military officers in working through the confoundingly manifold interrelations among all the decisions they have to make about equipment, tactics, and strategy, with the ultimate aim of maximizing an abstract quantity called "military worth." Weaver fully understood the fantastical nature of the computer, but regarded it as a compelling illustration of the lessons he wanted to convey about the potential of mathematical analysis in military decision-making.

Not long after the document's completion, a bona fide chance to implement those lessons arrived with the establishment of Project RAND in early 1946, which was soon reconfigured into the RAND Corporation, an independent, nonprofit contractor. John Williams, a mathematician who worked with Weaver during the war, later remembered being recruited to RAND by the Douglas Aircraft engineer Frank Collbohm, who was organizing the project. Williams recalled that Collbohm emphasized the "blue sky" nature of the enterprise: "Since it was peacetime, we would have the time to do things it was sensible to do. That had not been the case during the war, because we were just snowed by immediate emergencies all the time. He told me that he would like to have RAND permeated by the kind of analyses that the Applied Mathematics Panel had done during the war" (Bornet 1969). At RAND, Williams built up an Evaluation Section, which worked to translate the spirit of AMP's work into this new context. A January 1947 memorandum outlining a broad agenda for the section stated that it should "devise and use methods for evaluating means of warfare," stressing that the "almost boundless" complexity of the problem would require the application of a "diversity of skills," often in unexpected ways. As an example, it noted the "need for the economist is not confined to the situations usually designated by 'economic warfare.'" It also noted that "there is no particularly logical place at which to curtail the analysis, short of the limit imposed by inadequate information and understanding." That suggested a "broad principle" to guide the section in choosing what to work on: "A study should promise to increase information and understanding of the consequences of warfare operations."[3]

Soon thereafter, RAND launched the "Strategic Bombing Systems Analysis," a sprawling mathematical examination of a preferred design for the successor to the B-29 bomber, which would be specialized to carry out a nuclear strike on the Soviet Union. At that time, Boeing had already won the contract to develop the B-52, but its engineers were being sent repeatedly back to the drawing board as their designs failed to live up to army air force officers' continually shifting specifications. The difficulty of coformulating designs, specifications, and mission profiles was very much the sort of problem that mathematical analysis had the potential to resolve prior to incurring the expenses involved with advanced design and prototyping. The mathematician Edwin Paxson, who had also worked

3. "Program for the Evaluation Section of Project RAND," January 20, 1947, RAND Document RAD-26. RAND Corporation Library, Santa Monica, California

with Weaver during the war, led the effort, which absorbed three years and the efforts of a large fraction of RAND's staff. In the end, the air force, now an independent service branch, rejected RAND's recommendation to build a relatively inexpensive turboprop bomber in favor of a more expensive, jet-propelled aircraft (Collins 2002; Thomas 2015). Whether RAND or the air force was in some sense correct is difficult to gauge, as Boeing's B-52 fortunately never undertook its intended mission. While it proved a versatile aircraft and is still in service today, so is Russia's counterpart, the turboprop Tu-95 bomber. Meanwhile, RAND's perception that its analysis failed to provide persuasive answers to the choices the air force had to make sent it into a period of prolonged introspection over the reach and validity of such methods (Jardini 1996).

## Kenneth Arrow, Sequential Analysis, and Iterative Information Gathering

Returning to World War II, not long after the statistical group at Columbia began working on Cunningham's mathematical theory of combat, the US Navy presented it with a problem that was mathematically distinct but thematically quite similar. As Judy Klein (2000) has discussed in detail, military suppliers' quality control inspectors were facing as much pressure to pursue efficiency in testing as engineers developing new equipment. While it was already accepted practice to discontinue testing of a sample after enough failures had occurred to reject the lot, inspectors were also discontinuing testing after they had conducted enough tests to satisfy their own sense of whether the lot would pass muster. The question presented to the group was to determine exactly if and when testing of a sample can be legitimately stopped before it has been completed. While the problem initially fell to Allen Wallis and a young Milton Friedman, they quickly passed it along to their senior colleague, the Columbia University mathematical statistician Abraham Wald, who concluded the inspectors had indeed intuited an ultra-efficient testing procedure, which he formalized as "sequential analysis." In addition to prescribing a more efficient procedure, sequential analysis made explicit, interrogated, and overturned a hitherto tacit assumption of testing: that all tests would be conducted simultaneously, as in an agricultural experiment conducted using different plots of land, rather than in a sequence. This assumption implied that all the intellectual work of testing would take place during the design of a test and in interpreting the results afterward. Sequential testing, though, admitted the possibility of analysis during the testing process itself.

Yet the initial wartime formulation of sequential analysis also harbored its own uninterrogated assumptions, most notably that the very desirability of discontinuing a testing sequence derives from the fact that the costs of testing are nonzero and are therefore always implicitly balanced against the risk-associated costs of not testing any further. One of the people to whom this issue fell after the war was Arrow. Before the war, Arrow had been a student of Hotelling at Columbia, and during the war he worked in weather forecasting. After the war, still seeking a topic for his doctoral research, he briefly relocated to the Cowles Commission for Research in Economics, then based at the University of Chicago. During his stay at Cowles, Arrow met Abraham Girshick, an earlier student of Hotelling and a member of the wartime Statistical Research Group at Columbia University, who invited him and the Howard University mathematician David Blackwell to visit the RAND Corporation in the summer of 1948 (Arrow 2002). There, the three wrote an article they published in *Econometrica* titled "Bayes and Minimax Solutions of Sequential Decision Problems." The paper defines functions governing the termination of a testing sequence that unite within a single calculation the cost of undertaking an additional test with the risk-weighted costs associated with taking an action based on the tests conducted to that point. Although the paper is almost purely mathematical, it does hint at its applicability to economic problems, noting that the problem it describes is "closely allied to the economic problem of the rational behavior of an entrepreneur under conditions of uncertainty. At each point in time, the entrepreneur has the choice between entering into some imperfectly liquid commitment and holding part or all of his funds in cash pending the acquisition of additional information, the latter being costly because of the foregone profits" (Arrow, Blackwell, and Girshik 1949).

Arrow soon obtained a faculty position at Stanford but continued to spend subsequent summers at RAND. For further details on the intellectual culture of Stanford in this period, and Arrow's place within it, see the contribution of Beatrice Cherrier and Aurélien Saïdi in this volume. In the summer of 1950, Arrow attended a RAND conference on inventories at the invitation of Jacob Marschak. Together with the RAND mathematician Ted Harris, Arrow and Marschak developed a paper titled "Optimal Inventory Policy," published in *Econometrica* in 1951. The paper formally justifies optimal policies associated with two simple inventory problems before concentrating on a third: establishing an optimal inventory replenishment level and an optimal level at which the inventory should be replenished if inventories are below it after a predetermined interval of time. In the problem, demand during an interval is represented by a known probability distribution. Because the problem assumes inventories are durable, inventories not used during one interval may be reused in the next. Accordingly, an optimized decision to replenish must consider not only risk-weighted costs associated with inventory depletion in the upcoming interval but also, in principle, all future intervals. The problem is similar to sequential analysis in that it involves undertaking a risk calculation based on information, in this case a remaining inventory level, available at a moment in time. And the authors themselves pointed out that a further refinement of their treatment could actually incorporate sequential analysis by supposing the probability distribution of demand to be unknown but gradually discernible by taking a measurement of demand at the end of each interval (Arrow, Harris, and Marschak 1951; Arrow 2002; Klein 2007).

Arrow eventually came to understand that the prospect of gathering information through iterative testing had a profound economic significance, which he mused about at length in an address he gave to the 1956 annual meeting of the Operations Research Society of America (ORSA), titled "Decision Theory and Operations Research" (Arrow 1957). Regarding the term *operations research*, suffice it here to note that, although its meaning was highly variable in this period (Thomas 2015), Arrow took it to connote the development and refinement of theories of optimized decision-making and resource allocation for managerial applications. His conception encompassed inventory theory, which he had been working on for six years at that point and now took to be a representative problem of information gathering. Noting that future inventory replenishment decisions would benefit from information gained in the interim about inventory drawdown, he pointed out that decisions made in the present should take that anticipated learning process into account and hedge accordingly. However, departing from his more formalistic treatments of the subject, he admitted that it was not necessarily beneficial to make overly elaborate calculations about how to hedge. He remarked, "I think one could easily get a qualitative picture of the value to be placed on the stock of inventory at hand at the end of the period and put down an approximation that reflects the value with sufficient accuracy as far as the purpose on hand is concerned. Naturally, better results will be obtained by broadening and deepening the problem, by extending it in our inventory example to more time periods. But there is always a point where we must stop."

Arrow urged that, inasmuch as the decisions made in the present about sequential testing and inventory management took into account the value of information that could only be gained in the future, that thought process was fundamentally akin to the decisions that modelers themselves made as they developed their ideas. He remarked, "I would like to put forth the thesis that the open and tentative character of operations research, and of all scientific analysis, can be itself discussed in terms of decision theory. More specifically, I believe that the notions of decision analysis in sequential situations . . . can, if properly understood, be very revealing of the tentative and approximate nature of any particular solution to an operations-research problem." If any model and the calculated solution to it were bound to be provisional, it was important to reflect on what the purpose and value of a model being developed at that moment really was in order to decide how to formulate it and how it might be built up iteratively in subsequent studies. He insisted, for instance, that "formal over-simplified models which are not yet capable of being quantified may nevertheless be of great practical value." Elaborating elsewhere in his address on the "great values of theoretical model building" in cases in which the models outstrip the "computational possibilities of the moment or the data availabilities," Arrow said such models "will frequently enable us to see connections, to realize implications, and to specify which of the outcomes of the present situation will have an influence on the future." In addition, overly simplified models would "still enable us, when solved, to have a qualitative appreciation of the influence of our variables on the future"—including, he stressed, the value of information gathering. Arrow suggested it would be useful to model an actor's "deliberate policy" about whether to engage in record keeping and the "acquisition of information" based on whether the anticipated benefits of such acquisition outweighed the costs. Therefore, such decisions could be profitably incorporated into decision models as much as any other decision to expend or not expend resources. However, Arrow did not give any hint in his speech that at that time he was also thinking deeply about the implications that the costs of information gathering had for the economics of military research and development.

## Arrow on Information in R&D
## and Medical Care

At the same time that Arrow began to develop his ideas about modeling information gathering in the 1950s, he was also engaging with the principal work of the RAND Corporation. Complementarily to the organization's work in systems analysis, RAND's economists became interested in the problem of how to project the costs and benefits of cutting-edge technologies into the future. Recall that in its 1950 Strategic Bombing Systems Analysis, RAND unsuccessfully recommended the Air Force pursue an established turboprop-based design for the B-52 in view of the expense associated with the new technology of jet propulsion. However, RAND was also aware that as engineers became more acquainted with a technology, its price would eventually come down, making advanced technologies more attractive as longer-term investments. The principal instigator of work on this problem at RAND was the economist Armen Alchian (Arrow 2001). Alchian received his doctorate from Stanford in 1943 and worked as a statistician for the US Army Air Forces during the war. In 1946, he took root at the University of California, Los Angeles, and soon thereafter began consulting for RAND in nearby Santa Monica. Drawing on his wartime experience with aircraft production, Alchian (1949, 1950) focused much of his early work there on how to model "learning curves," that is, the evolution of cost-performance characteristics in aircraft production. Arrow and his wife, Selma, likewise wrote at least three papers on such curves in this period (Arrow and Arrow 1950a, 1950b; Arrow, Arrow, and Bradley 1951). As Matthieu Ballandonne (2015) has shown, this work formed the basis of Arrow's (1962) later foundational work on "learning by doing." It also indirectly formed the basis of Arrow's considerations on information and market structure.

As RAND began to grapple with the shortcomings of its Strategic Bombing Systems Analysis in the early 1950s, Alchian became one of the most trenchant critics of the organization's commitment to systems analysis as the centerpiece of its work. RAND's systems analysts regarded their work as valuable because it could aid in the design of complex systems such as aircraft by harmonizing requirements, design specifications, and design features before more intensive engineering work began. The frustrating and expensive process of repeatedly revising requirements, specifications, and designs for the B-52 was testament to the need for such analysis. Alchian, though, suspected that systems analysis was dangerous because it could lead to an illusory conviction that a final, most appropriate design could be produced without first going through an unavoidable period of trial and error. He illustrated his point in a 1952 memorandum by drawing an analogy with dining. "Research and Development decisions," he wrote, "are those of the Chef, who concocts new dishes and plans a menu of available alternative dishes, from which the Gourmet at a later time has the privilege of choosing in light of his tastes, companions, and income. A good Chef provides a broad menu—thereby assuring the Gourmet the opportunity to make the best selection. The difference between the task of the Chef and the Gourmet must be kept strictly distinct. To confound the two is as disastrous in the military as in the restaurant business." He urged that, rather than focus on a near-term timeframe, as the Strategic Bombing Systems Analysis had, it was important to devote more resources to R&D to increase the available options for the long term, lest the air force find itself prematurely committed to an inappropriate design and bearing the associated costs. "I would only argue that I fear we shall soon cease to be economizing gourmets with à la carte menus and become expensive, undernourished table d'hôte gourmands," he wrote (quoted in Alchian 1952).

The debate between Alchian and RAND's systems analysts reached its peak in 1953 and 1954. The systems analyst Edward Quade suggested in a memorandum that it might be advisable to assemble a course on how to develop and use systems analyses. He explained that air force contractors were becoming increasingly agitated about being undercompensated for development and design work on prospective aircraft that did not ultimately lead to a procurement contract. Some contractors had begun to recommend that the air force conduct systems analyses prior to awarding new development contracts. While Quade welcomed the enthusiasm, he reported there was concern at RAND that contractors were beginning to conduct low-quality analyses on their own to demonstrate the superiority of their wares. "There is little indication that industry has profited from RAND's mistakes," he wrote. He also argued that the military had been "oversold" on systems analysis and that it would be good to "disabuse the Air Force as to the technique and range of the method" (Quade 1953).

In a responding memorandum, Alchian and the RAND economist Reuben Kessel expressed their alarm at Quade's report that contractors were looking to systems analysis to resolve their concerns about undercompensated development work. They suggested that contractors were treating development as if it were a "loss leader" that would only become profitable once it resulted in a follow-on procurement contract. Alchian and Kessel were concerned contractors were becoming enthusiastic about systems analysis in the belief that by settling on preferred designs prior to development, it would help guarantee procurement. This, they argued, courted the danger Alchian had warned about earlier, that the air force and its contractors would be tempted into committing to a design before it was justifiable to do so. "Little boys and matches neither logically nor inevitably lead to fires, but the probability is distressingly high, if it's your boy and house," they wrote. For this reason they urged that any course RAND might offer should make clear that "systems analyses, unless used in an environment different from that which apparently now prevails, will do more harm than good in the development decision." They urged that more value needed to be ascribed to the pursuit of multiple development paths, arguing, "Inadequate compensation for development work is the reason developers feel inadequately compensated. . . . Therefore the cure is not in using systems analyses, however desirable that may be for other reasons; the cure is to break the link between development and procurement and make development pay" (Alchian and Kessel 1954).

In detailing plans for the course, Quade and the RAND economist Malcolm Hoag acknowledged the dangers Alchian and Kessel cited, but also turned the tables on their claims about the importance of diversity in investment in development projects, writing that they could not specify just how much diversity is enough. They wrote, "To hedge without limit by developing everything is, in view of the vast array of technically feasible choices, economically out of the question." Given that development choices would have to be made, they argued it would be necessary to make these choices "as carefully and as explicitly as possible, with no exclusion of alternatives arbitrarily or on the basis of petty considerations." This, in their view, was the entire point of systems analysis, which, they pointed out, did not mean that the "techniques and results" of analysis would be the same for development and procurement decisions, nor that the analysis would narrow potential design choices down to a single option (Quade and Hoag 1954). These sorts of considerations became an important part of their course, which was offered in 1955 and 1959, and adapted into a book published in 1964 (Quade 1964).

As David Hounshell (2000) has discussed in some detail, the debate between the economists and systems analysts at RAND opened up a line of work there on the economics of R&D, which emphasized the need for multiple, parallel lines of technological development. Arrow contributed to this work through a series of memoranda that he wrote in the latter half of the 1950s, focused on the question of how to foster the most satisfactory and productive relationships with contractors. In contrast with much of his work, which was highly formalistic, these memoranda were almost entirely qualitative discussions of what he regarded as the essential features of the topic. They drew heavily on an insight inherent in his and Alchian's earlier work on learning curves in airframe production: that design engineering is work in which valuable knowledge is gained through experience. He also drew explicit connections between this conception of engineering and the thinking about sequential information gathering that he was developing at the same time. In his first memorandum, "Economic Aspects of Military Research and Development" (Arrow 1955), he cast decisions about investment in a new technology in terms of the supply and demand for a commodity in which investments are made under conditions of uncertainty. However, he drew a contrast between this sort of uncertainty and the more familiar "irreducible" uncertainty that pervades investment in agricultural commodities, wherein factors such as weather can never been known except probabilistically. In R&D, Arrow argued, experimentation can access a stable underlying reality. He continued, "There therefore arises the possibility of sequential improvement of the information available or, to put it conversely, the reduction of uncertainty. The phenomenon is exactly the same as that in the sequential inspection of commodity lots where the decision to make further inspections can be better and better guided as more and more previous inspections have taken place."

Arrow leveraged this insight to reinforce Alchian's point that it is necessary to invest in a variety of lines of development, "gradually eliminating the less promising as more and more information is accumulated. At each stage," he went on, "we have information which will suggest expansion of certain lines of development and the curtailment or elimination of others." Knowing that investment in experimentation could reduce risk, it was inadvisable to invest in a single technology prematurely. These were essentially the same themes he would explore in his address to ORSA the following year: decisions in the present should be made in anticipation of future learning, and investment in information gathering should be regarded as a critical part of the calculus of investment. Here, though, Arrow also explored another theme: that there can be important barriers inhibiting the success of information gathering. In the case of the R&D process, he noted that different lines of development would be undertaken by different companies. If investment decisions were to be made "based on all available information," the development process could not be a decentralized one. The information gained by different companies would have to be shared with a central decision-making entity such as the military, which would make the decision about which to pursue and which to abandon.

Arrow drew a number of implications from this conception of the development process. Like Alchian, he stressed the importance of distinguishing development from production in order to fund a larger array of

risky development projects. He criticized the "universally accepted prop-
osition" that development and production should be undertaken by the
same company, which he warned could have "some very pernicious consequences," such as confining development only to those firms that were
large enough to undertake full-scale production. While he allowed that
joining production and development could indeed have advantages, especially when a development project is "of a very minor nature," he argued
that "as one goes further and further away from present models [of equip-
ment] there is a stronger and stronger case for divorcing development and
production or at least not restricting development to the companies now
engaged in the business of production." He suggested, for instance, that
the government might rely more heavily on specially sponsored "research
institutes" to conduct development projects. Alternatively, he also suggested that production companies might be coaxed to conduct more development projects by insuring them somehow against the risk of failure.
However, he also warned against compensating companies for unsuccess-
ful projects involving "a failure on the part of a firm or individual to do
the work successfully or to work hard enough at it." One possibility, he
wrote, would be to offer competitive prizes for "successful completion of
prototypes with prescribed specifications." In general, Arrow noted that,
through its monopsony power, the government "ideally could reproduce
through its economic power any institutional arrangement that it regarded
as optimal." However, he also lamented that government decision makers
were apt to feel an unjustified fear of supporting projects that ultimately
ended in failure.

Arrow expanded on his analysis of the design of R&D contracts in a
long 1958 RAND memorandum that he wrote with Alchian and the Stanford economist William Capron. While the bulk of the memorandum concerned a purported shortage of scientists and engineers the United States
was then experiencing, a short section dealt with contract structures as one
of the factors bearing on the perceived demand for their skills.[4] Discussing
the oft-used cost-plus-fixed-fee contract type, which mitigates the risk to
firms conducting R&D projects by reimbursing all the firm's costs, they
noted its "troublesome incentive effects." While, they observed, the possibility of earning follow-on contracts does create some long-run incentive
for strong performance, in the short run there are also poor incentives to
perform well and a perverse incentive to incur expenses that have "spill-

4 For background on this memorandum, see Arrow 2001.

over" benefits for the company's nongovernment work. Suggesting alternative arrangements, they wrote, "One can imagine a contract that provides for a fixed fee in any case, plus some percentage of the costs, plus additional compensation depending on the degree of success in the research work. Such a feature, known as 'coinsurance,' is employed in similar circumstances, such as insurance against medical costs, where it is desired to increase the incentive of the individual to economize." Once again, though, implementation was apt to be tripped up by political realities, since "where 'success' is so difficult to appraise objectively, the payment of additional compensation by the government will always be scrutinized suspiciously lest it reflect any bribery of government contracting officers."

Throughout his memoranda on R&D, Arrow's insistence on the need for the government to provide appropriate incentives and institutional structures to ensure adequate investment in development stood in explicit contrast with his conceptualization of the typical functioning of markets. In his 1955 memorandum, for instance, he drew a clear distinction between the need to actively coordinate the information flow between R&D projects with the "classical economic case of a world of certainty where the price system can take the place of the spread of detailed information." At that moment, Arrow (1953) had just published his now-well-known general equilibrium proof with Debreu, and had also recently delivered a talk in France on the role of securities in allocating risk alongside commodities in the market. He drew out the distinction between R&D and market action at length in a 1959 memorandum titled "Economic Welfare and the Allocation of Resources for Invention." In it, he pointed again to the problem of how the risks of R&D can be insured so that adequate development takes place while overcoming the "moral factor" that undermines the efficacy of insurance as a way to redistribute risk. In addition, he now spotlighted the difficulties in making information gained through R&D function as a commodity. Because, he argued, the knowledge products of R&D extend well beyond those that are effectively protected by patent law, they tend to become available to competitors essentially for free. For this reason, he warned, there is a diminished incentive for companies to bear the risks of R&D. Alternatively, if companies do perform R&D, they may impound the information they produce, in which case the full value of that information for society is not realized. For Arrow, all of this served to underscore once again the importance of government support for R&D while leaving unresolved such questions as how much the government should invest or what mechanisms of support it should employ.

Philip Mirowski and Edward Nik-Khah (2017) have argued that the conception of information as a commodity, and the identification of places where it fails to function as such, has played a critical role in motivating economists to establish market design as an important goal in their work. They further argue that an emphasis on the design of efficient markets is a defining characteristic of a powerful "neoliberal" ideology currently prevailing among economists and in society. For his part, from early on Arrow clearly conceived of the trade of information as a characteristic of an ideally functioning market. At the same time, though, he also stressed that the failure of information to function as a commodity cannot necessarily be ameliorated and that alternative structures are necessary to realize the full value of information.

Within a few years of his work on R&D economics for RAND, Arrow transplanted this view of uncertainty and information gathering into a new project on the economics of medical care that he pursued with support from the Ford Foundation. Whereas Arrow published his work on R&D in difficult-to-obtain RAND memoranda, he published his initial, similarly qualitative foray into medical care in the *American Economic Review* in 1963, and no doubt it is partly for this reason that it is much better known as a touchstone of his work in information economics. Introducing his analysis, Arrow wrote, "I will hold that virtually all the special features of this industry, in fact, stem from the prevalence of uncertainty." As in the case of R&D, he argued that the peculiarities of information as a commodity precluded the effective functioning market mechanisms. He wrote, "I propose here the view that, when the market fails to achieve an optimal state, society will, to some extent at least, recognize the gap, and nonmarket social institutions will arise attempting to bridge it." At this point in his text he inserted a footnote offering one of the few hints of the link between it and his prior work on military R&D, stating: "An important current situation in which normal market relations have had to be greatly modified in the presence of great risks is the production and procurement of modern weapons," citing the discussion of cost-plus-fixed-fee contracts in the memorandum he wrote with Alchian and Capron.

However, Arrow did not propose a one-to-one correspondence between R&D and medical care. Whereas in the case of R&D he regarded information as something a company was apt to swiftly lose to its competitors, in the case of medical care he regarded it as something that was almost impossible for a patient to obtain. He wrote, "Uncertainty as to the quality of the product is perhaps more intense here than in any other commodity. Recovery from disease is as unpredictable as is its incidence. In most commodities, the possibility of learning from one's own experience or that of others is strong because there is an adequate number of trials. In the case of severe illness, that is, in general, not true; the uncertainty due to inexperience is added to the intrinsic difficulty of prediction." He also noted the importance of the information disparities between patient and physician: "Because medical knowledge is so complicated, the information possessed by the physician as to the consequences and possibilities of treatment is necessarily very much greater than that of the patient, or at least so it is believed by both parties." Unlike in the case of R&D, where Arrow was equivocal about the value of insurance due to the potential effects of moral hazard on development activities, in medical care he regarded "the welfare case for insurance of all sorts" as "overwhelming" while noting the use of mechanisms such as co-insurance to encourage economizing.

Arrow also argued that in the medical profession, many aspects of physicians' professional apparatus and ethical norms that failed to adhere to market logic could be traced to the information disparity between physician and patient. He wrote, "Since the patient does not, at least in his belief, know as much as the physician, he cannot completely enforce standards of care. In part, he replaces direct observation by generalized belief in the ability of the physician. To put it another way, the social obligation for best practice is part of the commodity the physician sells, even though it is a part that is not subject to thoroughgoing inspection by the buyer. One consequence of such trust relations is that the physician cannot act, or at least appear to act, as if he is maximizing his income at every moment of time. As a signal to the buyer of his intentions to act as thoroughly in the buyer's behalf as possible, the physician avoids the obvious stigmata of profit-maximizing." Thus, he suggested, physicians charged patients variably depending on their ability to pay and discouraged price competition among themselves. They also worked to control the range of quality available in medical services. He observed, "If many qualities of a commodity are possible, it would usually happen in a competitive market that many qualities will be offered on the market, at suitably varying prices, to appeal to different tastes and incomes. Both licensing laws and standards of medical-school training have limited the possibilities of alternative qualities of medical care."

The degree to which the various strands of Arrow's work connected to each other has, I would argue, not been hitherto fully appreciated. That he could draw connections between sequential analysis, inventory control, industrial learning curves, risk reallocation, R&D policy, and the institutions and practices of the medical profession is testament to the fact that there was no unidirectional progress in his thought, for example, from qualitative description to formalized rigor. Rather, in his view, formalization could establish a conceptual appreciation for certain kinds of problems, such as the value of information and the problem of coping with risk, which could then be qualitatively analyzed as a key feature of certain sectors of economic activity. Although Arrow was without question one of the key figures in the transition to a more formalistic style of economics (Weintraub 2002, chap. 6; Düppe and Weintraub 2014), the methodological heterogeneity of his work suggests that such narratives should not dominate our understanding of his place in the profession's history.

## Conclusion

The progression of Arrow's work on information gathering—from formalistic treatments of sequential decision-making to qualitative explorations of the economics of R&D—paralleled the contemporaneous evolution of systems analysis at the RAND Corporation. As RAND continued to reflect on the failures of the Strategic Bombing Systems Analysis, it ultimately settled into a more heterogeneous methodology that integrated relatively small-scale mathematical analyses into larger, partially qualitative analytical frames. This transition was guided by RAND's head economist, Charles Hitch, who throughout the decade rejected the idea of seeking any sort of synoptically optimal design for a technological system, because the value and the very possibility of rigor at such an analytical scale would be undermined by limitations in analysts' investigative resources, time, computational power, and influence (Hitch and McKean 1960: 131). I have discussed this methodological transition in more detail elsewhere (Thomas 2015: chap. 28).

As with Arrow, though, historians have often taken work at RAND to be significant because it was a focal point for the development of various "tools" that soon exercised considerable influence in fields such as engineering, management, and the social sciences, including economics. Moreover, this influence has been linked to the emergence of a more general, rationalist mentality in postwar America that took methodological rigor to be tantamount to objectivity (Mirowski 2002; Amadae 2003; Isaac 2010; Erickson et al. 2013; Heyck 2015). The historian of technology Paul Edwards (1996) influentially characterized this mentality as a "closed world discourse" that was intimately related to Cold War attempts to engineer systems capable of monitoring and controlling any potential military threats. Historians' focus on technical tools is not unfounded, but we require a more-nuanced appreciation of exactly how and why those tools proved influential. I would argue that methods such as sequential analysis were regarded as powerful because they described both existing practices and ways to optimize them. This view accords with the recent observation of Catherine Herfeld (2018) that the adoption of these tools at the Cowles Commission was instrumental in turning its work from a descriptive to a normative methodology. It also accords with the concept of performativity as advanced by the sociologist Donald MacKenzie (2006) in his analysis of options pricing models, which argues that options traders adopted them not because they regarded them as inherently authoritative but because they described existing practices well enough that posited improvements, manifested as arbitrage opportunities, could be readily implemented or "performed."

However, I would further argue that, at least as important as the tools being developed in and around RAND was a newly enriched conceptual vocabulary that was being built up to describe a range of problems surrounding engineering, R&D management, and defense budgeting, many of which were not amenable to formalistic treatment. Although the existence of this vocabulary has never been sufficient to alleviate the varied ills of defense R&D (or, for that matter, of sectors such as medical care), it has been influential, and the issues it describes have continued to be important. For instance, the focus at RAND on keeping technological development options open until the risks associated with them have been reduced has come to be reflected in the use of "technology readiness levels" and "decision points" to govern R&D projects at agencies such as the National Aeronautics and Space Administration as well as the Defense Department. Even in the last few years, the Defense Department has placed a new emphasis on simulation, prototyping, and testing as a way to more swiftly identify promising designs for technicological systems that it believes will produce step changes in military capabilities (Griffin 2018). These more recent developments do not of course trace their heritage linearly from institutions such as RAND or individuals such as Arrow, but they do underscore the relevance of work that is now more than a half-century old.

# References

Alchian, Armen. 1949. "An Airframe Production Function." RAND Paper P-108. www.rand.org/pubs.html.

Alchian, Armen. 1950. "Reliability of Progress Curves in Airframe Production." RAND Research Memorandum RM-260-1. www.rand.org/pubs.html.

Alchian, A. A. 1952. "The Chef, Gourmet, and Gourmand." RAND Research Memorandum RM-798-PR. www.rand.org/pubs.html.

Alchian, Armen A., and Reuben A. Kessel. 1954. "A Proper Role of Systems Analysis." RAND Document D-2057. www.rand.org/pubs.html.

Alchian, A. A., K. J. Arrow, and W. M. Capron. 1958. "An Economic Analysis of the Market for Scientists and Engineers." RAND Research Memorandum RM-2190-RC. www.rand.org/pubs.html.

Amadae, S. M. 2003. *Rationalizing Capitalist Democracy: The Cold War Origins of Rational Choice Liberalism.* Chicago: University of Chicago Press.

Arrow, K. J. 1953. "Rôle des valeurs boursières pour la répartition la meilleure des risques." *Econométrie* 40: 41–47.

Arrow, K. J. 1955. "Economic Aspects of Military Research and Development." RAND Document D-3142. www.rand.org/pubs.html.

Arrow, Kenneth J. 1957. "Decision Theory and Operations Research." *Operations Research* 5, no. X: 289–92.

Arrow, Kenneth J. 1959. "Economic Welfare and the Allocation of Resources for Invention." RAND Paper P-1856-RC. www.rand.org/pubs.html.

Arrow, Kenneth J. 1962. "The Economic Implications of Learning by Doing." *Review of Economic Studies* 29, no. 3: 155–73.

Arrow, Kenneth J. 1963. "Uncertainty and the Welfare Economics of Medical Care." *American Economic Review* 53, no. 5: 941–73.

Arrow, Kenneth. 2001. "Armen Alchian's Contributions to NIE." *ISNIE Newsletter* 3, no. 2: 5–8.

Arrow, Kenneth J. 2002. "The Genesis of 'Optimal Inventory Policy.'" *Operations Research* 50, no. 1: 1–2.

Arrow, Kenneth, and Selma Arrow. 1950a. "A Critical Analysis of the Stanford Research Institute Report 'Cost-Performance Relationships for Airframes and Turbojet Engines.'" RAND Document D-714. RAND Corporation Library, Santa Monica, California.

Arrow, Kenneth, and Selma Arrow. 1950b. "Methodological Problems in Airframe Cost-Performance Studies." RAND Research Memorandum RM-456. RAND Corporation Library, Santa Monica, California

Arrow, K. J., S. S. Arrow, and H. R. Bradley. 1951. "Cost-Quality Relations in Bomber Airframes." RAND Research Memorandum RM-536. RAND Corporation Library, Santa Monica, California

Arrow, K. J., D. Blackwell, and M. A. Girshick. 1949. "Bayes and Minimax Solutions of Sequential Decision Problems." *Econometrica* 17, nos. 3–4: 213–44.

Arrow, Kenneth J., Theodore Harris, and Jacob Marschak. 1951. "Optimal Inventory Policy." *Econometrica* 19, no. 3: 523–32.

Ballandonne, Matthieu. 2015. "Creating Increasing Returns: The Genesis of Arrow's 'Learning by Doing' Article." *History of Political Economy* 47, no. 3: 449–79.

Bornet, Vaughn D. 1969. "John Williams: A Personal Reminiscence (August 1962)." RAND Document D-19036. RAND Corporation Library, Santa Monica, California.

Collins, Martin J. 2002. *Cold War Laboratory: RAND, the Air Force, and the American State, 1945–1950*. Washington, DC: Smithsonian Institution Press.

Düppe, Till, and E. Roy Weintraub. 2014. *Finding Equilibrium: Arrow, Debreu, McKenzie, and the Problem of Scientific Credit*. Princeton, NJ: Princeton University Press.

Edwards, Paul N. 1996. *The Closed World: Computers and the Politics of Discourse in Cold War America*. Cambridge, MA: MIT Press.

Erickson, Paul, Judy L. Klein, Lorraine Daston, Rebecca Lemov, Thomas Sturm, and Michael Gordin. 2013. *How Reason Almost Lost Its Mind: The Strange Career of Cold War Rationality*. Chicago: University of Chicago Press.

Griffin, Mike. 2018. "Statement before the Emerging Threats and Capabilities Subcommittee of the Senate Armed Services Committee on Technology Transfer and the Valley of Death, April 18, 2018." www.armed-services.senate.gov/imo/media/doc/Griffen_04-18-18.pdf.

Herfeld, Catherine. 2018. "From Theories of Human Behavior to Rules of Rational Choice: Tracing a Normative Turn at the Cowles Commission, 1943–54." *History of Political Economy* 50, no. 1: 1–48.

Heyck, Hunter. 2015. *Age of System: Understanding the Development of Modern Social Science*. Baltimore: Johns Hopkins University Press.

Hitch, Charles, and Roland N. McKean. 1960. *The Economics of Defense in the Nuclear Age*. Cambridge, MA: Harvard University Press.

Hounshell, David A. 2000. "The Medium Is the Message, or How Context Matters: The RAND Corporation Builds an Economics of Innovation, 1946–1962." In *Systems, Experts, and Computers: The Systems Approach in Management and Engineering, World War II and After*, edited by Agatha C. Hughes and Thomas P. Hughes, 255–310. Cambridge, MA: MIT Press.

Isaac, Joel. 2010. "Tool Shock: Technique and Epistemology in the Postwar Social Sciences." In *The Unsocial Social Science? Economics and Neighboring Disciplines since 1945*, edited by Roger E. Backhouse and Philippe Fontaine. *History of Political Economy* 42 (supplement): 133–64.

Jardini, David R. 1996. "Out of the Blue Yonder: The RAND Corporation's Diversification into Social Welfare Research." PhD diss., Carnegie Mellon University.

Klein, Judy L. 2000. "Economics for a Client: The Case of Statistical Quality Control and Sequential Analysis." In *Toward a History of Applied Mathematics*, edited by Roger E. Backhouse and Jeff Biddle. *History of Political Economy* 32 (supplement): 25–70.

Klein, Judy L. 2007. "Rules of Action for War and Recursive Optimization: Massée's 'Jeu des Réservoirs' and Arrow, Harris, and Marschak's 'Optimal Inventory Policy.'" citeseerx.ist.psu.edu/viewdoc/download?doi=10.1.1.416.2140&rep=rep1&type=pdf.

MacKenzie, Donald. 2006. *An Engine, Not a Camera: How Financial Models Shape Markets*. Cambridge, MA: MIT Press.

McGarry, Brendan W., and Heidi M. Peters. 2018. "Defense Primer: Planning, Programming, Budgeting and Execution (PPBE) Process." Congressional Research Service, In Focus, IF10429.

Mirowski, Philip. 2002. *Machine Dreams: Economics Becomes a Cyborg Science.* Cambridge: Cambridge University Press.

Mirowski, Philip, and Edward Nik-Khah. 2017. *The Knowledge We Have Lost in Information: The History of Information in Modern Economics.* Oxford: Oxford University Press.

Quade, E. S. 1953. "The Proposed RAND Course in Systems Analysis." RAND Document D-1991. RAND Corporation Library, Santa Monica, California.

Quade, E. S., and M. W. Hoag. 1954. "An Outline for the Proposed Course in the Appreciation of Systems Analysis." RAND Document D-2132. RAND Corporation Library, Santa Monica, California.

Quade, E. S., ed. 1964. *Analysis for Military Decisions.* Chicago: Rand McNally.

Thomas, William. 2015. *Rational Action: The Sciences of Policy in Britain and America, 1940–1960.* Cambridge, MA: MIT Press.

Weintraub, E. Roy. 2002. *How Economics Became a Mathematical Science.* Durham, NC: Duke University Press.

Young, Stephanie Caroline. 2010. "Power and the Purse: Defense Budgeting and American Politics, 1947–1972." PhD diss., University of California, Berkeley.

# Guy H. Orcutt's Engineering Microsimulation to Reengineer Society

Chung-Tang Cheng

> As soon as we introduce "synthesis" as well as "artifice," we enter
> the realm of engineering. For "synthetic" is often used in the broader
> sense of "designed" or "composed." We speak of engineering as
> concerned with "synthesis," while science is concerned with "analysis."
> —Herbert Simon, The Sciences of the Artificial (1969)

> I thought, "If you could represent a real population with a real sample,
> why couldn't we represent a theoretical population with a synthetic sample?
> Why couldn't we have a real sample representation of the real population
> at the start, and then move forward in time according to behavioral
> relationships applied to micro entities?" The sample no longer
> was real, once I started moving it. It was a synthetic one.
> —Guy Orcutt, interview with Duo Qin (1988)

Nowadays, microanalytic simulation (henceforth microsimulation) is widely applied by different government agencies and academic institutions to understand the consequences of demographic, tax, welfare, health, and redistributive policies.[1] Examples encompass the Policy Simulation

I would like to thank Mary Morgan, the special issue editors, two anonymous referees, and the participants at the 2019 *HOPE* Conference, for their invaluable suggestions. I am indebted to Duo Qin, who generously shared her interview notes with me. I am also grateful to Juan Acosta and Greta Seibel for their helpful comments at different phases of this work.

1. Even though they started off from different pasts, microsimulation is now often connected with "agent-based modeling," a more recent project in the economics toolbox. Developers of agent-based modeling also see microsimulation as their precursor—see, for instance, Gallegati, Palestrini, and Russo 2017: 15–17.

*History of Political Economy* 52 (annual suppl.)  DOI 10.1215/00182702-8718000

Model owned and used by the British Department for Work and Pensions, the EUROMOD, which analyzes tax-benefit policies of the European Union, and the Urban-Brookings Microsimulation Model constructed by the US Tax Policy Center. The Urban Institute played a crucial role in developing this technique for US policy evaluations. As a think tank founded in 1968 in the wake of Lyndon B. Johnson's War on Poverty, the institute's research centered on urban problems and the efficacy of federal welfare programs, for which it built simulation programs in cooperation with other agencies. During the early 1990s, microsimulation has been an essential policymaking tool for the federal government (Citro and Hanushek 1991: 1–2).[2] In 2019, the institute used six microsimulation programs, which span different policy areas from health insurance, transfer income, and social security benefit to social mobility.

Despite widely applied in policymaking, microsimulation as an empirical technique and its history in economics are still not sufficiently explored. Following Morgan's (2004; 2012, chap. 8) rediscovery, a key name to the story was Guy Orcutt, who first conceptualized economic microsimulation and implemented it back in the 1950s (Orcutt 1957, 1960; Orcutt et al. 1961). Orcutt also played a pivotal role in bringing microsimulation to the Urban Institute in the 1970s and served as the chief coordinator in developing one of its simulation programs, the Dynamic Simulation of Income Model (DYNASIM; Orcutt, Caldwell, and Wertheimer 1976). However, while Orcutt is more often remembered as an econometrician for his co-creation of the Cochrane-Orcutt estimator (Cochrane and Orcutt 1949), his more important role in the development of microsimulation has received little attention.

The story of Orcutt's microsimulation began with his background in engineering and physics and his fascination with Jan Tinbergen's approach. With these in mind, two senses of economic engineering were interconnected with Orcutt's career. First, based on his early attempt to design an electric calculation machine called the "regression analyser" (Orcutt 1948a), he developed the view that considering the national economy as an engineering feedback-loop could potentially solve the methodological pitfalls of the Cowles Commission approach. In that sense, Orcutt's first microsimulation, which he finished in 1961, was a rigorous start to take an engineering perspective to the analysis and synthesis of

2. Others are large-scale macroeconomic models, single-equation time-series models, cell-based models of population groups, econometric models of individual behavior, and large-scale microsimulation models.

the *socioeconomic system*. Second, microsimulation regained government attention in the late 1960s when an epistemic demand for program evaluation emerged. In retrospect, the 1976 DYNASIM was designed with the expectation that policymakers could use the simulation program for the purpose of *socioeconomic engineering*, for example, to decide which wage policies would efficiently reduce gender-wage gaps or to estimate the future caseload of welfare programs. Eventually, microsimulation developed from a product of Orcutt's dream to build an engineering Tinbergen-style model into an empirical tool used by practitioners to reengineer society.

## Orcutt's "Tinbergen Dream" and the Birth of Microsimulation in Economics

Guy Henderson Orcutt (1917–2006) was born in Homer, a small town in Michigan. As the son of a superintendent of electrical engineering at Michigan Alkali Company, he became interested in designing experiments with electronic circuits during his teenage years. After first enrolling in an engineering major at the University of Michigan, he switched to physics and mathematics. Orcutt graduated in 1939 and then stayed in Michigan to pursue the graduate degree in economics under the supervision of Arthur Smithies. Lacking an economics degree, the economics department required Orcutt to take five undergraduate economics courses in his first semester. In these courses, Orcutt met James Duesenberry, one of the class teachers and an advisee of Smithies. They soon developed a close friendship, along with fellow student Daniel Suits. Orcutt (1990: 7) recalled these stimulating friendships as "an enormous help to me in developing a commitment to my new field and in broadening and deepening my rather limited understanding of economic theory."

Building on his interest in engineering and his training in physics, Orcutt began to develop the idea of building an analog computational machine during his doctoral years, which he called the "regression analyser" (RA). The RA was designed as a combination of electrical circuits and resistances, in which both input and output were measured by voltmeters. Thus, when inputs varied, outputs could be calculated through its specific electrical properties. Initially, the prototype of the RA was the result of Orcutt's attempt to obtain numerical solutions in duopoly and spatial economic models. Later when his interest shifted from economic theory to econometrics, the prototype was applied to calculate regression coefficients. He started to engage with econometrics under the guidance of Smithies, who introduced him to the works of Eugen Slutsky, Trygve Haavelmo, and Jan Tinbergen. Among these canonical works, Orcutt was most fascinated by Tinbergen's (1939) macroeconomic modeling of the US national economy and was eager to pursue a Tinbergen-style approach. In this sense for Orcutt, designing the RA was not only to perform numerical calculations; he also believed that through the aid of a properly designed machine, he could create a large-scale socioeconomic system. Orcutt never lost this "Tinbergen dream"; later in life he reflected: "I always had the dream of doing something like Tinbergen did, to build a model which could cover all the system. I still have it."[3]

Despite proposing the preliminary design in his 1944 doctoral thesis "Statistical Methods and Tools for Finding Natural Laws in the Field of Economics," Orcutt had only finished the first workable version of the RA during his first employment at the Massachusetts Institute of Technology (1944–46). The building works were facilitated by the mathematics professor George Wadsworth and his laboratory as part of a weather-forecasting project for the US Army Air Forces. The size of the RA was about twelve by eighteen by twenty-four inches, with an oscilloscope for plotting scatter diagrams.[4] The RA accommodated up to three time series, with each up to thirty observations (Orcutt 1990: 10), and required forty to sixty seconds to calculate one simple regression.[5] The demonstration of this new machine took place at the 1945 annual Christmas meeting of the Econometric Society.[6]

During the summer of 1945, after Smithies's introduction, Orcutt wrote a research statement to Richard Stone, who was looking for new faculty members for the Department of Applied Economics (DAE) at the University of Cambridge.[7] The letter enclosed two proposals, one for his regression machine and its potentiality in applied economics and one for a "sampling experiment" to find a satisfactory test of significance for economic data. The idea of the latter was whether "what to expect by chance on the frequency distribution of correlations obtained between non-related

3. Duo Qin, interview with Guy Orcutt, 1988, summary, personal communication.

4. For the pictures, see Orcutt 1948a: 64, 69.

5. Orcutt to Stone, May 15, 1946, JRNS/3/1/96, Papers of John Richard Nicholas Stone, King's College Archive Centre, University of Cambridge. Hereafter cited as JRNS.

6. Since the 1950s, several machines were sequentially invented for modeling the economic system. Orcutt's RA finished in 1945 was a rather early attempt but only in calculations. For a history of using analog computers in economics, see Backhouse and Cherrier 2017.

7. Orcutt to Stone, August 22, 1945, JRNS.

series" could "exhibit the properties of continuity which we believe our real series to have."[8] Coming from the statistical tradition of Cambridge, Stone was sympathetic to Orcutt's proposal, which fit into the "English" sampling experiment.[9] He was also convinced that RA's emphasis on better computational efficiency would ultimately bring "immense value" to the DAE.[10] Therefore, when Stone went to visit Princeton for the following academic year, he stopped by MIT to meet Orcutt, and shortly after made him an offer as a senior researcher for the DAE. On November 1946, with his family and machine, Orcutt arrived at the University of Cambridge.

These years in the UK indeed proved worthwhile for Orcutt (1990: 10), who later remembered this period as "two of the most intellectually stimulating and productive years." Until 1948, he worked on the two original proposals along with statisticians and econometricians, including Stone, Roy C. Geary, Maurice G. Kendall, Maurice H. Quenouille, and Herman Wold. Four journal articles in time-series econometrics were published, in which the improved RA (Orcutt 1948a) had done most of the calculations. As Orcutt "was thinking very much of Tinbergen,"[11] his first published paper examined the autoregressive nature of Tinbergen's fifty-two economic time series. He concluded that an AR(2) model could best approximate the US economic time series (Orcutt 1948b; Qin and Gilbert 2001: 432–33). Then, using that AR(2) model, Orcutt and James (1948) generated a quasi-Tinbergen series with random numbers to test their correlations with the original series but found limited evidence on their statistical compatibility. The paper conjectured that a small sample and nonexperimental data like Tinbergen's series needed adjustments to eliminate its nonrandomness of the error term. Accordingly, the Cochrane-Orcutt transformation procedure was developed to improve biased least-square estimations (Cochrane and Orcutt 1949; Orcutt and Cochrane 1949).[12]

Orcutt joined Harvard in the fall of 1949, where he spent nine years mostly as an assistant professor. Since then, his econometric work in the

8. Chapter 3 of Orcutt's 1944 thesis tackled this idea without any empirical investigation, where he cited the Cambridge statistician G. U. Yule's (1926) "spurious correlation" as the primary reference of serial correlation (Orcutt 1944: 52). By then, he had also recognized the difference between economic series and random series through reading Slutsky's (1937) work on random summation (Qin, interview with Orcutt, 6).

9. This sampling-experiment tradition could be traced back to Yule 1927. His successors also inherited the notion and used random sampling technique to capture the behavior of time-series data. For a history of Yule's work, see Morgan 1990: chap. 3.1.

10. Stone to F. W. Lawfield, November 11, 1946, JRNS.

11. Qin, interview with Orcutt, personal communication.

12. For further discussions, see Epstein 1987: 146–47 and Qin and Gilbert 2001: 432–34.

UK, especially the Cochrane-Orcutt transformation, has become one of the "classics" among econometricians.[13] Based on his previous discovery on Tinbergen's data series, he turned increasingly critical of the Cowles Commission approach, which was mainly characterized by the simultaneous equation modeling (SEM) technique by T. C. Koopmans (1950) and its empirical exploration by Lawrence Klein (1950). Up till 1955, Orcutt wrote seven book reviews; two of them critically assessed the works of Koopmans and Klein (Orcutt 1951, 1952), by then accepted as Tinbergen's intellectual successors. With little empirical work but abundant reflective writings, the young Harvard econometrician began to question the usefulness of the SEM framework and aggregate-level information for policy evaluation. He found that a new empirical method was needed in modeling the national economy to solve those methodological pitfalls to reframe his "Tinbergen dream."

Orcutt elaborated his criticism of the Cowles paradigm through working on problems of *data*, *experiment*, and *recursivity*. First, he felt that aggregate economic time series suffered from insufficient information in either fulfilling statistical efficiency or exposing economic dynamics. He thus turned to endorse the need of searching for an alternative and credible data source, for instance, micro-level data (Orcutt 1951: 263).[14] Second, as predictions from the Cowles approach were based on multiple series of passive observation, it prevented model builders and policymakers from performing real experiments. By taking an analogy of experiments in electrical engineering, Orcutt (1952: 166) pessimistically elaborated this point: hoping to understand economic structures through the SEM framework "is somewhat analogous to that of giving a radio to a physicist and asking him to determine the operating characteristics of each component part merely by observing the radio as it plays but without being able in any way to take it apart or rearrange its circuits or perform experiments on it." In this view, the proper model of a national economy should have opened a possibility for socioeconomic engineers to design an actual experiment to unveil the structure of an economic system,[15]

13. Qin, interview with Orcutt, personal communication.

14. Around then, there were extensive empirical works identifying consumption structures using family expenditure surveys. For historical reviews in this literature, see Stigler 1954 and Thomas 1989. However, while these econometric works targeted solely the estimation of Keynesian consumption function, Orcutt's belief in the usage of micro-level data was more about applying it to construct a model of the macroeconomy. This pointed to the "aggregation problem" which is addressed later.

15. This idea implied that a properly designed machine could be isomorphic to an economic system fits into cybernetics literature of that time, although Orcutt did not use the phrase explicitly.

rather than merely provide observations without delving into micro-level entities. Third, influenced by Tinbergen and Wold, Orcutt believed that a model of the national economy must be recursive, so that the output was determined sequentially but not simultaneously (Morgan 2012: 318).[16] Those justifications not only characterized Orcutt's unease with the Cowles methodology but also signaled his turn to look for a micro-founded alternative later in the mid-1950s. However, until 1955, he still struggled with formulating a micro-founded analysis of national economy, since "there simply was no known way of satisfactorily aggregating relations about microcomponents into macroeconomic relations" (Orcutt 1990: 15).[17]

In 1956, Orcutt finally found the solution at his alma mater when he spent a summer fellowship at the Survey Research Center (SRC) of the University of Michigan. Benefiting from interactions with members such as James Morgan and another frequent visitor, James Tobin,[18] he came to understand the SRC's Survey of Consumer Finance as an excellent source of micro-level data that could be used to represent the real population. Furthermore, with representative samples, the Monte Carlo method could be applied to aggregate those micro-relationships.[19] This conceptualized methodological framework became realizable as a result of the progress made in high-speed digital computers. Starting from 1956, Orcutt served as Harvard Representative at the Computational Center for the New England College and Universities. After he had a chance to program the newest IBM 704 in this IBM-financed center, he knew that increasing computer capability could be the solution to the huge computational burden, as he recalled, "the concept of micro entities came to me much earlier, but it was until then I felt it was [sic] computationally feasible."[20]

16. Qin, interview with Orcutt, personal communication. For Wold's idea on recursiveness, see Morgan 1991.

17. Orcutt referred this to "a serious aggregation problem," as he was more concerned about the *empirical* validity when summing micro-level information into a representative macro scale. He was not, however, involved in the concurrent discussions on microfoundations in macroeconomics, which questioned the micro-macro relationship of Keynesian models and its *theoretical* root of economic agents, e.g., Lawrence Klein's aggregation program elaborated in Hoover 2012.

18 Both Morgan and Tobin had already worked on the SRC data since the early 1950s.

19 The Monte Carlo method has two roots, first, the 1920s English sampling experiments, and second, the 1940s postwar Thermonuclear Weaponry "H-bomb" project. While Orcutt was immersed in the former, he probably took the term *Monte Carlo* from the first academic paper on the Monte Carlo method by Los Alamos Laboratory (Metropolis and Ulam 1949), published in the same *Journal of the American Statistical Association* issue as Orcutt and Cochrane 1949.

20. Qin, interview with Orcutt, personal communication.

**First Trial: The 1961 Demographic
Microsimulation**

In 1957, Orcutt embarked on his first effort in microanalytic modeling
with his Harvard PhD students Martin Greenberger, John Korbel, and
Alice Rivlin. The new method—microsimulation—was introduced following two general accounts (Orcutt 1957, 1960) and was illustrated in the
final product: *Microanalysis of Socioeconomic Systems: A Simulation
Study* (Orcutt et al. 1961). Using the 1950 US population census and SRC's
1955 household surveys, this study formalized 4,580 US households
(10,358 individuals) as the initial population and then simulated their
aggregate trajectories of births, deaths, marriages, and divorces during
1950–60.[21] Each individual, called a "decision-making unit," would make
a demographic decision, based on different exogenous "status variables"
(e.g., sex, race, age) subject to a probability measure that was also specified based on the population census. The relationships between the probability measure and status variables were called the "operating characteristics" (OC). According to the OC, each individual with status variables
would be mapped to a probability measure presenting the likelihood of
actual behavior. As an example, Orcutt explained this concept through a
simple case of mortality rate. Suppose a specified probability of death
next month of a white man aged thirty-four years and seven months was
$P(male, white, 34y7m) = 0.0002$.

In this case, as the simulation started, this white man was drawn randomly to die by a chance of 0.02 percent. Otherwise, he had a 99.98 percent
chance of survival to the next month and reacted again to another mortality
measure $P(male, white, 34y8m)$. The process would repeat until the simulation ended. This study then aggregated the outcome of all such synthesized
individuals to obtain the "national" level.

In other words, the study consisted of three steps: *the OC, initial population*, and *the Monte Carlo method*. Through linear regressions, the US
population census was used to specify the OCs, that is, to calculate the
expected probability of death, birth, marriage, and divorce every month
for different groups of age, sex, and race. After a statistically representative population was constructed for April 1950 to April 1960, a monthly
demographic "event" would be designated to every individual through the
Markov process. During the event, the computer would generate a uni-

---

21. The simulation took about 150 hours on an IBM 704; for that, the computing hours were
guaranteed mostly from the New England College and Universities at MIT and the Littauer
Statistical Laboratory at Harvard.

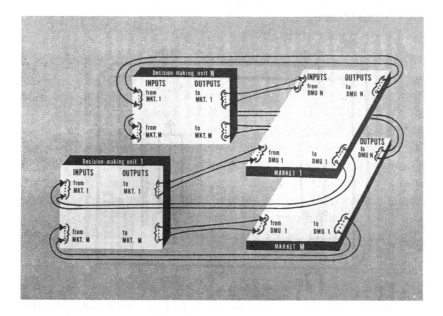

**Figure 1** The incomplete flow diagram of an economic system in microsimulation (Orcutt et al. 1961: 28)

form-distributed pseudo-random number from zero to one for every individual. The event was determined to happen if the generated number was smaller than the expected probability derived from the OC. This entire procedure of Monte Carlo method was designed and assembled by Greenberger, who also wrote the "random number generator" program to serve the task of the Markov process.

Based on the simple recipe above, a microsimulation framework contained a crucial assumption that the national economy could be disaggregated into micro-level behaviors and vice versa. Orcutt illustrated this idea by adopting an electric-engineering analogy in figure 1. The socioeconomic system could be presented as a closed feedback-loop that was "wired" by those inputs and outputs of markets and decision-making units. A decision-making unit under predetermined status variables would flow into a market and then process by the OC. The processed outcome would flow out as the input of that decision-making unit next period. In this sense, Orcutt emphasized that a microsimulation model was recursive: "There is no simultaneous interaction between units, and hence there are no simultaneous equations involving more than one unit at a time to be solved" (Orcutt et al. 1961: 26).

## Coming to Wisconsin:
## Social Systems Research Institute

In 1958, after a one-year initiation of microsimulation, Orcutt became more and more "restless" due not only to his rather slow promotion at Harvard but also to his desire for more resources for his grand project.[22] This was when Edwin Young, chairman of the economics department at the University of Wisconsin, offered Orcutt an excellent opportunity. By then the junior Wisconsin institutionalist was concerned that his home institution might deteriorate into a "third-rate department" due to the retirements of senior professors.[23] In response to the expected shortage, the recruitment committee decided to hire an "imaginative theorist-econometrician" who could bring the department a "renaissance" (Johnson 1993: 142). As such, Orcutt appeared to be on the top of the list after several discussions between Young and Peter Steiner, a Harvard alumni and young assistant professor recruited in 1957.[24] Young acquired a five-year grant of one hundred thousand dollars from the Wisconsin Alumni Research Foundation (WARF) to persuade Orcutt to come to Wisconsin, with the appealing offer that allowed him to establish a research center focusing on microsimulation.[25] After Young's visit to Harvard, Orcutt gave up his tenured professorship and moved to Madison with a doubled salary.[26]

The arrival of the Harvard econometrician sparked hope for departmental revival from the new recruitments: not only did a Harvard econometrician, Jack Johnston, and Orcutt's co-author Korbel follow him to Wisconsin, but his reputation also attracted many talented academics over the next few years, including Arthur Goldberger, Arnold Zellner, Martin

22. Laura Smail, interview with Edwin Young, 1978, 1981, transcript, Oral History Program, University Archives and Records Management Services, Madison, University of Wisconsin. Hereafter cited as OHP.

23. Smail, interview with Young, 1978, OHP.

24. Another key person who suggested Orcutt to Young was Sumner Slichter, who also knew Orcutt from Harvard.

25. At first, the WARF money was guaranteed mostly for natural science research. After Fred Harrington, a historian and a "rigorous proponent of social research," became assistant to President E. B. Fred in 1956, the WARF eventually began to allocate part of its budget to social science research (Solovey 1993).

26. Seymour Harris (1958), head of the economics department at Harvard, wrote to the *New York Times* about Orcutt's departure, "Many of the public universities are doing a splendid job and gaining in quality and prestige relative to private institutions. Last [academic] year one diverted a first-class economist from Harvard at double his Harvard salary." Young was typically impressed by Harris's complaint, "a place, no, kind of place like Wisconsin can take somebody away from Harvard. . . . They were really upset. . . . They didn't want to lose him" (Smail, interview with Young, 1981, OHP).

David, Charles Holt, Jan Kmenta, and Harold Watts. Outside the economics department, Orcutt helped to establish the statistics department by hiring the first chairman, George Box, in 1960 and by developing the new computer science department, where he served as an early faculty member (Orcutt 1990: 18). As Robert Lampman (1993: 145) lauded, "Bringing Guy Orcutt from Harvard—clearly the signal event in rebuilding the department—was parallel to bringing Richard T. Ely from Hopkins [in 1892]; in both cases the university announced an intention to invest heavily in the social studies. In each case the announcement was followed by a great burst of energy and new ideas."

In the fall of 1959, following by the launch of the Social Systems Research Institute (SSRI) at Wisconsin, Orcutt became the founding director. The aim of this new center was twofold. First was to build a compact microsimulation of the United States, an extension of Orcutt's dream. Second was to emulate the institutional model of the Institute of Social Research at Michigan;[27] Orcutt wanted the SSRI to act as a "holding company" of quantitative social sciences as well as an "umbrella institute" in mediating interdisciplinary researches.[28] Therefore, he tried to incorporate members from diverse backgrounds outside economics, such as sociology, anthropology, political science, regional and urban planning, and statistics. This goal was also reflected in its institutional structure. Initially, the institute started with a three-workshop system that turned into three research centers in 1962: the Systems Formulation and Methodology Center (led by Zellner), the Center for Household and Labor Market Research (led by Goldberger and later David), and the Center for Research on the Firms and Market (led by Steiner). Meanwhile, four new centers were also established: Research Policy and Operations (led by Holt), Financial and Fiscal Research, Social Behavior Research, and Demography and Ecology (SSRI 1963). Depending on their expertise, members of the SSRI were free to affiliate their memberships with those research centers focusing on complementary tasks. Each center also enjoyed its autonomy to organize research seminars and working paper series.

Since constructing a microanalytic model and doing quantitative social sciences required enormous computer power to handle the data work, Orcutt emphasized advancing the research infrastructure accordingly. As he put it, "Electronic computers are of tremendous importance in modern research in the social sciences. . . . The SSRI seeks to bridge the rather

27. Laura Smail, interview with Guy Orcutt, 1988, digital audio file, two tapes, OHP.
28. Laura Smail, interview with Martin David, 1981, digital audio file, two tapes, OHP.

large gap between social science and computer technology by maintaining a sizable staff of professional and student programmers" (SSRI 1963: 5). During 1962–63, over 40 percent of the budget was used to hire programmers and update contemporary computational devices such as the IBM 1460 and the CDC 3600.[29] In the spring of 1963, the Data Library was established to maintain all data on magnet tapes, which guaranteed its readability and accessibility.[30] Furthermore, inspired by Michigan's paradigm, the Wisconsin Survey Research Laboratory was established to conduct regional surveys through statewide interviews.

## Orcutt's Struggle at the SSRI

With capable econometricians, advanced computers, and a data and survey center, Orcutt's situation seemed ideal. Following the publication of his 1961 book on microsimulation, he moved to extend the microanalytic model to household behavior, that is, to identify the operating characteristics of household spending and consumption. During 1963–64, the research group contained two subgroups, one on the labor force and earning behavior led by Korbel and David, and one on the consumer and portfolio behavior led by Goldberger and Zellner (SSRI 1963: 8). Goldberger worked on the statistical nature of household expenditure on durable goods by analyzing Michigan's Survey of Consumer Finances (SCF). In the progress report presented at the 1961 annual AEA meeting, Goldberger and Lee (1962) found a stable pattern of household durable goods consumption using SCF data for 1951–60. They concluded that the reinterview of SCF and a new consumer survey conducted by the Wisconsin Survey Research Laboratory would provide useful references to specify the behavioral model of the household sector.

Orcutt (1962) presented a paper in the same 1961 AEA session, in which he argued for the need for microsimulation in economics. While reiterating its potential, he voiced a pragmatic concern that at most ten million dollars of governmental budgets per year should be allocated to his approach, while he predicted that the return to the country would "easily" be a billion dollars (240). Such emphasis reflected Orcutt's pressing need for external funding: the first-round WARF money would end in 1963, and therefore he had to seek other soft money to keep his project alive and to preserve the institute's autonomy.[31] From 1960 onward the

29. Author's calculation from SSRI 1963: 97.
30. See SSRI 1963: 7.
31. For Orcutt's struggle for funds, see Solovey 1993.

SSRI also received research grants from the National Science Foundation, the Ford Foundation, and the Brookings Institution, in addition to the WARF money. Among those grants, the three-year fund (1961–64) of $400,000 from the Ford Foundation was the most significant relief. During 1962–63, the Ford grant of $135,000 covered almost half of the annual budget of the SSRI (1963: 99).[32] Naturally, the biggest sponsor was expecting results from this huge investment, and Orcutt as principal investigator inevitably faced pressure to ensure sufficient research progress.

Around the first half of 1964, Orcutt and his research team finally began a big push to assemble household data into a computerized model.[33] However, the results were too unsatisfying to produce a workable program for the household sector. While progress stagnated, core members such as Zellner and Goldberger gradually focused on their econometric works instead of making the microsimulation practicable, as David recalled:

> Zellner concentrated a great deal of effort in trying to do we would call it a "cohort analysis" of data on households in which one would try to combine information from surveys with time-series data to produce results of considerably more detail than the pathbreaking econometric models of the time. . . . Zellner was pursuing this more aggregated philosophy and eschewed the notion of simulation modelling at the micro-level, which was really Guy Orcutt's dream. . . . his direction kind of moved off from Guy's. . . . Goldberger became increasingly interested in estimation problems and the theory of how econometrics proceeded and did some consolidation of that field.[34]

Why did these deviations occur? Part of the reason was that under the institutional setting of the SSRI, members with their own priorities lacked incentives to stay on systematic goals. As Lampman observed, "In the University there is remarkably little discipline possible in forming teams. . . . Guy had in mind something like the Manhattan Project, which brought together a group of people of different disciplines and they all did fit into the plan sent down from the top. . . . That kind of discipline was perhaps possible there, but not in an ordinary university setting."[35] A top-down approach to push microsimulation would ultimately contradict the idea of

32. Since then, the microsimulation was renamed to the Project MUSE (Simulation Models of the United States Economy) joint project with the Ford Foundation.

33. Orcutt to Shubik, May 28, 1964, folder: 1964 (3 of 4), box 10, Martin Shubik Papers, David M. Rubenstein Rare Book and Manuscript Library, Duke University.

34. Laura Smail, interview with David, OHP.

35. Laura Smail, interview with Robert Lampman, 1981, transcript, OHP.

the SSRI as a decentralized "umbrella" institute in which the university rather than the SSRI hired most of the affiliates. It was thus inevitable that he would confront a management problem, with staff members prioritizing their own research. In the end, Orcutt was disappointed by his research team's loss of interest in realizing microsimulation, instead researching what he considered "tangential products."[36] After 1964, his frustration became even more severe after the modest progress did not convince the Ford Foundation, which later withdrew its financial support. In 1964–65, Ford's extended grant had decreased to thirty-six thousand dollars without extension for the next year (SSRI 1965: 25). From 1965, under the new directorship of Holt, who shifted the institute's approach toward a more interdisciplinary focus, the microsimulation project was almost abandoned.[37] Since then, Orcutt was exhausted from fund-raising and administrative duties that confined the progress of microsimulation. After spending a year back at Harvard as visiting professor during 1965–66, he was determined to resign in 1966 "with deep regret" (Orcutt 1990: 19).

In retrospect, three reasons explain why Orcutt's vigorous attempt of microsimulation at Wisconsin did not succeed. First, as he noted in the final Ford report, the lack of "unrestricted, long-run support" had suffocated the SSRI and turned staff into "fund-raisers" (Solovey 1993: 183). Orcutt's complaint echoes what Martin David judged as him having "underestimated the enormous task."[38] The soft money from the Ford Foundation and the National Science Foundation was far less than Orcutt expected. For instance, while the SSRI gained a Ford grant for $400,000 in 1961, he had initially asked for $2.6 million in total from the Ford and NSF.[39] This financial shortage became even more pressing after the economics department failed to keep Zellner from departing for the University of Chicago in 1966. As Orcutt recalled, he started to worry about the "dim future" for his dream after losing the star econometrician, which truly harmed the SRRI in its ability to raise research funds from the university.[40]

Second, as Orcutt admitted, "the main difficulty was programming."[41] Unlike Harvard, the SSRI did not have a crucial programming technician

36. Smail, interview with David, OHP.

37. By then, Assistant to Chancellor Barbara Newell wrote to Chancellor Robben Fleming, saying that Holt was "very anxious" about the SSRI failing to serve its interdisciplinary task, and Orcutt "will not have a strong role in SSRI" (Smail, interview with Lampman, OHP).

38. Smail, interview with David, OHP.

39. Smail, interview with Orcutt, OHP.

40. Orcutt thought Zellner one of the "best at raising funds" (Smail, interview with Orcutt, OHP).

41. All quotations in this paragraph are from Smail, interview with Orcutt, OHP.

such as Greenberger, who in the 1961 microsimulation managed the entire simulation program by hiring staff to assemble the data into the computer. Despite the significant funds invested into acquiring capable computers and hiring programming staff, the project still lacked a suitable leader to integrate this infrastructure. He reflected, "We didn't have the muscle with respect to implementing it. . . . I never was able to find somebody who had enough capability to replace Martin Greenberger until later." Although he was desperate to bring Greenberger to Wisconsin, such efforts did not go as planned after Greenberger accepted the offer from MIT.

Third, another external explanation was the existence of an alternative paradigm, especially the contrasting approaches between Orcutt and Holt in the SSRI, as Lampman astutely observed: "They [Orcutt and Holt] were, in some sense, closer to engineering than to economics. The whole systems analyst approach is at some tangent to the mainline of economics. . . . It is much more a mechanistic, I guess I would put it, a mechanistic approach to economic phenomena."[42]

Despite sharing similar ideas on economic engineering, Orcutt and Holt applied quite different methodologies to modeling the national economy. Since the 1960s, empirical macroeconomics moved on from the Klein-Goldberger model to the Social Science Research Council (SSRC) model,[43] and by then, Holt was the primary developer of its computer program. Conversely, the microsimulation approach, in contrast to the SSRC model, was built on Orcutt's distrust of the Cowles aggregate methodology. Presumably, the SSRC model's growing reputation in evaluating policies pressured Orcutt to show that microsimulation could outperform it. This competitive nexus was implicitly addressed by Robert Summers when he challenged Orcutt's demand for governmental funds in the 1961 AEA meeting:

> The savings the economy might achieve with a successful model are indeed breathtaking, but there are lots of ways of saving large sums of money in a 525 billion dollar GNP economy where the federal budget is 90-odd billion. I am firmly of the view that there are many areas where the rate of return on the services of social scientists would be greater than that of the Wisconsin project when the actuarial risk of no-success is taken into account. (Summers, Suits, and Dingle 1962: 252)

42. Smail, interview with Lampman, OHP.
43. For a dynamic simulation of the Klein-Goldberger model, see Adelman and Adelman 1959.

Summer's unwillingness to support Orcutt's project reflected a common perception of microsimulation in the profession: why did governments need to risk investing money in a dicey microsimulation when there was a cheaper bundle of alternative models? Given that the SSRC model provided a cheaper and solvable alternative, Orcutt's project, which required an immense budget and time, seemed less worthwhile. Such contrast not only explained why, by then, mainstream economists were less keen on microsimulation, but perhaps substantiated why the Ford Foundation eventually lost patience and withdrew the funds.

### Urban Institute and the 1976 DYNASIM

On April 26, 1968, President Lyndon B. Johnson, in line with his War on Poverty, announced the launch of the Urban Institute in Washington, DC—a new think tank for the federal government to "renew our cities and transform the lives of people."[44] Based on the institutional model of RAND Corporation, the aim of this nonprofit quasi-governmental cooperation concentrated on urban problems such as poverty, housing, transportation, and education and provided solutions through technical assistances (Lindsay 1968: 1220; "Urban Institute" 1968: 368). William Gorham became the founding president and chief executive officer.[45] As a new RAND, the institute gathered researchers from different backgrounds, such as administrators, economists, city planners, operations analysts, architects, and engineers, to work on scientific analysis of policy implementation in urban areas (*Political Science* 1968: 13). Financially, the institute would receive 80 percent of funds from the US government and 20 percent from the Ford Foundation (Rosoff 1969: 20).[46] The support from the federal agencies was scheduled to be five million dollars for 1968 and expected to be ten to fifteen million dollars in the future (*Political Science* 1968: 13).

On Gorham's invitation, Orcutt joined the Urban Institute in 1968. During 1969–70, he went to Yale University as a visiting professor. In the

44. Lyndon B. Johnson, remarks at a meeting with the Board of Trustees of the Urban Institute, Gerhard Peters and John T. Woolley, American Presidency Project, University of California, Santa Barbara, www.presidency.ucsb.edu.

45. William Gorham (1930–) was a former staff member of the RAND Corporation during 1953–62, former assistant secretary of Department of Defense (1962–65) and of Department of Health, Education and Welfare (1965–68), president of the institute until 2000.

46. Leading sponsors included the Office of Economic Opportunity, the Department of Health, Education and Welfare, the National Science Foundation, and the Treasury Department.

summer of 1970, he was appointed by Yale as professor of economics and A. Whitney Griswold Professor of Urban Studies, where he stayed until his retirement in 1988. Until the new microsimulation project finished in 1976, he kept equivalent work duties between Yale and the institute in Washington.

With the massive financial injection from the federal government, Orcutt was able to continue his microanalytic modeling on the household sector at the Urban Institute—this time able to form an integrated team like the Manhattan Project, which included administrators, academics, and programmers, with the aid of improved high-speed computers. The new microsimulation project began in the fall of 1969 under the codirection of Orcutt and Harold Guthrie, and Orcutt served as the only full-time project director from 1972. After the frustration at Wisconsin, Orcutt's dream finally got adequate attention and funds from the government. The Urban Institute provided a perfect place to carry on his dream.[47]

The harvest of this project after seven years was *Policy Exploration through Microanalytic Simulation*, which presented the Dynamic Simulation of Income Model of the United States (Orcutt, Caldwell, and Wertheimer 1976).[48] DYNASIM was built on a PDP-10 computer at the Brookings Institution through the computer program MASH (Microanalytic Simulation of Households) designed by George Sadowsky.[49] As presented

47. Since 1968, the SRC published the first Panel Studies of Income Dynamics (PSID), which offered a more comprehensive survey on household income and was also used in the new project.

48. Apart from the main contributors Orcutt (main coordinator), Steven Caldwell (chap. 3 on death and immigration; chaps. 4–5 on family formation and dissolution; chap. 7 on geographic mobility; chap. 12 on demographic experiments), and Richard Wertheimer II (project manager; chap. 8 on labor sector; chap. 14 on women-wage experiments), the project also listed Steven Franklin (chap. 10 on income, wealth, and inheritance), Gary Hendricks (chap. 11 on Monte Carlo variability), Gerald Peabody (chap. 3 on birth; chap. 6 on education; chap. 13 on model interactions), James Smith (chap. 10), and Sheila Zedlewski (chap. 9 on disability and transfer payment; chap. 15 on divorce-on-income-distribution experiments). For those contents, see the discussions later.

49. For technical details of MASH, see Guthrie, et al. 1974: 126–37 and Sadowsky 1988. George Sadowsky (1936–) got a BA degree (1957) in mathematics from Harvard. As an expert in computer and programming, during 1962–65, he worked in the computer center and economics department at Yale for a year and then joined the graduate program in economics. His interest in microsimulation was stimulated by Orcutt's 1961 book and a course at Yale on gaming and simulation taught by Martin Shubik (Sadowsky 1988: iii–iv). During his graduate years, Sadowsky became a consultant to the Office of Tax Analysis of the US Treasury Department and introduced microsimulation to analyze the consequence of Revenue Act of 1964. In 1966, he went to the Brookings Institution and found the computer center where he was the first director. From 1970 to 1973, he moved to Urban Institute as senior research staff.

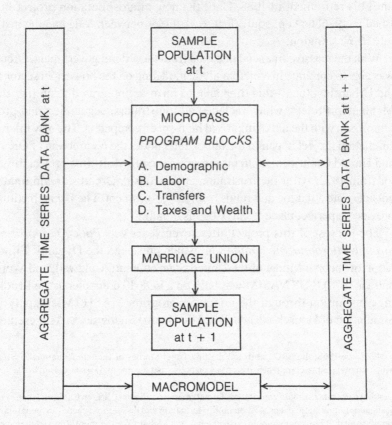

## RELATION OF MAJOR PROGRAM SECTORS TO UPDATING OF MICRO AND MACRO DATA FILES

**Figure 2**  The sectors of DYNASIM (Orcutt, Caldwell, and Wertheimer 1976: 28)

in figure 2, DYNASIM was modeled with three program sectors called "MICROPASS," "MARRIAGE UNION," and "MACROMODEL." These sectors were grouped into two routes: the up-down route demonstrated how population evolved through the MICROPASS and MARRIAGE UNION sector, and the left-right route accounted for the transition of aggregate economic time series by the MICROPASS and MACRO-MODEL sector. The former captured the simulated demographic trajectory of the total population, while the latter focused on the economic aspect of the decision-making units.

SCHEMATIC DESCRIPTION OF DYNASIM MACROMODEL

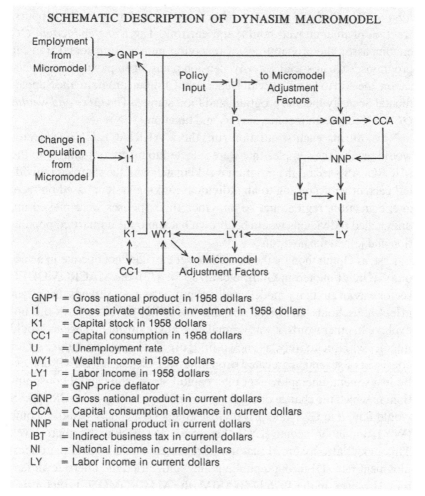

GNP1 = Gross national product in 1958 dollars
I1     = Gross private domestic investment in 1958 dollars
K1    = Capital stock in 1958 dollars
CC1   = Capital consumption in 1958 dollars
U      = Unemployment rate
WY1  = Wealth Income in 1958 dollars
LY1   = Labor Income in 1958 dollars
P      = GNP price deflator
GNP   = Gross national product in current dollars
CCA   = Capital consumption allowance in current dollars
NNP   = Net national product in current dollars
IBT    = Indirect business tax in current dollars
NI     = National income in current dollars
LY     = Labor income in current dollars

**Figure 3** The structure of MACROMODEL (Orcutt, Caldwell, and Wertheimer 1976: 37)

First, the MICROPASS sector contained four different blocks of operating characteristics, empirically specified from the US Vital Statistics, Current Population Survey, and the Panel Study of Income Dynamics from the University of Michigan. Those were demographic (chaps. 3–7), labor (chap. 8), transfer income (chap. 9), and taxes and wealth (chap. 10). The *demographic OC* considered birth, death, divorce, first marriage, remarriage as well as adding migration, disability, and education. The *labour OC* included wage rates, labor force participation, working hours, fraction of unemployed hours, and earning. The *transfer income OC* encompassed the probabilities of receiving money from social transfer programs, such as social security, pension plans, unemployment compensation, the Aid to Families with Dependent Children program, the Supplemental Security Income program, and food stamps. The *taxes and wealth OC* covered wealth income, saving, and taxation.[50]

Next, during each simulation run, the MARRIAGE UNION sector would receive the samples that were selected to marry or remarry in the MICROPASS sector, the program would match with the sampled individual each other according to an individual ranking system based on race, age, education, region, and so on. Once their spouses were picked up, unmatched individuals would be thrown back into the unmarried population and joined the next run.

Last, as Orcutt thought the household sector "does not operate in a vacuum" (Orcutt quoted in Guthrie et al. 1974: 113), the MACROMODEL sector was an auxiliary model used to capture the macro-trends that might affect households' decisions and that the MICROPASS sector did not explain. In other words, it was a simulation environment that agents would interact with recursively, as shown in figure 3. This macro-model sector consisted of several aggregated economic variables such as GNP, domestic investment, unemployment rate, capital stock, and capital consumption, in which the change of employment and population in MICROPASS would flow into GNP and private investment (I1), end as wealth income (WY1) and labor income (LY1), then again flow back to the micro-level. This model also assumed that the government could control the unemployment rate (U) through public policy and varied the micro-level factors. However, in the 1976 DYNASIM, the MACROMODEL sector was still developing and was not incorporated.

Based on this framework, five series of simulation experiments were performed, among which two of them concentrated on economic policy aspects.[51] One (chap. 14) examined how different labor-policy counterfactuals could eliminate gender-wage inequality. Three experimental scenarios were applied to square women's working conditions with men's: equal pay, equal hours, and equal hours and pay. After selecting a representative sample of four thousand people from the 1960 Census as an initial population, the trajectories of their incomes were simulated in a base run and then

50. Although specified, the 1976 DYNASIM did not include taxes and wealth OC.
51. Other series of experiments tested the possible errors of the Monte Carlo method (chap. 11), and population variations when the demographic OC altered (chaps. 12–13).

compared with three other experimental runs. The simulation results indicated that equalizing the wage between men and women would reshuffle the income redistributions from single men toward female-headed families, while increasing women's participation in the labor force would transfer a larger share of national income to husband-wife families (Orcutt, Caldwell, and Wertheimer 1974: 290–318). On the other hand, chapter 15 estimated the future cost of Aid to Families with Dependent Children (AFDC) program. Under the settings of a "static" and an "accelerating" divorce rate,[52] ten thousand representative samples from the 1970 Census were used to project the population dynamics and their incomes and earnings until 1984. Since 80 percent of AFDC recipients were female-headed families, from those predictions of population, the future financial caseload of AFDC program could be aggregated. This simulation showed that in 1984, the caseload of AFDC in the "accelerating" divorce-rate scene was estimated to be around a half million families larger than in the "static" scene (Orcutt, Caldwell, and Wertheimer 1976: 334).

## Microsimulation in Socioeconomic Engineering

Since President Johnson's War on Poverty, vast amounts of the federal budget were scheduled for this activist proposal, which was followed by a launch series of new program evaluation agencies, for example, the Office of Economic Opportunity in 1964; the Office of Assistant Secretary for Program Coordination (later renamed Planning and Evaluation) in 1965 in the Department of Health, Education, and Welfare; and the Urban Institute in 1968. It was often the case that those programs needed to be assessed quickly and systematically before their actual implementation so that the evidence could be used to convince Congress to pass annual budgets. As Orcutt observed, these evaluation officials were "dominated by quantitatively trained economists, many of whom had earlier engaged in systems analysis and operations research at the Department of Defense" (Orcutt et al. 1980: 81).[53] However, when this demand first appeared, contemporary statistical analysis could not serve this task. As Alice Rivlin (1971: 64) once concluded, without a credible analytic framework for understanding individual behaviors, statistical evaluations of education

52. The "static" divorce rate assumed the divorce rate was flat after 1974, and the "accelerating" divorce rate had 5 percent annual increment after 1974.

53. For instance, during that time William Gorham was assistant secretary for Program Coordination of the Department of Health, Education, and Welfare, and Alice Rivlin, Orcutt's former student and coauthor, was deputy assistant secretary and later assistant secretary.

programs still provided "discouraging" answers, as "the analysts can provide little useful information about the relative effectiveness of various educational methods or health delivery systems." This inadequacy thus induced a dilemma for the officials: they were encouraged to propose a reform while the consequences were mostly unknown. "They [administrators and social scientists] are afraid to admit that they do not know. And they may be wise. The Office of Economic Opportunity might have told Congress: 'We don't know whether preschool programs will work, or what kind would be best, but we have designed a program to find out.' But would they then have gotten the money?" (85).

During this period of dilemma, microsimulation technique was almost absent in program evaluations and underdeveloped because the higher-level officials who supervised the research budget were dubious about its financial viability and data accessibility. As Orcutt reflected, when he began to push microsimulation for the government agencies in the mid-1960s, even with Gorham's and Rivlin's support it was not sufficient to overturn the upper hierarchy's conservative mind-sets (Orcutt et al. 1980: 84). Fortunately, over several years, their reluctance diminished as a result of two successful practices. The first application of microsimulation in income transfer program by the Treasury Department was used for estimating tax revenue (Pechman 1965).[54] Second, in 1968, the creation of the President's Commission on Income Maintenance Program also initiated a tax microanalytic modeling project for transfer income (Wilensky 1970; McClung 1970). The commission's tax model became the prototype of the Urban Institute's first microsimulation program: Transfer Income Model (TRIM). Those examples convinced the officials that microsimulation could be an alternative tool to produce credible and timely evidence; they subsequently used the latter model to simulate different possibilities of President Richard Nixon's Family Assistance Plan (FAP), which was presented in Congress debates (Orcutt et al. 1980: 85). Such epistemic impact was noted by Daniel Moynihan, an adviser to Nixon and previous executive secretary of the Council of Urban Affairs, who argued that the simulation experiments of FAP had improved the quality of evidence and facilitated the Congress in reaching consensus.

By early 1969 a simulation model had been developed which permitted various versions of FAP to be "tested" and costs to be estimated. Most of this work was done by the Urban Institute, which made its informa-

54. Rivlin served as the collaborator and Sadowsky as the programming supervisor.

tion available to all who requested it. . . . This was a situation probably without precedent in the development of major social legislation; it disciplined and informed the debate for those in any degree disposed to restraint in the discussion of public issues. Once the President had made the proposal and congressional hearings were beginning, the Administration could in good conscience make statements about the effects it would have which never previously could have been made with any pretense to accuracy. (Moynihan 1973: 190)

Moynihan's impression explains why microsimulation began to be perceived as a useful empirical tool in fulfilling the demands for socioeconomic engineering. Through various simulation experiments, microsimulation aided officials in evaluating which redistributive policy would be beneficial for their optimum goals and which welfare program would be financially sensible for the government before spending significant amounts. For instance, in the case of tax models, the TRIM2 arguably reconciled the debate over the Family Support Act of 1988, and the Treasury tax simulation model played a crucial role in forming the Tax Reform Act of 1986 (Citro and Hanushek 1991: 3). Those usages were also usually combined with other models, such as TRIM2 and DYNASIM, which were applied to predict the short- and long-run effects under the 1983 Amendments to Social Security (Michel, Storey, and Zedlewski 1983). Among them, microsimulation constituted a unique epistemic source to reframe empirical knowledge and redirect policy implementation.

In this sense, microsimulation acted like a socioeconomic engine that allowed engine designers like Orcutt to scrutinize its inner structure more appropriately, as he put the analogy of an economic system to an engineering network:

If an engineer were given the job of predicting how a complicated electrical network would respond as numerous inputs were varied, he would want to know the components contained in the system, the way in which they are interconnected, and the operating characteristics of the individual components. If he were denied this information and given only very aggregate data about how total electric consumption, total power produced, and average voltage in the system varied over time, he might not regard the problem as completely insoluble, but he would certainly feel as though he were working blindfolded with both hands tied behind his back. (Orcutt et al. 1961: 6)

Responding to Orcutt's dream, microsimulation was initially created as a new engine in freeing both hands of socioeconomic engineers that enlarged our understanding of the economic system. After years of struggle, this engine finally benefited the customers and facilitated their abilities in reengineering society.

## References

Adelman, I., and F. L. Adelman. 1959. "The Dynamic Properties of the Klein-Goldberger Model." *Econometrica* 27, no. 4: 596–625.

Backhouse, R. E., and B. Cherrier. 2017. "'It's Computers, Stupid!' The Spread of Computers and the Changing Roles of Theoretical and Applied Economics." In *The Age of the Applied Economist: The Transformation of Economics since the 1970s*, edited by R. E. Backhouse and B. Cherrier. *History of Political Economy* 49 (supplement): 103–26.

Citro, C. F., and E. A. Hanushek, eds. 1991. *Technical Papers*. Vol. 2 of *Improving Information for Social Policy Decisions: The Uses of Microsimulation Modeling*. Washington, DC: National Academies Press.

Cochrane, D., and G. H. Orcutt. 1949. "Application of Least Squares Regression to Relationships Containing Auto-Correlated Error Terms." *Journal of the American Statistical Association* 44, no. 245: 32–61.

Epstein, R. J. 1987. *A History of Econometrics*. Amsterdam: North Holland.

Gallegati, M., A. Palestrini, and A. Russo, eds. 2017. *Introduction to Agent-Based Economics*. London: Academic Press.

Goldberger, A. S., and M. L. Lee. 1962. "Toward a Microanalytic Model of the Household Sector." *American Economic Review* 52, no. 2: 241–51.

Guthrie, H. W., G. Orcutt, S. Caldwell, G. E. Peabody, and G. Sadowsky. 1974. "Microanalytic Simulation of Household Behavior." In *The Role of the Computer in Economic and Social Research in Latin America*, edited by N. D. Ruggles, 109–38. Cambridge, MA: National Bureau of Economic Research.

Harris, S. E. 1958. "To Finance College Fees: Higher Tuition Payable in Long-Term Installments Proposed." *New York Times*, November 19.

Hoover, K. D. 2012. "Microfoundational Programs." In *Microfoundations Reconsidered: The Relationship of Micro and Macroeconomics in Historical Perspective*, edited by P. G. Duarte and G. T. Lima, 19–61. Cheltenham, UK: Edward Elgar.

Johnson, D. B. 1993. "Edwin Young." In *Economists at Wisconsin: 1892–1992*, edited by R. J. Lampman, 141–44. Madison: Board of Regents of the University of Wisconsin System.

Klein, L. R. 1950. *Economic Fluctuations in the United States, 1921–1941*. Cowles Commission Monograph 11. New York: Wiley.

Koopmans, T. C. 1950. *Statistical Inference in Dynamic Economic Models*. Cowles Commission Monograph 10. New York: Wiley.

Lampman, R. J. 1993. "Rebuilding and Expanding, 1958–1969." In *Economists at Wisconsin: 1892–1992*, edited by R. J. Lampman. Madison: Board of Regents of the University of Wisconsin System.

Lindsay, F. A. 1968. "Managerial Innovation and the Cities." *Daedalus* 97, no. 4: 1218–30.

McClung, N. 1970. "Estimates of Income Transfer Program Direct Effects." In *The President's Commission on Income Maintenance Programs, Technical Studies*. Washington, DC: US Government Printing Office.

Metropolis, N., and S. Ulam. 1949. "The Monte Carlo Method." *Journal of the American Statistical Association* 44, no. 247: 335–41.

Michel, R. C., J. R. Storey, and S. Zedlewski. 1983. *Saving Social Security: The Short- and Long-Run Effects of the 1983 Amendments*. Washington, DC: Urban Institute.

Morgan, M. S. 1990. *The History of Econometric Ideas*. Cambridge: Cambridge University Press.

Morgan, M. S. 1991. "The Stamping Out of Process Analysis in Econometrics." In *Appraising Economic Theories: Studies in the Methodology of Research Programs*, edited by N. de Marchi and M. Blaug, 237–63. Cheltenham, UK: Edward Elgar.

Morgan, M. S. 2004. "Simulation: The Birth of a Technology to Create 'Evidence' in Economics." *Revue d'Histoire des Sciences* 57, no. 2: 341–77.

Morgan, M. S. 2012. *The World in the Model: How Economists Work and Think*. Cambridge: Cambridge University Press.

Moynihan, D. P. 1973. *The Politics of a Guaranteed Income: The Nixon Administration and the Family Assistance Plan*. New York: Random House.

Orcutt, G. H. 1944. *Statistical Methods and Tools for Finding Natural Laws in the Field of Economics*. PhD diss., University of Michigan.

Orcutt, G. H. 1948a. "A New Regression Analyser." *Journal of the Royal Statistical Society: Series A (General)* 111, no. 1: 54–70.

Orcutt, G. II. 1948b. "A Study of the Autoregressive Nature of the Time Series Used for Tinbergen's Model of the Economic System of the United States, 1919–1932." *Journal of the Royal Statistical Society: Series B (Methodological)* 10, no. 1: 1–45.

Orcutt, G. H. 1951. Review of *Review of Economic Fluctuations in the United States*, by Lawrence R. Klein. *Review of Economics and Statistics* 33, no. 3: 261–63.

Orcutt, G. H. 1952. Review of *Review of Statistical Inference in Dynamic Economic Models*, by T. Koopmans. *American Economic Review* 42, no. 1: 165–69.

Orcutt, G. H. 1957. "A New Type of Socio-Economic System." *Review of Economics and Statistics* 39, no. 2: 116–23.

Orcutt, G. H. 1960. "Simulation of Economic Systems." *American Economic Review* 50, no. 5: 894–907.

Orcutt, G. H. 1962. "Microanalytic Models of the United States Economy: Need and Development." *American Economic Review* 52, no. 2: 229–40.

Orcutt, G. H. 1990. "From Engineering to Microsimulation: An Autobiographical Reflection." Special issue on Guy H. Orcutt, *Journal of Economic Behavior and Organization* 14, no. 1: 5–27.

Orcutt, G. H., S. Caldwell, and R. Wertheimer. 1976. *Policy Exploration through Microanalytic Simulation*. Washington, DC: Urban Institute.

Orcutt, G. H., and D. Cochrane. 1949. "A Sampling Study of the Merits of Auto-Regressive and Reduced Form Transformations in Regression Analysis." *Journal of the American Statistical Association* 44, no. 247: 356–72.

Orcutt, G. H., A. Glazer, R. Harris, and R. Wertheimer. 1980. "Microanalytic Modeling and the Analysis of Public Transfer Policies." In *Microeconomic Simulation Models for Public Policy Analysis*, edited by R. H. Haveman and K. Hollenbeck, 1: 81–106. New York: Academic.

Orcutt, G. H., M. Greenberger, J. Korbel, and A. M. Rivlin. 1961. *Microanalysis of Socioeconomic Systems: A Simulation Study*. New York: Harpers.

Orcutt, G. H., and S. F. James. 1948. "Testing the Significance of Correlation between Time Series." *Biometrika* 35, nos. 3–4: 397–413.

Pechman, J. A. 1965. "A New Tax Model for Revenue Estimating." In *Proceedings of a Symposium of Federal Taxation*. Washington, DC: American Bankers' Association.

*Political Science*. 1968. "The Profession." 1, no. 4: 12–18.

Qin, D., and C. L. Gilbert. 2001. "The Error Term in the History of Time Series Econometrics." *Econometric Theory* 17: 424–50.

Rivlin, A. M. 1971. *Systematic Thinking for Social Action*. Washington, DC: Brookings Institution.

Rosoff, J. I. 1969. "View from Washington: Reorganization, Consolidation—or Both?" *Family Planning Perspectives* 1, no. 1: 18–24.

Sadowsky, G. 1988. "Mash: A Computer System for Microanalytic Simulation for Policy Exploration." PhD diss., Yale University.

Slutsky, E. 1937. "The Summation of Random Causes as the Source of Cyclic Processes." *Econometrica* 5, no. 2: 105–46.

Social Systems Research Institute (SSRI). 1963. "Annual Report: Fiscal Year 1962–1963."

Social Systems Research Institute (SSRI). 1965. "Annual Report: Fiscal Year 1964–1965."

Solovey, M. 1993. "Guy Orcutt and the Social Systems Research Institute: Interdisciplinary Troubles." In *Economists at Wisconsin: 1892–1992*, edited by R. J. Lampman, 178–88. Madison: Board of Regents of the University of Wisconsin System.

Stigler, G. J. 1954. "The Early History of Empirical Studies of Consumer Behavior." *Journal of Political Economy* 62, no. 2: 95–113.

Summers, R., D. B. Suits, and M. E. Dingle. 1962. "Discussion." *American Economic Review* 52, no. 2: 252–58.

Thomas, J. J. 1989. "The Early Econometric History of the Consumption Function." *Oxford Economic Papers* 41, no. 1: 131–49.

Tinbergen, J. 1939. *Statistical Testing of Business-Cycle Theories*. Vol. 1: *A Method and Its Application to Investment Activity*. Vol. 2: *Business Cycles in the United States of America, 1919–1932*. Geneva: League of Nations.

Urban Institute. 1968. *Social Service Review* 42, no. 3: 368.

Wilensky, R. G. 1970. "An Income Transfer Computational Model." In *The President's Commission on Income Maintenance Programs, Technical Studies*. Washington, DC: US Government Printing Office.

Yule, G. U. 1926. "Why Do We Sometimes Get Nonsense-Correlations between Time-Series?—a Study in Sampling and the Nature of Time-Series." *Journal of the Royal Statistical Society* 89, no. 1: 1–63.

Yule, G. U. 1927. "On a Method of Investigating Periodicities in Disturbed Series, with Special Reference to Wolfer's Sunspot Numbers." *Philosophical Transactions of the Royal Society of London: Series A*, no. 226: 267–98.

# Economics and Engineering in
# Professional and National Cultures

# Redistributing Agency: The Control Roots of Spot Pricing of Electricity

Daniel Breslau

## Introduction: Control and the Market

Of the many connections between engineering and neoclassical economics, optimization is a particularly busy portal of commerce between the two fields. Engineers, in their pursuit of efficiency, are preoccupied with maximizing output and minimizing inputs. The market of microeconomics was also fashioned as an optimizing mechanism, optimizing aggregate outcomes among individual optimizers (Arrow 2008). It is therefore not a coincidence that the two arrive at equivalent results. Given the objective of the most efficient distribution, the greatest surplus at the lowest cost given a set of constraints, a central controller and a frictionless market arrive at the same result (Lerner 1947). With the development of mathematical tools the equivalence was strengthened, since the same mathematical equations that had to be solved in order to derive the optimal "program" of a central controller were also the analytic tools for describing the equilibrium outcome in a market economy (Dantzig 1963; Dorfman, Samuelson, and Solow 1958). And the tools developed for optimizing in cases of centralized control have been readily borrowed as tools for modeling the spontaneous optimization that is accomplished by economies under idealized conditions.

The case that is the subject of this article, the design of electricity markets and the development of the pricing technique that is now used in most

*History of Political Economy* 52 (annual suppl.) DOI 10.1215/00182702-8718023

liberalized wholesale electricity markets, features a more lively and open-ended exchange between these two contexts of optimization. Rather than transferring tools from the context of control to that of economic equili-bration, the engineers who led this effort were working on a hybrid that allocated agency among centralized controllers, automated and human, and distributed economic actors, thus blurring the distinction between them. As a consequence, they also blurred the respective jurisdictions of engineering and economics. The designed market is a hybrid of the engi-neer's control system, its explicit algorithm for processing signals and determining an optimal response, and the economist's multitude of dis-tributed utility maximizers. The specific division of labor between control and spontaneous equilibrium is subject to negotiation. Some control pro-cesses, such as the filtering of measurements and the estimation of a state space, are delegated to a central calculator. Other processers are distrib-uted to innumerable calculators who, on the basis of price signals calcu-lated by the central controller, conduct their own calculations to reach distributed decisions on production, consumption, and investment.

The hybrid structure of this case is typical of instances of market design, as expressed by the tension between the two components of the term, *mar-ket*, and *design*. It engages engineers in economic analysis and economists in the engineering of social institutions (Roth 2002). And it generally involves a negotiated redistribution of agency between a mechanism for centralized processing of information and calculation, and the information processing carried out by market participants. The design of the central mechanism, though often carried out by economists, resembles the engi-neer's design task, while economic analysis is applied to modeling and anticipating the actions of market participants (Guala 2001). The recent social science literature on market design has treated this relatively new area as the jurisdiction of economists, as they try with varying degrees of success to create institutions that have the properties, especially economic efficiency, of their idealized models (Nik-Khah 2008; Garcia-Parpet 2007; Breslau 2011). In the current case, however, the techniques, models, and concept of efficiency are provided by a team led by control engineers assuming the role of market designers. Because the constraints on optimi-zation in this case are the engineering constraints on the electricity grid, the calculation of prices incorporates the engineers' model of those constraints.

This article examines the origins and development of the mathematical framework for pricing electric power that today is incorporated in the locational marginal pricing (LMP) approach employed in numerous liberalized electricity markets. The account is based on analyses of the key publications and working papers through which the developmental work evolved and was publicized, as well as open-ended interviews with many of the central participants in the work and a range of engineers, economists, consumer advocates, and regulators who were involved in the design of the electricity market and its reception. The origins of the approach, and even the conditions for its possibility, emerged from the theory and practice of control engineering in the specific historical setting of the US electric power system from the early to mid-twentieth century. This is not to say that there was a firewall separating microeconomics from the theory and practice of control; engineering training and professional practice drew heavily though selectively on economic theory since the nineteenth century, and the foundational sources of economics in the works of engineers is well known. The point is that the innovations in pricing that are at the heart of electricity markets emerged from the experience, competence, and professional culture of power system control. Moreover, as I show, they were initially conceived as innovations in control, with no necessary connection to deregulation or justifications in free market thinking in economics. The engineers who initiated the work sought to incorporate the multitude of customers of electric utilities into the control system, rather than to replace centralized control with a market. I begin with a historical reconstruction of the central role of system controllers and the calculations they performed in the growth of the power system, and how the reforms proposed by a group of MIT engineers responded to a crisis in that system's growth.

## The Development of the Grid and the Controller's Craft

Since the work of Thomas Hughes (1983, 1987) on the subject, the electrical power system has been a paradigm for a sociotechnical system, that is, a system with mutually interacting and reinforcing components that are both social and technical. But this system is also a dynamic one. The parts do not simply function to preserve a static whole but put that whole in motion, at times achieving a degree of what Hughes calls technological momentum, as positive feedback loops among the components generate a growth process. Because the growth is the result of so many heterogeneous components, none have the ability to stop it; its momentum is irresistible by the will of the actors. It is not a major extension of this perspective to appreciate that the social actors themselves are, so to speak, caught up in the system. The system constitutes them, their perceptions and dispositions, not to mention their material interests, so that they are the last to conceive of an alternative to the system's dynamism.

The established historiography places technologies at the center of the growth machine. At the heart of the system was a set of generating technologies that seemed infinitely scalable and capable of continual improvements in efficiency. The turbine generator, initially powered by pressurized steam, when introduced in 1920 was an enormous improvement over piston-driven dynamos like those used in Thomas Edison's early lighting plants. It was more compact, lighter, durable, and seemed indefinitely scalable, with corresponding improvements in efficiency. The trajectory of these machines, in size and efficiency, permitted a corresponding growth in the load that could be served by large, centralized power stations (Hirsh 1989). The transmission grid, which started as a set of disconnected local systems, through the development of universal high-voltage alternating current, with a synchronized frequency, complemented the growth of the generators at its core. Voltages of 150 kilovolts by 1920, and approaching 400 kilovolts by midcentury, allowed power to be transmitted in bulk over long distances with limited losses. Rotary converters, in the pre–World War II era, allowed the transmission system to integrate every existing use of power: lighting, traction, and increasingly, industrial heating and machinery. As the system grew and integrated an increasingly diverse set of customers who used power at different hours of the day, the systems achieved greater efficiency and still-lower costs. Interties between systems allowed for further economizing as loads were further diversified.

Social organizational innovations also reinforced growth, strengthening the positive feedback. These consisted primarily of a system of regulation, first at the local and state level, and ultimately at the federal level for the regulation of interstate commerce in electric power (Glaeser 1957). Regulation played several important roles for the growth regime. It allowed utilities to be legitimately shielded from competition. It harmonized the growing power system with the financial system by providing a predictable return on investment, assuring that investor-owned utilities were "going concerns." This was especially important in reducing risk and the costs of capital in an industry that requires enormous up-front investments relative to modest revenue streams. But for its success, regulation also depended on the continual advance of the growth regime itself. Regulation is an adversarial process, pitting conflicting interests of producers and multiple groups of consumers. A successful regulatory system is one that contains those latent conflicts. As many have commented, the best friend of regulators in this regard was the continual growth of the system, with continual improvement in efficiency and reduction of costs (Anderson 1981; Gormley 1983).

The system was further buttressed by innovative financial techniques. From its early years, electric power was an outlier among major industries in the size of initial investments relative to the revenue streams created by those investments. The enormous initial costs of power plants and transmission lines introduced a chronic problem of attracting capital. Because of the long planning and construction horizons and the much longer duration it would take to recover investments after a plant was built, investors were acutely sensitive to risks. Even within a system of regulation that allowed investors to recover the costs of plants by charging their customers, capital flowed into the industry slowly. Regulation, by protecting smaller utilities from competition, could also put up a barrier to consolidation (Hausman and Neufeld 2011). The growth envisaged by the developers of the power system would require a financial structure to overcome the risks and to channel investment to the grid. Although the Commonwealth Edison magnate Samuel Insull is often credited with developing the industry's financial structure, as with other features of the system, the investment grid was the result of a set of nearly simultaneous and overlapping innovations that eventually emerged into a financial structure that was isomorphic across the industry (Lambert 2015; Hughes 1983).

The techniques for pricing electricity to final consumers also reinforced the growth regime. Regulation determined utilities' "revenue requirements" for the sake of recovering capital investments, providing a return adequate to attract capital, and covering the industry's variable production costs. But the tariff structure, by which utilities would be allowed to meet their revenue requirements, was the result of a separate set of considerations. Beginning in the years of adoption of electric utility regulation, between 1905 and 1915, utilities were allowed to satisfy their revenue requirements through a system of prices that discriminated across classes of customers, but which were designed to maximize market penetration, without regard to improving the efficiency with which the utility's resources were used. For industrial and commercial customers, this consisted of a rate consisting mostly of a demand charge based on the customer's peak use of power during the billing period, with a small charge for each unit of power consumed. For residential customers, more numerous but each with relatively small demand, utilities were granted a tariff based almost entirely on a per-kilowatt-hour "volumetric charge." Notably, despite the existence of metering technologies that could track each customer's contribution to peak demand, a rate system that would charge based on time-specific use was roundly rejected by the largest players in the industry (Yakubovich, Granovetter, and McGuire 2005). Efficiency could be achieved by extending and diversifying the system; prices should not inhibit growth. For large customers, linking their bill to their own peak use, and thus the capital costs of supplying power through their own isolated facilities, encouraged their decision to connect to the utility's grid (Neufeld 1987).

## Control for Growth

A full accounting of the elements of the growth model must add to these technological and institutional elements the knowledge and practices of the human controllers who operated the system in real time. As Julie Cohn (2017) has recently described in acute detail, the growth regime that persisted for the first seventy years of the twentieth century would not have been possible without the continual development of techniques for controlling the flows of power on the ever-expanding grid. The economic logic of interconnection was irresistible due to its massive effects on load factors and efficiency. The sheer growth of power systems, by expanding the system's geographic footprint, diversifying load, and diversifying power sources, provided the potential for new economies, even as load was left to develop according to its own logic. But the realization of those efficiencies required much more than adding an interconnection to the physical grid. These investments presupposed the ability to control flows of power in a way that would realize their benefits and allow for continued integration and growth of the grid.

An essential element of the growth regime, and what Hughes (1987) calls the momentum of this sociotechnical system, was therefore the work of system controllers. The engineers operating the system, along with the devices developed to assist them, allowed the efficiencies of larger and more diversified systems to be cashed in. They accomplished this primarily through the practice of economic dispatch, or "economy loading." Economic dispatch is the practice of meeting the current load using the lowest-cost combination of generating sources. Often, the practice is described in terms of a stack of generators, arranged in order of cost per unit of power output, for instance, dollars per kilowatt-hour, from lowest to highest. At low loads, operators will dispatch only the lowest cost sources, such as hydropower and nuclear. As load increases, due to seasonal factors, or simply the daily cycle, more costly sources will be dispatched, coal and natural gas, with inefficient but quickly activated "peaking" generators the last to be called on, as their name suggests, during the small number of hours when demand for power, or load, is at its peak.

Early attempts at economic dispatch, during the first half of the twentieth century, proceeded by simply considering the generators on a system in terms of their heat rates, the energy input, measured in BTUs, required to generate a unit, usually a kilowatt-hour, of power. The lower the heat rate, the more economical the generating unit. Early practices, on relatively small power systems, consisted of considering the power plants in terms of their heat rates, dispatching the most efficient units first, until they were producing power at their maximum capacity, and then successively dispatching less efficient units as the system's total load increased (Stahl 1931). In a process that would be repeated past midcentury, analyses soon showed that this technique was suboptimal, that it did not come close to the most economical use of resources. An improved approximation relied on proportionally dispatching plants as load increased, with a larger but constant proportion of the additional load coming from the more efficient plants.

With the growth and increasing interconnection of power systems, economic dispatch became a problem for calculation, for an explicit numerical result, rather than a practical skill of adjusting the output in response to changing load. As systems grew, controllers had to increasingly take into account the features of the transmission system, particularly line losses, which are a function of the length of the transmission line and the safe operating capacity of transmission lines. The same features that made the power system increasingly economical made the control problem increasingly complex. To continue to realize the efficiencies of a larger and more integrated grid, controllers had to solve increasingly complex optimization problems. Before the availability of digital computers to calculate optimal dispatch, power systems used analog computers that could be configured as scale models of a power system. Greater computing power and advances in calculation techniques, chiefly linear programing, extended the capacity of controllers to realize lowest-cost dispatch on an ever-growing and diversifying grid (Cohn 2015). Dispatch starts months in advance, with load forecasts based on weather forecasts, economic analyses, historic growth, new construction of plants, and planned outages or retirements of existing plants. Operators construct day-ahead schedules specifying which generating units will be committed the following day and what levels of generation will be required for each hour throughout the day. And engineers do not simply dispatch generators according to a queue, by which the lower-cost generators are operating at capacity before a higher-cost unit is dispatched. The efficiencies of generators vary depending on their output. So, in dispatching plants, engineers need to compare alternate sources based on their current output and the cost of drawing an additional unit of power from them. And they must take into account the location of the plant, which affects cost through the effects of grid congestion or the losses of power when it is transmitted over long distances. Thus the art and science of economic dispatch is really a process of calculating the output of each generator on the system, given its location, operating characteristic, so as to serve the existing load at the lowest cost.

## Crisis of the Growth Model

When historians of the power system refer to the growth regime or the growth model, they are implying that growth, and the expectation of growth, was a constitutive feature of the industry and its system as a whole. As Hughes hinted with the concept of technological momentum, it was inherently a dynamic system. Rather than a sequence of static equilibria, the system operated at any moment only with the promise of future growth. Its financial structure was predicated on a predicted path of growing load and revenues. Regulators required growth forecasts, which they scrutinized closely, when granting permits for new investments in power plants, allowing the developer to recover the cost of the investment by billing their customers. The rate structure lacked economic justification if one views the system in static equilibrium; it was inherently a forward-looking structure, which could be justified only in the way it facilitated rapid market penetration. And the commercial peace in relations of producers to consumers was likewise made possible and guaranteed by the growth model. The power of the industry in regulatory proceedings, which makes the industry a paradigmatic case of regulatory capture, was tolerated by customers and political authorities only because of the promise of continued growth, efficiency, and reduced costs.

Beginning in the middle of the 1960s, this regime of growth in the electric power system in the United States reached an impasse (Hirsh 1999: 55–70; Lifset 2014b). Improvements in efficiency had arrived at a plateau as generators approached the theoretical limit of 48 percent thermal efficiency. In an effort to wring more power out of each dollar invested, utilities attempted to construct ever larger power plants, also finding a declining marginal return as the larger designs raised new problems of maintenance and reliability. The innovation of dual-cycle turbines, which reused waste heat from combustion turbines to power a second, steam-driven, turbine, squeezed a few additional percentage points of efficiency, but likewise arrived at what is still recognized as a hard limit. The "last hope" of a system founded on continual growth, nuclear power, likewise failed to sustain the trajectory of cost economies of previous decades as the cost of building nuclear plants spiraled. The environmental movement, which had its first successes in legislating protections by the late 1960s, introduced further limitations on the continuous growth model. Finally, the crisis in supplies of oil and natural gas brought higher costs of generating electricity, since generation using these two fuels had proliferated in the previous decade owing to the abundance and low prices of oil and gas.

As is typical of a crisis, elements of the existing system that were taken for granted, and were even necessary for the system's growth, are redefined as problems. A constitutive feature of the power system had been the practice of treating short-term load, the demand for power at any moment, as a given, as an exogenous condition to which system operators had to adjust. As mentioned earlier, the pricing system adopted in the early twentieth century enshrined load following, as did the entire craft of the system operator, and the marketing of electric power that allowed the grid to cover the North American continent. This basic condition shaped the professional outlook of operators, as well as the tools and techniques at their disposal. The load-following character of the power system, which had been eagerly adopted under the growth model, was now seen as an obstacle to the realization of efficiencies. The ferment of pricing ideas, and a combined intellectual and practical disruption of existing pricing systems, corresponded exactly with the crisis of the growth model. The literature blossomed in the early 1970s, at the same time as utilities, without inspiration from formal economic analyses, initiated small-scale programs and experiments in varying the price of power to induce greater efficiencies in the timing of consumption.

### Fred Schweppe and the MIT Group:
### A Control-Engineering Solution

It was this crisis of the growth model that concerned a group of engineers at MIT in the 1970s, as they focused their attention on finding new efficiencies within the control system. They were acutely aware that this problem was simultaneously technical and political, and advocated for their approach on the grounds that it would transcend what had become a zero-sum regulatory game between utilities and their customers. They motivated their far-reaching reform with a comprehensive critique of the historical legacy of the growth model:

> The failure of most present-day utility-customer transactions to meet today's needs can be traced to their historical foundations. They were established by individuals unconcerned with power system control and operation, during a time when communication and computation were very expensive, when there was less incentive to use electricity in an efficient fashion, and when cross-subsidies were of limited concern to society. (Schweppe et al. 1988: 3–9)

The control engineering reform would address the technical and social impasses of the power system. On the one hand, it meant refinements to the control system that would boost capacity factors and lower costs. On the other hand, it would restore peace to relations between utilities, their residential customers, and even more importantly, their commercial and industrial customers (Lifset 2014a; Hirsh 1999). It was the interruption of the growth regime that had surfaced tensions that had been latent only as long as rates continued their downward trajectory. The solution proposed by Fred Schweppe's group, rooted in practices of power system control, was more comprehensive, even radical, than the many proposed reforms that were confined to tariff design.

At the center of the MIT group was Schweppe, a control engineer who first joined MIT as a member of the Lincoln Laboratory, an R&D shop working exclusively on US Department of Defense contracts (Freeman and Lincoln Laboratory 1995). At the Lincoln Lab, Schweppe would likely have been involved with its central pursuit, the development of missile defense systems. Here the conception of the control problem as a system of stochastic differential equations would have been a common currency, as would have been the representation of that system as a state space (Bennett 1993: 202–3; MacKenzie 1990).

With his move in the mid-1960s to the Department of Electrical Engineering, and the Energy Lab, Schweppe quickly took on the task of bringing practice in the operation of power systems to the standards of control engineering and the capacities of advanced computers. The foundational task in this project was to reconstruct the power system as an object of state-of-the-art control theory and practice, namely, as a state space. Marcel Boumans sketches the history of these techniques in his contribution to this volume. An entire power system, such as a regional grid under the control of a monopoly utility, had to be represented as a vector of state variables from which one could, with the aid of computers, derive the power flows between all nodes, or buses, on the grid. By representing the power system as a state space, where the state variables represent the voltage magnitudes and phase angles at every bus on the system, Schweppe could import techniques of filtering, estimation, and prediction from control engineering.

By 1968, Schweppe and a small number of collaborators had developed an algorithm for power system state estimation using weighted least squares. The technique allowed system controllers, human and computers, to derive the best estimate of the power flows across an entire system. Controllers needed to know this state, captured in a vector of voltages and phase angles of all buses in the system, in order to plan economic dispatch and to maintain security. Previously, controllers would construct a representation of the full set of power flows using metered readings of the power being injected into the system and removed from the system at each of the buses. But, especially with the increasing size and complexity of these systems, this "power-flow" approach was prone to endemic sources of error. A single missing or flawed meter would, and often did, invalidate the entire power-flow study. Schweppe saw that the problem of representing the state of the power system was analogous to many control engineering problems, once the system was understood as a state space. Rather than rely on a complete set of power flow measurements, the state could be estimated from a large quantity of incomplete, redundant, and noisy measurements. These included injections of power, data from line flow meters, and the status of switches throughout the power system. Combined with the vast computing power now available to controllers, Schweppe's technique provided a far-superior snapshot of the entire system. The technique soon became a standard feature of computational methods in power-system control (Abur and Gómez Expósito 2004; Wu 1990; Schweppe and Wildes 1970). Based on the state-space representation, controllers could then use dynamic programming to find the optimal, economic dispatch (Grainger and Stevenson 1994). It was through the perspective that Schweppe and his associates viewed the combined technological and political impasse of power systems.

Schweppe and his group at the MIT Energy Lab targeted the load-following nature of power systems, which had been a deeply embedded, and usually unspoken, assumption of the growth model of power systems. Initially, with the adoption of a time-invariant pricing scheme in the early twentieth century, load following was a deliberate policy, driven by the growth model. Utilities chose load following due to their preference for growth and market penetration over efficiency. As long as efficiencies were realized elsewhere, load following would allow for unbridled growth (Yakubovich, Granovetter, and McGuire 2005). But as the growth model, figuratively and literally, ran out of steam, the implicit assumption that load should be an exogenous input, allowed to develop and change according to consumers' needs, and that it was the power system's imperative to meet it, was made explicit and problematic. Utilities had relied on diversification of load to realize better load factors and greater efficiency. But the slow growth of the system indicated that the limits to diversity were also being reached. And this meant that the role of diversity in improving load factors was also near exhaustion. Engineers, economists, and other would-be reformers now identified load following as an obstacle to higher load factors and lower costs. In the longer term, systems had to be prepared for a peak load that was much higher than the load that had to be served most of the time. The system required enormous investments in generators that were used for only a small proportion of the time. In the shorter, day-to-day and hour-to-hour scale, load following led to suboptimal use of resources and controllers scrambled to meet random changes in load, and responses to frequency changes in the grid often departed from the most economical use of available resources. The low capacity factors of the existing fleet of power plants, indicating their low total output relative to their full capacity, had become a frontier in the search for efficiencies.

## Homeostatic Control

Equipped with the state-space approach to the power system, Schweppe proposed a comprehensive solution that amounted to a radical change in the control system at the heart of the power grid. From his position as a leading control engineer, Schweppe sketched an expansion of control theory that he argued would help break the deadlock in regulatory politics and benefit producers and consumers of power alike. He introduced the approach, which he called "homeostatic control," around 1978 in a seminar of the MIT energy lab. Homeostatic control is derived from a biological metaphor, that of an organism. The organism maintains its internal state in the face of a changing environment. For instance, it can refer to the way that organisms maintain their body temperature as the environmental temperature changes unexpectedly. When the environmental temperature increases, temperature receptors send information to a controlling device, the central nervous system. The control center then sends control signals to the units of the organism, generally in the form of hormones through the endocrine system, or through quicker nervous impulses. Through processes of negative feedback, the system, a living organism, is returned to its initial homeostatic state. Schweppe defined his task as the application of this kind of logic to the electric power system. The kinds of environmental disturbances to this system could be rapid increases in temperature, and the increased load as home, commercial, and industrial cooling systems are added to the existing background demand for power. Or, a large generator could experience problems or be shut down unexpectedly. Downed transmission and distribution lines can cause a local system failure. In all these cases, changes in the system environment are registered as changes in the system's frequency, or changes in flows of power. Receptors, to adhere to the biological metaphor, monitor frequency and power flows and can either respond locally or convey information to the system's nerve center.

As Schweppe put it, his aim was "an efficient, internally-correcting control scheme" (Schweppe et al. 1980: 1151). Schweppe initially approached the issue with respect to the classic problem of frequency control. Frequency, like body temperature or blood pressure, must be maintained within a narrow range for the power system to operate. Sudden changes to load or to output will upset the balance of load and generation and reduce frequency, if load exceeds generation, or less often increases frequency with a flux of generation relative to load. Frequency regulation had been a purely load-following affair, accomplished through quick adjustments in generator output. In a presentation to the Utility Systems Program seminar in the Energy Lab, Schweppe introduced the idea of homeostatic control as a way to bring load, the consumers of electric power, into the frequency regulation problem. He proposed sending frequency signals to electricity-using devices that would then adjust their load to regulate frequency—reducing load or even shutting off when frequency was low and resuming when frequency was marginally above the system frequency of 60 Hz. Joined by colleague Richard Tabors, an economist trained in operations research, and a group of engineers and graduate students, the group developed this concept into a proposed device called a FAPER, or Frequency Adaptive Power Energy Rescheduler. The FAPER only needs to monitor the local frequency; the frequency becomes a signal. It would work in a way that is analogous to automatic governors that had been placed on generators since the early twentieth century, and would replace those governors. In response to changes in frequency, the FAPER would cycle selected power-consuming equipment on and off. A fleet of FAPERs distributed across a power system's customers would reduce costs for the system by obviating the need for governors on power plants to continually adjust to changing frequency, and the need for automatic generation control for a control area of the grid. They reasoned that this would largely do away with the problems confronted by generations of engineers, of how to maintain scheduled flows on tie-lines while regulating frequency. It would liberate the system to simply serve load at the lowest cost, without unexpected departures from the lowest cost dispatch for the sake of frequency regulation. The system's homeostasis, the biological metaphor for maintenance of standard frequency, would be spontaneously realized by a myriad of mutually sensing and adjusting agents, the FAPERs themselves. The paradigm case for application of the FAPER was electric heating, for both industrial applications and residential space and water heating. Heating, the Schweppe group argued, requires energy rather than power; the demand is for a fixed quantity of energy over a time interval. Unlike an electric motor, which uses electricity for power and requires adequate power at the moment that it is functioning, as long as heating elements have heated within an acceptable range, they can be cycled on and off randomly while maintaining temperature within that range (Schweppe et al. 1980). Energy-using applications, through the FAPER, could easily adjust their load in order to regulate frequency.

### Spot Pricing

The logic of the homeostatic metaphor lent itself to frequency regulation, but soon the group around Schweppe begin mapping the metaphor onto the role of price as a control signal. The shift in focus to spot pricing corresponded with the addition of a Harvard-trained engineer, Michael Caramanis, and Roger Bohn, an economics PhD student at Harvard's Sloan School of Business, to the group. While the FAPER involved the response of distributed automated devices, the use of price signals brought homeostatic control into the domain of economic analysis. As load increased, customers would be signaled, through prices, to reduce load. Thus customers would be brought into the control system. Load data would be processed through state estimation models to provide a signal to controllers who would calculate economic dispatch orders. Customers would be signaled of the state of the system through prices. The combination of these complementary control functions would maintain the system as efficiently as possible within its secure operating limits. Homeostatic control has some clear affinities with economic ideas, particularly those in the Austrian tradition dealing with self-organization. The turn to the use of prices to achieve spontaneous and optimal control of the power system echoes Ludwig von Mises's catallactics as well as Friedrich Hayek's ideas about spontaneous order. But these affinities are almost certainly post hoc, with Schweppe's inspiration coming from the cybernetic theory that had been so important for mathematical engineering and was noted as early as Wiener's influential first book on the topic (Wiener 1948; see also Boumans, this volume). Ivan Boldyrev (this volume) points to another, apparently independent case, of metaphorical extension of the biological organism to engineering control systems.

Homeostatic control was adopted by the group as a generative principle for a series of papers distributed among the core members of the group. In their initial presentation of homeostatic control, the authors refrained from advocating a specific method for calculating prices. Their preoccupation was not with optimal price signals but with a range of possible pricing systems, to accomplish a range of control objectives. All the proposed pricing alternatives had the general property of increasing prices as the demand for power increased. But, recognizing that the monopoly utility was not a market, that prices were the product of a central calculator and not countless interactions among buyers and sellers, they understood the pricing method as a policy decision rather than a spontaneous outcome of an impersonal market equilibrium. For instance, one proposal based prices on the average total cost for the entire system, combining capital costs with average variable costs (Schweppe et al. 1980: 1157). Selection of a pricing algorithm would ultimately be based on the desired effect of pricing. Spot pricing was therefore initially an administrative procedure. The electricity marketplace was a space in which a central calculator, the computer that monitored the state of flows on the system, would iteratively derive prices from the state of the grid. The consumers would then respond to the prices, and in iterative fashion, the new state would provide the basis for updated prices.

With addition of Caramanis and Bohn, the group pivoted from pricing as an element of homeostatic control to the calculation of optimal spot prices. They had now joined the idea of prices as a control signal with welfare economics results on the efficiency of marginal cost-based pricing. The terminology, too, was shifting, as papers from the group gradually ceased to evoke homeostatic control and adopted the term *spot pricing*. The term was an apt one in distinguishing the group's recommended approach from virtually all other pricing systems then in use, including the introduction of time-varying prices on a limited scale (Reynolds and Creighton 1980). Even the experiments in time-varying prices in France, described by Gillaume Yon (in this volume), based price calculations on historic load curves. Spot pricing based prices strictly on the current state of load, thus extending the system operator's perspective, the system as a static state-space of power flows, to the calculation of prices. As Caramanis, Bohn, and Schweppe argued in the initial exposition of the approach, spot pricing was a kind of limit to which other proposals for time-varying prices had aspired, but without eliminating remaining inefficiencies. Spot pricing "is shown to encompass and achieve more fully the objectives of rate structures and load management techniques proposed so far" (Caramanis, Bohn, and Schweppe 1982: 3234).

Economic theory alone was therefore insufficient for deriving the prices that economic theory prescribed. The task required a thorough knowledge of the physical limits and engineering practices of the power grid, and the mathematical representations of the state space, the grid, and its power flows. And it is from those practices and that knowledge that Schweppe and his associates derived a pricing system that would ultimately have an economic justification. The prices were based on quantities that are derived when the state is estimated and the optimal loading, the economic dispatch, of the system is found. In the solution to a problem of optimization under constraint using any of a range of methods employing Lagrange multipliers, each constraint is multiplied by a figure representing the incremental change in the objective function with an incremental relaxation of the constraint. In the case of optimizing dispatch of electric power, the paramount constraint is the total load—the quantity of power demanded, with other constraints due to the configuration and safe operating limits of the transmission grid. When the objective function is for total cost, as in the case of economic dispatch, these Lagrange multipliers, conventionally denoted by the Greek letter lambda, are estimates of the cost of an incremental relaxation of a constraint. For purposes of economic dispatch, controllers are most interested in the multiplier that represents the additional cost of one additional unit of load. System controllers carefully tracked this "system lambda" as a way to gauge the load relative to the system's resources; it represented the incremental cost, the shadow price, of providing a particular load, usually the incremental cost of the most expensive generator dispatched at a given moment. They could also calculate the effects of congestion on costs by lambdas indicating the shadow price of congestion at a particular location on the grid. Schweppe et al. (1988: 175), in their book on spot pricing, noted that the equations they developed for calculating prices at each system bus are analogues of the tools of system operators: "Readers with a power system background in economic dispatch and optimal load flow (with line flow constraints) will find that the equations of this chapter look familiar. This is to be expected, since such power system theory motivated their development." In a limited sense, the central controller embodies Walras's auctioneer, announcing prices each period. But this controller is more than an auctioneer, since, in addition to calculating equilibrium prices, she must plan optimal dispatch, taking into account not only the bid schedules of participants but the range of generating resources, the physical configuration of the grid, and its safe operating limits.

Schweppe's team recognized that they had leveraged the equivalence of optimization via central control and optimization of a perfectly competitive market. The centralized optimization could supply the prices that would theoretically be arrived at by a competitive market. And instead of feeding those signals to the central controller, they could be turned into price signals for electricity customers. In each one-hour time period, prices would be updated based on load at the end of the previous time period, so demand during each hour would respond to prices at the beginning of the hour and would then be used to derive the price for the next hour. In an interview with the author, an economist on Schweppe's team describes how the pricing problem recapitulated the engineering problem: "And essentially the prices that came out of it were the shadow prices of the engineering constraints on the electric power system. So that was the theory. We wrote down all the key constraints on the power system, and then we set them up as a maximization problem and looked at their shadow prices. And then we said well what if you interpret these shadow prices as real prices and actually start applying them to things. Can you control the power system in this way?" The same economist certified the result: "I was able to bless it and say yes this was consistent with economic theory in all regards" (Caramanis, Schweppe, and Tabors 1983).

The "marketplace" envisioned by the Schweppe group was decidedly not a market in the economic sense. It lacked basic features of a market and is therefore better described as a pricing model. Revenues based on marginal costs are likely to be insufficient to cover the industry's large fixed costs, particularly for generators at the margin. Later electricity market proposals expected that scarcity rents, during periods of peak demand when prices could rise to multiples of the marginal cost of generation, would provide the revenues to cover fixed costs. The MIT group proposed a more direct solution. Those investments would still be subject to a regulatory process, where utilities would seek approval for new plants, and those plants would become part of their rate base. The spot pricing model included an adjustment for "revenue reconciliation," a correction that is not a part of any liberalized electricity model today, to assure that total revenues received by a utility would cover revenue requirements, namely, its costs plus a return on investors' capital. Regulators would no longer approve the specific short-term rate that was charged to customers, but would approve the mechanism for calculating prices, and would justify total revenues in terms of the utility's "rate base." This also meant that investment in new power plants would continue to be subject to a regulatory process. In the chapter on revenue reconciliation, Schweppe and his group proposed a menu of possible ways to force the revenues paid by consumers at spot prices to equal the utility's revenue requirement as determined in the regulatory process. Some of these involved recalculating prices by including the revenue requirement as a kind of reverse budget constraint; total expenditures of customers were constrained to go no lower than the revenue requirement. However, the authors recommended an approach based on a revolving fund, in which revenues above the requirement would be deposited, and would be debited in case of a shortfall in revenues. Thus customers would still be presented with prices approximating short-term marginal costs.

It is possible that the provision for revenue reconciliation was added in anticipation of objections from utilities, who would naturally be concerned that the spot pricing systems would not necessarily deliver returns to their investors or cover their own operating costs. As one of the authors reflected, in a 2013 interview, "We knew that we were introducing distortions into the prices and that would affect behavior. But everybody who we talked to about deregulation said that no existing utility is willing to play that game unless it can pay off its sunk costs." This concern may have been prescient, as the question of revenue adequacy has been, and continues to be, one of the most contentious political issues around electricity markets. When competitive wholesale markets were instituted in parts of the United States a decade after the publication of the spot pricing book, no revenue reconciliation was contemplated, since that would defeat the purpose of competition. It was expected that generators at the margin, if they were truly necessary, would recover their costs during periods of peak demand, when prices would rise well above their marginal costs, yielding "scarcity rents." But the market participants and regulators continue to struggle over the adequacy of market revenues for supporting necessary investment (Breslau 2013).

## Selling the Model

Tabors assumed the role of the public face of the spot pricing program, activating a network of connections in an effort to scale up the framework of spot pricing. Schweppe died unexpectedly in 1987, but the remaining members of the spot pricing group continued these efforts through a consulting firm they formed, Tabor, Caramanis, and Associates, in 1988. They consulted with electrical utilities, regulators, large industrial electricity customers, and industry groups. Their efforts to interest engineers, through the industry-funded Electrical Power Research Institute, were not successful. Electrical engineers, and their organizations, resisted the concept of homeostatic control, and later the proposal for marginal-cost-based spot pricing. This can be understood as simultaneously a matter of shielding their professional jurisdiction and responding to an affront to their intellectual outlook. When Schweppe and his associates, principally Tabors, presented their model to the Electrical Power Research Institute, "we got a pretty dramatic cold shoulder out of EPRI. There are some incredible quotes from the number two guy at EPRI, who came to the Foxboro conference, and wrote us a letter back and said that as far as he was concerned, spot pricing, or, in those days, homeostatic control, was the analogue of giving everybody on a 747 a joystick and expecting them to be able to land the airplane." Engineers, concerned above all with the secure operation of the system, chafed at the idea of transferring control of flows of power to the multitudes of customers. Because the system had developed with the embedded assumption of load following, their procedures depended on a highly predictable load. The response to prices was liable to invalidate their planning, including the advance commitment of generating units and day-ahead economic dispatch plans. They did not trust the ability of the proposed system to predict the response of consumers to price changes. The redistribution of agency recommended by Schweppe and his colleagues went too far.

The response from electric utilities was not much more positive. The initial efforts of the Schweppe group to find allies was focused on utilities, and trying to sell them on instituting spot prices. The conviction all along had been that spot prices would save money for both utilities and their customers, but utilities were very hesitant to restructure their pricing and billing practices in a way that could make their revenues less predictable. The group worked briefly with the Southern Company, then and now one of the country's largest regulated utilities, as well as Niagara Mohawk, a utility in New York State, now a subsidiary of the UK-based National Grid. At best, firms such as Detroit Edison were willing to pilot spot pricing for selected groups of very large customers.

Potential adopters in industry were not difficult to identify. These were industrial firms with electricity-using processes that could be scheduled at any time. In Schweppe's words, their demand was for energy, not power. For instance, firms that liquefied gases for industrial applications simply needed a total amount of electricity, which they could take at any time: "That is literally just a big storage tank and a compressor. You can run the damn thing whenever you want, right? So it's a perfect example of, if you have time-variant, significantly time-varying rates, you know, and they don't care when they squeeze it, don't turn the darn thing on when the price is high. Make stuff when the price is low." Kodak's plant in Rochester, another example, consumed power largely for molding plastic parts. But parts could be produced in large quantities overnight for assembly during daytime hours. If Kodak would lobby the utility from which it purchased power to introduce time-varying prices, it could realize savings by shifting its consumption to off-peak and therefore low-cost hours. There were also efforts to develop new techniques of load forecasting that would allow operators to accurately anticipate the responses to spot prices and plan accordingly (David 1988).

Ultimately, no utility implemented spot pricing as described by the Schweppe group. There were a few programs, such as the pilot programs by large California utilities, that adopted a spot pricing algorithm for selected large customers, industrial and commercial firms, in the mid-1980s (Garcia and Runnels 1985). But despite the efforts of Tabors and his associates to promote their concept, it was never adopted as an approach to systemwide control. The unpredictable feedback loops that would be activated if all power customers, including large industries, reacted to changing prices in real time, were intolerable for system operators whose work was premised on a relatively predictable load, prior scheduling of dispatch, and incremental real-time adjustments.

## Conclusions

The market design envisioned by Schweppe and his collaborators, with the spot pricing algorithm at its core, can be understood as a control system with agency distributed between a central calculator and a myriad of independent price-responsive actors. The division of agency, and the construction of the agents themselves, parallels the division of labor between the engineering work to develop the control techniques for state estimation, economic dispatch, and price calculation; and the economic work of modeling the consumer response to price changes and the efficiency of the market design. The particular division of labor put forth by the Schweppe group was ultimately not adopted by the power industry or supported by regulators. With the advent of deregulation in the 1990s, the Schweppe model had even less of a chance. In the one discussion of deregulation in the classic 1988 book, the four authors suggested that the spot pricing system could be extended to a deregulated market by completely severing the price calculator from both buyers and sellers, so that all market participants would be making decisions in response to hourly spot prices. In an interview, a figure who would be involved in the design for wholesale markets that was eventually adopted, describes a common reaction to the book's proposal: "The central coordinator would announce the prices and everybody would make their own independent decisions, and then everything would work. And when you discuss this idea with system operators, they had a heart attack. They just said, 'What are you talking about?' Because they could see the lights going out quite rapidly if we tried to actually implement that."

The solution, or at least the one currently in place in a large and growing number of power systems internationally, retains the price-calculating approach of the MIT group, but differs in its allocation of agency. As is practiced nearly universally, the central controller uses techniques of economic dispatch and price calculation based on those developed at MIT two decades earlier, but within a design that expands the role of central control while circumscribing the agency of the many buyers and sellers. In this design, buyers and sellers submit bids and offers one day in advance of the trading, specifying quantities and prices. The system operator uses the bids to calculate optimal dispatch and the prices that will be charged, based on the lambdas of the dispatch model, for every hour of the following day. Rather than trading for all the power transacted in real time, most of the transactions have already been determined in the day-ahead market. In real-time, a small amount of power is transacted and prices calculated every five minutes, for deviations from the day-ahead schedule. This is apparently a way to organize the relationship of central calculation to distributed, market-based, control that could satisfy the industry's powerful stakeholders. But once again, it was the underlying equivalence between the optimal allocation and the theoretical market equilibrium that allowed for a reallocation of agency.

## References

Abur, Ali, and Antonio Gómez Expósito. 2004. *Power System State Estimation: Theory and Implementation*. New York: Marcel Dekker.

Anderson, Douglas D. 1981. *Regulatory Politics and Electric Utilities: A Case Study in Political Economy*. Boston: Auburn House.

Arrow, Kenneth J. 2008. "George Dantzig in the Development of Economic Analysis." Special issue in memory of George B. Dantzig, *Discrete Optimization* 5, no. 2: 159–67. doi.org/10.1016/j.disopt.2006.11.007.

Bennett, S. 1993. *A History of Control Engineering, 1930–1955*. Stevenage, UK: P. Peregrinus on behalf of the Institution of Electrical Engineers, London.

Breslau, Daniel. 2011. "What Do Market Designers Do When They Design Markets? Economists as Consultants to the Redesign of Wholesale Electricity Markets in the U.S." In *Social Knowledge in the Making*, edited by Charles Camic, Neil Gross, and Michèle Lamont, 379–403. Chicago: University of Chicago Press.

Breslau, Daniel. 2013. "Designing a Market-like Entity: Economics in the Politics of Market Formation." *Social Studies of Science* 43, no. 6: 829–51. doi.org/10.1177/0306312713493962.

Caramanis, M. C., R. E. Bohn, and F. C. Schweppe. 1982. "Optimal Spot Pricing: Practice and Theory." *IEEE Transactions on Power Apparatus and Systems* PAS-101, no. 9: 3234–45. doi.org/10.1109/TPAS.1982.317507.

Caramanis, Michael C., Fred C. Schweppe, and Richard D. Tabors. 1983. "Spot Pricing and Its Relation to Other Load Management Methods." dspace.mit.edu/handle/1721.1/60591.

Cohn, Julie A. 2015. "Transitions from Analog to Digital Computing in Electric Power Systems." *IEEE Annals of the History of Computing* 37, no. 3: 32–43. doi.org/10.1109/MAHC.2015.37.

Cohn, Julie A. 2017. *The Grid: Biography of an American Technology*. Cambridge, MA: MIT Press.

Dantzig, George B. 1963. *Linear Programming and Extensions*. Princeton, NJ: Princeton University Press.

David, A. K. 1988. "Load Forecasting under Spot Pricing." *Transmission and Distribution IEE Proceedings C—Generation* 135, no. 5: 369–77. doi.org/10.1049/ip-c.1988.0048.

Dorfman, Robert, Paul A. Samuelson, and Robert M. Solow. 1958. *Linear Programming and Economic Analysis*. New York: McGraw-Hill.

Freeman, Eva C., and Lincoln Laboratory, eds. 1995. *MIT Lincoln Laboratory: Technology in the National Interest*. Lexington, MA: Lincoln Laboratory, Massachusetts Institute of Technology.

Garcia, E. V., and J. E. Runnels. 1985. "The Utility Perspective of Spot Pricing." *IEEE Transactions on Power Apparatus and Systems* PAS-104, no. 6: 1391–93. doi.org/10.1109/TPAS.1985.319232.

Garcia-Parpet, Marie-France. 2007. "The Social Construction of a Perfect Market: The Strawberry Auction at Fontaines-En-Sologne." In *Do Economists Make Markets? On the Performativity of Economics*, edited by Donald A. MacKenzie, Fabian Muniesa, and Lucia Siu, 20–53. Princeton, NJ: Princeton University Press.

Glaeser, Martin Gustav. 1957. *Public Utilities in American Capitalism*. New York: Macmillan.

Gormley, William T. 1983. *The Politics of Public Utility Regulation*. Pittsburgh, PA: University of Pittsburgh Press.

Grainger, John J., and William D. Stevenson. 1994. *Power System Analysis*. New York: McGraw-Hill.

Guala, Francesco. 2001. "Building Economic Machines: The FCC Auctions." *Studies in History and Philosophy of Science* 32, no. 3: 453–77.

Hausman, William J., and John L. Neufeld. 2011. "How Politics, Economics, and Institutions Shaped Electric Utility Regulation in the United States: 1879–2009." *Business History* 53, no. 5: 723–46. doi.org/10.1080/00076791.2011.599589.

Hirsh, Richard F. 1989. *Technology and Transformation in the American Electric Utility Industry*. New York: Cambridge University Press.

Hirsh, Richard F. 1999. *Power Loss: The Origins of Deregulation and Restructuring in the American Electric Utility System*. Cambridge, MA: MIT Press.

Hughes, Thomas P. 1983. *Networks of Power: Electrification in Western Society*. Baltimore: Johns Hopkins University Press.

Hughes, Thomas P. 1987. "The Evolution of Large Technological Systems." In *The Social Construction of Technological Systems: New Directions in the Sociology and History of Technology*, edited by Wiebe E. Bijker, Thomas P. Hughes, and Trevor Pinch, 51–82. Cambridge, MA: MIT Press.

Lambert, Jeremiah D. 2015. *The Power Brokers: The Struggle to Shape and Control the Electric Power Industry*. Cambridge, MA: MIT Press. search.ebscohost.com/login.aspx?direct=true&scope=site&db=nlebk&db=nlabk&AN=1058793.

Lerner, Abba Ptachya. 1947. *The Economics of Control: Principles of Welfare Economics*. New York: Macmillan.

Lifset, Robert D. 2014a. "A New Understanding of the American Energy Crisis of the 1970s." *Historical Social Research / Historische Sozialforschung* 39, no. 4: 22–42.

Lifset, Robert D. 2014b. "A New Understanding of the American Energy Crisis of the 1970s." *Eine Neue Interpretation Der U.S.-Amerikanischen Energiekrise Der 1970er Jahre* 39, no. 4: 22–42. doi.org/10.12759/hsr.39.2014.4.22–42.

MacKenzie, Donald. 1990. *Inventing Accuracy: A Historical Sociology of Nuclear Missile Guidance*. Cambridge, MA: MIT Press.

Neufeld, John L. 1987. "Price Discrimination and the Adoption of the Electricity Demand Charge." *Journal of Economic History* 47, no. 3: 693–709.

Nik-Khah, Edward. 2008. "A Tale of Two Auctions." *Journal of Institutional Economics* 4, no. 1: 73–97.

Reynolds, S. P., and T. E. Creighton. 1980. "Time-of-Use Rates for Very Large Customers on the Pacific Gas and Electric Company System." *IEEE Transactions on Power Apparatus and Systems* PAS-99, no. 1: 147–51. doi.org/10.1109/TPAS .1980.319621.

Roth, Alvin E. 2002. "The Economist as Engineer: Game Theory, Experimental Economics, and Computation as Tools of Design Economics." *Econometrica* 70, no. 4: 1341–78.

Schweppe, F. C., R. D. Tabors, J. L. Kirtley, H. R. Outhred, F. H. Pickel, and A. J. Cox. 1980. "Homeostatic Utility Control." *IEEE Transactions on Power Apparatus and Systems* PAS-99, no. 3: 1151–63. doi.org/10.1109/TPAS.1980.319745.

Schweppe, Fred C., Michael C. Caramanis, Richard D. Tabors, and Roger E. Bohn. 1988. *Spot Pricing of Electricity*. Boston: Kluwer Academic.

Schweppe, Fred C., and J. Wildes. 1970. "Power System Static-State Estimation, Part I: Exact Model." *IEEE Transactions on Power Apparatus and Systems* PAS-89, no. 1: 120–25. doi.org/10.1109/TPAS.1970.292678.

Stahl, E. C. M. 1931. "Economic Loading of Generating Stations." *Electrical Engineering* 50, no. 9: 722–27. doi.org/10.1109/EE.1931.6429418.

Wiener, Norbert. 1948. *Cybernetics, or, Control and Communication in the Animal and the Machine*. New York: Wiley and Sons.

Wu, Felix F. 1990. "Power System State Estimation: A Survey." *International Journal of Electrical Power and Energy Systems* 12, no. 2: 80–87. doi.org/10.1016/0142-0615(90)90003-T.

Yakubovich, Valery, Mark Granovetter, and Patrick McGuire. 2005. "Electric Charges: The Social Construction of Rate Systems." *Theory & Society* 34, nos. 5–6: 579–612.

# Building a National Machine: The Pricing of Electricity in Postwar France

Guillaume Yon

In the mid-1960s, Pierre Massé, then head of the Commissariat général au Plan, the agency in charge of French economic and social planning (usually abbreviated as the Plan), published a book to explain the rationale behind the French postwar planning experience (Massé 1965). Massé was an engineer who entered the École Polytechnique in 1916 and graduated from the École des Ponts et Chaussées in 1922.[1] In the interwar period, he designed and oversaw the construction of some of the largest hydroelectric dams in France. When the whole electricity industry was nationalized in 1946, and Électricité de France (EDF) was created, he became the director of equipment before moving to the Plan in 1959, until 1969. At least two times in his book, Massé (1965: 44–54, 162–87) develops the reasoning I propose to analyze below. This allows me to introduce how this article intends to approach the question of the economics and engineering nexus.

I thank Pedro Garcia Duarte and Yann Giraud for inviting me to the *HOPE* conference, a fascinating experience of intense discussion. All the participants at the conference and two anonymous reviewers provided great advice and many insights for this paper, and food for thought for the years to come. I also thank the members of the Department III at the Max Planck Institute in Berlin, where a first draft of this paper was written, and Mary Morgan and Véra Ehrenstein, for numerous discussions on the topic and invaluable support from the first steps of the research to the final version.

    1. On Massé's career, see his autobiography (Massé 1984).

*History of Political Economy* 52 (annual suppl.)  DOI 10.1215/00182702-8718035

Massé starts with what he calls the basic tenet of economic theory, formulated, according to him, by Léon Walras and Vilfredo Pareto, which he considers "a remarkable intellectual construction" of atomistic producers and consumers immersed in an environment they do not know well and do not need to know. All they get from this environment are simple and clear signals, namely, prices. Consumers adapt their demand to these signals in order to maximize their utility, while producers adapt their production plans to the signals in order to maximize their profit. Massé praises this intellectual construction on two different grounds. First, he acknowledges the ability of the market thus defined to efficiently perform short-term adjustments. A new operating decision made by a producer, or an investment shortly implemented, will, through a new price, trigger a quick reaction on the demand side. Conversely, a small change in consumers' preferences will be shortly carried to producers through price signals and generate an adaptation of the supply side. Second, Massé adds to the efficiency argument a political one. The Walrasian construction is democratic. The price reflects the costs of production and conveys all the information on a new good to the consumers. Consumers freely respond by expressing their level of demand for that good. The price mechanism constantly organizes a plebiscite, and the market gives people what they want.

For Massé, the main limit of this construction becomes obvious when one adopts the engineering perspective. Large-scale and capital-intensive investments, like hydroelectric dams, canals that connect two large river basins, tunnels or railroads, have no market. They cannot rely on automatic signals and consumers' preferences, and they entail too many uncertainties. Public authorities providing public infrastructures are not the only ones facing this limit. Private firms encounter the same issue, for example, when a steel producer discusses the opportunity of developing a new conveyor chain technology, or a car manufacturer the launch of a new model (with its associated new assembly line methods).

Massé interprets the socialist calculation debate as diverging responses to this very problem. He rejects Oskar Lange's solution. As the head of the French planning agency and former director of equipment of a firm that managed the whole French electricity market, Massé considers that a central planning board that would equate all prices to marginal costs, effectively running a Walrasian auction and trying to compute through a trial-and-error process a general equilibrium, would have to greatly simplify the multiple preferences of consumers and the aims of producers. Moreover, the central planning board would have to rely on a great deal of authority and police to enforce the chosen plan. Simplification and enforcement both impede freedom.

But Massé also emphasizes some crucial elements, based on his own and his colleagues' engineering work, that are absent from the solely theoretical solution put forward by Maurice Allais and Gérard Debreu. This might seem surprising. Massé, Allais, an engineer with the same training as Massé, and Debreu, a PhD student of Allais, are usually considered to be all on the same page. Yet Massé argues that his experience at EDF and then at the Plan in postwar France adds, in some important aspects, to the theories of Allais or Debreu. The present article aims to explain why and how, by describing the EDF experience on pricing electricity based on the so-called long-term marginal cost.

Massé summarizes the bulk of the innovation as follows. He writes that the solution to the problem of long-term investment decisions was presented in its most sophisticated form by Kenneth Arrow and Debreu. Against Lange's authoritarian solution, their reasoning extends the sovereignty of the consumer to decisions about the future, through the idea of complete (or "generalized" in Massé's words) markets. The basic idea is that uncertainty means multiple possible futures, hence the introduction of multiple commodities with different prices that can be traded separately. Each commodity and the associated price are time- and state-of-the-world dependent (i.e., the delivery of one unit of a specific good if a specific but uncertain state realizes at a specific future date). This is a theory of securities traded on financial markets. The theory extends the sovereignty of the consumer to his or her probability estimates, his or her appetite for risk and for deferred satisfaction. The theory does so through the sole means of a price that the consumer is willing to pay.

For Massé, this extension of liberalism, individual freedom, and sovereignty paradoxically destroys the very notion of sovereignty. Producers and consumers practically make no enlightened decisions anymore; they are just robots reacting to signals sent by financial markets. Here Massé (1965: 184) quotes Debreu: the producer does not need to engage in thoughtful and balanced calculations; she just needs to announce a production plan, acknowledge the response of the stock market, and adapt. In addition to this paradoxical destruction of informed decisions about the future, Massé emphasizes that this theory implies a huge confidence in the ability of prices to convey reliable information. Price signals might be easily manipulated by powerful vested interests. Small miscommunications of information through prices might trigger catastrophic collective malinvestment, with long-lasting effects. Thus, although backed by obvious antiauthoritarian motives, the consequences of relying solely on an anonymous, dispersed price mechanism are potentially huge.

Massé does not believe that prices can tell the truth about what people really want, especially in the long run, when large infrastructural projects are involved. In place of such an automatic mechanism, he proposes a conscious decision. Technologies and preferences, or, in Massé's words, productive processes and consumption behaviors, are not outside the realm of the market, with no constraints on them. They are the object of an informed political decision. This decision, then, requires economic techniques like linear programming to conciliate all its requirements in a coherent technical project. Long-term marginal cost pricing, then, works as a set of administrative instructions, designed in order to shape the behavior of users in the long run, according to the decisions made in the realm of production. The market does not supersede politics, rather, it is a tool to realize complex political decisions (Massé 1965: 165). What Massé calls "the plan of the nation" provides every citizen with an image of a desirable collective future to work for, far from the automated response to price signals.

Finally, Massé specifies that his is not a radical solution, but a practical and empirical one. It is therefore less prone to theorization than the solution proposed by Lange or by Debreu (Massé 1965: 49). Massé's solution was epitomized not by a full-fledged theory but by a practice, the long-term marginal-cost pricing policy at EDF. The present article is devoted to the description of this practice.

## Preliminaries: Two Traditions in Economic Engineering

Before turning to the details of marginal cost pricing at EDF, I would like to briefly explain why I think that the emphasis put by Massé on long-term and large-scale investments is relevant for the topic of this volume. The economic and engineering nexus is often considered through the lens of the critical narrative provided by Philip Mirowski and Edward Nik-Khah (2017). These authors tell a story that starts with the socialist calculation debate. They show how the political agenda that aimed at demonstrating the superiority of the free market system over socialism, and its subsequent encounter with the computer technology in Cold War America (with Hayek as the link), shaped a new vision of the market as an information processor. The market is able to process information scattered across many actors fumbling in the dark; the output is nothing but the truth about what people really want (the authors name it "market epistemology"). The market supersedes lengthy political discussions, compromises, and enlightened consents. Mirowski and Nik-Khah add that this tradition actually produced a form of economic engineering narrowly focused on the technical details of the informational properties of markets and short-term matching problems. According to these two authors, this leaves ample room for the intervention of powerful vested interests.

The critique formulated by Mirowski and Nik-Khah echoes strangely the one made by Massé in 1965. The project that explicitly aimed at extending the sovereignty of the consumer appears to end paradoxically in a vision of the consumer as an automaton reacting to price signals. The consumer does not make any informed decisions or express a collective will for the future. Mirowski and Nik-Khah add that this shift within economics produced a form of economic engineering focused on the technical details of the informational properties of markets and short-term matching problems, leaving ample room for the intervention of powerful vested interests. This outcome is in contradiction with the project of extending the sovereignty of consumers and the realm of freedom, echoing Massé's intuition.

The specificity of the economics and engineering nexus in postwar France, its difference from contemporary epistemologies of economic engineering, has often gone unnoticed in the literature. The latter rightly emphasized the importance of Keynesian policies and "indicative planning," that is, the circulation of information across the state, private firms and trade unions, implemented through the construction of a complete and consistent national accounting system (Fourquet 1980; Rosanvallon 1987; Desrosières 1999). If these policies were important, they were only part of the story. As developed by Massé (1965: 164), these policies were crucial to deal with cycles and disequilibrium, in order to come back to an equilibrium or to "defend" it. An excessive focus on Keynesian policies would miss the crucial groundwork of defining and implementing future equilibrium through the design and construction of large infrastructures.

Interestingly enough, the literature on the EDF case emphasizes neither the nevertheless crucial innovations introduced in Allais's and Debreu's theories through the engineering practices, nor the critique of the grand Walrasian scheme, clearly stated by Massé. Robert Frost (1985, 1991) considers that the project of EDF's engineers was to apply scrupulously and rigidly the general equilibrium theory, as restated by Allais during the war, to the electricity sector, in order to mimic perfect competition in the absence of competition and fight the powerful communist trade union.

The aim was to avoid the socialization of the newly created public monopoly, a first step toward the socialization of the whole French economy. Frost suggests that the use of economics by EDF's engineers, especially marginal-cost pricing, turned out to be nothing but a sophisticated smokescreen hiding a policy in favor of large, electro-intensive industrial users and in disfavor of urban domestic users (the workers).

Martin Chick (2002, 2007: chaps. 4, 5) interprets the practice of marginal cost pricing at EDF as the birthplace of the contemporary practice of peak-load pricing. EDF's engineers, because of the centralized structure of the firm, the importance of capital-intensive sources of production (hydropower), and the influence of Allais, developed a visionary understanding of economic rationality through the implementation of peak-load pricing. They drew a straightforward link between consumption (especially during peak hours) and costs, signaling through prices the costs of production to users (something not achieved by their British counterparts). Chick concludes that EDF's pricing policy was an application of the general equilibrium theory, and this early application explains why public pressure for privatization in the 1970s was less intense in France than in the UK. EDF, organized around the use of marginal cost pricing, was considered efficient and economically rational, whereas the British electricity industry was commonly branded as inefficient and plagued with opaque political bargains.

Frost's and Chick's narratives both analyze EDF pricing policy as the direct application of Allais's theory and as a way to mimic a competitive equilibrium. Both authors see the EDF case from the vantage point of a liberalized and perfectly competitive model of the market. They both interpret the work of EDF's engineers as the hidden origin of this version of the market, either to criticize it (Frost) or to praise its rationality (Chick). If, as historians, we do not believe in teleology, and if we want to stress the specificity of an epoch, we need to interpret the work of EDF's engineers in their own terms and context. I argue that their articulation of economics and engineering was different from the economic engineering of competitive markets dominant today. Frost's and Chick's narratives miss a crucial point: the use of cost and price calculations for the design and construction of an infrastructure. This is the crucial point made by Massé: for EDF's engineers, productive processes and the uses of electricity were not already defined and taken for granted, or formed outside the realm of the market. Their aim was not just to signal, correctly and without distortion, existing and transparent costs of production to users, as I show in the first section above. Instead, EDF's engineers deployed economic calculations to make politically informed decisions on the design of technologies of production and on the future strategic uses of electricity, as I show in the next two sections. Finally, as the last two sections of the article demonstrate, the prices thus calculated served as administrative instructions sent to users in order to shape their uses (their nature, location, and time) in the long run.

## The Problem of the Long Term

A seminal paper by Marcel Boiteux, a young engineer at EDF, staged very well the specificity of his and his colleagues' practice by introducing the central notion of long-term marginal cost (Boiteux 1949a).[2] Boiteux (1987) put it in a nutshell when he wrote that long-term marginal cost pricing allowed EDF to use prices as tools to realize an investment policy. His reasoning revolved around the idea that marginal costs cannot be directly calculated. The cost of an additional kilowatt-hour does not exist if a plant operates at full capacity; but if it does not operate at full capacity, then its marginal cost is zero (letting a little bit more water flow through the turbine does not cost anything). His intuition was that marginal costs could, however, be calculated indirectly, if one knew and wanted to ensure a satisfying equilibrium between production, transport, and the load curve (that expresses the variation of the quantity of kilowatt-hours over time) demanded by users. Thus, long-term marginal costs, and the prices deduced from these costs, would be defined as a response to an investment plan, a dispatch (the movements of energy through the grid), and a concerted forecast of the future load profile. Prices were to be designed to trigger the users' behaviors that would support and be adapted to the realization of an equipment plan (the construction of new plants). Long-term marginal cost pricing considered consumers central components of a machine under development, to whom instructions were transmitted through prices.

Boiteux opened his 1949 paper with a general image borrowed from Allais: the image of an economy governed by the principles of competitive planning (*planification concurrentielle*). Allais was an engineer by training. He graduated from the École Polytechnique in the early 1930s. He quickly focused on teaching and conducting research, mostly at the École des Mines. During the war, he published an imposing book, À la recherche d'une discipline économique (*The Search for an Economic Discipline*) (Allais 1944), which brought together all the findings of the marginalist school inspired by Walras, and connected these findings to the

2. For an English translation, see Boiteux 1960b.

industrial problems of the time. Once translated and turned into papers, the book gave Allais the Nobel Prize in 1988. After the war, Allais's seminar used to gather members of the state corps of engineers in charge of running industrial sectors that had been nationalized (engineers from the national railroads company, the national coal mining company, the national gas company), as well as private companies. It was in this seminar that Gabriel Dessus, in charge of pricing at EDF, met and hired Boiteux, one of Allais's PhD students, to help him establish the pricing policy of the new public monopoly (Boiteux 1993). Dessus was not versed in economic theory like Allais. He was a graduate from the École Polytechnique, too, but like Massé he had a long and successful career as an actual engineer before joining EDF. Before the war, Dessus had been working in one of the most important private electricity companies, the one that distributed a large part of the electricity consumed in the Paris area, the Compagnie parisienne de distribution d'électricité. There, Dessus collaborated with two engineers, Charles Malégarie and Paul Stasi (Dessus hired the latter to work with him and Boiteux at EDF), who pioneered the use of marginal costs techniques for power production management (Malégarie 1947).

The image borrowed by Boiteux from Allais is as follows. Allais wanted to mathematically demonstrate the equivalence between Walras's general equilibrium theory and the optimal state of an economy as defined by Pareto. For Allais, an economy is at an optimal state when all the goods and services are priced at their marginal cost (the production cost of one additional unit). Dessus (1949) provides us with an apologue that illustrates this reasoning. For its future production, a steel work in Saint-Étienne (an industrial city and a mining center in the Massif Central, eastern central France) can choose between an electric arc furnace or a fuel-based blast furnace. If the price at which oil is sold to the company were artificially inflated and the price of electricity artificially decreased, the investment decision would be in favor of electricity. This means that, at the level and from the perspective of the national reconstruction, resources would be used to build more hydropower dams in order to satisfy the steel work, while in fact fewer resources could have been used to provide the same service to the company through an increased exploitation of oil. Moving away from marginal costs generates a waste of resources, when the same service can be provided with fewer resources by matching prices with marginal costs.

Allais's theory requires the generalization of two types of equivalence: of the production factors through their cost and of consumers' satisfaction through prices. The theory considers the national economy as a whole, with all its markets (its productive processes), and aims at finding the allocation of production factors (capital and labor as measured by costs) that maximizes the global satisfaction of consumers in this economy (measured by the prices that consumers are willing to pay). Marginal cost pricing ensures the maximum efficiency of the production factors; these are allocated between the different sectors of the economy in order to produce the maximum satisfaction for all the consumers. This is why Allais called this reasoning *théorie du rendement social*. As suggested by Dessus's example, wastage happens if one turns away from marginal costs, because it would have been possible to produce the same service at a lower cost by using fewer resources.

Boiteux (1948) expanded on this idea through a series of nested examples. A given necessity might be satisfied by different uses of electric power. For instance, there are different ways to heat water with electricity. One of them is to use a storage device that heats water during off-peak hours, at night, when production is less costly. But the same necessity (heating water) might be satisfied by using other energy sources, such as a gas heater and coal-based collective heating. And then, the need for hot water might be in balance with other individual and industrial necessities. If, in each of these situations, producers displayed the production cost of one additional unit, individuals and industrials could consider the intensity of their needs in light of these costs. The demand established at this price measures this intensity. If individuals and industrials required more production, they would derive a satisfaction exceeding the price they are willing to pay (if not, they would not have required additional units). Setting prices at marginal costs is supposed to make sure that consumers' satisfaction is not inferior to the cost collectively incurred by the nation to satisfy these needs. Boiteux wrote that in Allais's world, the prices must tell the costs as clocks tell the time. According to Boiteux, this is a principle of productivity and maximum efficiency for the nation (an optimal state): it would not be possible to produce more satisfaction with the available productive resources.

Allais's grand scheme, presented above, was not implemented though. Time and history were reintroduced through costs calculation, when Boiteux faced the material thickness of the concrete production processes used by EDF. The next step in Boiteux's reasoning was the study of marginal costs in electricity production based on available technologies (Boiteux 1949b). In the electricity sector, the cost for producing one additional unit was either almost zero (for installations not operating at full capacity) or indeterminate (for those operating at full capacity, it was impossible to produce one additional unit without endangering the equipment). These prices, Allais's prices, could not be made sense of. They supposed that a new installation would be built as soon as existing installations were saturated at very low prices, because these prices would equate the production costs at the very moment when the demand would be expressed.

To solve this absurdity, Boiteux's innovation consisted in introducing time, especially the future, through the new concept of long-term or development marginal cost. Instead of building a new plant once the last one would be saturated at prices equating the instantaneous marginal costs of Allais's theory, Boiteux exploited the indeterminacy of marginal costs associated with an installation operating at full capacity in order to set these costs differently. He called for oversaturating the installations and increasing the prices to contain the demand at the level of capacity of existing plants. If the demand increased and its intensity rose, the prices would contain it. How far? Up to a moment when the demand would be sufficiently intense to finance the readaptation of the production system, that is, its development. At this level of prices, demand would be able to cover the development cost throughout the construction of new plants. Given that this reasoning applied to saturated installations for which marginal costs were indeterminate, Boiteux suggested that this new kind of price was the marginal cost calculated by taking into account the long-term readaptation of the productive system.

Optimal prices were those that guaranteed the financing of future installations, that is, EDF's investments. This implied that the system, whose development would be supported by electricity consumers, ought to be defined. Boiteux specified that this support might not be perfect; it only needed to be satisfactory. Prices would manipulate the load curve in such a way as to sufficiently finance the investment plan of the country's electricity sector over a given period, which would be defined as the time needed to develop, commission, and amortize the new plants. The intuition was as follows: to conduct/induce a demand that remained free (it was not a centrally administered rationing system, users' decisions were decentralized) toward the support of a production system to be planned.

## Design

To better understand the significance of Boiteux's innovation, let us come back to the problem to which he provided a decisive solution. The problem originated from the nationalization and the creation of the Plan at the end of the Second World War: how to write an engineering project for the production of electricity, by combining many types of materials, in order to produce useful effects and achieve specific objectives, under various constraints imposed by a range of different actors? I argue here that EDF's engineers grappled with the problem of designing a very large machine.

When EDF was created, in 1946, defining its objectives (the services that the public monopoly ought to deliver) was not particularly difficult. Within and beyond the company, there was a broad consensus that production and consumption should be strongly encouraged. Electricity production was considered a major bottleneck of the French economy and the first obstacle to overcome in order to modernize the country. The nationalization aimed at allowing a vigorous increase of electricity uses. EDF's engineers did not start by analyzing an existing demand. Such an analysis would have made no sense in a country that had been destroyed by the war. Instead, they made a decision on a load curve that would need to be satisfied. This decision was named "the law of the doubling every 10 years."[3] Surprisingly, this drastic increase of production was not anticipated by taking demand and price into consideration. Rather, it rested on statistical observations of the American situation, which was considered the modern, developed economy to be imitated.

Estimates derived from this US benchmark were corrected and adjusted based on inquiries among industrial users and during consultations organized by the Plan and its different councils. The purpose of these discussions was not to listen to the requests of French employers, who had been discredited (Kuisel 1981). For the engineers who resisted Nazi Germany and then came to power with the Liberation of France, most employers represented the small provincial risk-adverse firms of the Third Republic, the profit seekers during the crisis of the 1930s, and the cowardly economic collaborators with Germany in the 1940s. The consultations aimed, for the Plan, at establishing industrial objectives based on the existing forces of the French economy; they were not held to register private requests and claims. From the objectives the Plan eventually established, electricity needs (quantities of kilowatt-hour) could be deduced, and this gave EDF a production target.

The target, the load curve, was thus set. For EDF, then, the focus was on the choice of the production means. EDF's department of equipment was tasked with combining different material equipment to produce the

3. For a presentation, see Boiteux 1956, sec. 1.

given load curve. The department was led by Massé (1953), for whom "the object/aim of a national company such as Électricité de France is to provide the collectivity with the services it expects from the company, and to provide these services at the lowest costs through an appropriate combination of various techniques" (my translation). The aim was the production of an artifact, a machine, that is, the provision of services obtained from the careful assemblage of material means. But EDF's engineers were not independent craftsmen, and their work included an additional difficulty: the satisfaction of multiple constraints.

If in 1946 the definition of the services to be provided by EDF was consensual, Massé's account shows that the problem resided in the combination of the production means. The issue revealed the existence of multiple, contradicting requirements, a situation that echoes the different councils of the king discussing a technical project in eighteenth-century France, as described by Hélène Vérin (1993). In the late 1940s, early 1950s, disagreements about the production of electricity revolved around the choice between hydropower dams and thermal plants. The company's engineers, especially Massé, had been trained in the construction of dams. The Plan was on the same page. Its mission was to equip the country and build a national industrial heritage. As pointed out by the military, hydropower was a national source of energy, while the French coal mines located in the north and east of the territory tended to be quickly lost during conflicts (the wars with Germany, and the threat of tanks coming from the USSR). EDF's department of equipment, together with the department of research, both concerned with long-term strategy, also argued that dam reservoirs allowed the engineers to turn off the costly coal plants during peak load, that their exploitation cost was low, and that they benefited from free work provided by the sun and the clouds (evaporation and precipitation).

However, EDF's division of exploitation and the sales representatives of the company (much more worried about the present situation and directly facing users) opposed the idea of relying so heavily on dams. The needs in electricity were too large and the building time of a dam was about ten years, while thermal plans could be commissioned much faster, within five years, sometimes even less. The Ministry of Finance supported the latter position given the very high investment required by the hydraulic program. It clearly preferred low-investment thermal plants. Besides the dams versus thermal plants debate, another controversy was raging within the Plan over the use of coal versus oil. Coal was national, yet oil was cheap. The debate had a strong geopolitical dimension too. Oil had been discovered in Algeria, but the French overseas department was starting to fight for its independence. Therefore, the technical project elaborated by EDF's engineers had to balance various constraints, from investment cost to security and geopolitical concerns.

The division headed by Massé did exactly what would be expected from state engineers: they calculated a technical project and determined the services (the shape of the load curve) that would be provided by different combinations of material equipment (hydropower, with or without reservoirs; thermal, coal-based or oil-based) to satisfy EDF's supervisory authorities and their multiple requirements. Massé's team decided on the building, or not, of plants, including their size and location, by comparing discounted costs. This means that debates, corrections, and decisions revolved around costs, which costs should be taken into account and how to evaluate them, and the choice of the discount rate.

### The Technical Project

The plan, the calculated project of the machine, the set of solutions to the problem described in the previous section, took shape in the first half of the 1950s. In what follows I sketch how, through a calculation that could combine a large variety of exigencies, the engineers' reasoning developed and evolved (Boiteux 1957).

The initial idea was to develop thermal power generation with the purchase of large generators in the United States, larger than those constructed by private companies in France before the war. The argument was these large generators consumed fewer calories per kilowatt-hour and required fewer employees. But this choice needed to take into account another constraint in the calculation: the pollution emitted by these generators. The calculation incorporated a geographic sensibility. By assigning to power plants near Paris an increased cost that included a substantial depollution cost (about 4 percent of the plant's cost), it was decided that these plants would not be built near any urban centers.

The decision in favor of thermal power was based on the growing cost of hydropower energy. Building new dams was increasingly costly, while resources were rare in postwar France. The best sites were already equipped and the available ones would require more efforts and involve more uncertainties. Given that EDF benefited from the guarantee of the state, the banks might be willing to provide loans at an interest rate as low as 4 percent. At this rate, the building of dams, a rather costly initial investment (unlike thermal power, which becomes costly in operation because of the cost of fuel), could be profitable. Thus, at this rate, a large portion of the savings would be absorbed by EDF, to the detriment of other sectors that did not benefit from the reassuring status of a national monopoly. Therefore the interest rate had to be set in light of at least two phenomena: on the one hand, the will to direct a portion of available savings toward the electricity sector, and on the other hand, the total volume of savings available for investment, which was linked to governmental decisions to encourage saving over immediate consumption. The rate that was eventually chosen in the cost calculation, 7 percent, was set by the Plan after a series of consultations. This rate was sensibly higher from the one at which EDF could have "naturally" borrowed. Yet, even at this higher rate, EDF was absorbing about 5.5 percent of national investments in the mid-1950s (Boiteux 1960a).

The connected decisions evoked above built on a key assumption: the price of thermal units would decrease thanks to massive imports of hydrocarbons, especially oil, at low cost. This was, again, both a decision about which productive processes to develop and a bet. Right after the nationalization, thermal generation was obtained from coal, but it was expected that French coal mines would soon close as their productivity was declining, while miners' salaries were increasing. This expectation pushed for hydropower, which yet was considered by the Plan a costly option, giving too much weight to electric needs and undermining the development of other economic sectors. The situation appeared in a different light with the anticipation that thermal power could be developed based on imported oil and gas. A balance might thus be reached between a limited volume available for investment and massive equipment providing basic production. Each of these bets translated into a future cost. Converted into prices, these costs could become tools for action and coordination.

The calculations performed in the first half of the 1950s introduced considerable changes compared to the prewar period and the situation during the nationalization. These changes were guided by the will to recast the place of hydropower in electricity production, and substitute it with large thermal plants that would be built far from urban centers (e.g., the Parisian consumption basin) in the eastern and northern mining regions of the French territory, or near coastal ports where the imports of hydrocarbons would arrive (Le Havre in Normandy, Fos-sur-Mer on the Mediterranean Sea). A strategic decision was made to limit the flows of investment in the electric sector by relying on the hope for low-cost oil. This decision implied that large thermal plants would provide the production base by operating almost constantly, at a very high number of hours per year.

Once the decision was made to build large thermal plants in areas where coal and oil were easily available, in order to rapidly equip the nation at the lowest midterm investment cost, a new problem arose: the satisfaction of peak demand. Building large installations (thermal ones and later, perhaps, nuclear ones) would make sense only if they formed the production base and were able to operate at a very high number of hours per year. But building this production capacity to meet the highest demand, winter evenings' peak load, for a few hours a day and only during a few months was not compatible with the requirements of the Plan for the use of the nation's savings. This tension resulted in a new calculative twist figured out by EDF's engineers: to redefine and transform the role of hydropower.

The hydropower plants of the three main mountain massifs in the south of France originally operated in isolation. Their size had been set to supply high needs in winter, when the water level is low, which means that, in summer, production was in large surplus. This regime had encouraged the development of a specific industrial geography. The Alpine valleys, for example, had attracted many energy-intensive plants (aluminum, cement, chemicals). A specific organization of supply and demand was in place there, with industrial clients agreeing to reduce their production in winter in exchange for lower prices in summer. Concerning the new role of hydropower, the intuition of EDF's engineers was as follows: thermal plants in the Parisian region would be a new type of "client" for hydropower plants in the south of France, which would now be interconnected. This interconnection would imply two things. First, as soon as the hydropower plants generated some surplus, which in the past had no value and was sold off locally, this surplus would acquire a higher economic value by turning off thermal plants and saving coal. Second, the water in the dam's reservoir would also acquire a higher value, as it could be stored during the summer months and consumed in the winter. Therefore, the seasonal peak demand in the Parisian region could be supplied, and the need to construct plants operating at full capacity only a few hours a year was offset. In a nutshell, EDF's engineers concluded that hydropower should be used to satisfy peak load in Paris.

Many advantages were expected to unfold from this decision. It reduced the need for costly new investments in hydropower equipment. Interconnection meant that it was not necessary to cover all the needs of the southern industrial region with hydropower only, which required very large installations able to produce enough electricity during winter and huge surplus in the summer. Instead, it would be possible, when needed, to transport electricity generated by the future large thermal plants in the north of France. At the same time, this investment choice would not impede the development of the hydropower program. Boiteux recalled that hydropower was a national energy. It could counterbalance the dependence on oil imports guided by the low-cost hypothesis and, to a certain extent, ensure France's energy sovereignty. Besides, the building of dams was a highly structured industry, and it mattered to continue this program, which, since the 1920s, had developed specialized equipment and a skilled workforce. These qualitative considerations could be easily factored into the calculation by assigning a high value to hydropower kilowatt-hours produced during peak load. This compensated for the cost of transporting electricity, encouraged the development of interconnection, decreased the cost of hydropower, and secured its place in the future system.

Thus a multitude of choices and constraints was shaping the future of the French electricity sector, and the calculated plan articulated these constraints and strategic choices, in order to draw the project of an integrated machine for the production, transport, and distribution of electricity. The whole hydropower sector could not be shut down overnight. Marginal cost pricing did not fully determine the place of the electricity sector in the national economy; this place was decided in consultation with the Plan through an interest rate. For EDF's engineers, calculating costs and prices aimed at finding the few parameters that would enable the concrete realization of a project fulfilling the various conditions presented above. These conditions amounted to a series of strategic bets and interrelated opportunities. The decision was made to rely on a basis of thermal power plants in the north and east of the country, both fast to implement and requiring few starting investments. This decision made sense only in interaction with a new exploitation doctrine for the hydropower potential of the south and its reservoirs. The French hydropower potential was reframed to satisfy domestic peak-load uses in Paris.

## Building

The concept of long-term marginal cost was a nodal point in the system of electricity provisioning because it enabled the operationalization of this project through a set of prices that would frame behaviors.

Boiteux (1952) described the method for translating investment planning into a pricing policy, the one used to compute the *tarif vert* (green tariff) released in 1956, as follows. The main idea since 1949 was to equal the price with the cost of producing one additional unit. But the aim was now to ensure the production of this additional unit in the long run, which implied readjusting and developing EDF's production capacities. In other words, prices would trigger the demand that would satisfactorily meet the electricity generation portfolio. The computation method started with Paris in the winter. Paris was surrounded by a loop of thermal power plants, a legacy of the Compagnie parisienne de distribution d'électricité. Dessus was one of its directors before the war and knew its production processes very well. EDF's engineers determined as a first approximation that this thermal loop worked independently from the rest of the grid. Relying on this imperfect but useful hypothesis, it became easy to know the value of marginal costs, apart from peak-load hours. One just needed to ask the dispatcher of the Paris region. As Dessus nicely put it: an imperfect measure is better than none, and *ex post* verifications and cross-checks are always possible.

Apart from peak hours, production costs and prices for the Parisian area were set at the operating cost of the least efficient thermal power plant, the last plant to be started. These costs were low but higher than the costs of more productive plants started first to meet the demand. Therefore, prices equivalent to the exploitation costs of the least productive plant financed a part of the full costs of the other plants. In peak hours, however, the situation was different, and the demand was responsible for the total size of EDF's production capacity, that is, the total amount of electricity produced. At these very specific moments, an increase in production would require the construction of a new thermal plant in the Parisian area, which would be particularly expensive. In the calculation, peak demand thus incurred an additional cost: a fixed premium of four thousand francs per kilowatt-hour. Boiteux and Paul Stasi, his assistant, then just needed to follow the existing flows of energy and, depending on the time of the day, add (if Paris imports) or subtract (if Paris exports) the costs of transport to the prices for the Parisian area, in order to obtain the prices at any point of the French territory.

As anticipated by Dessus, *ex post* verifications and cross-checks did matter. Again, apart from peak hours, the prices calculated for Lille, a major city in the north of France supplied by its own thermal loop, were deduced from the Parisian prices and had to coincide with the operating costs of the least productive plant in Lille. And so on . . . Boiteux and Stasi were particularly concerned with coherence in the long run. Tracing the flows of energy, they obtained a result where the east and the north of

France, where coal mines were located, would import electricity from Paris. Given the design choices discussed in the previous section, EDF's engineers decided to set lower prices, already equivalent to future production costs, once these regions were fully equipped. This adjustment aimed at increasing demand to support the development of the envisioned capacity. The same correction was applied to the south of France and its hydropower plants because in the initial calculation conducted in 1952, this region was not exporting enough electricity. Lastly, similar adjustments were made for the selected future oil ports: Bordeaux, Fos-sur-Mer near Marseille, Le Havre, and Dunkerque. It was expected that oil refining would develop and chemical companies would settle in these port cities. A certain capacity of electricity production was thus required to sustain this development. The power plants would be located in the immediate vicinity of their input (imported oil) and their users (oil products processing, in the broadest sense). This land-use planning rested on a strategic bet on lower oil prices in the long run, especially in comparison with the increasing price of national coal (due to decreasing productivity of national mines and increasing miners' wages). This strategic bet was partly a geopolitical one too, a consequence of the decision made by the French government to explore and intensively exploit the large oil discovery made in the Algerian desert.

Boiteux and Stasi insisted on the importance of verification. "The satisfactory equilibrium" is the one that reflects "the durable characteristics of costs" in a given region (Boiteux and Stasi 1952). The initial calculation built on the existing system, with a focus on the Parisian region. This aimed to create some kind of coherence and guarantee a certain realism, in order to compute prices that would not lead to the collapse of the network. Verification then came in to modify these costs, to ensure coverage and flows of energy that would correspond to the long-term plan, not in real time but on average. In Paris, one objective was to allow the off-peak demand to develop by benefiting from low prices (set at the exploitation cost). But the main objective was to flatten the peak period demand through the double effects of higher kilowatt-hours and a fixed premium, while financing the development of the thermal plants that would provide the base production for the region. The aim was to contain a certain type of demand (peak demand in Paris, i.e., domestic uses) and encourage imports from dams and plants near coal mines to satisfy it.

This articulation in the reasoning is central to the argument of this article. First, the calculation of marginal costs for peak periods supposed an investment plan. The power plant that would be commissioned next needed to be known in advance. Boiteux and Stasi even stated that time frames should be longer, and marginal costs should integrate eight-to-ten-year plans, in order to send out a clear pricing message to consumers and reduce the commercial and organizational costs associated with rewriting the pricing contracts. In practice, they relied on the department of equipment headed by Massé and the constraints and strategies described in the previous section. Second, the calculation of marginal costs and their propagation across the whole territory also required knowing the flows of electricity in the long term. And again, Boiteux and Stasi relied on the division of equipment, which was in charge of calculating these equilibriums as outputs of various constraints and bets.

We see here what it meant, for EDF's engineers, to calculate marginal costs (and thus prices) indirectly, based on the intuition formalized by Boiteux in 1949. These costs were not observable in accounting books. They implied the future equilibrium of a production-transport network, the commissioning of not-yet-existing equipment and subsequent flows of energy, and the shaping of the load curve to reach this future equilibrium. That Paris, the capital of the country, was chosen as the starting point of the calculation is telling. Propagated from Paris to the rest of the national territory, marginal costs acted as administrative instructions. These instructions transmitted information about the development and the construction of the network to consumers, especially industrial companies, who were part and parcel of the construction process. Their own industrial projects aligned with the broader project of the Plan. EDF pricing policy was essential to this convergence.

### Prices as Administrative Instructions

When they came out with this new pricing structure, called the green tariff, Boiteux and Stasi said that EDF was not selling kilowatt-hours anymore but different electric commodities. Indeed, electricity prices entailed three interrelated features according to which they could be differentiated: the fixed premium (linked to the amount of power subscribed), the region, and the consumption time. These differentiations were meant to act on the uses of electricity.

While domestic uses (responsible for peak demand) were contained, what Boiteux and Stasi called the long uses were strongly encouraged. This meant the power-intensive industries. The fixed premium was linked to the length of the period of use; the longer the uses, the cheaper the fixed premium. Moreover, differences in prices were linked to the time of consumption, which added another discount for long users, as power-intensive industries tended to consume electricity at night, when it was cheap.

The regional differentiations of prices aimed at producing various complex effects. This was the reason sophisticated calculations were required and intensively used at EDF. Calculations enabled the simultaneous combination of multiple constraints through the writing of systems of equations. I would like to emphasize one of the main effects EDF's engineers wanted to produce as they were trying to find the numbers. With the green tariff, areas in the south of France faced a significant price increase, whereas areas in the north and east of the country experienced a significant price decrease that reflected the lower costs of upcoming efficient thermal power plants built on top of mines' workings. Price differentiations according to the time of the day, or levels of fixed premium per kilowatt-hour, aimed at supporting long industrial uses, and price differentiations according to the region of consumption, aimed at commanding the location of the heavy industry. The goal was to trigger a move from the Alps to mining areas in the north and the east of France. It can be argued that EDF's engineers sought to modify the French industrial geography.

The three differentiation criteria combined to reorganize the definition of priority needs: light manufacturing had developed in the south thanks to the surplus of hydropower and was now constrained in order to encourage the heavy industry in the north of France.

The pricing policy more specifically targeted peak demands through two mechanisms. If subscribers agreed to stop consuming during peak hours, then their fixed premium would be reduced. Subscribers might also decrease consumption during these peak hours when kilowatt-hours were particularly expensive, because they were priced at the exploitation cost of the least productive plants. EDF's engineers were acutely aware of the importance of the effects generated by the pricing policy. Labor-intensive industries, such as textile manufacturing, which consumed electricity during the day, would be negatively affected, unless they chose to switch to night work. The same consequences were visible for domestic consumers, who used electricity to cook and light their homes in the evening and to heat them in the winter. Changing consumption times and deciding on momentary shutdowns (what the heavy industry employing little workforce was able to do) was not really an option for domestic consumers and labor-intensive industries.

Potentially increasing workers' night shifts and trying to minimize domestic consumptions were seen as acceptable consequences because the priorities were elsewhere (Massé 1958). The green tariff enabled a 5 percent decrease of the national peak demand. Besides, the minimization of peak load reduced the use of the least efficient plants that consumed more coal. The reduction in the amount of coal required was estimated around seven hundred tons per day during the six winter months, a period when coal was usually imported from the United States. In other words, with the explicit consent of the government, the green tariff redefined the priority needs vital to the nation, among different types of industry and between industrial and domestic uses, in such a way as to limit investments (a scarce resource in a reconstruction economy) and save on coal, especially imported coal.

On a more general level, the result was an adaptable and decentralized program that can be summarized as follows. The Alpine valleys, the cradle of electrochemistry, metallurgy, and aluminum production, were remote, isolated, difficult to access, too distant from their markets and from urban concentrations where the workforce was to be found. This was the idea that prevailed at the Plan. Its different councils had elaborated a vision: as praised in the press and ministries, the future of the French economy would rely on two key areas that suffered a lot during the war, Le Havre, a port in Normandy along the English Channel, and the Lorraine, an area in eastern France (Rioux 1980: chap. 11). The latter was integrated into Germany; the Allied landing took place near the former. Yet, and this was the Plan's vision, hydrocarbons would soon supply Le Havre, attracting industries, while coal mines in Lorraine would, simultaneously, be modernized and integrated into the emerging European Coal and Steel Community, turning France into a vast workshop, as Jean Monnet, one of Europe's "founding fathers," put it.[4] EDF pricing policy was one of the contracts that organized this vast construction site by issuing specific instructions.

## Conclusion

EDF's engineers strongly believed in the aim of the nationalization of the electricity sector that took place in the immediate aftermath of the war (Picard, Beltran, and Bungener 1985: chaps. 1, 2). They considered the prewar situation, with numerous small producers in competition with each other in a low-regulation environment, as an obstacle to the high level of coordination and investment required for reconstructing and modernizing the country's productive processes.

4. Alain Desrosières (1999) shows that a distinctive feature of French planning was to consider the whole national economy as a single firm.

But the available solutions appeared to them as insufficient to achieve this goal. First, they were aware of the socialist calculation debate going on in the interwar period, and they did not believe in the concrete possibility of a fully centralized economic calculation performed by an authoritarian planning board, in order to achieve Pareto efficiency (Boiteux 1948). Second, they used the Arrow-Debreu general equilibrium theory as an "intellectual construction," a tool to enquire into and and solve practical, large-scale engineering problems (Massé 1965: chap. 5). The nationwide design, planned development, and management of the interconnection of capital-intensive and rainfall-dependent hydropower with fuel intensive thermal power, to satisfy a demand varying over time that needed to grow, was seen as the topical exemplar of this type of problem. Lastly, they saw the indicative planning that was applied in many European countries at the time (including France) as useful, but too modest and too defensive.

EDF's engineers invented their own solution, yet not from scratch. They drew on a rich tradition of state engineering. State engineers emerged in eighteenth-century France; their task was to design fortresses or warships. They invented optimization techniques to accommodate multiple technical and political constraints in a single coherent design, and then developed cost and price calculations to control and monitor the work of contractors in construction sites (Vérin 1993). In the nineteenth century, the machines that were of interest to the state were not so much weapons and warships but industrial processes (Vatin 1993). Optimization broadens to encompass the monitoring of the behavior of future users, through pricing, as in the debates on the design of bridges or railroads (Grall 2004). The techniques that the state engineers invented were formally very close to marginalist tools, but the aim was different. State engineers of the nineteenth century were suspicious of the grand Walrasian scheme (Vatin 2008). Their aim was not to build a general theory of market equilibrium but to optimize concrete existing machines. All this engineering work was performed for the state. Since the eighteenth century, state engineers thus made an explicit connection between the design and construction of large infrastructure and state-building processes (Foucault 2004; Smith 1990; Mukerji 2009). They never considered that the market, even properly engineered, or the straightforward application of cost-benefit analysis could replace politics, especially when large infrastructure and associated land-use planning debates were involved (Porter 1995).

This inheritance, transmitted mainly through the École Polytechnique, explains the divergence from a different tradition that paved the way to the contemporary form of economic engineering. For the latter, a market properly engineered can tell the truth about consumers' preferences and supersede politics (Mirowski and Nik-Khah 2017). Technologies and preferences are formed outside the realm of the market. The scope of the intervention made by the economist turned engineer is very narrow. EDF's engineers embodied the divergence from this vision. As engineers, they used linear programming techniques to make decisions on the detailed design of power plants and transmission lines, and then used long-term marginal cost pricing to shape the consumers' behavior in order to match the decisions made on the long-term development of production and uses for the whole country. As state engineers, their cost and price calculations paid specific attention to the politics of land-use planning: industrial regional development, movements of population, definition of the valuable "resources" of each part of the territory.

As Edmond Malinvaud (2001), a prominent state engineer, indicates in his memoir, this set of practices was progressively dismantled from the 1970s on, first by the critique of technocracy and growing environmental concerns, and second by globalization, which made this conscious direction of infrastructural developments more difficult to achieve. The intellectual project behind the European Common Market and other international institutions like the WTO was explicitly to get rid of the preeminence of nation-states through the construction of global markets (Slobodian 2018). Furthermore, decolonization made EDF more dependent on global markets for its oil supply. EDF also became more dependent on global financial markets, when President Valéry Giscard d'Estaing asked EDF to borrow money on international financial markets in order to launch the nuclear program in the mid-1970s (Chick 2003: 91–93). The idea that the competitive (financial) market can tell the truth about consumers' preferences, without any previous political agreement on long-term technological choices, land-use planning, and consumption practices, took center stage in economics. It paved the way to a different kind of economic engineering, focused on short-term information processing and market microstructure, away from the concrete materiality and territoriality of productive processes.[5] This is, I think, a general and ongoing tension between two different traditions in economic engineering, with broad political implications.

5. Daniel Breslau, in this volume, describes in detail this shift in the US electricity market in the 1980s, a shift motivated by the will to empower consumers through spot pricing. Breslau's brilliant analysis of the reaction of the engineers to this project is particularly telling. For the engineers, transferring control of flows of power to the multitudes of customers was "the analogue of giving everybody on a 747 a joystick and expecting them to be able to land the airplane." Replace the airplane by the plan of the nation, and you have Massé's words quoted in the introduction.

## References

Allais, Maurice. 1944. *À la recherche d'une discipline économique.* Paris: Imprimerie nationale.

Boiteux, Marcel. 1948. *Économie concurrentielle planifiée: La politique des prix.* Archives EDF 891 066, Archives nationales de France, Paris.

Boiteux, Marcel. 1949a. "La tarification des demandes en pointe." *Revue générale de l'électricité,* no. 58: 321–40.

Boiteux, Marcel. 1949b. *La tarification des demandes en pointes.* Archives EDF 891 067, Archives nationales de France, Paris.

Boiteux, Marcel. 1956. "Le choix des équipements de production électrique." *Revue française de recherche opérationnelle* 1, no. 1: 45–60.

Boiteux, Marcel. 1957. *Le tarif vert d'Électricité de France.* Archives EDF 891 070, Archives nationales de France, Paris.

Boiteux, Marcel. 1960a. "L'énergie électrique: Données, problèmes et perspectives." *Annales des Mines,* no. 10: 631–50.

Boiteux, Marcel. 1960b. "Peak-Load Pricing." *Journal of Business* 33, no. 2: 157–79.

Boiteux, Marcel. 1987. "Le calcul économique dans l'entreprise électrique." *Revue de l'énergie,* no. 390: 81–88.

Boiteux, Marcel. 1993. *Haute tension.* Paris: Odile Jacob.

Boiteux, Marcel, and Paul Stasi. 1952. *Sur la détermination des prix de revient de développement dans un système interconnecté de production-distribution.* EDF Archives 891 066, Archives nationales de France, Paris.

Chick, Martin. 2002. "Le Tarif Vert Retrouvé: The Marginal Cost Concept and the Pricing of Electricity in Britain and France, 1945–1970." *Energy Journal* 23, no. 1: 97–116.

Chick, Martin. 2003. "Productivité, politique tarifaire et investissement dans les entreprises électriques nationalisées françaises et britanniques, 1945–1973." *Annales historiques de l'électricité* 1, no. 1: 53–69.

Chick, Martin. 2007. *Electricity and Energy Policy in Britain, France, and the United States since 1945.* Cheltenham, UK: Edward Elgar.

Desrosières, Alain. 1999. "La commission et l'équation: Une comparaison des Plans français et néerlandais entre 1945 et 1980." *Genèses,* no. 34: 28–52.

Dessus, Gabriel. 1949. *Sur les tarifications d'intérêt général dans les services publics industriels.* Archives EDF 891 066, Archives nationales de France, Paris.

Foucault, Michel. 2004. *Sécurité, territoire, population: Cours au Collège de France 1977–1978.* Paris: Gallimard / Le Seuil.

Fourquet, François. 1980. *Les comptes de la puissance: Histoire de la comptabilité nationale et du plan.* Paris: Éditions Recherches.

Frost, Robert. 1985. "Economists as Nationalised Sector Managers: Reforms of the Electrical Rate Structure in France, 1946–1969." *Cambridge Journal of Economics,* no. 9: 285–300.

Frost, Robert. 1991. *Alternating Currents: Nationalized Power in France, 1946–1970.* Ithaca, NY: Cornell University Press.

Grall, Bernard. 2004. *Économie de forces et production d'utilités: L'émergence du calcul économique chez les ingénieurs des Ponts et Chaussées (1831–1891)*. Rennes: Presses Universitaires de Rennes.

Kuisel, Richard. 1981. *Capitalism and the State in Modern France: Renovation and Economic Management in the Twentieth Century*. New York: Cambridge University Press.

Malégarie, Charles. 1947. *L'électricité à Paris*. Paris: Librairie polytechnique Ch. Béranger.

Malinvaud, Edmond. 2001. "Some Ethical and Methodological Convictions." *American Economist* 45, no. 1: 3–16.

Massé, Pierre. 1953. "Les investissements électriques." *Revue de statistique appliquée* 1, nos. 3–4: 119–29.

Massé, Pierre. 1958. "Quelques incidences économiques du tarif vert." *Revue française de l'énergie* 97, no. 9: 392–95.

Massé, Pierre. 1965. *Le plan ou l'anti-hasard*. Paris: Gallimard.

Massé, Pierre. 1984. *Aléas et progrès: Entre Candide et Cassandre*. Paris: Economica.

Mirowski, Philip, and Edward Nik-Khah. 2017. *The Knowledge We Have Lost in Information: The History of Information in Modern Economics*. Oxford: Oxford University Press.

Mukerji, Chandra. 2009. *Impossible Engineering: Technology and Territoriality on the Canal du Midi*. Princeton, NJ: Princeton University Press.

Picard, Pierre, Alain Beltran, and Martine Bungener. 1985. *Histoires de l'EDF: Comment se sont prises les decisions de 1946 à nos jours*. Paris: Dunod.

Porter, Theodore. 1995. *Trust in Numbers: The Pursuit of Objectivity in Science and Public Life*. Princeton, NJ: Princeton University Press.

Rioux, Jean-Pierre. 1980. *La France de la Quatrième République: L'ardeur et la nécessité (1944–1952)*. Paris: Seuil.

Rosanvallon, Pierre. 1987. "Histoire des idées Keynésiennes en France." *Revue Française d'Economie* 2, no. 4: 22–56.

Slobodian, Quinn. 2018. *Globalists: The End of Empire and the Birth of Neoliberalism*. Cambridge, MA: Harvard University Press.

Smith, Cecil O. 1990. "The Longest Run: Public Engineers and Planning in France." *American Historical Review* 95, no. 3: 657–92.

Vatin, François. 1993. *Le travail, économie et physique (1780–1830)*. Paris: Presses Universitaires de France.

Vatin, François. 2008. "L'esprit d'ingénieur: Pensée calculatoire et éthique économique." *Revue Française de Socio-économie* 1, no. 1: 131–52.

Vérin, Hélène. 1993. *La gloire des ingénieurs: L'intelligence technique du XVIe au XVIIIe siècle*. Paris: Albin Michel.

# Realities of Formalization: How Soviet Scholars Moved from Control Engineering to the General Theory of Choice

Ivan Boldyrev

## 1. Introduction: Being among Soviet Engineers

Postwar Soviet Union was, in a sense, a country of engineers—both due to its ambitions to engineer the new society and because for the tasks of expanding its state-owned (military-)industrial complex, a large number of engineering staff was a *conditio sine qua non*.

The involvement of engineers in solving technical tasks had a natural connection to economic challenges. Suffice it to say that the most well-known early Soviet economic growth model (Feldman [1928] 1964) was created by an engineer, Grigory Feldman (1884–1958). The engineers should also be credited with the priority in formulating the idea of more precise quantitative appraisals of investment projects—a crucial topic for the postwar Soviet economic discussion (Zauberman 1967: 140).

After the purges of the 1930s, which began with the infamous Industrial Party Trial, when the engineers of the older generation were accused of sabotage and forced to publicly confess their guilt, the state started to oversee and control this class that was responsible for—and, in a sense, was embodying—the technical infrastructure of the totalitarian machine.

I am deeply grateful to Fuad Aleskerov, Salvador Barberà, Olessia Kirtchik, Michel Le Breton, Mark Levin, Boris Mirkin, Lev Rozonoer, the participants of the 2019 *HOPE* annual conference, the two anonymous referees, and the editors of the *HOPE* volume, Pedro Garcia Duarte and Yann Giraud. This research has been funded by the Canadian Research Council for the Social Sciences (SSHRC) "Insight development" grant (with Till Düppe as the principal investigator).

*History of Political Economy* 52 (annual suppl.)  DOI 10.1215/00182702-8718052

A mass production of engineers that began in the 1930s is now analyzed with considerably less enthusiasm (Graham 1996) than it was perceived before. Their education was, for the most part, quite narrow (unlike the one of their predecessors), and their real work was limited by the daily technical issues of the specific industry they were trained for. The same goes for the mass outlook of the engineering intelligentsia: in the Stalin times, their interests were severely limited by purely technological concerns, and the "permitted" discourses never invoked any real social, political, or ethical considerations.

By the period of stagnation in the 1970s, a whole new generation of the ITR (*injenerno-teknicheskiye rabotniki*, engineering-technical workers) had emerged, with a diverse and sometimes more subversive weltanschauung. At the same time, the educational pattern faced a natural challenge of overproduction and mismatch. In the virtual absence or suppression of the private sector, almost everyone became an "engineer." This group with fuzzy borders, fulfilling a plethora of social roles, could even be characterized as coinciding with the Soviet middle class (see various approaches to the analysis in Kryshtanovskaya 1989; Lipovetsky 2013; Tamas 2013; and Abramov 2017).

Within the Soviet technical intelligentsia, a diversity of ideologies, intellectual commitments, and strategies of relations with the bureaucratic powers (Gerovitch 2008) was a norm—and this concerned its engagement with economic knowledge as well. In the context of severe ideological pressure, when the subject matter of standard economics (markets) was definitely not on the agenda for decades, it was only natural that economic ideas were developed in methodologically heterogeneous environments and were marked by a certain eclecticism (Boldyrev and Kirtchik 2017). One important tendency was the emergence of "economic cybernetics" and, generally, the growing legitimacy of "mathematical methods" in economic analysis, to which engineers definitely contributed. In what follows, I assume that "engineers" who are the focus of this article refer not just to "technical experts" but to those individuals who, having a background in the applied sciences / mathematics, became *academics* and got interested, along with engineering problems, in the fields directly or indirectly associated with economics.

I deal with one particular group of Soviet scholars led by a control engineer and an applied mathematician, Mark Aronovich Aizerman (1913–1992). So far, in the recent histories of Soviet cybernetics, mathematical economics, and related fields (Gerovitch 2002; Boldyrev and Kirtchik

2014, 2017; Hands 2016; Leeds 2016; Peters 2016; Rindzevičiūtė 2016), this group was not considered in detail. It was Olessia Kirtchik (2019) who first addressed its work focusing on the models developed by Emmanuil Braverman, one of the members of Aizerman's group. However, the contexts and the overall direction of its work deserve a closer examination. Why did Aizerman's group start doing research related to economics? What were the constraints they were facing? And what kind of academic culture emerged as a result of this engagement?

## 2. Aizerman's Group: The Beginnings

Aizerman was a key force behind the major intellectual and institutional developments this article is focusing on, so it makes sense to consider his career in more detail.

After graduating from the major Soviet engineering school, the Bauman Institute, in 1937, he started working at NATI (Academic Auto-Tractor Institute). In 1937, career tracks were characteristically "easy" (there was a lack of human resources due to emigration and the waves of repressions), and immediately upon entering NATI, Aizerman became "a head of the lab." He completed his first dissertation (analogous to a PhD in engineering—"candidate of technical sciences") in 1939, rejecting the offer to defend his diploma project as such a dissertation. While in 1937 the results were only the development prototypes of automobile engines based on liquefied gas, in 1939 Aizerman actually installed such engines on various existing Soviet car types.

In 1939, a new research institution within the Soviet Academy of Sciences was created (the one with which Aizerman would associate his whole subsequent career), the Institute of Automatics/Automation and Remote Control (Institut Avtomatiki i Telemekhaniki, or IAT; since 1969 Institut Problem Upravleniya,[1] or IPU), preceded by the lab that had been founded as early as 1934.[2] Aizerman was among the first researchers to join the institute, where he started working on his second—habilitation, "doctor of technical sciences"—thesis on the "stability of a class of non-linear automatic control systems." (He would defend it only after the war,

---

1. The term *upravleniye* refers to "control" (also as a mathematical term applied in the theory due to Lev Pontryagin in the 1960s), but also, importantly, to "management" and "governance." See Kirtchik 2019. The standard rendering was "institute of control sciences."

2. Comparable institutions in the United States and Germany were created in 1936 and 1939, respectively (Bissell 1998).

in 1946.) The creation of the IAT was followed by an inaugural conference gathering various scholars who worked on the theory of automatic control and thus consolidating Soviet control engineering.

Aizerman's supervisors and major influences before and after the war were an important physicist and applied mathematician, Aleksandr Andronov, and an engineer working in automatic regulation theory, Georgy Shchipanov.[3] In 1939, the institute also became home for Nikolai Luzin, one of the greatest Soviet mathematicians, who was persecuted during the infamous Luzin affair in 1936 (Demidov and Levshin 1999) and was jobless at that time.

While the influence of Andronov and Shchipanov defined the initial direction of Aizerman's research at the IPU, Luzin reinforced Aizerman's mathematical sensibilities.[4] One can say that, without having a degree in mathematics, Aizerman became an applied mathematician (all his subsequent works, including those connected to economics, are fairly sophisticated from a mathematical viewpoint).

The war (1941–45) was a break in Aizerman's research—but also made him work on military tasks (such as studying the mechanical features of the trophy German tanks or improving the famous tank T-34) at the proving ground near Moscow. After the war, Aizerman was involved in automation and control theory, and in its application in introducing automation devices and systems into various industries.

Aizerman's primary interest was in the "theory of automatic regulation"—in fact, cybernetics of technical devices. While in the 1930s Aizerman's focus was on the automation of internal combustion engines—both for military and nonmilitary purposes—he later moved to theoretical problems of automatic regulation/control.

3. On Andronov, see Bissell 1998. Shchipanov was expelled from the institute in 1939 for the paper he had published establishing the attempt to build a system of automatic control in which external perturbations would amount to zero. For the ideological background, see Bissell 1999. Aizerman wrote a letter in support of Shchipanov and had a suitcase ready at home with clothes and other things necessary in case he was arrested (Aleskerov 2018). After the big purges of 1936–38, this was a common behavior. Quite uncommon, however, was the courage with which Aizerman defended his teacher.

4. Aizerman was doing individual studies with Luzin in 1939–41 by meeting him several times a week (Aleskerov et al. 2003: 28, 32). This connection is crucial, since Aizerman had never had any deep mathematical training before. Note that prominent Soviet mathematical economists were, for the most part, either mathematicians by training (like Leonid Kantorovich) or got additional mathematical training (examples are Victor Polterovich and Braverman, who, after getting a degree in engineering, obtained a second degree in mathematics at Moscow State University [see Boldyrev and Kirtchik 2014; and Kirtchik 2019]).

At the end of the 1950s, partly following the widespread interest in cybernetics in the Soviet Union, Aizerman started working on the more abstract theory of automata. In 1962, Laboratory 25 was created, headed by Aizerman and officially called "laboratory of theory and methods of constructing automata." The new members were coming from different schools, notably from the Moscow Institute of Physics and Technology (PhysTech).[5]

The theory of automata has been basic for cybernetics. Aizerman and his collaborators were mostly interested in what certain abstract logical machines could do. In particular, after having learned of Frank Rosenblatt's (1958) construction of the "perceptron"—the first learning machine imitating the working of the brain, they got interested in how this machine could actually work. It was Braverman who initiated a new research program on the question of how machines can *learn*.[6] Braverman's formalisms for the problems of image recognition and the "method of potential functions" (describing the impact of a given perceived point on the other points) suggested by another researcher of Lab 25, Lev Rozonoer, led to the new approach in data analysis and became a key research direction over the years to come (Aizerman, Braverman, and Rozonoer 1964).

For Aizerman, these learning mechanisms in producing the patterns and classes of arbitrary elements constituted the important element of the general cybernetic problem—the problem of control (Aleskerov et al. 2003: 127). From modeling the algorithms of visual perception and automatic classification (or cluster analysis / image recognition without a "teacher"), his interests moved to applying this idea to understanding the *living systems*, in particular, control in the muscles of animals and humans, as well as the mechanisms of human perception. This, of course,

5. Since 1953, Aizerman was teaching at PhysTech and in 1964–78 held a chair of theoretical mechanics there.

6. On Braverman, image recognition, and the role of this research for economics in the context of cybernetics, data science, and disequilibrium analysis, see a detailed account in Kirtchik 2019. Importantly, image recognition turned out to be very popular at the institute: at the same time, in another lab of the IPU, headed (till 1971) by Alexander Lerner, somewhat different methods were suggested by Vladimir Vapnik and Alexey Chervonenkis, who started to work in 1962 and made important contributions to computational learning theory. In fact, Chervonenkis's work was initially inspired by Aizerman's lectures at PhysTech (Chervonenks n.d.). After the fall, Vapnik, who is now one of the world's most famous data scientists, went to the United States, and somewhat later Chervonenkis became a professor in London; they received prestigious awards for their contributions (e.g., John von Neumann Prize for Vapnik, who perfected his methods while working with AT&T in the 1990s, and partly incorporating Braverman's and Lev Rozonoer's insights).

was influenced by the work of Norbert Wiener, which was at that time already widely debated in the Soviet Union, followed by the visit of Wiener himself in 1960 (see Gerovitch 2002; Peters 2016).

But this new field required, among other things, a new methodology. "Being an expert in the theory of control in technical systems, [Aizerman] discovered, that an adequate language in studying the control principles in living systems is the language of biological experiments. This understanding involved a radical rethinking of the ways how an engineer should study the system of control" (Andreeva and Muchnik, quoted in Aleskerov et al. 2003: 162).

Instead of what we now call calibration, when the theoretical model is the first step in constructing and experimentally testing a technical device, the new methodology involved a direct experimental study of the living systems as its primary aim and its major source of information and theoretical insights. This was not the first interdisciplinary leap of Aizerman, but it was a crucial one, clearly involving the new experimental techniques and an extraordinary openness toward other sciences. In 1963, Aizerman launched a seminar called "Extension of the Capabilities of Automata," in which mathematicians, biologists, psychologists,[7] medical experts, and cyberneticians all shared their experiences.

Overall, in this research, image recognition was tied to the problem of using the learning mechanisms in the systems of control. The challenge was to understand how this can work in a machine—and how to actually build the machine capable of image recognition. Animals and humans served as living models for this research.

Despite his primarily theoretical interests, Aizerman was willing, throughout his career, to combine the pure and the applied, and to make the one inform the other. For example, in the 1960s, Aizerman's lab cooperated with NIITeplopribor—a research institute associated with the Soviet Ministry of Mechanical Engineering and Instrumentation—in helping create automation devices for various industries. In particular, with several colleagues he created and implemented a unified system of elements for industrial pneumatic (using the compressed air energy) control. In 1964, together with his colleagues from the research division he was heading, and with some others, Aizerman was awarded the prestigious Lenin Prize for the advancement of technology.

7. Aizerman was even in contact with Alexei Leontiev, the head of Soviet school of "activity theory" in psychology (Aleskerov et al. 2003: 148).

### 3. Lab 25 Turns to Economics

The IPU in general and Aizerman's lab in particular were—both geographically[8] and conceptually[9]—not so far away from Soviet mathematical economics. Aron Katsenelinboigen at the Central Economic-Mathematical Institute (CEMI) and Braverman at the IPU were those individuals who were insisting on building and working with mathematical models of economic processes. In 1974, "control of complex socio-economic systems" became part of an official research agenda at the IPU (Kirtchik 2019).

What kind of mathematical modeling was involved? On the one hand, Braverman was enthusiastic about data science: the techniques for finding patterns in the data, such as cluster analysis, were a natural outgrowth of his interest in automatic classification. On the other, he was seriously engaging in fix-price disequilibrium economics. Braverman found a kindred spirit in Boris Mirkin, at that time an applied mathematician working in the economics research institute in Novosibirsk. (He would later become an internationally acclaimed computer scientist.)[10]

Somewhat unexpected in this story, however, is that neither the algorithms for data analysis nor the cybernetic disequilibrium fixed-prices models were to become the focus of Aizerman's research. Instead, he turned to the field that defined the major research direction of the lab till the end of his life and beyond: *the theory of choice.*

It was Mirkin who provided the first book-length treatment of the collective choice problems. Mirkin's book was inspired by Braverman, who felt that while the lab was going to change the topic and move closer to "mathematical social sciences," no ingenious and authoritative summary of the work done in the field was available. Mirkin collaborated with another Lab 25 researcher, Andrei Malishevski, who was as fascinated with the topic as Mirkin himself and was a meticulous editor of Mirkin's manuscript. The book was completed in 1972 and published in 1974.

Inspired in part by the approach of John G. Kemeny and J. Laurie Snell (1962), the book he had translated into Russian, Mirkin (1974) treated the

---

8. The institute's building is not far from the building of CEMI, the major research institution in Moscow devoted to mathematical economics.

9. Vadim Trapeznikov, a head of the institute in 1951–87, participated in the public economic discussion as early as 1964 (Kirtchik 2019).

10. One of the Lab 25 fellows, Ilya Muchnik, came to Novosibirsk for a joint project on data analysis with the sociologist Tatyana Zaslavskaya (again, a soon-to-be central figure in Soviet sociological research) and quickly saw that Mirkin was interested and competent in measurement theory and classification algorithms. See the recollections in Rozonoer et al. 2018.

issue in quite a general (and much more extensive) way. For him, collective choice was a specific way to frame the *aggregation problem*, whereby the nature of aggregation could remain unspecified. It could be an aggregation of votes—which would lead to a formal political theory, or an aggregation of individual preferences—which would amount to the analysis of aggregate demand. Expert judgments, optimization criteria, or classification parameters (in factor analysis)—all these sets of data could become inputs in the system performing the "collective choice," that is, essentially, aggregation of "individual" heterogeneous data. He termed it "group choice" to stress that *collective* involves active bargaining, coalitions, and, generally, interdependency of its individual parts, while *group* is just a set of fully autonomous elements (Mirkin 2019).

Mirkin actually disliked mathematical economics, but was well versed in the theory of binary relations and was fascinated by the opportunity to use qualitative mathematics to analyze sociological and psychological data. In fact, he first encountered this problem while trying to find an approach to the economic problems he was confronted with in Novosibirsk: how to aggregate the data coming from different divisions of an enterprise and how to form an integral parameter or an index in the analysis of sociological data from surveys (Mirkin n.d.).

Mirkin's book contained quite up-to-date material on preferences, voting, Arrow impossibility theorem, as well as general equilibrium and game theory.[11] (The most recent results in mathematical economics were treated as special cases or problems in the text.) Again, decision theory here emerged out of the work in data analysis, and only in discussing game-theoretic methods did Mirkin (1974) grudgingly assume that here, when dealing with humans, we need to take into account their "reflexive" ability to change their states.[12]

This book, which became widely known in the Soviet community even beyond mathematical economics, along with a clear interest of various leading members of the lab (mostly Braverman and Malishevski) and the institute as a whole, motivated Aizerman to finally turn to mathematical economics and choice theory. However, he was not happy with this move and hoped to avoid the "ideological" field of economics (Mark Levin,

11. It was very quickly translated into English and edited by the American decision and utility theorist (and a researcher at AT&T Bell) Peter Fishburn, who at that time was also working on general choice theory. See Mirkin 1974.

12. In an introduction, Mirkin also mentions the "Western" normative notion of welfare economics and its importance for a socialist system.

pers. comm.): in fact, doing "economics" and not political economy in the Soviet Union was obviously an ideologically suspect activity. Still, both Braverman and Malishevski had more than a theoretical interest in modeling human behavior and social systems.

While Braverman, in his disequilibrium analysis, was willing to create algorithms and to literally do "economic cybernetics," in line with his previous work in pattern recognition, and using the notions of feedback, learning, and adjustment, Aizerman was less enthusiastic both about immediate applications of this work and about their (essentially neoclassical) theoretical foundations.[13]

Thus, while Braverman and Malishevski served as bridging figures between Lab 25 and other institutions of formal economics in the USSR, Aizerman's style of work was quite different from standard interests and concerns of Soviet mathematical economists. In particular, he was skeptical of Kantorovich's theory of optimal planning and other models that were being developed at the end of the 1960s and the beginning of the 1970s, predominantly at CEMI. Instead, he was inspired by the ideas of Herbert Simon that were much closer to his interdisciplinary vision.[14]

What kind of vision did Aizerman subscribe to? In 1974, he gave a talk at the All-Union conference on automatic control, titled "Human and Collective as Elements of a Control System." He framed this talk as a reflection on the new tendencies in control theory, in which one moves from treating humans as controllers to looking at them as elements of the system itself. In this, Aizerman proceeded to what he called "behavioral models"—and referred to a broad range of approaches authored both by Soviet and by non-Soviet mathematical economists. In these models, the most important issue for him was the idea of a *scalar criterion in decision-making*. Whether decisions are taken following a scalar, or a vector, of various factors, could be settled only by experimental research, but Aizerman's (1975: 87) position was rather skeptical: "Although the experimental work in this field is only beginning, even the first results make

13. Braverman's untimely death in 1977 was important for Lab 25's subsequent development: although his work was taken up by Mark Levin (Braverman and Levin 1981; Makarov, Levin, and Rubinov 1995), Levin has not become a researcher at Lab 25; its research profile changed and since then was mostly defined by Aizerman and Malishevski.

14. Simon's "The Sciences of the Artificial" (1969) was translated into Russian as early as 1972, but Aizerman could have heard of Simon's approach already in 1956, during his first visit to the United States (Aleskerov 2019). Indeed, Simon's wide-ranging interests in control theory, learning processes, and rationality paralleled those of Aizerman and his team. However, I have not found references to Simon in Aizerman's published work on choice theory.

rather plausible the claim that the situations, in which one can really assume the existence of one criterion (and even several criteria!) when choosing an alternative, are relatively rare and of special nature." It is this lack of a singular criterion governing an action that, for Aizerman, distinguishes humans and groups as elements of the control systems from technical apparatuses, and thus social systems from technical ones. Other important aspects of this fundamental distinction are, for Aizerman, the possibility of opportunism ("cheating the system," in his parlance); the option to create coalitions that would defy the expectations of the system; and the ability of agents to take account of the system as a whole. Characteristically, the first two features are illustrated with the examples of contemporaneous economic theory (Aizerman refers to Allan Gibbard's [1973] theorem on the inevitability of cheating for the case of individual opportunism, and to the theory of cooperative games, in the case of coalitions), while the third one, which sounds like a version of rational expectations / efficient markets story, is only illustrated by the work of a Soviet (and US) social scientist Vladimir Lefebvre (1936–2020).

Aizerman's research in the theory of choice began—and, in a sense, ended—with addressing the most fundamental question of (micro)economics: the basic formalisms of rationality (Aleskerov 2018). The major instrument for him was, however, not the standard utility functions but the so-called choice functions, in the sense of Arrow 1959, Sen 1971, and Plott 1973.[15] While for microeconomists these issues were important primarily as a foundation for demand theory, Aizerman recognized the conceptual difficulties of what he later described as a "classical" theory of choice and preferred the more general language of choice functions. While the "classical" approach cares only for those choice functions that could be generated by a "rational" (in some sense) preference ordering and unambiguously connected to a maximization of certain utility function and/or representation of a binary relation, for Aizerman, some problems required a more general formulation. In particular, he was thinking about the examples of choice in which a simple binary comparison is not adequate, because the preferences between two alternatives depend on alternatives *from the same choice set*. Hence the choice functions Aizerman investigated, following Sen 1971, were set-valued, rather than "element-valued." Contrary to the "classical" approach focusing on how to preserve the exclusive dependence of choice on the specific features of the

15. Simply put, a choice function maps a set of alternatives (a choice set) onto the set of those alternatives that are actually chosen.

chosen alternative—and in this sense, context-independently[16]—Aizerman suggested that a more general formulation is needed.

With his collaborators, notably with Malishevski, a decision theorist and operations researcher, Aizerman created the new classification of the choice functions and the new language for the general theory of choice (Aizerman and Malishevski 1981). One of the examples they worked with were so-called hyperrelations, an object purportedly more general than standard binary relations in pairwise comparisons of alternatives. This analysis involved the possibility of comparing one alternative with a set of other alternatives (Aleskerov et al. 2003). Aizerman called it "non-classical" choice: "Classical logic of choice, which in its pure form is embodied in an abstract pair-dominant mechanism, relies on binary structures. . . . In contrast, examples of non-classical logic of choice . . . have as their structures more complex, $n$-ary relations" (Aizerman and Aleskerov 1990: 117).[17]

Using this logic, the standard microeconomic problem of preference revelation (and, inversely, of preferences rationalizing choice) was also reformulated, with the choice being defined not by preferences reducing it to a set of pairwise comparisons but by a set of "elementary" choice functions, into which the one we "observe," the "revealed" choice function, can be decomposed (Aizerman and Aleskerov 1990: 67–68).

In the beginning of the 1980s, Aizerman started to work on the theory of collective (social) choice. When Fuad Aleskerov came to the lab in 1975, two topics were suggested to him: theory of optimal control and collective choice theory. Aleskerov had just earned a degree in mathematics, and while the optimal control theory was familiar to him (by that time, it had been already the part of curriculum), he remembered his shock after learning that economic—and, generally, social—problems could be addressed as rigorously as he felt was necessary. So Aleskerov opted for the choice

16. The key to this independence is the so-called independence of irrelevant alternatives axiom, first formulated by John von Neumann and Oskar Morgenstern (1944) and later widely used in choice theory, in particular, by Arrow (1951). For Aizerman and his colleagues (1977), analogous to this in the standard microeconomic framework was the weak axiom of revealed preference. In a slightly different context (in dealing with individual preferences and not with their aggregation), Aizerman's approach was perceived in the social choice community as rejecting the strategy of imposing the conditions of the "internal consistency of choice" independently of any context. As Sen (1993: 499) argues, "Being consistent or not consistent is not the kind of thing that can happen to choice functions without interpretation—without a presumption about the context that takes us beyond the choices themselves," that is, brings us to motivations, norms, values, objectives, and the like.

17. Pairwise domination implies that "any 'reasonably arranged' choice mechanism should be equivalent to the mechanism of choosing the 'best' (dominating) variants according to some binary relation of superiority (domination)" (Aizerman 1985: 239).

theory.[18] Together, Aizerman and Aleskerov formalized collective choice in terms of choice functions and formulated the "locality" condition (analogous to Arrow's independence axiom). Overall, their major idea was to formalize the *context-dependence of choice* in the general case, to demonstrate that the standard rational choice procedures of elemental comparisons (underlying the standard optimization techniques and algorithms as well) should be regarded as a special case of a more general construct. This allowed them to redescribe important issues in the theory of voting, such as the "menu-dependent preferences" (Sen 1995).

## 4. Lab 25 as a Collective Machine:
## The Elements of the Research Culture

How did Lab 25 actually work? To better understand its singular role in the Soviet academic context, we need to briefly touch on the research practices and modes of communication among its members.

Perhaps the most salient feature of the academic culture fostered by Aizerman was a collective way of doing research. Never a member of the Communist Party, Aizerman, who in his youth participated in one of the early communes and retained humanistic socialist views till the end of his life, was a true *communist of ideas*. For any new set of problems, a huge new research direction was explored by creating a seminar (Aleskerov et al. 2003: 112), a practice Aizerman might also have inherited from Andronov's weekly seminars on the theory of automatic control.

For Aizerman, a careful and an efficient organization of research groups belonged to the science proper (Rozonoer 2003: 245). He would often say that the value of a scientist is a value of "his" lab. Within the lab, as many of its former and current members say, there was no real competition or fear of plagiarism. Rather, the researchers cooperated and supported each other, while Aizerman himself was contributing decisively to everything written/published by the lab members. At the same time—perhaps in line with Arrow's impossibility theorem he so thoroughly investigated—Aizerman could be a rather authoritarian person, and while he focused on the maximum efficiency in the work of the lab (and supported all the members accordingly), the criteria, the aims, the direction of research in the lab were clearly defined by Aizerman alone.

18. Aizerman himself was not very enthusiastic about applying Pontryagin's optimal control theory to economic modeling and did not pursue it further himself—perhaps following, as suggested to me by Roy Weintraub, a general dissatisfaction with these topics in the West.

Another element of this culture was *interdisciplinarity*. Aizerman considered himself as someone who maps the new territory, gets some new results, and then switches to another topic. These changes of perspective that, as indicated above, could be quite radical also clearly involved constant learning. The scope was literally breathtaking: "As long as I can remember, he [Aizerman] learned the basics of mathematical logic, theory of stochastic processes, electrophysiology, principles of mathematical economics, and elements of relativist physics" (Rozonoer 2003: 246).

This learning was also collective: people were appointed to study new fields and the relevant literature to subsequently deliver lectures in small groups. This division of labor was believed to enhance academic efficiency. This type of teamwork could also be associated with some features of Aizerman's research program: to unify and codify the language in the general theory of choice.[19]

Aizerman's lab was not just growing: when it was clear that a certain topic outgrew the capacity of a single lab and the interests of colleagues began to diverge, a new lab was created, while Aizerman continued to work with a smaller collective on a set of issues that was on the agenda.

It was this outstanding curiosity and constant search for new topics that partly explains why Aizerman, unlike other Soviet operations researchers, never engaged with any big military or related projects after the war—such as missile regulation or the space program headed by Sergei Korolev (Boris Petrov from the IAT was collaborating with Korolev on that in the 1950s–1960s), and did not allow the researchers from his lab to work on them (Mark Levin, pers. comm.). These projects would have meant much for a career, but would have limited the freedom to choose the subjects for his work and to travel abroad. This was even more important in the specific Soviet context, to which I now turn.

## 5. Permeability and Constraints
## of the Iron Curtain

Soviet science was notoriously isolated from the international scene. However, this general situation and the well-known complications encountered by the majority of Soviet scientists when trying to contact—or, even more so, to receive recognition from—their foreign peers played out differently in different contexts.

19. Various individuals in a group thus started speaking the same theoretical language that further reinforced the need to streamline and standardize the terminology. I thank Salvador Barberà for making this clear to me.

Aizerman's lab was from the beginning a part of an international research network. Despite the fact that Aizerman was of Jewish origin and never was a party member, his authority both in Soviet science and among numerous colleagues abroad, as well as his visible loyalty, helped him to organize international communication and to travel a lot himself.[20] In 1960, the first huge world congress of an important association of control engineers, International Federation of Automatic Control (IFAC), was held in Moscow. At that time, its president was Alexander Letov, an engineer and an applied mathematician who was one of the founders of IFAC. It was there that Norbert Wiener gave a keynote; Rudolf Kálmán first presented the idea of the Kálmán filter, estimating the state of the system over time; a leading Soviet mathematician, Pontryagin, and his team presented their theory of optimal control and the maximum principle (Pontryagin et al. 1962);[21] and an American operation researcher, Richard Bellman, gave a talk on his results in dynamic programming.[22] At that time, Aizerman established a contact—and developed a friendship—with Bellman. In fact, Aizerman was among the first Soviet visitors to the RAND Corporation, where Bellman worked in the 1960s.

Aizerman established an international reputation quite quickly: his lectures on the theory of automatic control were translated into English (Aizerman 1963), and in the 1970s, his colleagues immigrating to the United States were getting positions in prestigious institutions.[23] After he changed the direction of his research, new colleagues were to appear. In 1967, Aizerman organized an international symposium on image recognition and related problems and gathered lots of scholars from all over the world. Since the 1970s, when choice theory was on the agenda, his international partners had been Charles Plott, who then became one of the founders of modern experimental economics, and other mathematical economists and social choice theorists (Salvador Barberà, Bernard Monjardet, and Amartya Sen). Further contacts included the mathematical economist David

20. However, he claimed that the "energy conversion efficiency" in trying to obtain permissions for travel did not exceed 20 percent (Isaev 2003: 278). Rozonoer (n.d.) explains this by Aizerman's good relations with the administrative bureaucracy of the institute whom he always invited to go abroad with him, thus creating an "incentive compatibility."

21. Despite his increasing anti-Semitism, Pontryagin was on good terms with Aizerman (cf. a letter of recommendation and evidence that he was a visitor at Aizerman's seminars in Aleskerov et al. 2003: 57, 280)—as he was with Aizerman's teacher Andronov (Dahan 2004).

22. Judy Klein, Marcel Boumans, and Béatrice Cherrier and Aurélien Saïdi (all in this volume) discuss the relevance of these authors to postwar developments of economics in the United States.

23. Interestingly, they all landed in engineering departments (Anatoliy Yashin at Duke, Semyon Meerkov at Michigan, and Muchnik at Rutgers).

Gale; the mechanism designer Theodore Groves; the game theorist and political scientist Steven Brams; and the political theorists Richard D. McKelvey, Norman Schofield, and Thomas Schwartz. They exchanged working papers and offprints, and, very rarely, would visit each other's institutions or meet at the conferences. The publication issue was somewhat more tricky: even in the 1980s, the culture of preparing and sending papers to international professional journals (in mathematical economics and social choice/decision theory) was not firmly established: many results appeared in Soviet outlets, and the work of the group was thus not really visible in the international research community. This clearly marked a limit to its integration into the mainstream.

At the same time, despite Aizerman's loyalty, the political constraints were pervasive. Suffice it to say that the letters Aleskerov and others received from abroad had been opened before they reached them. Someone reported to have seen a book sent around 1985–86 by Brams with a dedication to Aleskerov, in the semiclassified division of the INION library.[24] It was redirected there without notifying the receiver.

Of course the IPU group's interest in collective decision was anything but innocuous from the ideological point of view. Importantly, the analysis of collective decision-making quite naturally led Aizerman's group not just to social choice but also to the formal political theory—a discipline that could never be openly practiced in the USSR, where political science was replaced by "scientific communism." Two anecdotes should illustrate the contexts of Aizerman's work.

The first one is that of subversion. At the beginning of the 1970s, Malishevski, who was close to the Soviet dissidents and, in particular, to Andrei Sakharov,[25] proved a theorem demonstrating that if one uses a "total" majority rule (a group decision is taken if all members but one are in favor of it), one can always redistribute a finite amount of resource by taking it from one agent, giving most of the resource to the others, and retaining a small share with the one performing redistribution. Reiterating this procedure yields what Mirkin (1974) calls a "total majority path" (the

24. All-Union Institute of Scientific Information in Social Sciences. Brams never inquired about the book, believing that Aleskerov did not reply simply because he had not liked it (Aleskerov 2019).

25. Katsenelinboigen recollected that in the 1960s, Malishevski made a copy of the Russian edition of Samuelson's *Economics* (which was published in 1964, but the number of copies was limited and the book was available only in academic libraries) and was popularizing it among his colleagues at the IAT (Malishevski 1998: 521), as if inviting them to go all the way from *Economics* to the *Foundations of Economic Analysis*. Note that J. R. Hicks's *Value and Capital* was first published in Russian translation only in 1988.

term was Malishevski's suggestion): at each step a different agent is "robbed" by the collective majority vote, each step is preferred by the majority to the previous one, and the system itself might even become "poorer," since every time a share of resources may be appropriated by the one who manages the vote. Only high-brow mathematical formalism seemed to have saved Mirkin from the fury of censors.[26]

Another anecdote demonstrates how pervasive ideological fear was even into the 1980s. In 1981, Aizerman together with Aleskerov started to work on the issues surrounding Arrow's impossibility theorem. When discussing the paper draft, Aizerman insisted that the terms *dictator* and *oligarchy*— used by, among others, Sen (1970) and even Mirkin (1974)—be replaced. Aleskerov did not understand the reason for this excessive caution, and he remembers Aizerman eventually saying, with a note of sadness: "I have spent 70 years with this regime, and I will not allow you to ruin your life and career because of the two words that will surely be misunderstood" (see the story in Aleskerov 2005). In the published paper (Aizerman and Aleskerov 1983), the terms used are *decisive voter* and a *decisive group* (although in the footnotes, they do refer to the standard terminology).

Thus, despite the porousness of the Iron Curtain and despite Aizerman's exemplary academic reputation both inside and outside the country, the Soviet epistemic regime did pose sufficient constraints on the ways that the ideas were formulated and communicated. But what kind of knowledge did these forms of academic life eventually create?

### 6. Experiments: The Missing Link?

If one tries to make sense of Aizerman's—and thus his lab's—evolving interests and commitments, two aspects turn out to be worthy of attention. First, the change had a specific direction. From modeling the *mechanical* systems, Aizerman switched to the analysis of *living* systems and abstract problems of cybernetics. Then, in the 1970s, living systems receded to the background (the group working on these issues became a separate lab), and,

26. "Formalism" was an attitude that helped Aizerman as well. When asked to sign collective letters denouncing something, he found refuge in demanding materials to be able to get acquainted with the phenomenon he was asked to publicly condemn together with his colleagues. Not being a Communist Party member helped, too: he was not beholden to the "party discipline" (Rozonoer 2003: 248). This "formalistic" attitude enabled Aizerman to stay away from the Soviet collective campaigns without becoming a dissident. Interestingly, the formalism as a methodological strategy could also have nurtured the collective research culture of Lab 25—in a way similar to the logical positivist context described in Daston and Galison 2007: chap. 5. I am grateful to a referee for this reference.

after some experimentation, the focus moved to modeling *social* systems.[27]

Second, and related to that: the interdisciplinary agenda of Aizerman's lab was of quite specific nature. On the one hand, Aizerman was open to virtually any kind of problem. Moreover, he posed the problems in non-standard ways. But when it came to actually solving them, the work was following the patterns characteristic of deductive mathematical thinking: those of formalization and generalization. In various fields—from control engineering to cybernetics of living systems to choice theory, Aizerman himself and his colleagues were actually attracted by *theoretical* challenges.[28] But while the link between the pure and the applied was quite straightforward in the case of mechanical systems and more or less understandable (although somewhat less so) in the case of living organisms (the lab was involved in several projects in "medical cybernetics"—both exploring the control processes in muscles and creating the first algorithms to analyze the medical data), the social interactions posed the biggest problem. What was the approach of Aizerman and his colleagues?

As I have shown above, the ambition was to build a more general theory and to formalize the insights that suggested this generality. The apparatus of choice functions was the language Aizerman found most appropriate for addressing this problem. Thus he both questioned the validity of the "classical" rationality and used a deductive approach: from the more abstract, more general perspective that would incorporate the classical idea as a special case.

This process might seem curious for a student of twentieth-century economics, since we know that the many challenges to the standard model of rationality eventually led to the rise of behavioral and experimental economics. But neither Aizerman nor his collaborators were—or could become—economic experimentalists.

At the same time, experimental research did play a role in Aizerman's career. Experiments were part of his research activities from the beginning: to study and to regulate the pressure in the liquefied gas engines,

27. Aleskerov does not share my interpretation and believes instead that, although this rendering is accurate, it does not reveal any teleology. Rather, the change of interests was due to Aizerman's exceptional curiosity and propensity to change the disciplinary frameworks. Perhaps our positions can be reconciled in that Aizerman himself might not have seen or planned this transformation of interests in this particular way.

28. At the IPU, Aizerman also had the reputation of a theorist, which attracted to him individuals with similar sensibilities, such as Rozonoer (n.d.).

one needed to perform lots of experimental work. Aizerman's "bionics" program—the study of the control processes in animals and humans—was also based on the experiments the lab researchers performed for many years. But this was still not exactly the experimental *economics* in the form it was initiated by Vernon Smith and Plott in the United States.

In 1986, upon returning from a visit to Plott in Caltech, Aleskerov suggested that they do experiments as well.[29] Aizerman fully supported this initiative: the lab members ran several experiments and published a summary of results in a conference proceedings (Aleskerov et al. 1986). Thus Aleskerov could be considered one of the first Soviet experimental economists. However, he never went further.

Why, despite Aizerman's support and, generally, perfect initial conditions, did the group not adopt the experimentalist program—following the path of Plott himself, who turned from doing pure social choice theory to experimental economics? One reason is, clearly, Aizerman's own proclivities.

In March–April 1987, the Committee on Contributions of Behavioral and Social Sciences to the Prevention of Nuclear War, represented by its members, the behavioral scientists Herbert Simon and William Estes, as well as the political scientist Robert Axelrod and a couple of staff members, visited the Soviet Union and talked to the major scholars in eight research institutes, including IPU. In the report they prepared, they summarized their meeting with Aizerman in the following way.

Aizerman's research is on the theory of choice, voting, and agenda control. It is mathematical and computer modeling work on the logic of choice, and is expanding classical rationality from comparisons of pairs (which have problems of transitivity) to more general choice functions. He is interested in the problem of organizing agendas for collective discussion so as not to manipulate voters as [at?] the USSR institutes voting procedures. Almost all the group's work is published in English as well as Russian, and some involves collaborations with U.S. scholars, such as Charles Plott and Thomas Schwartz. In response to questions, Aizerman said his group is concerned with attentional effects, which he described as the "effect of context"; no empirical work is now going on, but he

29. The 1985 visit to Caltech left some important traces. In particular, Leonid Hurwicz (1986: 75), who also presented at a conference there, acknowledged that he was inspired to pursue the choice functions approach by Aizerman and his team in one of his papers devoted to the implementation of social choice rules. Barberà (email to Ivan Boldyrev, July 6, 2019) recalls how both men quickly established contact and engaged in an intensive dialogue.

hopes to begin some. Aizerman wants to extend the work to the problem of cooperation, which he calls the "theory of agreement."[30]

So in 1987 still no empirical work was being done. While Plott was interested in testing the existing economic theories and—somewhat later—testing new policies and improving market design, in the Soviet case, apart from obvious ideological limitations, two essential factors were missing. First, there was no established community of economists potentially interested in experiments and grouped around some kind of a mainstream paradigm of human behavior/rationality (Boldyrev and Kirtchik 2017).[31] Second, there were no markets and no real competitive political system to apply any insights either from market design or from social choice models. Around 1975, Mirkin publicly asked his Novosibirsk boss, Abel Aganbegyan, whether the analysis of group choice, voting theory, and the like can ever be applied in the better design of collective decision-making—and received a definitely negative answer that discouraged him. In 1983–86, when Aizerman was presenting the first results on collective choice theory in various academic institutions, his lectures attracted hundreds of colleagues (Aleskerov 2005). The interest in formal political theory was amazing, which probably reflected the situation of growing uncertainty and growing demand for various new discourses in the social sciences (in particular in political science) so characteristic of perestroika and the first post-Soviet years.

Absent any theoretical or policy interest, the research funds to perform experiments were also missing. Despite that Aizerman, Malishevski,[32] Aleskerov, and other members of the team were driven by much more general theoretical concerns, the contexts mattered as well: once the Soviet Union ceased to exist, Aleskerov contributed to the work of the first huge center of experimental and behavioral economics in Russia

30. Report, Committee on Contributions of Behavioral and Social Sciences to the Prevention of Nuclear War, May 4, 1987, p. 11, Series VI: Consulting—1942–2000, box 48, folder 3694, Herbert A. Simon Papers, Carnegie Mellon University, Pittsburgh, PA.

31. For example, Plott (2012: 296) came to the insights very similar to those of Aizerman—but inspired by the US public choice tradition: "Buchanan was right [in his criticism of Arrow]: there is no need to restrict the theory to processes that operate on two-element sets and once that assumption is discarded . . . a completely different frontier is opened." Another example is Arrow's work in the economics of R&D and medical care discussed by William Thomas in this volume.

32. Malishevski suffered from depression and committed suicide in 1997. His and some others' premature deaths mark huge missed opportunities for new research during the post-Soviet period.

organized by Alexis Belianin at Moscow's Higher School of Economics, which became a site of collaboration between economists, psychologists, and political scientists.

## 7. Conclusion: The Engineering Cultures in Soviet Mathematical Economics?

Overall, Soviet economics was an isolated form of knowledge. Even in its mathematical mode, it could not be a part of an increasingly internationalizing field—be it general "economics" or its particular branches.[33] However, what was true for the whole was not true for some of its parts, such as the Aizerman group. Its members were not just well versed in the most up-to-date literature but were also contacting the "bourgeois" economists and political scientists and publishing in English. Despite all the constraints discussed above, Aizerman's lab was one of the most internationalized groups in Soviet mathematical social sciences. By the beginning of the 1980s, it had already established a reputation among social choice and decision theorists. Although Aizerman's team has never been a group of "full-fledged" economists, the work it was doing stood on a par with the most advanced economic and decision theory in the West.[34]

So why did this group of engineers embark on the study of economics? The story told here has revealed a plethora of different motivations—the sheer curiosity and the feeling that new results may be obtained; the ambition of reformulating the whole theory of choice and thus the foundations of the behavioral science; the search for new methods in data analysis; and the move from the cybernetics of mechanical and living systems to that of a social system. Of particular importance was Aizerman's tendency to regularly and entirely reorient his research agenda.

It is curious, however, that Aizerman and his colleagues, being open to virtually any kind of question and keen to do interdisciplinary work, produced for the most part results that were very abstract and followed the mathematicians' quest for ever higher generality and formalization—working on the *foundations* of (micro)economics and rationality. This work could be placed at the heart of the formal theory discussed in the

33. Several notable exceptions (see, among others, Boldyrev and Kirtchik 2014) only confirm the rule.

34. The group members were not the only ones doing social choice theory in the USSR, but the other authors were isolated and driven by other (sub-)disciplinary contexts. See Aleskerov 2005.

aftermath of Arrow's impossibility theorem. As a political theory, how-ever, it sounded even more subversive for the Soviet context than "mathe-matical economics," which still could legitimize itself with the recourse to Kantorovich's theory of "optimal planning."

The formalisms suggested by Aizerman's group, although being criti-cal of the "classical" rationality, which nowadays seems to be abandoned, and moreover, being accepted by the economics mainstream, never really gained traction and have not become a standard in the social choice liter-ature.[35] Aizerman also could not—and perhaps did not want to—be a part of the "experimental turn" in economics, although this type of "eco-nomic engineering" could have been the way to fully integrate his and some of his colleagues' engineering background, on the one hand, and their theoretical aspirations, on the other. To engage with experimental markets and to apply the insights of mechanism design—the very essence of economics as "social engineering"—were hardly possible in the period of Soviet stagnation.

Thus, judging with hindsight, one of Mark Aizerman's most successful (social) engineering achievements was the team he established at Labora-tory 25. After his death, Lab 25, headed now by Aleskerov, remains one of the most productive centers at the IPU and belongs to the very few research groups in the post-Soviet world actively working on formal polit-ical science, social choice, and decision theory.

## References

Abramov, Roman. 2017. "Soviet Engineering and Technical Intellectuals from the 1960s to the 1980s: Searching for the Boundaries of Collective Consciousness" (in Russian). *Vestnik instituta sotsiologii* 8, no. 1: 115–30.

Aizerman, Mark A. 1963. *Theory of Automatic Control*. Oxford: Pergamon.

Aizerman, Mark A. 1975. "Human and Collective as Elements of the Control Sys-tem" (in Russian). *Avtomatika i Telemekhanika* 36, no. 5: 83–96.

Aizerman, Mark A. 1985. "New Problems in the General Choice Theory: Review of a Research Trend." *Social Choice and Welfare* 2: 235–82.

Aizerman, Mark A., Emmanuil M. Braverman, and Lev I. Rozonoer. 1964. "Theoret-ical Foundation of Potential Functions Method in Pattern Recognition" (in Rus-sian). *Avtomatika i Telemekhanika* 25, no. 6: 917–36.

35. One reason might be, as Sen (1995: 95) argues in the context of voting theory, that "using choice functions as inputs is much more demanding on voters and on the system of 'counting' than is the use of rankings of each voter with menu-dependence assumed away. In fact, using choice functions as inputs may be infeasible in practice in many types of exer-cises." See also Aizerman and Aleskerov 1986 (this paper first emerged as a Caltech working paper); Aleskerov 2002.

Aizerman, Mark A., Nikolay V. Zavalishin, and Evgeny S. Piatniskii. 1977. "Global Function of Sets in the Theory of Alternative Selection." *Automation and Remote Control* 38, no. 3: 393–406.

Aizerman, Mark A., and Fuad T. Aleskerov. 1983. "The Arrow Problem in the Group Choice Theory (the Problem Analysis)." *Automation and Remote Control* 44, no. 9: 1211–32.

Aizerman, Mark A., and Fuad T. Aleskerov. 1986. "Voting Operators in the Space of Choice Functions." *Mathematical Social Sciences* 11, no. 3: 201–42.

Aizerman, Mark A., and Fuad T. Aleskerov. 1990. *Choice of Variants: Elements of a Theory* (in Russian). Moscow: Nauka. Published in English as: *Theory of Choice*. Amsterdam: North-Holland, 1995.

Aizerman, Mark A., and Andrei V. Malishevski. 1981. "General Theory of Best Variants Choice: Some Aspects." *IEEE Trans Automatic Control*, AC-26: 1030–40.

Aleskerov, Fuad T. 2002. "Categories of Arrovian Voting Schemes." In vol. 1 of *Handbook of Social Choice and Welfare*, edited by Kenneth J. Arrow, Amartya Sen, and Kotaro Suzumura, 95–129. Amsterdam: Elsevier.

Aleskerov, Fuad T. 2005. "The History of Social Choice in Russia and the Soviet Union." *Social Choice and Welfare* 25, nos. 2–3: 419–31.

Aleskerov, Fuad T. 2018 Interview by Olessia Kirtchik, Moscow, January 31.

Aleskerov, Fuad T. 2019. Interview by Ivan Boldyrev, Moscow-Nijmegen, February 12.

Aleskerov, Fuad T., et al. 2003. *Mark Aronovich Aizerman (1913–1992)* (in Russian). Moscow: Fizmatlit.

Aleskerov, Fuad T., Vladimir I. Volskiy, and Zoya M. Lezina. 1986. "Experimental Modeling of the Market Processes." In *Proceedings of the All-Union Conference on Modeling Economic Experiments* (in Russian), 171–72. Moscow: GKNT.

Andreeva, Ekaterina A., and Ilya B. Muchnik. 2003. "In Search of the Adequate Language for Studying the Principles of Control in Living Systems." In *Mark Aronovich Aizerman (1913 – 1992)* (in Russian), 160–98. Moscow: Fizmatlit.

Arrow, Kenneth. 1951. *Social Choice and Individual Values*. New York: Wiley.

Arrow, Kenneth. 1959. "Rational Choice Functions and Orderings." *Economica* 26, no. 102: 121–27.

Bissell, Chris C. 1998. "A. A. Andronov and the Development of Soviet Control Engineering." *IEEE Control Systems* 18, no. 1: 56–62.

Bissell, Chris C. 1999. "Control Engineering in the Former U.S.S.R.: Some Ideological Aspects of the Early Years." *IEEE Control Systems* 19, no. 1: 111–17.

Boldyrev, Ivan, and Olessia Kirtchik. 2014. "General Equilibrium Theory behind the Iron Curtain: The Case of Victor Polterovich." *History of Political Economy* 46, no. 3: 435–61.

Boldyrev, Ivan, and Olessia Kirtchik. 2017. "The Cultures of 'Mathematical Economics' in the Postwar Soviet Union: More Than a Method, Less Than a Discipline." *Studies in History and Philosophy of Science, Part A* 63: 1–10.

Braverman, Emmanuil M., and Mark J. Levin. 1981. *Disequilibrium Models of Economic Systems* (n Russian). Moscow: Nauka.

Chervonenkis, Alexey. n.d. Interview by Marina Pyatnitskaya and Vladislav Yurchenko, Moscow. www.youtube.com/watch?v=x8XVOFOqSEI&list=PL6VRZz38 PrqNTSJx9HHDn51fgnc_Mr_fb&index=22.

Dahan Dalmedico, Amy (with Irina Gouzevitch). 2004. "Early Developments of Nonlinear Science in Soviet Russia: The Andronov School at Gor'kiy." *Science in Context* 17, nos. 1–2: 235–66.

Daston, Lorraine, and Peter Galison. 2007. *Objectivity*. New York: Zone Books.

Demidov, Sergei, and Boris Levshin, eds. 1999. *The Case of Academician Nikolay Nikolaevich Luzin* (in Russian). Saint Petersburg: RKhGI.

Feldman, Grigory A. (1928) 1964. "On the Theory of Growth Rates of National Income." In *Foundations of Soviet Strategy for Economic Growth,* edited by Nicolas Spulber, 174–99. Bloomington: Indiana University Press.

Gerovitch, Slava. 2002. *From Newspeak to Cyberspeak: A History of Soviet Cybernetics*. Cambridge, MA: MIT Press.

Gerovitch, Slava. 2008. "Stalin's Rocket Designers' Leap into Space: The Technical Intelligentsia Faces the Thaw." In "Intelligentsia Science: The Russian Century, 1860–1960," special issue. *Osiris*, 2nd ser., no. 23: 189–209.

Gibbard, Allan. 1973. "Manipulation of Voting Schemes: A General Result." *Econometrica* 41, no. 4: 587–601.

Graham, Loren R. 1996. *The Ghost of the Executed Engineer: Technology and the Fall of the Soviet Union*. Cambridge, MA: Harvard University Press.

Hands, D. Wade. 2016. "Crossing in the Night of the Cold War: Alternative Visions and Related Tensions in Western and Soviet General Equilibrium Theory." *History of Economic Ideas* 24: 51–74.

Hurwicz, Leonid. 1986. "On the Implementation of Social Choice Rules in Irrational Societies." In vol. 1 of *Social Choice and Public Decision Making: Essays in Honor of Kenneth J. Arrow,* edited by Walter P. Heller, Ross M. Starr, and David A. Starrett, 75–96. Cambridge: Cambridge University Press.

Isaev, Vyacheslav K. 2003. "M. A. Aizerman and PhysTech." In *Mark Aronovich Aizerman (1913 – 1992),* (in Russian), 266–88. Moscow: Fizmatlit.

Kemeny, John G., and J. Laurie Snell. 1962. *Mathematical Models in the Social Sciences*. Boston: Ginn.

Kirtchik, Olessia. 2019. "From Pattern Recognition to Economic Disequilibrium: Emmanuil Braverman's Theory of Control of the Soviet Economy." In *Economic Knowledge in Socialism, 1945–1989*, edited by Till Düppe and Ivan Boldyrev. *History of Political Economy* 51 (supplement): 180–203.

Kryshtanovskaya, Olga. 1989. *Engineers: The Evolution and Development of a Professional Group* (in Russian). Moscow: Nauka.

Leeds, Adam. 2016. "Dreams in Cybernetic Fugue: Cold War Technoscience, the Intelligentsia, and the Birth of Soviet Mathematical Economics." *Historical Studies in the Natural Sciences* 46, no. 5: 633–68.

Lipovetsky, Mark. 2013. "The Poetics of ITR Discourse: In the 1960s and Beyond." *Ab Imperio*, no. 1: 109–41.

Makarov, Valery L., Mark I. Levin, and Alexander M. Rubinov. 1995. *Mathematical Economic Theory: Pure and Mixed Types of Economic Mechanisms*. Amsterdam: Elsevier.

Malishevski, Andrei. 1998. *Qualitative Models in the Theory of Complex Systems* (in Russian). Moscow: Nauka.

Mirkin, Boris G. 1974. *The Problem of Group Choice* (in Russian). Moscow: Nauka. Published in English as *Group Choice*. New York: Wiley, 1979.

Mirkin, Boris G. 2019. Interview by Ivan Boldyrev, Moscow-Nijmegen, March 14.

Mirkin, Boris G. n.d. Interview by Dmitry Zavigelskiy. www.youtube.com/watch ?v=jlJDwdSrZeQ.

Peters, Benjamin. 2016. *How Not to Network a Nation: The Uneasy History of the Soviet Internet*. Cambridge, MA: MIT Press.

Plott, Charles. 1973. "Path Independence, Rationality, and Social Choice." *Econometrica* 41, no. 6: 1075–91.

Plott, Charles. 2012. "Personal Reflections on the Influence of Buchanan, Tullock, and *The Calculus of Consent*." *Public Choice* 152, nos. 3–4: 293–98.

Pontryagin, Lev S., Vladimir G. Boltyanskii, Revaz V. Gamkredlidze, and Evgeny F. Mishchenko. 1962. *The Mathematical Theory of Optimal Processes*. New York: Wiley.

Rindzevičiūtė, Egle. 2016. *The Power of Systems: How Policy Sciences Opened Up the Cold War World*. Ithaca, NY: Cornell University Press.

Rosenblatt, Frank. 1958. "The Perceptron: A Probabilistic Model for Information Storage and Organization in the Brain." *Psychological Review* 65, no. 6: 386–408.

Rozonoer, Lev I. n.d. Interview by Marina Pyatnitskaya and Vladislav Yurchenko. youtube/yWVDn_luyOE.

Rozonoer, Lev I. 2002. "The Way I Remember Him." In *Mark Aronovich Aizerman (1912 – 1992)*, 244–51. Published in Russian. Moscow: Fizmatlit.

Rozonoer, Lev I., Boris G. Mirkin, and Ilya Muchnik, eds. 2018. *Braverman Readings in Machine Learning: Key Ideas from Inception to Current State: Lecture Notes in Artificial Intelligence*, vol. 11100. New York: Springer.

Sen, Amartya. 1970. *Collective Choice and Social Welfare*. San Francisco: Holden-Day.

Sen, Amartya. 1971. "Choice Functions and Revealed Preference." *Review of Economic Studies* 38, no. 3: 307–17.

Sen, Amartya. 1993. "Internal Consistency of Choice." *Econometrica* 61, no. 3: 495–521.

Sen, Amartya. 1995. "How to Judge Voting Schemes." *Journal of Economic Perspectives* 9, no. 1: 91–99.

Tamas, Pal. 2013. "Was the Soviet Engineer So Unique?" *Ab Imperio*, no. 1: 189–94.

Von Neumann, John, and Oskar Morgenstern. 1944. *Theory of Games and Economic Behavior*. Princeton, NJ: Princeton University Press.

Zauberman, Alfred. 1967. *Aspects of Planometrics*. London: Athlone.

# Technocratic Economics:
# An Afterword

Mary S. Morgan

Twentieth-century economics can be characterized by two contrasting modes of economic-engineering: one is the design mode of engineering focused on creating technologies that engineer change; the other is the tool-based engineering mode of problem-solving. In earlier work, I suggested that economics became something of an engineering science in the twentieth century, without recognizing very clearly those different modes.[1] There were several strands to my argument then that still, in retrospect, remain important and might now be more firmly pressed, but also reassessed. First, I argued economics developed more tool-based methods of working compared to the political economy of earlier centuries: mathematics, statistics and modeling. These tools were not just for the practices

I thank the editors of this special issue, Pedro Garcia Duarte and Yann Giraud, for inviting me both to the *HOPE* workshop and to contribute this final piece to their special issue. Thanks also go to Dominic Berry for materials on engineering design; to Malcolm Rutherford (for ideas from our collaboration in the earlier projects); to participants in the special issue workshop for rekindling my interest; to Marcel Boumans (from whom I have learned to appreciate the engineering elements in economics); and to David Warsh and the editors for comments on a draft of this piece.

    1. The first paper outlining this argument was made with Malcolm Rutherford in a special *HOPE* issue (1998) on American economics in the twentieth century. This was substantially reworked and extended beyond the American context for the *Cambridge History of Science* series, in an essay of 2003 commissioned by Ted Porter and Dorothy Ross (editors of the volume on the history of social sciences). In this version of the argument, I have been sparse in referencing works within the history of economics, and only indicative with references beyond our field.

*History of Political Economy* 52 (annual suppl.)  DOI 10.1215/00182702-8718067

inside economic science, but also ones that could be used in policy work. Second, although "the economy" had been conceived as a unit of its own in earlier times, its object-like quality seemed more assured by the middle of the twentieth century in the sense that economists conceived of it as a sufficiently material system that intervention in its workings was thought possible, and moreover that those technologies developed for understanding economies could also be repositioned for intervention. Third, the events of the middle century, beginning with the critical problems of the Great Depression, fostered a stronger sense of responsibility of economists over the well-being of economic life—for that depression was unambiguously an economic outcome, not the fallout of political events such as revolutions and wars. This attitude carried economists into the successful running of wartime economies, economic reconstruction after World War II, and participation in international economic agencies responsible for the health of the international economy and developmental processes in national economies.

Timing is critical here.[2] It was that same younger generation who were developing those tool-based modes of work in the interwar and war period—and who developed such an active sense of responsibility because of the challenging contexts—who grew their ambitions to engineer a better economic world in the design-based mode. They gained confidence that such actions could be successful following their active participation in various kinds of technical war work, both using economics and otherwise. Such experience in the 1920s–1950s involved a variety of economics technologies in an engineering mode: that is, technologies of analysis ("cameras") that doubled as technologies of intervention, control, and rationing "engines": input-output matrices to sort out labor supply systems, macroeconomic modeling and national income accounting to figure out fiscal policy and planning, and so on.[3] I refer to these as "technologies" because they embody, and their use depends on, both human know-how (knowledge and experience) and material systems. This combination of objectification of the economy, tools and technologies and associated

2. Of course, there were earlier idealist economists who took those responsibilities seriously (such as the progressives in the United States and Fabians in the UK), other groups who were serious about state action (the cameralists in Germany, and perhaps the fiscal state analysts of Italy), other traditions steeped in engineering and economics (as in France), and individuals (such as Thorstein Veblen) advocating an engineering mentality. The point to be appreciated here is the timing and combination of such stances with technical changes in economics. A good comparative national study across all these elements is surely needed.

3. I return later to this language of cameras and machines taken from MacKenzie 2006.

expertise, and a sense of public responsibility created something I understood then as an engineering approach to the economy and in economics, and which I now want to acknowledge as involving both problem-solving and design-based modes of doing economics.

I stand by this argument, and perhaps it is clearer in its restatement here than it was then, either in its early form of 1998 or its more developed form of 2003. Now I would stress even more strongly how the exigencies of history—both economic and political—have shaped these developments. The history of tool development—the adoption of mathematics, statistics, and models—has sometimes been told as a largely internalist story (possibly even Whiggish), picturing economists driven by scientistic ambitions for greater rigor and greater objectivity from the late nineteenth century into the 1920s. But it was never entirely so. Indeed, the development of such tools was strongly connected not just (1) to the (arguably) new phenomenon of business cycles (and other kinds of economic cycles) but (2) to the burgeoning growth of data as statistical evidence both for theory testing (in econometric models) and for policy usage in fields such as agricultural and industrial economics, and (3) in creating accounts that were generic or model-based, and more closely focused on particular problems, rather than in examining and appealing to general laws.

It is now well established that it was only during the middle of the twentieth century that this tool-based economics became more thoroughly spread within, and across, the economics field during the same period that the economic and political contexts became really important to the identity of economists. So, while the explanation for any individual economist's tool-development may of course lie in personal circumstances, training, resources, and so forth, those personal attributes, talents, and ambitions needed rich grounds to flourish. Those economists had to be noticed, and their tools needed and employed both for scientific understanding and for interventions. This narrative of economics in engineering mode could not have been generated merely by individual stories of engineers or physicists turning into economists; those stories are surely relevant but are nowhere near sufficient.

There is now a significant way in which, from the vantage point of the twenty-first century, I want to reshape this argument to separate out these engineering modes more effectively, as well as to extend the account of the development of tools. That the papers in the *HOPE* workshop and this volume seem to coalesce around the mid-twentieth century might be taken as evidence for my original thesis. But in taking that longer view, such concentration might point to a narrative not of continuous rise but of differential paths in these two engineering modes.

For the design mode, the early 1950s seem to be well endowed with positive econo-engineering ambitions, and some level of successful interventions evident in the Marshall Plan for reconstruction after World War II, in the ECLA program of import-substitution industrialization in Latin America, and in countless individual country development plans in that period. In the 1950s and 1960s, design reengineering ambitions were found everywhere, manifest in the general belief in "planning," not just for socialist states, but for all economies. American client states were sold planning for democracy just as Soviet ones were sold planning for socialism. "Planning" was the universal language not just for economic reconstruction, and management at the macro-level in Western European countries, but for any "modernization" program in the developing world, as well as for local and regional economic projects worldwide.

Perhaps the height of confidence in this design mode was the 1960s, a period of utopian dreams to change economic worlds alongside a belief in economic expertise to achieve those changes: economic design-engineering was embedded in theory and in practice. It is one of the most striking realizations from studying colonial-independence events of the early 1960s that their elites believed that they could create new economies to match their newly independent political status. Ambitions to design their economic futures were magnificent. Cuba under Che Guevara aimed to engineer socialist planning based on advanced American managerial accounting techniques (Yaffe 2009). Nigeria aimed for democratic planning based on Tinbergian processes of consultation and using National Income Accounting numbers to enforce plan consistencies (Morgan 2008). Sudanese elites argued whether their new state should continue in a mother-offspring colonial commodity-supply economy, or develop its own regional economies, or go into fuller partnership with Egypt—each of which would have involved different forms of reconfigurations of the economy (Young 2017). Design-engineering these economic projects proved more problematic, but progressed much further into action than armchair dreams. A useful contrast is provided in the experiences of reverse engineering the transition from communist to capitalist societies in the 1990s. These desires prompted well-needed discussion of how to do this, how fast the transition should be, when to start, which order to do things in, and so forth. And despite the confidence of some economists who were invited in to help, it was seen as fraught with more doubts and more immediate difficulties than the earlier ex-colonial experiences. These doubts were well founded, given the subsequent problematic experiences of transition in many of those economies.

The notion of engineering design that these ex-colonial, developmental, projects involved was positive and creative, and expected economists to conceive of how those economies could be, and could function, by searching for "clearly conceived forms which are well adapted to given contexts," to quote one of the gurus of industrial design of the period, Christopher Alexander (1964). Such hopeful framing can be compared with ideas coming from Herbert Simon in the same period (1969), who saw the design problem as focused on the means and tools of "changing existing circumstances into preferred ones," which seems better to reflect the mind-set of those later, less confident, projects of transformation. We might say that where Alexander was more concerned with the object to be designed, Simon was more concerned with the environment of the object (though both of course understood that both elements were involved).

How do these ideas relate to the history of economics? The infertility of economics in dealing with the recent Global Financial Crisis (GFC) of 2008–9 and its aftermath seemed to match the equivalent lack of analytical confidence and failure of economic agencies in dealing with the events of 1929–33 and the Great Depression. But the loss of innocence in the possibility of economic expertise to re-engineer an economy in Alexander's design mode had set in well before this GFC. This is well understood by economic historians, even if not so well recognized by economists. The 1970s had provided the first major set of problems for such reengineering dreams. The collapse of the postwar, fixed-exchange-rate system (based on gold and the dollar, established at Bretton Woods) saw not just the replacement of monetarism for Keynesianism but revealed the more recalcitrant practical, national and international, economic difficulties of floating exchange rates and debt crises: part of the environment in Simon's terms. Two of the most interesting episodes of thinking about economics in terms of design-reengineering the economy as a unit are the 1970s stagflation and the long stagnation in the Japanese economy nearer the end of the century. These occurred well before the GFC, but like that latter event, were ones for which economists seemed to have no well-tried explanations and had to reframe their thinking in order to make such explanations and solutions. An economic machine cannot be mended without understanding how it works, nor can circumstances be changed at will. And when managing, or fine-tuning, or mending the economy failed—either the circumstances had to be changed, as Simon suggested, or redesigning the system entailed rethinking the object, as Alexander would have it, in order to design new technologies fit for the changed circumstances.[4] This double problem was well exemplified when, in the 1980s and 1990s, economists were at the forefront in replacing 1960s design-engineering modes of development planning with older-fashioned recipes of fiscal and monetarist rectitude. These older recipes in the new environment created such stress (and increasing poverty levels) in a number of developing economies that they were largely abandoned. But it is significant that they were abandoned in favor not of some new utopian redesigns but of the use of the other mode of economic engineering, using more narrowly focused, tool-based, interventions rather than technologies for wholesale redesign.

So the overall narrative I suggest here sees a rise in the midcentury and then a fall in the ambitions and domain of economic actions, where the latter fall can be characterized as a change from design-engineering to problem-solving engineering. This is most easily recognized in the changes in the self-identity of economists that occurred over the course of the twentieth century. John Maynard Keynes earlier portrayed economists as dentists, and Esther Duflo more recently labeled economists as plumbers. Both labels portray economists as professionals, with expertise in diagnosis and intervention, but of a very focused kind, namely, to recognize and to fix specific problems. This identity is a far cry from the midcentury dreams of creating "modern" economies, or reconstructing war-torn and heavily damaged economies. The dentist/plumber identity points to that alternative kind of econo-engineering, using tool-based accounts and tool-based interventions, and in more problem-focused ways. This is not a narrative of macroeconomic interventions giving way to microeconomic ones, but rather an account of a different mode in recognizing and solving economic problems via economic engineering interventions. These could be using modelling tools (e.g., to fix tax rates to reduce cigarette consumption, or to design auctions of licenses), or—to take more recent examples—behavioral economics tools of nudging (to make people pay taxes), or even field experimental tools (to trial specific poverty reduction measures). But the critical point is that they adopt the same hands-on, practical problem-solving mode akin to that analogous mode of engineering: tinkering, fixing, improving, and seeking small design changes—getting things to work in the most economic way, a far cry from redesigning whole economies. In retrospect, the narrative arc I have painted is not entirely discerning, for the

---

4. One of the most thoughtful accounts of the generic processes of reframing—taking into account the actors, theories, and timing—is by Peter Hall (1993), in treating the switch from Keynesianism to monetarism.

two modes are not substitutes for each other. And, going back to my earlier narrative, it may well be that it is the midcentury period in which the development of such tools is most active even while the use of technologies in design mode is also at its height. Why? Perhaps because design-engineering relies on tool-based engineering to make it work. So both approaches are actively developing in parallel in midcentury, while the grand design project comes in and fades away.

In the long run, economists have always played roles in the public and policy domain, hence the original label of political economy. Our understanding of mercantilists, physiocrats, cameralists, and so forth are pitched within an earlier framework that economics is for, and about, state action. Their earlier problem-solving tools of the fiscal and regulatory state have not disappeared, and may well have been refashioned even while new ones are developed and used. But this public usage is not what is important to the narratives in this volume, which are much more concerned with how new tools in this second problem-solving engineering mode are made, and in the processes and contexts of their development. This requires serious thinking about historical framing, as is evident in the articles in this volume. As they recognize, it does not work well to presume that economists simply pinched their tools from engineers or engineering, either with confidence or under the thrall of some inferiority complex. The latter would simply replace an account framed for the late nineteenth century about economists being infected by scientistic desires, with one where technocratic ambitions were dominant. The articles in the volume also suggest we should avoid the awkward notion that what economists were doing was "simply" applying mathematics. Apart from the problem that mathematics is many different things, and so a choice always needs to be made as to the relevant mathematics, the question remains how to apply it? Mathematics is not simply applied to economics as an iron is applied to a wrinkled shirt to make it fit to wear. We know from the work of a wide range of philosophers and historians of science (including those of economics) that the means of doing science, the methods, the formulas, the templates, even the framings, are rarely transferred from one science and applied to a new subject area without some transformation or adaptation, with possible gains and losses in the new home.[5] Nor does it give us much insight to

5. For a few examples, in which many further resources are referenced, see Maasen et al. 1995 on transfers between biology and social sciences; Porter 1986 on the transfers of statistical thinking in the nineteenth century (including physics and social sciences); Herfeld and Lisciandra (2019), on template and model transfers; and Morgan 2012 (chap. 5) on analogical model transfers into economics.

think of economists simply as borrowing tools from another science or even being in a "trading zone," for historians' accounts of such trading zones habitually ignore something that economists do know, namely, that trade involves exchange. Maybe there is exchange—but we rarely get an account of the other side of the bargain; we often know only a one-way transfer in or through the "boundary zone" (a more usable notion). Nevertheless, all transfers—like metaphors and analogies—come with baggage, and the articles here are alert to this issue.

What about the tools? The articles in this volume prompt me to frame these histories of econo-engineering initiatives as ones of tool forging, which enable us to focus not on the borrowing but on the activities and outcomes of making tools workable in, and for, economics. This framing brings back agency to the economists, who may have forged tools for their own purposes on their own account; or they may have found tools used elsewhere and taken them to be refashioned into usable things to solve economists' technical problems. This framing leaves open whether the tool is borrowed or transferred, comes via translation or analogy, or is the result of a shotgun marriage or theft. Yet, giving back agency to the economists does not mean ignoring the specific resources—in people, in ideas, in techniques, and in individuals or groups from other fields—that economists drew on. Nor does it avoid questions about intersections and interactions between different professions—sometimes these tools did indeed come ready-made from engineers, or were forged in collaborations with engineers. But they could also be the result of economists' engineering mind-set: focusing on problem-solving, and picking out and developing "the right tools for the job" (Clarke and Fujimura 1992). And here is where the framing of the present volume is particularly helpful, focusing attention as it does in its section headings on the importance of institutional and professional overlaps in places and ideas. And then—in the individual contributions—we see what actually happened in the forging of tools in those places where economists and engineers, or (perhaps more likely) where their problems and solutions, met.

Focusing on the meeting up of problems and solutions creates its own new questions about understanding in the intersections. Sometimes, as for the several examples on utilities' production and pricing, the partnership of engineers and economists is very close, close in terms of sharing problems and creating tools. But we should beware whether those two professional groups had the same understandings and concept set. Thus *costs*, *prices*, *efficiency*, and *value* all have commonsense usages. They are also technical terms and conceptual terms for economists meeting engineers over issues of deciding pricing for a utility.[6] And while economists have separate notions of costs and prices, it is less evident that engineers do. The same tools may be compatible with different concepts, and the same concepts may be consistent with different tools. Where different professional groups come up with different figures for something, one suspects that they may have held different concepts as well as different methods of calculation.

These examples and observations point to a salient, and often neglected, issue. Tools in science are not neutral; they are not independent of subject content. The tools of economics are not like hammers to hit nails, but are forged to fit securely into economics at levels of representations such as equations, and in analytical processes and modes of calculations. So, in cases where tools of representation and analysis from engineering lead the formulation of economic tools (rather than follow them), their usage is more likely to infect the ways economists understand the economic phenomena they investigate and treat with those tools. Without being conscious of it, they are likely to construct their understanding with those engineering ideas in mind. In other cases, tools are forged especially to fit economics, as for example the development of econometric tools were made to fit the special characteristics of economic data and theory—and those tools differed markedly from those forged to fit psychometrics (both diverged, in different ways, from the standard statistical models and techniques of the time). Thus the forging and use of tools with joint economic and engineering characteristics in this midcentury period—by "mashups," or collusions, or shotgun marriages—seem particularly evident in characterizing problems, tasks, and questions about maximizing, efficiency, dynamic processes, feedback systems, and so on. Of course these can be understood as both economic and engineering ideas. Perhaps they may also be linked to the well-attested change of definition of economics toward a focus on efficiency in the use of scarce resources that we know took over during the twentieth century. Yet older notions of economics, and questions of growth and distribution and stability, were still dominant in macroeconomics and development economics (particularly in that broad notion of planning). It would be as misplaced to suppose that the development of the tool-based engineering mode in economics was a neoliberal conspiracy as to suggest that economists have blindly taken and misapplied ideas in other periods from physics or evolutionary biology.

---

6. The elephant in the room is surely to ask where was "accounting" in these costing-pricing intersections?

It may be less immediately exciting, but more interesting and rewarding, to frame this history of economic-engineering intersections and interactions within a broader historical question about the twentieth-century performativity of economics. Although performativity studies in sociology of economics have largely focused on microeconomic and financial markets, we can use that notion to frame all these different modes of economic-engineering as attempts to make the world more like the theories and models economists have of that world, whether this involved creating a socialist or capitalist state, or figuring out the pricing rule for electricity. Invoking the language of performativity is neither to propose, nor to give in to, a social constructivist account of economics, but the opposite—because remaking the economic world has been the aim of these economic-engineering interventions. If economists succeeded in using their tools and technologies to change economic performance, it was not because of some stealthy hidden agenda by economists, but due to explicit ambitions. Performativity in this guise is not just about tracing economic ideas into policy, but the next big step of how those ideas get remade on the ground—and here is where economic-engineering really matters. For such ambitions, it is worth adapting Donald MacKenzie's book title that invites us to see economics as "an engine not a camera." I find it more apt to suggest that economics, particularly in its design mode of engineering, is both "a camera and an engine," and even, perhaps, that its effectiveness as an engine depends on the quality of its cameras. In following the tools and technologies in use, we surely will find interventions which have proved more or less dangerous, more or less efficacious, more or less successful in reaching their aims, and prompting more or fewer externalities. Remaking the economic world depends not just on creative design of technologies and the forging of tools, but on their usage. Of course, as our histories show, not all technologies and tools are well designed or well used.

## References

Alexander, Christopher. 1964. *Notes on the Synthesis of Form.* Cambridge, MA: Harvard University Press.

Clarke, Adele E., and Joan H. Fujimura. 1992. *The Right Tools for the Job: At Work in Twentieth-Century Life Sciences.* Princeton, NJ: Princeton University Press.

Hall, Peter A. 1993. "Policy Paradigms, Social Learning, and the State." *Comparative Politics* 25, no. 3: 275–96.

Herfeld, Catherine, and Chiara Lisciandra. 2019. "Editorial." In "Knowledge Transfer and Its Contexts," edited by Catherine Herfeld and Chiara Lisciandra, special issue, *Studies in the History and Philosophy of Science, Part A* 77: 1–10.

Maasen, S., E. Mendelsohn, and P. Weingart, eds. 1995. *Biology as Society, Society as Biology: Metaphors*. Sociology of Science Yearbook 1994, vol. 18. Amsterdam: Kluwer.

MacKenzie, Donald. 2006. *An Engine, Not a Camera*. Cambridge, MA: MIT Press.

Morgan, Mary S. 2003. "Economics." In *The Cambridge History of Science, Volume 7: The Modern Social Sciences*, edited by T. Porter and D. Ross, 275–305. Cambridge: Cambridge University Press.

Morgan, Mary S. 2008. "'On a Mission' with Mutable Mobiles." Working Paper 34, *The Nature of Evidence: How Well Do "Facts" Travel?* project, Department of Economic History, LSE.

Morgan, Mary S. 2012. *The World in the Model*. Cambridge: Cambridge University Press.

Morgan, Mary S., and Malcolm Rutherford. 1998. "American Economics: The Character of Transformation." In *The Transformation of American Economics: From Interwar Pluralism to Post-War Neoclassicism*, edited by Mary S. Morgan and Malcolm Rutherford. *History of Political Economy* 30 (supplement): 1–26.

Simon, Herbert A. 1969. *The Sciences of the Artificial*. Cambridge, MA: MIT Press.

Yaffe, Helen. 2009. *Che Guevara: The Economics of Revolution*. Basingstoke: Palgrave-Macmillan.

Young, Alden. 2017. *Transforming Sudan: Decolonization, Economic Development, and State Formation*. Cambridge: Cambridge University Press.

# Contributors

**Amy Sue Bix** is professor of history at Iowa State University. Her 2013 book, *Girls Coming to Tech: A History of American Engineering Education for Women*, won the 2015 Margaret Rossiter Prize from the History of Science Society, as well as 2015's IEEE-USA Award for Distinguished Literary Contributions, and 2014's Betty Vetter Award for Research from WEPAN (the Women in Engineering ProActive Network). Bix has written widely on many topics in the history of science, technology, and medicine, including *Inventing Ourselves out of Jobs? America's Debate over Technological Unemployment, 1929–1981* (2000). Her book in progress is "Recruiting Engineer Jane and Astrophysicist Amy: American STEM Advocacy for Girls, 1965–2015."

**David Ian Blockley** is an emeritus professor of civil engineering of the University of Bristol, UK. He is a fellow of the Royal Academy of Engineering and was president of the Institution of Structural Engineers 2001–2. He has written over 170 papers and 7 books and has won several technical awards including the Telford Gold Medal of the Institution of Civil Engineers.

**Ivan Boldyrev** is assistant professor of history and philosophy of economics at the Radboud University Nijmegen, the Netherlands. He is a philosopher and a historian of ideas with wide-ranging interests, including the history and philosophy of recent economics, German idealism, and critical theory. He is the coeditor (with Till Düppe) of *Economic Knowledge in Socialism, 1945–89* (2020), and (with Ekaterina Svetlova) *Enacting Dismal Science: New Perspectives on the Performativity of Economics* (2016). Other publications include papers in professional journals and two books: *Ernst Bloch and His Contemporaries* (2014), and (with Carsten Herrmann-Pillath) *Hegel, Institutions, and Economics* (2014).

*History of Political Economy* 52 (annual suppl.) DOI 10.1215/00182702-8831745
Copyright 2020 by Duke University Press

**Marcel Boumans** is Pierson professor of history of economics at Utrecht University. His main research focus is on understanding empirical research practices in social science from a combined historical and philosophy perspective. He is particularly interested in the practices of measurement and modelling and the role of mathematics in social science. Because models are not complete as sources of knowledge for sciences outside the laboratory, additional expert judgements are needed. This is the topic of his most recent monograph *Science outside the Laboratory* (2015). His current research project "Vision and Visualization" explores how expert judgments (views) are made and how they could be validated, particularly in those research practices where visualizations are built or used.

**Daniel Breslau** is associate professor in the Department of Science, Technology, and Society at Virginia Tech. He is the author of numerous articles on the history and sociology of the human sciences, and is currently working on a book on the science and politics of electricity market design.

**Chung-Tang Cheng** is a PhD candidate in economic history at the London School of Economics and was a research fellow at the Center for the History of Political Economy at Duke University for the 2018–19 academic year. His thesis investigates how econometricians have used micro-level data to produce empirical knowledge since the postwar era.

**Beatrice Cherrier** is a historian of economics at CNRS, THEMA, University of Cergy Pontoise and an associate professor at Ecole Polytechnique. She researches the history of applied economics in the last decades, including the rise of applied fields such as urban and public economics, and macroeconomics. She is also interested in the relationships between the rise of applied work and the changing status of women in economics.

**Pedro Garcia Duarte** is senior research fellow at INSPER, Brazil, and researches the technical transformations of economics in the twentieth century, particularly after World War II, with a special interest on the history of macroeconomics. He published several articles on this topic in leading journals on the history of economics, coedited the book *Microfoundations Reconsidered: The Relationship of Micro and Macroeconomics in Historical Perspective* (2012), and has been a guest editor, with Marcel Boumans, of the symposium "The History of Macroeconometric Modeling," published in 2019 in *HOPE*. He is coeditor of the *Journal of the History of Economic Thought* since 2018, and the co-organizer of the History of Recent Economics Conference (HISRECO).

**Yann Giraud** is professor of economics at CY Cergy Paris Université and a researcher at Agora (EA 7392), Center for Research in Civilizations, History, Literature and Heritage. His research is mostly concerned with the role of visual language as well as with issues of knowledge transmission and vulgarization in economics and the larger social sciences during the twentieth century. His articles have appeared in such journals as *History of Political Economy, Journal of the History of Economic Thought,* and *History of Science.* He co-organizes the History of Recent Economics Conference (HISRECO).

**Judy L. Klein** is professor of economics, emerita, at Mary Baldwin University in Virginia. She is the author of *Statistical Visions in Time: A History of Time Series Analysis, 1662–1938* (1997), coeditor of *The Age of Economic Measurement* (2001), and coauthor of *How Reason Almost Lost Its Mind: The Strange Career of Cold War Rationality* (2013). She is completing a book on how US military needs during World War II and the Cold War steered applied mathematicians to an economic way of thinking about scarce resources, including limited computational resources, and how economists incorporated the resultant modeling strategies into their models.

**Mary S. Morgan** is the Albert O. Hirschman professor of history and philosophy of economics at the London School of Economics; she is an elected fellow of the British Academy, and an overseas fellow of the Royal Dutch Academy of Arts and Sciences. Her past research has focused on the history and philosophy of the practices of the social sciences, particularly economics (models, measurements, observation, experiments, and so forth). Her two most recent books are *The World in the Model* (2012) and *How Well Do Facts Travel?* (2011). She is currently working on poverty measurement and the performativity of economics in remaking the economic world. She leads a large Narrative Science project: www.narrative-science.org/.

**Aurélien Saïdi**, trained in economic theory, is the author of several articles on complex macroeconomic dynamics, as well as on the history of macroeconomics. He is an associate professor and a vice president for digital affairs at the University of Paris Nanterre. He currently researches the intellectual, institutional, and political conditions for the development of scientific communities and the production of economic knowledge, in particular in macroeconomics.

**Thomas A. Stapleford** is associate professor in the Program of Liberal Studies at the University of Notre Dame, where he works on the history of the human sciences, especially economics. He is the author of *The Cost of Living in America: A Political History of Economic Statistics* (2009) and coeditor of *Building Chicago Economics: New Perspectives on the History of America's Most Powerful Economics Program* (2011). His articles have appeared in the *Journal of American History, Isis: Journal of the History of Science Society,* and *History of Political Economy,* among other venues.

**William Thomas** is a senior science policy analyst at the American Institute of Physics in College Park, Maryland, and writes for AIP's publication, *FYI Science Policy News.* He earned a PhD in the history of science from Harvard University in 2007 and is the author of *Rational Action: The Sciences of Policy in Britain and America, 1940–1960* (2015).

**Guillaume Yon** is a LSE fellow at the Department of Economic History, London School of Economics and Political Science. His book on the implications of optimization in the electricity sector for the theory, practice, and politics of economic planning in postwar France is in preparation.

# Index

Abromovitz, Moses, 96–97
adaptive expectations model, 135
agent-based modeling.
     *See* microsimulation
Aizerman, Mark Aronovich
  as applied mathematician, 273
  applied theoretical work, 275
  automatic regulation theory,
     273–74
  behavioral models, 278–79
  Caltech visit, 287
  career of, 271–72
  choice theory, 277, 279–81, 286,
     288
  collective research, 281
  experimental research, 286–88,
     290
  formalism, 285n26
  influences, 273, 278
  at Institute of Automatics, 272–73,
     281–82
  interdisciplinarity, 282, 286

international partners, 283–84
living systems, 274–75, 286
mathematical training, 273n4
political constraints, 284–85
political courage, 273n3
reputation, 283, 286n28
research reorientations, 289
social systems, 286
Alchian, Armen, 178–82, 184
Alchon, Guy, 15
Aleskcrov, Fuad
  on Aizerman's curiosity, 286n7
  choice theory, 280–81
  collaborations with Aizerman,
     285
  experimental economics, 287
  mail intercepted by Soviet
     government, 284
  post-Soviet research, 288–89
Alexander, Christopher, 298–99
Allais, Maurice, 247, 249–53
Allen, R. G. D., 135

*History of Political Economy* 52 (annual suppl.)  DOI 10.1215/00182702-8831757
Copyright 2020 by Duke University Press

PQV181164

ISBN-13: 978-1-4780-1162-0

9 781478 011620

Cover Credit:
Photograph by Andreas Feininger, 1942, Farm Security
Administration/Office of War Information Photograph
Collection, US Library of Congress.